ABORIGINAL HEALTH AND HISTORY

ABORIGINAL HEALTH AND HISTORY

Power and Prejudice in Remote Australia

ERNEST HUNTER

Regional Psychiatrist, Aboriginal and Torres Strait Islander Mental Health, Peninsula and Torres Strait Regional Health Authority, Cairns.

CAMBRIDGE UNIVERSITY PRESS

Published by the Press Syndicate of the University of Cambridge
The Pitt Building, Trumpington Street, Cambridge CB2 1RP, UK
40 West 20th Street, New York, NY 10011-4211, USA
10 Stamford Road, Oakleigh, Melbourne, Victoria 3166, Australia

Printed in Hong Kong by Colorcraft

National Library of Australia cataloguing in publication data
Hunter, Ernest M.
Aboriginal health and history.
Bibliography.
Includes index.
ISBN 0 521 41629 9.
ISBN 0 521 447607 (pbk)
[1]. Aborigines, Australian – Western Australia – Kimberley – Mortality.
[2]. Aborigines, Australian – Western Australia – Kimberley – Suicidal behavior.
[3]. Aborigines, Australian – Western Australia – Kimberley – Social conditions.
[4]. Aborigines, Australian – Western Australia – Kimberley – Alcohol use. I. Title.
304.64089991509414

Library of Congress cataloguing in publication data
Hunter, Ernest, 1952–
Aboriginal health and history: power and prejudice in remote Australia/Ernest Hunter.
Includes bibliographical references and index.
ISBN 0–521–41629–9 (hard back)
1. Australian aborigines – Mental health – Australia – Kimberley Region (W.A.)
2. Australian aborigines – Australia – Kimberley Region (W.A.) – Social conditions.
3. Power (Social sciences). 4. Control (Psychology). I. Title.
[DNLM: 1. Aborigines – history – Western Australia. 2. Aborigines – psychology – Western
Australia. 3. Health Status – Western Australia. 4. Power (Psychology). 5. Social Problems
– Western Australia. 6. Prejudice. WA 305 H945aj]
RC451.5.A95H85 1993
362.2′0422′089991509414 – dc20
DNLM/DLC
for Library of Congress   92–49158
CIP

A catalogue record for this book is available from the British Library

ISBN 0 521 41629 9 hardback
ISBN 0 521 447607 paperback

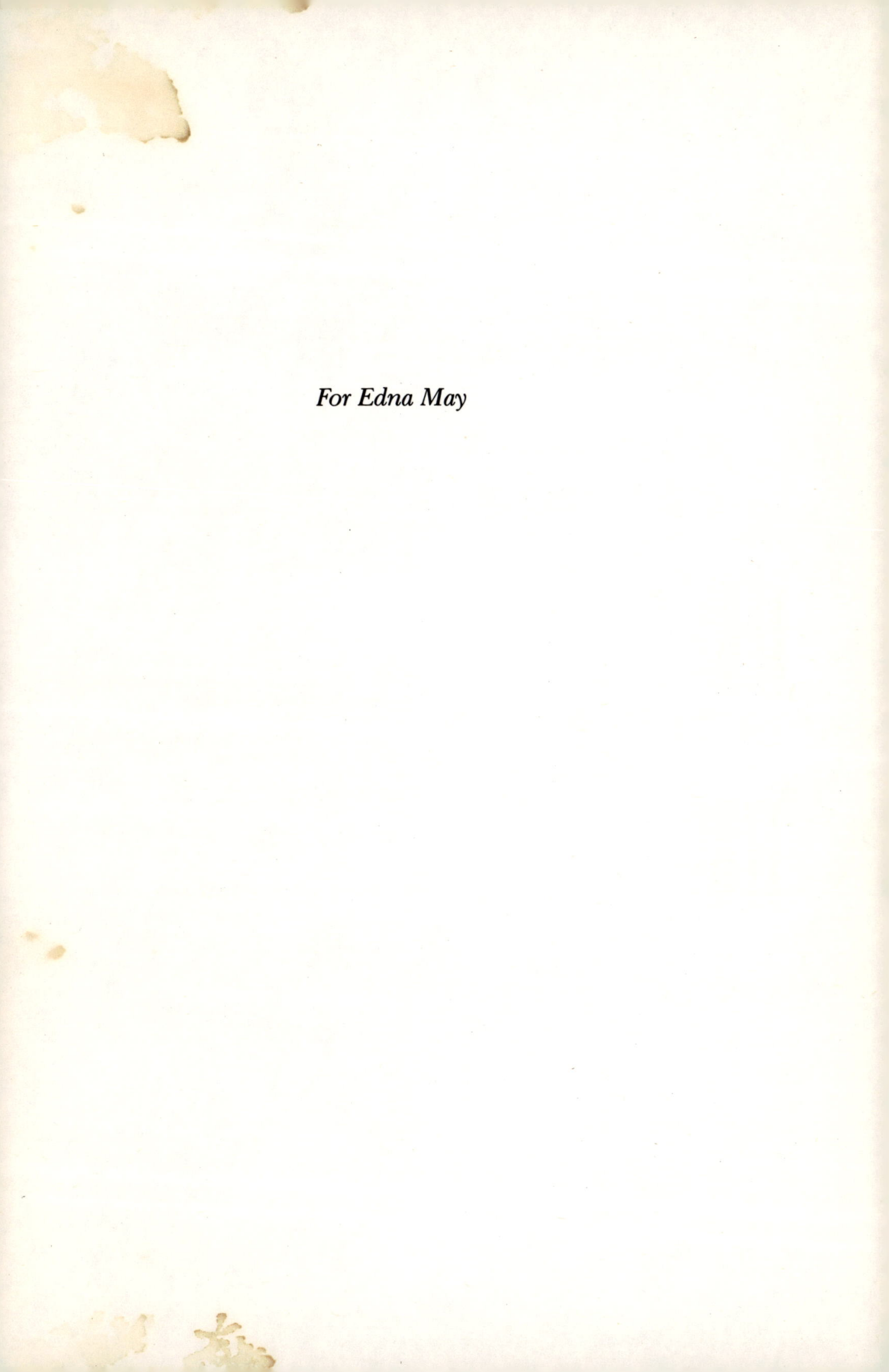

For Edna May

Contents

9   Structures and Change   254

Figures

Figures

Tables

Preface

Power courses and pulses across remote Australia. Where once symbols were coded in the land to sustain and guide its guardians, they are now obvious to all. Microwave and satellite dishes have supplanted the wind-powered bore as the technological icons of the outback — remote Australia is no longer isolated Australia. The pulsing rhythms of the generator and the crepitation of distant videos keep the night at bay in even the most remote Aboriginal communities. While power remains central to Aboriginal life, both the cultural symbols, and its negotiation and articulation, are changing. The rerouting of the powerlines within and between Aboriginal groups, and between Aborigines and the wider Australian society, has far-reaching consequences. The Aboriginal flag adorns and bedecks garments and buildings as a communication of a prideful identity, a statement and a challenge. However, these transformations have not taken place without casualties and this work examines some of the behavioural outcomes for this group that have emerged over the last three decades, drawing from one region of remote Aboriginal Australia — the Kimberley.

The Aboriginal informants and subjects, whose cooperation was essential to this work, are too numerous too list. Their help is gratefully acknowledged. Particular thanks are extended to Elsta Foy, Iris Prouse, Richard and Alice Hunter, Jimmy Chi, Susie Gilbert, Jack Mulardy, Nipper Tabagee, Sandy Paddy, Aubrey Tigan, Aboriginal Health Workers, and ex-patients of the Derby leprosarium. Among other Kimberley residents to whom I owe gratitude are Father 'Mac', Father McKelson, Brother Peter Negus and the Catholic and State school teachers of the region, Sarah Yu, Susan Laird, Sisters Francis and Antoinette, and the staff of Communicable Disease Control and Community Health Services. Those outside the region include John Cawte, Lawson Holman, Rose Ellis, Mary

Anne Jebb, Richard Smith, Colin Tatz, Roderic Campbell and Patricia Fagan. The research was funded in part by the New South Wales Institute of Psychiatry and the Commonwealth Department of Community Services and Health. Other institutions assisting were the Broome Regional Aboriginal Medical Service, the University of New South Wales, the Health Department of Western Australia, the National Drug and Alcohol Research Centre, CSIRO Division of Human Nutrition, the Western Australian Departments of Police and Corrections, and of the Registrar General, the *Aboriginal and Islander Health Worker Journal*, the Ellard practice of Northside Clinic and the Aboriginal Medical Service (Redfern). For data analysis and more I am in debt to Wayne Hall. Permission to use previously published material was given by the *Australian and New Zealand Journal of Psychiatry*, the *Medical Journal of Australia*, *Social Science and Medicine*, *Australian Psychologist*, the *Aboriginal Health Information Bulletin*, and the *Australian Journal of Social Issues*. Finally, the research would not have been conceived and could not have proceeded without the guidance and encouragement of my brother, Randolph Spargo. There are many left unmentioned — thanks.

CHAPTER 1

Caduceus and Clipboard

SETTING AND SET

Beyond Australia's northern horizon, submerged by time and rising seas, is another coastline. Somewhere along that slowly shifting shore prehistoric wanderers welcomed the certainty of solid ground — the first footprints of Homo sapiens marked the sand and were washed away. Perhaps slow curious eyes followed them, or furtive, frightened, fluttering glimpses. The ancestors of the ancestors, markers of the land, had entered the rhythm of change, caught in the moods of this land, transformed by it across the centuries and transforming it. Those earliest landfalls, perhaps over 50 000 years ago, may have been off the Kimberley region of Western Australia. To reach the Sunda Shelf, even at the lowest level of the seas, would have required a sea-crossing of some 87 kilometres (Flood 1983). For the survivors of that journey into the unknown there was no return.

THE REGION

Age-scarred and rugged, with colours drained by a relentless sun, the weathered landscape of the Kimberley seems to declare its resistance to change. However, beneath lies a hidden story of geological change. The sandstones and shales of the plateaux testify to ancient forces, while the sediments beneath the sandy country of the west and east Kimberley tell of more recent transformations (Petheram & Kok 1986). The region is vast, even by Australian standards, and remote. It is over 2000 kilometres by road from Perth to Broome in the south-west Kimberley and another 1000 kilometres to Kununurra in the north-east, near the Northern Territory border. Few travellers venture far from the single sealed road, the National Highway, beyond which lies an expanse of nearly half-a-million square kilometres (figure 1.1).

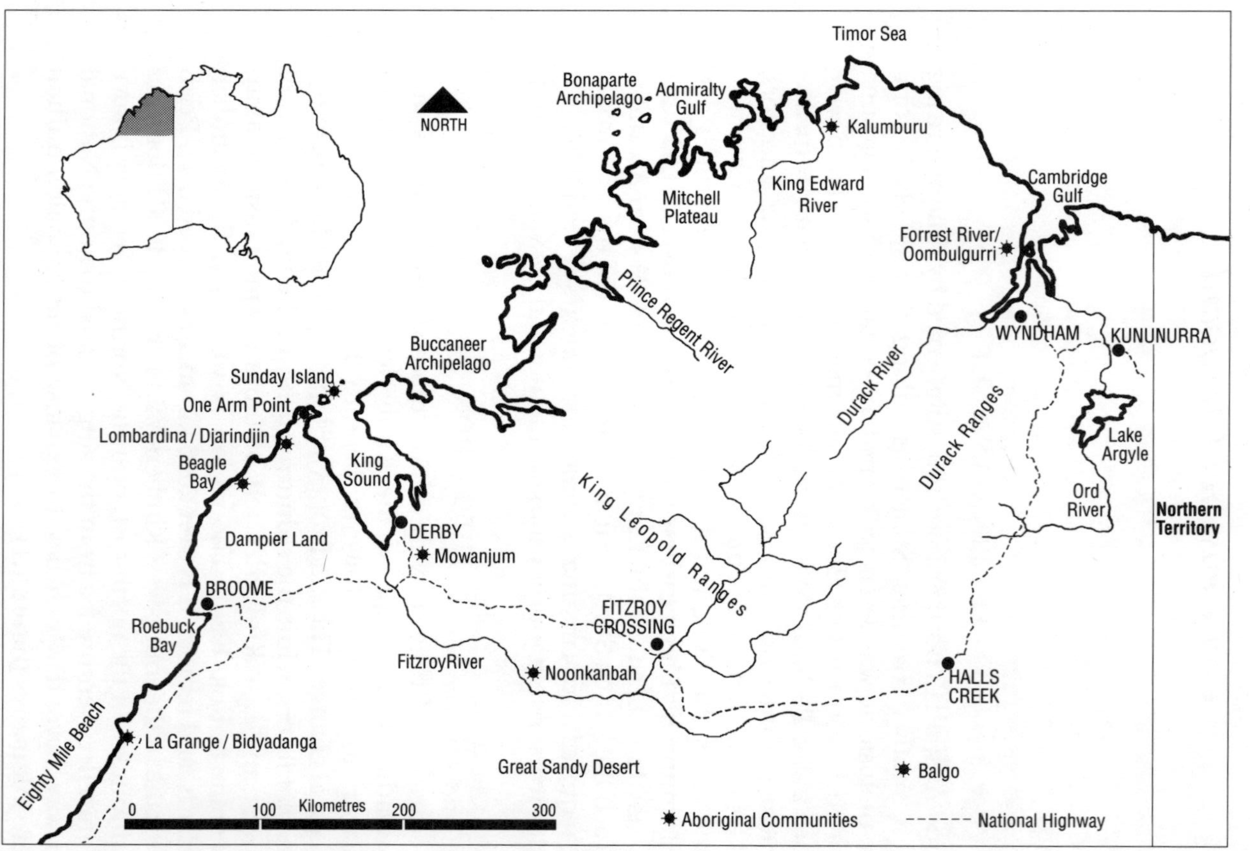

Figure 1.1 *Map of the Kimberley region, Western Australia*

The coastline of the Kimberley region is divided by the mangrove-lined waters of King Sound. Draining the Fitzroy River, low mud-islands emerge and disappear in its 10-metre brown tides. From the entrance to the Sound at the tip of the Dampier Land peninsula, the Indian Ocean pulses over gentle bays and wide tidal beaches, which give way southwards to the dazzling, uninterrupted shoreline of Eighty Mile Beach, where the Great Sandy Desert confronts the sea. North from King Sound the spectacular Buccaneer and Bonaparte archipelagoes stand as rocky sentinels before a tortuous shoreline. Here the sea surges through narrow channels to hidden inlets. The coast is wild, beautiful and deserted.

To the east, rising to some 800 metres, the deeply etched sandstone and basalt Kimberley plateau spreads over almost a third of the region. From the air the gently rolling, weathered hills seem barren through most of the year — the radiated heat trapped in a dull, stifling haze. At ground level, spinifex, grass and scattered gum-trees appear like the scrawny vestiges of some former epoch, struggling between rock and stone; struggling perhaps, but also wonderfully adapted. Following the monsoonal deluges of the 'wet' (December to March), these surfaces explode into a profusion of life. Swollen rivers carve deeper through tortuous gorges, whose shadows shelter hidden subtropical realms. Towards the ocean to the west and north sharp escarpments, cut deeply by tidal inlets, border the plateau. To the south and east the massif gives way through the rugged King Leopold and Durack ranges (the former containing Mount Ord, at 930 m the highest point in the Kimberley) to the savannas and grassland plains of the Fitzroy and Ord river basins.

These fertile corridors attracted and guided European pastoralists, who have in turn transformed the land. They initially arrived in the 1860s, and by the First World War there were some 700 000 cattle and 300 000 sheep in the Kimberley (Petheram & Kok 1986). Over-stocking and inadequate attention to pasture management rapidly resulted in soft riverbanks crumbling under-hoof, in deep gullies sweeping away the fragile topsoil during the summer floods. From a wild torrent swelling to the horizon across the floodplains during the 'wet', the Fitzroy contracts to a chain of long, silent waterholes, flood-strewn debris high in the river gums attesting to the river's moods. Away from the muted green corridors of the watercourse, the plain is grass, spinifex, dust and endless ranks of anthills raised to the sky.

South from the Fitzroy the transition is less abrupt. The monsoons that deliver up to 1500 mm of rainfall in one season to the north-west of the plateau are far less generous or predictable moving inland. South of Halls Creek annual falls of less than 400 mm mark the southern limits of the cattle industry. Increasingly arid, the unyielding plain and stunted growth hide contrasts. Temperatures can fall below freezing during the cloudless, sparkling nights of the dry season, rising to the high thirties during the shimmering heat of the day. In the wake of heavy rains, the mesa-studded plains of the south-east are unable to drain the saturated land. Rivers suddenly fill and bodies of water materialise. Barren of even their usual sparse cover, dead trees disappearing to the horizon tell of these lakes' pulsations. Further to the south and east begin the sandhills of the Great Sandy Desert carving across the base of the Kimberley to the ocean.

GUIDING FRAMES

From the 1980s the Kimberley has been home to roughly equal numbers of Aborigines and non-Aborigines. While living in the same space, they are in many ways in different worlds. This is reflected in the region's economies. That of the dominant culture is based on growth, including: mining (gold, iron, zinc, silver, lead, diamonds, marble; with known deposits of uranium, copper-platinum, and bauxite); marine resources (particularly pearling); cattle (over 90 leases averaging 350 hectares, two-thirds of which are owned by corporations from outside the region); agriculture (small-scale horticulture focused about Kununurra); tourism (now bringing perhaps over 200 000 visitors a year); and government services (Aborigines, in this sense, being a resource).

The Aboriginal economy, save for a small urban subgroup, is primarily domestic, static, and based on welfare. Thus, there are glaring disparities in disposable income and in credit (other than internal 'credit', most Aborigines of the Kimberley are functionally excluded from the credit resources of the wider society). Aborigines of the region are economically poor — and often powerless.

Contemporary powerlessness — its roots and history; its manifestations and articulation; its consequences and perpetuation — threads through and links the sections of this study. The focus of this study is the Aborigines of the Kimberley; but it does not pretend to speak for them, or to present an 'Aboriginal view'. It is a non-Aboriginal perspective. There have been many studies with such a perspective before, and more will follow. However, while the field of Aboriginal studies has historically discounted Aboriginal opinions, that situation has changed, with the development of a powerful Aboriginal voice producing its own constructions of 'Aboriginality' and of non-Aboriginal cultures. Hopefully, works such as this one and others by Aboriginal writers will stimulate a dialectical process of mutual exploration and understanding.

There are serious problems in generalising from one region of Aboriginal Australia to another, in particular from remote Australia to urban populations. This work is based on a particular region that, itself, contains enormous diversity: its findings may not be relevant to the unique circumstances of other regions and populations. On the other hand, they may. The study demonstrates that patterns of Aboriginal ill-health in the Kimberley are powerfully influenced by social factors that are embedded in the particular history of the region. This is true for mental health generally — a point frequently missed by psychiatrists constrained by their metropolitan professional identity:

> Tearing the subject from history, rendering him a passive actor, a judgmental dope, out of touch with the real rhythms and reasons of his behaviour, is the production of each psychiatrist experiencing and rationally reacting to, therein constituting, the professionally organised domain of psychiatry. (Robillard 1987 : xvi)

This work proceeds from the premise that the analysis of health demands a knowledge of the historical forces defining its social context. The following chapters trace an outline for this task. Chapter 2 presents an overview of forces affecting Aborigines in the region since the arrival of Europeans and Chapter 3 sketches the development of health services in the region. While these sections are quite detailed, as LeVine has commented regarding cross-cultural variation in psychosocial adaptation: 'a full understanding necessarily requires both historical reconstructions and the analysis of current function' (1982 : 164).

Disciplinary divergences

I have trained and worked predominantly in clinical psychiatry, and my orientation is informed by that exposure. Soon after arriving in the Kimberley in March 1987, I found that my ascribed professional identity substantially determined the attitudes and expectations, not only of Aborigines, but of workers from other disciplines. In a situation not unique to researchers in remote Australia, the tension between psychiatry and the social sciences has long allowed only an uneasy rapprochement: 'the relationship between sociology and psychiatry often takes the form of a superficial acceptance of the ideas of the one by the other, or the acceptance of the authority of the one by the other' (Doerner 1981 : 2).

Psychiatry is in a particularly sensitive position in that it deals with issues that overlap the fields of interest of the social sciences. As a subdiscipline within medicine it is frequently construed as reflecting the supposedly narrow positivist perspectives of the physical and natural sciences, inappropriate for the study of systems of meaning. However, as a discipline that engages its subjects on the level of emotions and feelings, psychiatry of necessity *is* concerned with systems of meaning and with intersubjectivity. While the ascendancy of biological theories and the 'medical model' of mental illness is transforming both research and practice in general psychiatry, the cross-cultural subdiscipline is in the opposite direction — from foregrounding biology to emphasising cultural explanations.

Despite this, or as a consequence, with growth into a similar domain of interest, particularly in the limited field within Australia, differences are accentuated in defining 'territory'. This is frequently articulated in terms of emic versus etic distinctions. Derived from linguistics and extended to cultural research, emic approaches (from 'phonemic') explain observed behaviour using constructs from within the culture, whereas etic approaches (from 'phonetic') utilise external criteria imposed by the researcher in an attempt to generate universal categories (Davidson 1977). In contrasting these orientations, Berry (1980) indicated that an emic approach: studies behaviour from within the system; examines only one culture; uncovers structure; and generates criteria relative to internal characteristics. By contrast, an etic approach: studies behaviour from a position outside the system; examines many cultures, comparing them; imposes structure; and generates criteria considered absolute or universal. However, Jahoda (1977) has pointed out that any cultural system is composed of overlapping and interlocking systems at different levels. He questioned whether an analysis is possible within one system without reference to another, and whether a researcher (who generally is not and cannot become a member of the system under study) can provide an analysis from 'inside the system'.

In the field of Aboriginal studies Biernoff has opposed the emic approaches of anthropology to the etic analyses of psychiatry in the interpretation of 'aberrant' Aboriginal behaviour. Acknowledging that 'identifiable symptoms and aberrant behaviour do occur and are recognised as abnormal by both Aborigines and psychiatrists' (Biernoff 1982 : 149), he suggested that 'it is but a small step from explaining psychopathology in cultural terms, to describing culture in psychopathological terms' (ibid : 150).

While the trend to pathologise culture is not unique to psychiatry, in that discipline it arises primarily in settings with limited cross-cultural exposure. In the fields of cross-cultural psychiatry and psychology there is intense and active debate on these issues. The emic–etic distinction is clearly of major concern; cross-cultural psychiatry contrasts these orientations as ethnopsychiatry versus comparative psychiatry (Lipsedge 1989). While the corpus of psychiatric writing on Aborigines is limited, there are examples of both approaches. One may compare the etic analysis of 'voodoo death' by Eastwell (1982) and the 'fear of sorcery syndrome' by Reser and Eastwell (1981), to the emic analysis of the 'Groote Island syndrome' by Cawte (1984). Spiro provided a salutary caveat: 'that cultural frames make emic, or intra-cultural, sense does not imply, however, that they are immune from valid cross-cultural, or etic, judgement, let alone that they are the primary, if not the exclusive, determinants of what social actors think and feel or how they behave' (1984 : 329).

Psychiatry clearly brings certain biases to the cross-cultural situation. Kleinman (1987) has repeatedly drawn attention to the ethno-medico-centricism of the discipline and the particular problems of cross-cultural instruments, indicating, for example, that the approach to the diagnosis of depression exemplified by the Diagnostic and Statistical Manual of Mental Disorders of the American Psychiatric Association (DSM–III and its scion DSM–IIIR) minimises emic aspects (Kleinman & Good 1985). This is necessarily the case; for, as classificatory tools to guide treatment by comparison of like constellations of symptoms and behaviours, such nosologies rest on an etic foundation. As taxonomies, diagnostic systems are culturally determined, identifying clinical conditions that are themselves culturally constituted and embedded in a social context: 'a medical and psychiatric diagnostic system is a cultural object that constitutes abstract clinical entities based on distinctive symbolic conventions' (Fabrega 1987 : 392).

With many conditions but few clearly defined causes and even fewer confirmatory tests, psychiatric praxis rests on such labelling, indeed: 'underlying all of its powers, institutions and technologies — has been one sustaining psychiatric act: diagnosis' (Reich 1981 : 62). Within the field there are both pragmatic and magical functions of such labels. It is the latter, the transmutation of description to disorder, the confusion of 'things with the names we give them' (Biller 1976 : 5) that causes friction between psychiatry and the other social sciences. Instruments such as DSM–III, which have come to signify for psychiatry's detractors the profession's inflexibility, do not adequately take into account the culturally constituted idioms of distress that inform, for example, possession states (Obeyesekere 1970) and sickness behaviour (Nichter 1981) in non-European contexts, or the social role of sickness among Aborigines (Nathan & Japanangka 1983). In tradition-oriented Aboriginal Australia this includes the use of the projective mechanisms of sorcery (Reid 1983) and ritual (Kaberry 1973 [1939]) in dealing with stress and danger. However, in pointing out psychiatry's potential for pathologising culture, Biernoff has not considered that a significant proportion of clinical work in exotic situations is the identification and treatment of organic disorders, all too easily ascribed to cultural factors (Hunter & Allan 1986). Denying or minimising disorder or disease in a cross-cultural context is disarmingly easy and dangerous. There is no simple solution, one strives for an openness to the cultural dimensions of human existence while retaining clinical vigilance.

METHODOLOGIES

The sign proclaimed plainly and simply: 'No doctors allowed'. There was no easy explanation of this perplexing message for the eminent American researchers who had travelled to Balgo, one of the most remote Aboriginal communities in the Kimberley. The specificity was unavoidable: not whites (or *gudiyas*), or miners, or politicians, or bureaucrats — but doctors. This prohibition challenged the expectations of 'privileged access' that presumed an interculturally shared valuation of doctors as caring and appreciated.

In that community, Aborigines clearly did not resonate with that professionally self-serving construction.

The sign was on the door of the art centre, one of a few conspicuously intact buildings surrounded by gutted, tumbling dwellings and ramshackle windbreaks. Nearby, my international colleagues saw Aboriginal Australians and their dogs retreating from the early afternoon heat and dust. By any definition the residents of this isolated ex-mission settlement were, and remain, in terms of money and resources, poor. Judging from the arid countryside and the state of disrepair in the community, there appeared little likelihood of changing that economic situation — unless, perhaps, through painting.

Gugadja (Kukatja) artists had first adopted non-traditional media in the late 1970s. By 1986 Balgo art was being exhibited at the Art Gallery of Western Australia and further afield. Entrepreneurs soon 'discovered' this untapped resource and were quick to take advantage of artists who were unaware of the 'value' of their productions in the metropolitan markets of the south. Thus, the connection to the sign. At the time of our visit the government clinic staff had been withdrawn owing to vandalism and perceived 'threats', continuing services being provided through the Royal Flying Doctor Service. Our Aboriginal informants explained that doctors, flown out at a time of great need for brief clinics, had been unavailable on several occasions for consultation. Instead, we were told, they had been seeking out artworks and purchasing them at bargain prices.

Episodes of such professional confrontation were rare during the course of my research in the Kimberley. When they did occur, however, they were reminders that the work I was engaged in was socially and historically located. A non-Aboriginal, urban, economically privileged professional, I was engaged in the immediately asymmetric process of Aboriginal health research. Indeed, in the course of medical work it is impossible to discard the expectations and behaviours that constitute one's professional identity. To the extent that one wishes to minimise the distorting effects of such ascribed or enacted attributes, one must acknowledge and question their impact on communication and interpretation.

RESEARCH: PATHS AND MAZES

Fieldwork for this study took place between March 1987 and November 1989. While the planning stage reflected my medical background and psychiatric training, the orientation gradually changed to accommodate unforeseen circumstances. Such divergences resulted from the logistics of fieldwork and were a consequence of dialectical reformations based on emerging material. No rigid research protocol existed.

The most important shift in focus occurred at the outset. This study was initially conceived as an emic analysis of suicide within a discrete Aboriginal population, but I soon realised the problems inherent in such an endeavour. Additionally, to more accurately delineate the dimensions of Kimberley Aboriginal suicide, a review of death certificates was undertaken. While suicide emerged, as expected, it was found to be embedded in and eclipsed by dramatic regionwide increases in Aboriginal mortality from a variety of non-natural causes. At the same time that the mortality review was under way, I was attempting to become familiar with the Aboriginal history of the region. I quickly recognised that this task was essential to understanding the results of the mortality study. Emerging from this preliminary experience was a sociohistorical orientation that became the unifying frame for all subsequent work, including the large random sample survey that was conducted during the last eighteen months in the region. In the following chapters I will describe in detail the methodologies used in the various sections of this study. Given what has been said thus far regarding the non-linearity of this research, a brief overview is here provided which will allow the reader to follow the path taken, including some of the digressions.

Research proposals often bear scant resemblance to subsequent fieldwork. I arrived in Broome with a proposal submitted the year before to the New South Wales Institute of Psychiatry entitled: 'Psychiatric morbidity and the emergence of suicide in a remote Aboriginal population'. With hindsight, that proposal reflected a naive optimism, the aim being:

> To generate a psychiatric morbidity profile of an Aboriginal population in a remote area of Australia, components of which were surveyed using short stay techniques twenty years previously, with particular attention to depression; suicide and suicide-equivalent behaviour; the psychosocial antecedents of this; and the cultural and subcultural interpretations of these behaviours.

This agenda rapidly gave way to practical considerations. A period of 'being there' and becoming known was a necessary precursor to formal 'researching'. I was told that it would take about a year to be accepted sufficiently by Kimberley Aborigines to do the work I planned. At that stage a year seemed unreasonably long. I believed that, having worked in the Kimberley as a medical student in the early 1970s, and in cross-cultural settings in the Pacific, my acceptance by the local Aboriginal community would be expedited. That background proved helpful in anticipating the climatic and social rigours of the Kimberley; it was irrelevant, however, in terms of allaying suspicions of the intruder.

Ultimately, my entry into Aboriginal communities was most powerfully supported by my brother, Dr Randolph Spargo. A veteran of 23 years in the Kimberley with the Health Department of Western Australia, his work had taken him frequently to every community in the region. While functional access still demanded time and a willingness to give (largely in terms of services), my being related to him clearly influenced attitudes towards me. Acceptance in many remote Aboriginal settings requires that one is somehow located in the social framework. My brother, as 'Old Man' (an honorific of sorts suggesting one is a stayer rather than transitory) was socially located. As a consequence, my location and conditional acceptance, was facilitated, and for the duration of the research, regardless of introductions, I was 'young Spargs'.

MORTALITY REVIEW

To identify the suicides that had occurred in the region, and to generate a comprehensive picture of Aboriginal mortality, a review of deaths was undertaken. This required examining the registers of deaths in each of the four regional centres within the Kimberley, as well as checking through deceased hospital files, burial records, and coronial reports in Perth. A period of 30 years was selected, as this covered 15 years before and after all Aborigines in the Kimberley obtained full citizenship rights. Access to the death registers also provided an opportunity to examine recorded deaths as far back as the 1880s.

SUICIDES AND CELLS

While thus engaged, I began to gather further information about those suicides that had occurred in Broome Shire, both through discussions with informants and, unexpectedly, as a result of being approached by relatives and acquaintances of earlier suicides who had heard of the research. Community concern was obvious from the beginning, and heightened by reports in the media of a series of six deaths, allegedly by suicide, of young Aboriginal males in custody in Queensland. Letters patent, empowering the Royal Commission into Aboriginal Deaths in Custody, were subsequently issued in October 1987. 'Black Deaths' emerged in the lead-up to the Bicentennial celebrations as a symbol of Aboriginal disadvantage in Australian society. Buffeted by cresting waves of public disapprobation, politicians and bureaucrats sought sanctuary in a variety of conciliatory and usually expedient gestures, exemplified in Western Australia by the setting up of a parallel 'Interim Inquiry Into Aboriginal Deaths in Custody', established in November 1987.

Although I was only months into the research on Aboriginal suicide, a field which had few workers but sudden intense public interest, it was tempting to assume the role of the expert the media demanded. The confidence built by such ascriptions of expertise at least facilitated access in one area where entry has been problematic. Two of the Kimberley suicides had occurred while in custody in Broome, and I proposed a short study in the police-cells. Obtaining official permission took some time and effort; however, the Police Department of Western Australia thereafter was consistently helpful.

Even so, police sensitivity to my daily presence in the cells was obvious. On my first day the sergeant pointed to a recent newspaper article pinned to the notice board. 'Prison victims leave Aborigines seething: Black vow to murder police', ran the headline to Norm Aisbett's column in the now defunct *Western Mail* (20–22 November 1987 p. 4). Mr Aisbett has subsequently expressed his regret for the sensationalist and irresponsible article (personal communication, January 1989), but at the time it resonated with public opinion, which was as much anti-police as it was pro-Aboriginal.

A young policeman one afternoon demonstrated his ambivalence about my presence. I had arrived during the change in shifts when most staff, including Aboriginal police aides, were present. The recently arrived constable asked in a voice ensured of an audience throughout the main office area 'Doc, how come blackfellows haven't got AIDS?'. Unprepared and off-guard, my silence was amplified by the stillness of an attentive audience. I shifted uneasily (presumably as was hoped) and he, without looking up, provided his sardonic solution: 'the government hasn't given it to them'. This non-exchange achieved three purposes. He had made a statement about Aborigines, with the silence in the room implying general (white) assent. Furthermore, the AIDS *double entendre* humiliated the Aboriginal police aides and gave them no option but to be either tacitly complicit or be accused of being humourless and 'sensitive'. Not least of all, the intrusive 'doc' was publicly put in his place.

The study involved interviewing 100 detained Aborigines over a period of two months. Seeing that alcohol emerged as an important factor among the suicides examined out of custody, it became a focus of the lock-up study. The resulting patterns of findings indicated widespread and serious behavioural and psychological correlates of drinking among those detained. The further question was raised: Are these Aborigines, in their patterns and correlates of alcohol consumption, typical of Aborigines in the wider Kimberley society? Simple observation suggested that this was not so. Turning to the literature on Aborigines and alcohol, little reliable quantitative information was found, with none addressing the Kimberley. As a consequence I decided to attempt a population-based survey.

PILOT COMMUNITY SURVEYS

Moving from making the decision to executing the survey proved difficult for a number of reasons, not the least of which was personal inexperience. Two alternative strategies were initially considered and trialled in distinct but similar communities situated approximately 20 kilometres apart and over 200 kilometres from the nearest town. The first community, which will be called Mosquito Creek, was the site of an informant-based approach.

Informant-based methodology

At the time of the study (late 1987) the population of Mosquito Creek was approximately 320 full-time residents, with a further floating population that numbered about 100 people. The first visit coincided with an AIDS education campaign during which the opportunity was taken to approach the council and gain its approval for a study. During a second visit all medical charts were reviewed, with information recorded suggestive of psychiatric and alcohol-related disorders, including nurses' observations, consultation records, medical evacuation reports, hospitalisation summaries and assessments.

Discussions with the community health nurse, Aboriginal health-workers and school representatives extended this data-base.

During the third and longest stay, the Psychiatric Morbidity Census utilised by Cawte and Nurcombe as part of the short-stay psychiatric field team approach on Mornington Island was completed (Cawte 1972). This instrument was designed to elicit diagnostic information about adults and children from informants. After consultation with the council, it was decided that the most appropriate way to proceed was to approach two male and female representatives of each of the family groups in the community. Thus, 29 interviews were conducted in the informants' homes, at times including other members of the households, with opportunities taken to digress into other aspects of local life. Incidental activities such as fishing, gatherings around a fire at night, sitting outside the store, or giving someone a lift home, were also used to gather information. The childhood questionnaire was also filled out by the eight teachers at the school.

Following the survey different sources were compared. In order to be given a diagnosis, an individual had to have either a highly suggestive picture, or be identified by several sources. A designation of alcohol misuse was arrived at by identifying 'problem drinkers' and 'episodic heavy drinkers'. The former had to have either medical or psychiatric complications of drinking, or to be identified as causing major social disruption when drunk. The episodic heavy drinkers were heavy consumers when in town, and often arrested. However, as arrests for 'drunk' were generally considered a 'little problem' (versus 'big problems' that resulted in gaol sentences), it was decided that this group be separately classified.

The results of this trial survey will not be presented in detail.[1] The major findings included a higher prevalence of problem drinking among adult males (32 per cent) than females (5 per cent), and of conduct disorders among boys (7 per cent) than among girls (none). The findings were compared to those presented by Cawte (1972) from Mornington Island, and by Kamien (1978) from Bourke. However, despite the fact that all investigators in these three studies were psychiatrists, and two (Nurcombe and this writer) were child psychiatrists, this comparison raised problems. The studies were separated by two decades and utilised different methodologies and diagnostic categories, and were of populations with their own unique characteristics.

The benefits were experiential. Aboriginal informants were co-operative and helpful and appeared to enjoy the opportunity to bring up concerns of their own. For a novice researcher it provided object lessons in the limitations of metropolitan clinical training. Developing cross-cultural communication skills is a process that never reaches completion, the essential element being contact. Every contact is another lesson. However, by the time this survey was completed it was clear that the informant-based methodology was unsatisfactory.

Practically, the results could not be generalised beyond Mosquito Creek as comparable replication required a similar social structure. In addition, changing diagnostic patterns confound comparisons. Indeed, as Kleinman and Good stated of affective disorders 'the history of psychiatry is strewn with "nosologies", or systems of categorisation of depression' (1985). The process is compounded in cross-cultural settings. Kleinman clearly articulated the problem as the 'category fallacy':

> A category fallacy is the reification of a nosological category developed for a particular cultural group that is then applied to members of another culture for whom it lacks coherence and its validity has not been established. (1987 : 452)[2]

Instrument-based methodology

As the informant-based and diagnosis-oriented approach was clearly inadequate, an instrument-based study was conducted, involving an evaluation of symptoms of anxiety and depression in the second community. With the enormous differences in levels of education, proficiency with English and degree of acculturation across the region, the instrument chosen had to be simple and clear. Some 20 kilometres from Mosquito Creek was a community that I shall call Cockatoo Flats, the site of the second pilot study.

The council at Cockatoo Flats had been approached for their approval during the initial journey to Mosquito Creek. On a second visit all medical files for the population of approximately 250 residents, which included a floating population of around 75 people, were reviewed; the nurse and health-worker there were also interviewed in the same way as had been done at Mosquito Creek. The instrument chosen was the Self Reporting Questionnaire-20 (SRQ-20), designed to be read by the interviewer as a screening instrument for psychiatric morbidity in primary health care settings.[3] The SRQ-20 had been administered by Aboriginal social work students to a sample of 109 patients attending the Aboriginal Medical Service in Perth (Spencer 1986). Spencer commented on problems associated with interpretation, and in a comment recalling Kleinman's 'category fallacy' advised 'caution in interpreting certain responses as indicating psychiatric pathology when they were in fact more likely to be cultural responses to anomie and demoralisation' (Spencer 1986 : 480).

In preparation, the SRQ-20 was administered to health-worker students at the Aboriginal Medical Service in Broome. Suggestions regarding terminology were solicited from them, and from six health-workers, to include individuals from different regions of the Kimberley. Of the 103 individuals whose charts were reviewed, 85 were approached for interview, with only two declining to participate.

On the basis of the chart reviews and discussions with informants, diagnoses were made, as at Mosquito Creek. One in two of the males and one in seven of the females were considered to be problem drinkers. When the results of the 83 SRQ-20 interviews were examined, it was found that there was a tendency for females to admit to more items than men, and for those with problem drinking or other diagnosis, regardless of sex, to score above those without problem drinking or other diagnoses.

While it was clear that an instrument-based approach was acceptable in this setting, the SRQ-20 was not the desired instrument. For females the sensitivity and specificity were similar to those reported in earlier studies. However, for the males this was not the case. The impression gained during the course of the study was that, while the subjects were generally at ease answering and elaborating on the items, difficulty arose with the dichotomous choices. In addition, the non-specific nature of the SRQ-20 was limiting. Thus, while the methods employed at Mosquito Creek and Cockatoo Flats were not subsequently used, the experiences were valuable. Several other avenues, including attempts to explore 'locus of control' and 'anomie' were explored and abandoned without such extensive consideration.

Teacher questionnaire

One of the digressions arose from a comment by the headmaster of the school at One Arm Point on the tip of the Dampier Land peninsula, who stated that the male pupils under-achieved by comparison to the girls, and also that they seemed to be smaller. Surprisingly, anthropometric and laboratory measures were available to check the latter observation. In relation to the observations on under-achievement, a brief questionnaire regarding sex differences in students' performance was distributed to the teachers at the school, and later to teachers at predominantly Aboriginal schools throughout the region.

POPULATION-BASED SURVEY

Coincidence and serendipity may influence the research process more than many researchers are wont to acknowledge. Their welcome rays of light fell across the path of this researcher at several crucial junctures. One such occasion followed soon after the completion of the pilot surveys. Dr Richard Smith of the CSIRO Division of Human Nutrition had contacted my brother, with whom he had earlier collaborated, requesting help with a survey of hypertension and related issues among Kimberley Aborigines. The aim in this study was to examine a large random sample of Aborigines from across the Kimberley, an exercise which had not previously been attempted. As it was known that alcohol-use was related to the variables of interest, an estimation of consumption was necessary. So, just when I was lamenting my lack of progress and despairing at ever undertaking a comprehensive population survey, I was approached for that very purpose. The first meeting to develop an instrument was held in Derby in September 1987. It was suggested that the whole process would take six to nine months — a schedule that was informed largely by naivety. Two years later we were still on the road.

Questionnaire for Alcohol Research in the Kimberley

The first interviews using the new instrument didn't take place until February 1988. In the intervening months consultation with professionals, Aboriginal acquaintances, health-workers and students had resulted in a considerably larger but more workable instrument. Aboriginal visitors to my brother's house often found themselves as subjects for the latest version, frequently contributing their thoughts on idiom and style. An example of this process was the adapting of the successor to the SRQ-20, the Hopkins Symptom Checklist-25 (HSCL-25), which became one part of the new instrument.

The HSCL-25 was preferred to the SRQ-20 as a means of generating an index of current symptoms of depression and anxiety. As noted earlier, the dichotomous variables of the SRQ-20 had caused trouble. The HSCL-25 scores on a four-point Likert scale for each of 10 questions regarding anxiety, and 15 items relating to depressive symptoms. The flexibility offered by a continuum made this clearly more acceptable to informants. The difficulty was how to provide a scale meaningful to subjects, many of whom were illiterate. The solution emerged from recognising the fine visual discriminatory skills of Aborigines, which are matched by artistic skills, particularly the sensitive manipulation of abstract symbols. After being shown a painting by a gifted Gugadja (Kukatja) artist, I produced an abstract scale for the HSCL-25. Space, number, density and intensity were varied in this scale which, when tried in different settings, was understood and responded to with alacrity.

Ethical issues

By February 1988 development of the Questionnaire for Alcohol Research in the Kimberley (QARK) and the cardiovascular/dietary questionnaire was completed. The random sample contained 638 Kimberley residents of Aboriginal descent. Nineteen months were spent in the field, covering over 100 000 kilometres, with interviews conducted in 32 sites (usually on several occasions at each site). The format and the interviewers remained the same throughout.

In retrospect, many aspects of this research might have been undertaken differently. The ethics of, and procedures for conducting research in Aboriginal communities have since been debated widely. At that time the issues which were systematically addressed were: consent on an institutional, community (where possible), and individual level; and the provision of feedback to participants, agencies and communities.

Consent

After ethics committee approval from the CSIRO and the Western Australian Department of Health had been obtained, communities were contacted and the research described. In some settings local institutional clearance was also sought (for example, from the

Broome Regional Aboriginal Medical Service). After arriving in the community, we explained the work to the council and to the local health-workers. Twenty-two chairpersons were met with, among whom eight had been selected as part of the random sample. During our stay in a community, services were usually delivered. We often spent more time attending to medical problems than in conducting research. This was acknowledged and accepted as part of the research agenda. Where possible, the clinic was used for the interviews. However, as the research equipment was capable of running on batteries, it was not uncommon to work out-of-doors.

Obtaining informed consent from participants, particularly more tradition-oriented individuals, presented specific difficulties. Wherever possible the two sections of the study (cardiovascular/dietary and alcohol/psychosocial) were conducted in parallel, the subjects moving from one to the other. With the help of local health-workers, two interviewees were located and the research described to them over tea and biscuits. At the end of the session the subjects were again asked if there were questions; areas that appeared confusing were clarified. We then asked them if we could 'keep their story' and added that, if not, they could take the papers. At times relatives, partners or health-workers accompanied the subjects and occasionally assisted with explanations. While this approach appeared to provide the best prospects for obtaining meaningful informed consent, it is likely that for some elderly individuals comprehension remained poor. There is no simple solution.

Feedback
Feedback proceeded on five levels, beginning at the time of interview: face-to-face with the participants; a letter sent to each subject; discussions of the ongoing findings with the community councils and health-workers; a regionwide tour in May 1990; and a written simple language description. Following each interview, the results were discussed and advice given on problems that may have emerged. At times we initiated medical treatment and, in exceptional circumstances, organised hospitalisation. The participants were advised that a letter would arrive for them within a couple of months and, where it seemed appropriate, permission was obtained to send a copy of that to the sister or doctor at the local clinic.

The letter contained all the gathered medical information including anthropometry, blood pressure, laboratory and electrocardiographic results, with comments and suggestions on how particular problems might be addressed. This information was complex. However, while simplicity in language was sought, no attempt was made to restrict content based on estimations of the participant's level of comprehension. It was felt that all subjects had a right to complete information, and that restrictions discriminated against those who were tradition-oriented or illiterate. All informants were told where they could take the letters for further clarification. Subsequent reports from doctors, nurses and health-workers proved that this option was frequently exercised.

On return visits, feedback was provided to the health-workers and community members. In the regionwide tour, in May 1990, 12 publicised talks were delivered. Two-thirds of the approximately 500 people who attended these meetings were Aborigines. The local Aboriginal radio station in Kununurra also broadcast a review of the results.

Responses to the presentations were universally positive and included requests for documentation, as a result of which a simple language booklet was later produced (Smith, Hunter, Spargo & Hall 1990). The information was presented on two levels, each of which related to simple graphics. A basic level aimed at interested community members, with a somewhat more detailed description provided for community workers and agencies. Some 300 copies of this document were forwarded to communities, agencies and interested individuals. During another tour of the region, in October 1991, a survey was conducted to examine the degree of awareness of the research by both subjects and agency workers, and the opportunity taken to again disseminate the findings.

Analyses

Fieldwork clearly forms the guts of any research endeavour and requires particular skills and tolerance for uncertainty and ambiguity. However, making sense of the entrails, discriminating meaning in the patterns and profiles that tantalisingly or teasingly remain hidden, requires a different vision and expertise. As the data-base for this last section of the research grew to un-anticipated dimensions, the need for sophisticated analysis was glaringly apparent. The cardiovascular/dietary section of the research was examined by CSIRO in Adelaide. For the statistical expertise necessary to analyse the QARK, I turned to the National Drug and Alcohol Research Centre (NDARC) in Sydney.

Probably the most fortuitous coincidence of the Kimberley research occurred thousands of kilometres away from the region, in my meeting and collaborating with Professor Wayne Hall at NDARC. The insight, enthusiasm and intellectual rigour he brought to the task ensured my lasting admiration and appreciation. The resulting monograph contains a full description of the data-analytic strategies and a comprehensive documentation of the results (Hunter, Hall & Spargo 1991).

FRUITFUL DIGRESSIONS

This adumbration of the research process hopefully demonstrates the metamorphoses that occurred. The description outlines only the 'formal' approaches. More was learnt than is evident from the 'hard data'. Ongoing observation in diverse settings was critical, as was recognition and acknowledgement of informants as experts in their own right. This demanded a willingness to follow paths that threatened to meander from whatever the primary path of the research at that time appeared to be. Three such digressions leading to the examination of issues that will be covered in some detail later are informative.

One night in 1987 a group of Aborigines from a remote community arrived at my brother's house in high spirits. They came to sit and talk, drink beer and celebrate the good fortune of one of their members. It is well known that my brother regularly bets on horses, and our guests announced that their lucky man had won several thousand dollars at cards. The party, and the sharing, was beginning. Being relatively new in the Kimberley, I was curious about such abundance in the midst of scarcity. Obviously, the money had been won from others who probably had little to spare. Furthermore, it was soon revealed that the beneficiary of this good fortune was a frequent winner. The party eventually moved on, growing all the while. I was left with questions, which ultimately led to a study of gambling based on discussions with informants and attendance at various gaming venues.

Around Christmas another young Aborigine arrived at the door. It was immediately clear that this man's life had not been marked by such good fortune. He appeared battered and was 'fully drunk', dressed only in a pair of pants. Unable to articulate his reasons for coming, he sank into a seat. Mapped onto his chest and arms were dozens of keloid scars of various ages and sizes. In their random, jagged patterns they bore no resemblance to the traditional cicatrices that I had often seen on older Aborigines. As I turned to the other Aborigines who were sitting with us at the table, my question was anticipated with a gesture. An older woman, dragging her hand across her chest in imitation of a knife, announced, 'he's this one'. Once I became aware, I began to notice others: 'cutters' were then regularly encountered at the house. Certain social characteristics appeared to be common among this group of young adults, which led to an examination of non-traditional self-mutilation and the inclusion of questions relating to this behaviour in the QARK.

The third issue arose as a result of another visit much later in my stay. I was asked to assist in setting up for a party at the house of an Aboriginal acquaintance. Some time later I was sitting talking to an elderly woman when a fight broke out. I rose to see a man lying unconscious on the ground while another repeatedly kicked his head. The others present appeared to stand back and did not intervene. I do not remember how my appraisal of the situation proceeded; however, I attempted to resuscitate the prostrate figure. While bending over him I was the target of another well-placed kick. I woke up in hospital some 12 hours later. On many occasions I had observed violence (both Aboriginal and non-Aboriginal) and its consequences while in the Kimberley. However, this was a potent reminder that researchers are implicated in the social situations they purport to study.

The perpetrator later turned up on our random sample list and I interviewed him. Subsequently he was repeatedly in fights; following a brutal assault on an Aboriginal police aide, he was the victim of police violence in which, ironically, my brother was called on to intercede. These experiences led to thinking about the circumstances of violence, how it appeared to be changing, and its location in an intercultural context.

In the following chapters the results of the various sections of the research will be presented. The alcohol consumption data from the QARK is contained in chapter 5 (on alcohol). However, other sociodemographic, family and psychological material from the

QARK is interpolated into the relevant chapters. The next two chapters develop the historical frame essential to understanding this continuing research.

NOTES

1. For full documentation of the results of the surveys at both communities see the MD thesis, 'Just happy': Myths and realities of Aboriginal health in isolated Australia, University of New South Wales 1989.
2. Kleinman cites the DSM–III diagnosis of dysthymic disorder, which in contexts such as large sections of Aboriginal Australia, may represent a medicalisation of social problems, where:

   > severe economic, political and health constraints create endemic feelings of hopelessness and helplessness, where demoralisation and despair are responses to real conditions of chronic deprivation and persistent loss, where powerlessness is not a cognitive distortion but an accurate mapping of one's place in an oppressive social system, and where moral, religious and political configurations of such problems have coherence for the local population, but psychiatric categories do not. This state of chronic demoralisation, furthermore, is not infrequently associated with anaemia and other physiological effects of malnutrition and chronic tropical disorders that mirror the DSM–III symptoms of Dysthymic Disorder. (1987 : 452)

3. This instrument had been produced for a World Health Organisation Collaborative Study based on consensual selection of 20 items from four instruments to detect non-psychotic symptomatology, and four items designed to detect psychotic symptoms (Harding, De Arango, Baltazar, Climent, Ibrahim, Ladrigo-Ignacio, Murthy, Srinivasa & Wig 1980).

CHAPTER 2

Time

INTRODUCTION

Reading Battye's 1915 history of the north-west, one is seduced by the illusion of progress in the early development of the region. The time of writing was a period of high feelings for king and country. Given his imperialist sentiments, his preoccupation with territorial expansion and economic development is not surprising. Here was the fringe of the empire, the expansion of which both testified to and justified the rule of order and reason. However, for Aborigines of the Kimberley, order and reason in the early experiences of contact with Europeans was probably as illusory as the imperial policies formulated on their behalf, which provided that they be brought the benefits of Christianity and civilisation, be accorded full status as British subjects, and have their physical well-being fully protected (Long 1979). The stories of Aborigines in the Kimberley must be stripped of this veneer of progress and promises.

Documented history constitutes only a fraction of the millennia of Aboriginal occupation of the region. Groups continued to make first contact with European culture, thus entering 'history', well into this century. The consequences for those Aborigines emerging from the Western Desert to the mission at La Grange in the 1960s and 1970s bore scant resemblance to the experiences of Aborigines adapting to the arrival of settlers a century earlier. Aboriginal experiences of Europeans in the Kimberley must thus be seen in both diachronic and synchronic perspective. Certain areas were settled by Europeans more than a century ago, and most residents can identify historical events that have informed contemporary race relations. From the record of legislation, commissions and reports, a chronology emerges that is presented as historical reality. Two problems are posed by this narrative. First, it is a construction that was written and is read, for the most part, by Europeans, and serves their interests. Second, Aboriginal experience of European presence does not exist as a simple unfolding, a gradually increasing contact with and knowledge of the intruders:

> There was not a single moment of contact, not a dramatic confrontation, but a prolonged adjustment in response to changing circumstances — not a clash between one well-defined 'culture' and another well-defined 'culture' but a succession of changes during which each of the two 'cultures' itself underwent change. (Hasluck 1988 : 5)

Meining (in Healy 1978) identified four zones typical of the moving frontier of nineteenth century imperialism. Each of those zones had characteristic patterns of interaction with indigenous peoples that produced, reinforced and were, in turn, reinforced by prevailing stereotypes. The most disturbed zone, the 'European zone', included in New South Wales such melancholy figures as Bungaree (who sailed with Matthew Flinders, and visited the Kimberley in 1817 with Phillip Parker King [Macknight 1969]). By contrast, Pemulwuy in New South Wales and, later, Pigeon (Sandawara) in the Kimberley, represented the resistance (or treachery, depending on interpretation) of the 'frontier zone'. Beyond, according to Meining's schema, lay the 'disrupted native zone', only briefly contacted, but already experiencing the destabilising impact of population movements and introduced diseases. At the greatest remove from 'civilisation' lay the 'undisturbed region', populated in differing visions by 'noble savages' or bloodthirsty villains. As Healy noted, 'in the perception of Europeans a different kind of Aborigine inhabited each area' (1978 : 109), the most isolated regions being the interest of philanthropy (and later anthropology); the frontier zone, of colonial politics.

The images of Aborigines emanating from these settings clearly differed. Those responsible for such constructions did not acknowledge that they, and their subjects, were part of a process of social transformation. In the Kimberley there was no order to settlement: the front of European intrusion advanced unevenly and in waves; until recently non-Aborigines remained few in number and scattered. Until the 1960s most of the information emanating from the region was typical of a frontier zone, as it was provided by explorers, pastoralists, missionaries and government 'protectors'. Not only were such constructions non-Aboriginal, they were by and large non-reflective.

There are Aboriginal myths of contact (Kolig 1979) and European myths, the meanings of each determined by the needs and experiences of each group. Certain European myths, such as the early views of Aboriginal unrelatedness to the land, were clearly self-serving. Likewise, contemporary interpretation of the historical record is influenced by the prevailing social and political climate. Regardless, examination of the 'recorded events' has more than heuristic interest. However, as it is impossible to explore the history of the Kimberley in isolation, events outside the region which were of importance in shaping the course of Aboriginal–European relations will be interpolated.

Geographic boundaries and economic incentives constrained and channelled European intrusion into the Kimberley. The four broad regions determining the pace and course of this intrusion were, in order of increasing inaccessibility: the coast and islands; the fertile river valleys; the hill country; and the desert. Prior to settlement, there were Aboriginal populations throughout the region. These groups existed as relatively independent but interacting speech communities (northern Australia contained the greatest linguistic diversity on the continent) comprised of up to several hundred persons each (Vaszolyi 1979). Language acted as the mechanism of inclusion/exclusion for traditional land-usage groups and was a core element of identity (Kolig 1977). Complex networks of sanctioned relationships, restrictions and taboos gave structure to these groups, power being invested through religion rather than with secular leaders (Kolig 1982; Mol 1982).

Arriving Europeans were blind to the complexities of these Aboriginal societies. Their incursions into Aboriginal territories were made for many reasons, there being five broad, overlapping and interacting incentives: exploration and territorial acquisition; economic investment; missionary interests; government services; and, most recently, tourism. Before examining those processes and their consequences, the history of legislation and events affecting Aborigines throughout Western Australia is reviewed.

ACTS AND ACTORS

Before the first settlers arrived in the north, legislation formulated in Britain and the distant capitals of the south was defining the roles to be allocated to Aborigines in the European vision of the region.

With its economic viability marginal from the outset, Western Australia demanded convicts to support the foundering economy well after other colonies had ceased transportation (Hughes 1987). However, the British government prohibited the use of convict labour above the twenty-sixth parallel of latitude. While policy initially responded to events in the south, Aboriginal labour supply in the north ultimately became a central issue.

By the time settlers arrived in the Kimberley legislation already existed controlling various aspects of the lives of Aborigines and the nature of European relations with them. Recurring concerns were alcohol — the supply of which was prohibited to 'Aboriginal natives' in 1843 — and 'miscegenation'.

Policy was not clearly defined until the 1870s, formulated in response to events in the north. Subsequent legislation continued to be guided by the principles of paramountcy (of European interests) and protection, which became formalised in the 1873 Pearl Shell Fishery Regulation Act (Marchant 1981). In the century since, legislation has reflected fundamental shifts in policy, including the very definition of who is an Aborigine. Control and containment characterised the period to the turn of the century, with protection through isolation guiding policy until the Second World War, following which assimilation became official policy. This has in turn given way to self-management and self-determination.

Throughout, certain concerns, particularly the anticipated imminent 'passing of the Aborigine', and the spectre of an increasing population of 'half-castes', permeated political debate until the post-Second World War period. Legislative changes until that time systematically increased control over almost every facet of Aboriginal life. With varied degrees of interest and enthusiasm, the law-makers and experts in Perth deliberated and made decisions about Aborigines of the Kimberley.

In 1882 and 1884 investigations were undertaken with relevance for the Kimberley. The Fairbairn report of 1882 was produced in response to hostilities towards pastoralists in the Murchison and Gascoyne regions of the central coast. While suggesting that Europeans in the region may have been responsible for the Aborigines' actions, the report nevertheless broadly supported the pastoralists (Woenne 1979). Local European opinion was exemplified by the testimony of Charles F Gale, who suggested that: 'if the government shut their eyes for six months and let the settlers deal with the natives in their own way it would stop the depredations effectively' (in Haebich 1988 : 97). Gale was later to become chief protector of Aborigines from 1908 to 1915. The Forrest Commission of 1884 reported in detail on the conditions of Aborigines at Rottnest Island prison and briefly dealt with a range of other issues. The general thrust of the report implied that Aborigines were dying out and were of limited capacities and potential (Woenne 1979).

In September 1886 the Aborigines Protection Act created the Aborigines Protection Board under the auspices of the Colonial Office, including in the definition of 'Aboriginal natives' all half-castes living with Aborigines (Haebich 1988). The year before, J B Gribble, an Anglican missionary, had arrived in Western Australia from the Murrumbidgee region of New South Wales. He proceeded to an inspection tour of the Gascoyne region, and in his subsequent public criticisms of the treatment of Aborigines, *Dark Deeds in a Sunny Land or Blacks and Whites in North-West Australia*, published in 1905, alienated himself from both the pastoralists and the government. The reports were eagerly devoured in Britain and the eastern States, causing embarrassment for the administration in the west. His accusations regarding the cruel death in detention of Thackabiddy were first published by the *West Australian* but later retracted by the paper, which led to a law-suit by Gribble which, when lost, precipitated his departure from the colony (Hunt 1987). In his alienation from, and attack on the establishment, Gribble has come to be seen in the west as an early crusader against the abuses of Aborigines. In the east, where he was perceived as very much part of the missionary establishment, he has subsequently been portrayed as ineffectual and repressive (Read 1988).

Local government was, thus, clearly sensitive to negative criticism from Britain. The 1889 Constitution Act granted self-government to Western Australia; however, Section 70 ensured that 'native affairs' remained the responsibility of the imperial government, the only such exception among the new colonies of Australia. Rowley suggested that the 1886 Act itself was 'drafted so as to satisfy administrative consciences in Britain' (1972a : 242). John Forrest, the first premier (1890–1900), opposed the Aborigines Protection Board that had resulted from the 1886 Act. He bitterly resented the restrictions of Section 70, which granted one per cent of State revenue or £5000 annually as a safeguard for Aborigines, to be administered by the Board. In 1897 the one per cent clause was repealed — by means that have subsequently been claimed to have been illegal (McLeod n.d. : 9) — and the Aborigines Protection Board was abolished, being replaced by the Aborigines Department with Forrest as its head until 1900. In the same year Aborigines in Australia were excluded from the census by the Commonwealth Constitution Act and officially became uncounted non-citizens.

Forrest appointed H C Prinsep as the first Chief Protector of Aborigines. With no previous experience, Prinsep was preoccupied with the increasing mixed-descent population, and defined a policy that was interventionist and separatist. In this he was influenced by the 1897 Aborigines Protection and Restriction of Sale of Opium Act (Queensland), which extended control over Aborigines in Queensland. In 1902 the prohibition of sale of alcohol to 'Aboriginal natives' was extended to half-castes who associated with natives, and in 1905 to all Aborigines regardless of descent (Haebich 1988). While Prinsep was pressing for a bill similar to the Queensland law, adverse publicity about the treatment of Aborigines in the north-west resulted in the Roth Royal Commission, which delivered its findings in 1905. W E Roth, who had been instrumental in defining the Queensland bill, identified widespread abuses. While he only interviewed three Aborigines, he pointed to maladministration of the Aborigines Department and Police Department, and reinforced the need for protection (Woenne 1979). He advised the implementation of Prinsep's 1904 bill, which was the basis of the 1905 Aborigines Act, although that Act did not include his recommendations for a minimum wage for Aborigines. It did give greater powers to the Department, the Protector becoming the guardian of all 'illegitimate' Aboriginal children up to the age of 16 years, with right of removal. It also controlled movement, property, employment, marriage, access to firearms, residence, public behaviour, supply of alcohol, and allowed summary arrest. Police, as honorary protectors, were thus granted massive powers over Aborigines (Haebich 1988).

In 1908 Charles Gale became Chief Protector — the same man who had suggested extreme remedies at the time of the Fairbairn inquiry; he had also chaired the 1908 Royal Commission which exonerated members of the Canning exploration party from allegations of immorality and maltreatment of Aborigines. He continued the policies of isolation, which included setting up, with the Department of Health, the lock hospitals in the north. Legislation in 1909 allowed any local justice of the peace to send half-caste children less than eight years of age to a mission. In pursuit of tighter controls over cohabitation and access to alcohol, Gale pushed through the 1911 Aborigines Act Amending Act, which further increased the powers of his office. According to Jacobs (1990), Gale's aim was to shift the economic burden of Aborigines from the Department to stations. This period was one of great change in the south of Western Australia. The collapse of gold-mining together with the government investment in intensive agriculture which resulted in 55 000 Britons arriving in the State between 1903 and 1915, both combined to undermine the role of Aborigines in the pastoral industry of the south-west (Haebich 1988). Returning soldiers added to the economic malaise, public sentiment hardening towards the increasingly vulnerable southern Aboriginal population.

In 1915 Commissioner Underwood appointed A O Neville, previously secretary for Immigration, as Chief Protector of Aborigines. Like his predecessors he had no previous experience, but ushered in 'a new period in the administration of Aboriginal affairs in Western Australia characterised by aggressive leadership, strict implementation of the 1905 Act and unprecedented interference in the lives of Aborigines' (Haebich 1988 : 153). Neville remained the guiding hand of the Department from 1915 to 1940, save for the period 1920–1926, when he was secretary of the Department of the North-West. He expanded and centralised control over Aborigines throughout the State. Maintaining a tight rein, he initially welcomed anthropological research in the Kimberley, but later used his powers to prevent work critical of the directions of the Department. His relationship with the missions also soured, and southern Aborigines were increasingly moved onto government settlements (Moore River and Carrolup).

During Neville's tenure events in the Kimberley had repercussions for Aborigines throughout Western Australia. In 1926 Billy Hay, a white stockman on Nulla Nulla station, was speared and killed on the banks of the Durack River in the East Kimberley. The subsequent retaliation in May 1926 resulted in the deaths of at least 11 Aborigines in what became known as the 'Onmalmeri massacre'. E R B Gribble (the son of J B Gribble) was at the time at the nearby Anglican mission at Forrest River. Following the discovery of the charred remains, his persistent demands to have the matter investigated culminated in the Wood Royal Commission, which was empowered in January 1927. The investigation was hampered by local European resistance from the start, and those responsible received only censure. Gribble himself was ostracised and alienated from the Aborigines Department, despite Neville himself having earlier called for action in a speech to the Women's Services Guild. Ultimately, on the recommendation of A P Elkin to the Australian Board of Missions, Gribble was removed. The final report of the Commission pointed to collusion between police and pastoralists in the north, but also for the first time questioned the prevailing wisdom that Aborigines would die out, identifying their importance as a labour resource in the region (Woenne 1979). In the aftermath of the Commission, Neville continued to push for further controls over Aborigines of mixed-descent and for an increase in the age of guardianship by means of the 1929 Aborigines Act Amending Bill, which was at that time defeated but became the basis for the 1936 Act (Haebich 1988).

Through the 1920s Neville attempted to reduce the role of the missions, but in the early 1930s they found an ally in Mary Montgomery Bennett, a writer and ex-matron of Forrest River mission. The policies of the government, and Neville, were attacked, culminating in the presentation to a London conference of the British Commonwealth League in June 1933, of accusations of slavery and abuses of Aboriginal women in the north. On 30 August 1933 Coverley, the Labor member for Kimberley, pointed out the ensuing publicity in the British and local press and called for a Royal Commission to examine the administration of the Department.

The resulting 1934 Moseley Royal Commission was the first to take substantial evidence from Aborigines. Moseley's 26 recommendations included: the appointment of divisional protectors as permanent officials; a reduction of the number of honorary protectors and abolition of police protectors; compulsory medical examinations; the establishment of a leprosarium; a medical fund for employed Aborigines; and a variety of provisions for rationing (Moseley 1935). The report did not question the policies of protection, and the ensuing 1936 Native Administration Act, ironically, widened the power of the new Department of Native Affairs, with Neville, architect of the Act, the first commissioner of Native Affairs.

In April 1937, near the end of his term of office, Neville attended the inaugural national meeting of protectors and commissioners in Canberra and put forward the position he had been moving towards over several years — that the future for Aborigines lay in absorption into the dominant population through 'miscegenation' (Elkin 1979). General opinion was slowly changing, with the debate moving into a public arena as it became clear that, rather than dying out, the Aboriginal population was increasing. The mounting pressure for federal control of Aboriginal affairs was resisted by the wartime commissioner, F I Bray (1940–1947), and by the minister for the North-West, Coverley.

In the south, the conditions at the government concentration centre at Moore River contributed to the passage of the 1944 Natives (Citizenship Rights) Act, which made it marginally easier for Aborigines to obtain conditional citizenship, provided they were able to prove they had dissolved tribal and native associations and were fit and proper citizens (Howard 1981). In the same year a Commonwealth Referendum, which included a clause allowing the Commonwealth to legislate for Aborigines, was defeated, though it achieved majority support in Western Australia (Elkin 1979). Later in the 1940s the 'Pindan movement', inspired by Don McLeod in the Pilbara, resulted in the first industrial action by Aborigines in the north (Rowley 1972a; McLeod n.d.).

During the tenure of commissioner S G Middleton (1948–1962), the policies of assimilation, encouraged by post-war immigration and Elkin's influence, became paramount. Following changes at the Commonwealth level, in 1954 the Native Welfare Act reconstituted the State Department of Native Affairs as the Department of Native Welfare. The director of Native Affairs, thus, became the director of Welfare in an attempt to bring all disadvantaged Australians under the same welfare umbrella (Hasluck 1988). Aborigines throughout Western Australia were influenced by changes at the national level, with the lifting of restrictions on Commonwealth social services in 1960, and the right to voluntary enrolment in Commonwealth and State elections following in 1961 and 1962. In Western Australia, the 1963 Native Welfare Act removed the remaining restrictions, save drinking rights, which remained in force in the Kimberley until 1971. The policy of assimilation was clearly stated by Hasluck at the 1961 Commonwealth and State ministers conference in Canberra:

> The policy of assimilation means in view of all Australian governments that all aborigines and part-aborigines are expected eventually to attain the same manner of living as other Australians and to live as members of a single Australian community enjoying the same rights and privileges, accepting the same responsibilities, observing the same customs

and influenced by the same beliefs, hopes and loyalties as other Australians. Thus, any special measures taken for aborigines and part-aborigines are regarded as temporary measures, not based on colour but intended to meet their need for special care and assistance to protect them from any ill effects of sudden change and to assist them to make the transition from one stage to another in such a way as will be favourable to their future social, economic and political advancement. (1961 : 1)

The Commonwealth Referendum of 1967 followed a period of intense political activity by the Federal Council for the Advancement of Aborigines and Torres Strait Islanders. With support from both the Liberal–Country Party coalition and the Labor opposition, the resulting amendments gave the Commonwealth the power to make laws for Aborigines nationally (section 51), and to include Aborigines in the census (section 127). While passed with a 90 per cent Yes-vote nationally, the electorates with the highest proportion of No-votes were those with substantial Aboriginal populations: the State with the highest No-vote being Western Australia (19 per cent); and the electorate of Kalgoorlie, in which the Kimberley is located, polled a 29 per cent No-vote, the nation's highest (Bennett 1985).

Following the referendum, Prime Minister Holt established a three-member Council for Aboriginal Affairs under H C Coombs. An explosion of activity followed, with the 'tent Embassy' in 1972 bringing Aborigines' demands (with bureaucratic and police responses) into the living-rooms of 'White Australia'. The subsequent Labor government sped up the pace of change, with Gough Whitlam establishing the Department of Aboriginal Affairs in 1972. The formation of the National Aboriginal Consultative Committee in 1973 was followed by calls for a National Aboriginal Congress in the following year in a failed attempt to gain Aboriginal control of the Department of Aboriginal Affairs itself (Jones & Hill-Burnett 1982). With the 'new era' of self-determination came a growth in the bureaucracy:

In less than ten years the new Department had proliferated all over the continent, with warrens on every bare hillside — a Central Office in Canberra, Regional and Area offices in all States and at least a dozen commissions, councils, conferences and institutes studying, arguing, consulting and drawing their travelling allowances and sitting fees. Money glistened everywhere like flowers in the desert after rain. (Hasluck 1988 : 124)

In Western Australia in 1972 the State Department of Native Welfare split to become the Department of Community Welfare and the

Aboriginal Affairs Planning Authority. Administrative changes were accompanied by an increasing public awareness of Aboriginal grievances. The Furnell Commission of 1973 was the first Western Australian commission occurring in response to Aboriginal demands, emphasising the shift in focus from assimilation to self-determination (Woenne 1979), with the Laverton Royal Commission of 1976 returning to confrontations between police and Aborigines.

In the 1970s a new Aboriginal political voice emerged, with events in northern Australia prominent. In the 1977 State elections, the first with substantial Kimberley Aboriginal participation, the Court of Disputed returns upheld an objection by the Labor candidate, Ernie Bridge, a local Aboriginal pastoralist, on the basis of practices which had prejudiced Aboriginal voters. Although Bridge had only been narrowly defeated by Alan Ridge, the Liberal candidate, it was Ridge who was returned in the subsequent by-election (Tatz 1979; Bennett 1989). Nevertheless, these controversies emphasised Aborigines' presence on the political stage.

In the Northern Territory the 1962 Yirrkala bark petition, the 1967 Gurintji walk-off at Wave Hill and the 1968 Blackburn land-rights case instituted a new level of Aboriginal activism affecting Aborigines nationally. The subsequent 1973 Woodward Land Rights Commission culminated in the 1976 Aboriginal Land Rights (Northern Territory) Act, stimulating demands for similar legislation elsewhere. Contemporaneously, the federal government set up the Aboriginal Land Fund Commission (ALFC) in 1974, to facilitate the purchase of land by Aboriginal groups on the open market. By the end of the 1970s seven Kimberley properties had been purchased under this plan, with the Kimberley Land Council functioning from 1978. Two years later, on Noonkanbah, property purchased by the ALFC, Premier Court's Liberal government supported mining interests against the objections of traditional and new owners, focusing national attention on the Kimberley. Subsequently, the Labor government of Brian Burke appointed Paul Seaman to head the Aboriginal Land Inquiry. Ultimately, his recommendations supporting land-rights were rejected. Instead, the government opted for land grants involving freehold title without inalienable rights with the passage of the Western Australian Aboriginal Land Act (1985). In spite of this, land-rights continued to symbolise the nationwide demands for autonomous control.

NEW ARRIVALS IN AN OLD LAND

EXPLORATION

European 'pre-settlement intrusion' in the west Kimberley spanned the period from the mid-seventeenth to the nineteenth century, and in the east Kimberley from 1819 to 1884 (Clement 1987). However, the first Europeans to sight the region were probably Portuguese in the sixteenth century and the Dutch through the following century. William Dampier, the first Briton to reach New Holland, careened his vessel, *Cygnet*, at Karrakatta Bay on King Sound in 1688 (Marchant 1988). The accounts of his circumnavigation brought fame and benefactors. With the support of the Admiralty, he returned to the western Australian coast in command of the *Roebuck* in 1697. His observations of Aboriginal life have been coloured by his privateering, and overshadowed by the often quoted negative comparisons with the 'Hodmadods of Monomatapa' that are found in his manuscript which was written considerably later (Marchant 1988).[1] His detailed descriptions, for example of Bardi life and communal fishing techniques, provided a picture recognisable into this century (Mulvaney 1989). These accounts influenced such later luminaries as Joseph Banks, who commented on 'the prejudices which we had built on Dampier's account' (in O'Brian 1988 : 124) while off the coast of New South Wales in 1770.

During the voyage of the *Roebuck* an Aborigine was shot near Shark Bay following the spearing of a sailor — the first casualty of British contact. It was there that Dampier identified pearlshell, anticipating the discovery of pearls by Helpman at the same site in 1850. French navigators also came; Baudin visiting the area of La Grange in 1802, and Freycinet in 1808. The first systematic explorations were those of Phillip Parker King in 1817, 1819 and 1821 in the *Mermaid*, and J C Wickham in the *Beagle* in 1837.

George Grey was the first to venture beyond the coastal fringe of the Kimberley. Those who had preceded him had had little impact on the Aboriginal population, generally returning to their ports of origin with pessimistic reports. During the wet of 1837–1838 Grey explored the Glenelg area of the northern Kimberley. He made extensive observations of the land and local Aboriginal groups. On several occasions conflict arose, and he was himself wounded. Despite near calamity, and unaware of the enormous seasonal variations, he returned with buoyant accounts of the grazing potential. His reports, and those of A C Gregory in 1861, who described good range land in the east Kimberley, were to change the perception of the region. This was enhanced with the discovery of pearls, and by the sighting of guano by Stokes on the Abrolhos Islands during another voyage of the *Beagle* in 1840. While exploration would continue, there were now reasons to stay. Early documents reflected the economic incentives, Aborigines being incidental observations: 'Most of the Australian land explorers were not particularly reflective men, and the Aborigines that came through their journals were undifferentiated stick creatures. They were men whose acts swamped their thoughts' (Healy 1978 : 160).

SETTLEMENT: GOLD, CATTLE, PEARLS, CONVERTS

Mining

Guano mining, which started in 1850 and continued sporadically on the Lacepede and, later, Abrolhos islands until 1904, had little impact on Aborigines. During the explorations of Alexander Forrest, who traversed the Kimberley to the Ord River in 1879, Fenton-Hill, a mining and geological surveyor, speculated on the possibility of gold in the upper Fitzroy region (Clement 1987). The rush that eventually brought thousands of European prospectors to the region followed the discovery of gold over 800 kilometres inland by Charles Hall and Jack Slattery in August 1885 at what became known as Halls Creek. Derby (founded in 1883, the same year as Broome) and Wyndham (1886) served as entry points for the miners. Along with the relatively large number of Europeans came discriminatory legislation: miners' rights were denied to 'Asiatics and Africans' (Battye 1987 [1915]). A century after the brief gold rush, systematic exploration and major ventures such as the Argyle diamond mine, have had substantial impact on Aboriginal communities.

Cattle

Historically, cattle and pearling represented the two major economic forces and thus, owing to their particular needs — land and labour — the main points of contact and conflict. In 1864, 140 settlers arrived with sheep at Camden Harbour, south of present-day Broome, which was, however, abandoned the following year. A later attempt, made further north at Roebuck Bay, also failed, with the deaths of the two leaders following conflict with local Aborigines. Maitland Brown (later a notable Western Australian politician) led an armed party in reprisal, which killed 20 Aborigines on Roebuck Plains. This was only the first of a series of punitive expeditions. Sheep were finally successfully introduced to Yeeda station near Derby in 1881.

The period of greatest pastoral expansion lasted from the 1880s to the First World War, with graziers moving along the Fitzroy valley from the west. The east Kimberley was settled in three major overland treks lasting more than two years each, in which the Duracks, Macdonalds and Buchanans brought their herds of cattle from Queensland to the Ord. While passing explorers had relatively little direct impact on Aboriginal life, settlement brought a different level of interaction as Aborigines resisted this expropriation of their land and its resources. The consequences of resistance were grave. The 'resistance' of Pigeon (Sandawara), which followed the killing of Constable Richardson, lasted three years until his death in 1897. It provided a pretext for a systematic campaign to pacify the Bunaba people of the Fitzroy valley.[2] With herds increasing and replacing native game around the waterholes, 'criminal' spearing of cattle was inevitable, initiating further conflict.

Aboriginal hostility was clearly seen as a threat to the expansion of the cattle industry. While the government was responsible for 'native welfare' and 'protection', it was also charged with providing for the safety and enterprise of the pastoralists. The dilemma was compounded by the absence of any mechanisms for enforcing government policy in remote regions, and resulted in the pastoralists' demands for authority to maintain 'order', which led to the 1882 Fairbairn report. Exemplifying the paradox, the 1886 Act empowered police as 'honorary protectors'.

With the land settled and in the control of the graziers, the concerns turned to labour. Rapidly developing skills, Aborigines became valued as a resource. The seasonal cycles and nature of cattle work, involving a mobile existence related to a tangible food resource, was not entirely alien to traditional land/resource-utilisation patterns (McGrath 1987). Identification with the activities of the cattle industry, particularly important for males, was a source of considerable esteem and provided relative safety compared to the dangers of resistance.

For the pastoralists, such identification and subsequent dependence also reduced the killing of stock by Aborigines, for which the government had had to provide compensation. The costs of this, and of imprisonment, at times requiring removal to Rottnest Island off Fremantle, were prohibitive. The conflict of Aboriginal 'protection' versus pastoral expansion was superficially resolved by the setting up of government stations at Moola Bulla in 1910 and Munja in 1927. These stations, and ration depots such as Violet Valley (1911), were conceived to reduce this expenditure. They acted as collection points for Aboriginal offenders from throughout the Kimberley, absconders being liable to punishment and forced to return by the police. Adults and children could be imprisoned for three months under the Masters and Servants Act, in power until 1892, following which, under the 'Whipping Act', a local justice of the peace could sentence recalcitrant Aborigines to a flogging. Such legislation compounded isolation and Aborigines were further removed from the events of the wider Australian society: 'The stations of the North-West were temporarily immune from historical events, and the Aborigines who lived on, and moved around, those stations were further removed. The essence of their existence was ahistorical' (Healy 1978 : 152).

Laws formulated far to the south, supervised by rarely seen travelling inspectors and honorary protectors, were of little relevance to the life of Kimberley station Aborigines. During the period of quiet that followed settlement and 'pacification' (1930s–1960s) several patterns emerged in the relationship between pastoralists and Aborigines. The first and most progressive (though clearly paternalistic) may be called the 'good pastoralist', for whom there was a long-term family investment in an area and in its people. Stations such as Mount Elizabeth, Argyle and Rosewood fall into this group, with basic education being provided to Aborigines. Jack Kilfoyle on Rosewood developed a pension scheme for long-term workers in the 1960s ahead of government initiatives. For the second group, 'benevolent dictators', there was also a 'responsible' attitude, but based on a feudal relationship to Aborigines as property that went with station ownership. Lulugai, Fossil Downs and Mount House were typical. The last group consisted generally of absentee landlords without an enduring personal relationship to the station. Certain of the managers, such as Vic Jones at Gogo, were long-term residents who generated fierce loyalties among their workers and were more typical of the second group. Others, particularly those part of corporate structures, which became dominant from the 1960s, demonstrated a utilitarian relationship to both land and Aborigines, with little regard for workers' health, safety or well-being beyond that which expedited profit.

Aboriginal women on the stations had additional roles within the homestead. As servants they learnt skills, including language. As sexual partners they at times had a degree of social mobility unavailable to males, but often at a cost. While some lived in stable relationships despite prohibitive laws and attitudes, many were treated as chattels, as Gribble observed: 'in certain places the choicest bit of hospitality that could be tendered to a visitor was the finest looking blackgirl' (1987 [1905]: 51). As intermediaries between homestead and camp, the relationship between Aboriginal men and women was affected:

> Although the white men arrived womanless, their guns and goods meant they gained access to Aboriginal females. The story starts with Aborigines in control of a world upon which Europeans had started to encroach. It concludes in a loss of power, and emphasises male Aboriginal loss of their women. (McGrath 1987 : 3)

The arrival of European women transformed inter-racial relationships, particularly at the higher levels of the 'pastoral aristocracy'. The gross asymmetries of intercultural power are no more glaringly evident than in the domain of inter-racial sexual contact. While Aboriginal men were relatively powerless against demands for their women, the control of the sexuality of European women became symbolic of racial superiority (Hunt 1986). Inter-racial relationships involving white men were frowned on, but such unions involving white women were unthinkable.

The Second World War emphasised the importance of Aboriginal workers in the north. In 1941 Aborigines living north of the twentieth parallel were forbidden to travel south of that line. This was ostensibly to limit the spread of leprosy but McCorquodale (1985) suggested that the real purpose was to protect the labour-vulnerable pastoral industry of the north. During the early decades of the century unionists in Western Australia had resisted attempts by Aborigines to enter the workforce (Haebich 1988). Using the rationale that money only caused problems for Aborigines, payment to Aboriginal pastoral workers in the Kimberley was withheld until the 1950s, although some Pilbara workers were paid in the 1930s.

The issues were clearly articulated in parliament by Coverley: 'Money is a curse to the native but there are places where the employment of natives is contingent upon their being paid certain wages, and we find where the line of demarcation exists, which is perhaps about Broome, that the question of wages is a serious problem' (1933: 649).

Mounting pressure for equal wages for Aboriginal pastoral workers during the 1960s in the Northern Territory led to the North Australian Workers' Union case before the Conciliation and Arbitration Commission. In December 1968, following the Wave Hill walk-off and soon after the Commonwealth Referendum, award wages, with the implicit recognition of labour value, were extended to Aboriginal workers in the Northern Territory, precipitating major demographic changes. However, in the Kimberley the population shifts from stations to the town fringes had already begun. Innovative technology in the 1960s brought a gradual erosion of reliance on Aboriginal labour: the fencing of cattle runs, bores for fixed watering points, road transportation and, finally, aerial mustering — all of which had been compounded by the economic consequences of an American embargo on Australian lean beef during the Johnson administration. Stations were also gradually passing from family hands to corporate control, in which 'owners were replaced by managers, long-lasting relationships were ended, managers were strangers thrust upon the Aboriginal population' (Spargo 1981). In the Kimberley the costs of signing Aboriginal workers up to be covered by the award, and a 'slow workers provision' allowing some employers to pay sub-award wages, ensured continuing disparities in wages. Regardless, the relationship between pastoralists and Aboriginal workers was changing:

> the 'equal wage' decision had had the effect therefore of replacing an ill defined (but usually understood) obligation on the pastoralists to provide modest support for a whole Aboriginal group in return for the labour of a few, with a precise and larger, but limited, obligation towards the individuals actually employed. (Coombs 1978 : 10)

The evictions and walk-offs from the stations to centres like Fitzroy Crossing were unplanned, displacing many communities from station life, which had at least allowed an identification with land and tradition. At the same time as struggling to deal with the psychological impact of dispossession, the moves were associated for many with the introduction of a cash economy, and alcohol. Many

Europeans saw the Aboriginal casualties of this sudden transition as justifying their earlier paternalism.

Pearling

The history of the pearlshell and pearling industry in the Kimberley is entwined with that of the pastoral industry, many pastoralists themselves having interests in pearling (Hunt 1986). As on stations, remoteness and reliance on Aboriginal labour defined the relationships with Aborigines. The focus of pearling moved from Shark Bay in the 1860s to the fertile beds south of Roebuck Bay in the 1870s. Nominal responsibility for controlling the use of 'native labour' came from Great Britain. The ban on the use of females and children in 1871, and the Pearl Shell Fishery Regulation Act (1873), were attempts to counter forced recruitment (blackbirding[3]), which was rife during the 1870s and 1880s. Gribble recorded the report of David Carly, whose description of labour recruiting practices in 1872 demonstrates the impotence of legislation:

> I have seen numbers of natives brought in from the interior, and some of them had never before seen the face of a white man, and they were compelled to put their hand to a pen and make a cross which they never could understand, and having done this they were then slaves for life, or as long as they were good for pearl diving. Their rations consisted only of a little flour when they are engaged in pearling. (1987 [1905] : 50)

Rapid expansion of the industry and high mortality ensured the demand for Aboriginal workers until the development of diving suits and compressors (1887) allowed deep-sea harvesting, and resulted in the reliance on an Asian workforce. At its height, before the First World War, over 400 luggers and more than 3000 indentured labourers were based in Broome. Demands made of coastal Aborigines changed, from men to women. As early as 1844 the colony had introduced legislation to 'prevent the enticing away the Girls of the Aboriginal Race from School, or from any Service in which they are employed' (McCorquodale 1985 : 108). Legislation supposedly to protect Aboriginal women from abuses added a powerful and enduring sexist component to official government attitudes. The Aborigines Act of 1905 prohibited Aboriginal women being within two miles (3.2 km) of a creek used by pearlers at night, bans on cohabitation remaining in force until 1953. The cumulative weight of such measures and attitudes towards a woman of Aboriginal descent was described by McCorquodale:

> First, she was considered of dubious moral character, a legislative whore, unworthy as a guardian of her own child who could be taken from her and kept in an institution. She could be sent to a school to be instilled in Christianity and service; if she were unsatisfactory at her task she could be beaten; her employer was not permitted to be Asiatic or Negro; she was subject to unannounced inspection by police or the Superintendent; unless she married a white she was not exempt from the Act; if she failed to marry a white, but lived with him, he and she were guilty of a criminal offence. Her movements within the State, within districts, even within a reserve or camp were circumscribed, particularly if pearling or trading vessels were nearby; she possessed no citizenship rights and could not qualify for exemption as a returned serviceman. (1985 : 130)

Such 'protective' legislation did little to stem the abuses of Aboriginal women, particularly as the powerful enticements offered by white and Asian men made Aboriginal women, and at times their men, colluding partners. However, while the pearling industry enjoyed only a relatively brief primacy in the white economic growth of the Kimberley, its social impact has been enduring. Among the large group of 'coloureds' descended from Europeans and Asian indentured labour, a proportion did not identify primarily as Aboriginal, producing a tripartite ethnic community. According to Hasluck, in Broome: 'the half-caste child was born into a separate half-caste community and grew up almost as a member of a distinct race' (1988 : 49). Coverley voiced alarm about the growing coloured population to parliament, with warnings on a familiar theme:

> The position at Broome is positively alarming. An endeavour was made by the residents of Broome and those in control of the allocation of areas for certain purposes in that township — I refer to the local authorities — to keep the whites, blacks and coloured races separate. Broome town is generally recognized as the coloured quarter. The Japanese and the Chinese have their respective areas and their different streets. Then there are the Koepangers, the Malays, and, in addition the mixture of all of them. On the other hand, the aborigines and the half castes, by virtue of their being domestics, have found their way into the homes of the white people themselves. The trouble is that they have been allowed, and encouraged to become landowners, with the result that the position to-day is serious. There is no line of demarcation in Broome to show where the white people begin and where the aborigines, as residents, end. Being the owners of land in Broome, it has followed that certain of the coloured races have been permitted to build homes within the

area formerly proclaimed for whites alone. There is not only the growing menace of the half-caste, but there is the additional difficulty of the coloured person who represents a mixture of the Japanese, Malay, Chinese and other races. (1933 : 651)

The relationship between full-descent Aborigines and those of mixed-descent was influenced by legislation which offered citizenship to those among the latter who distanced themselves from Aboriginal culture. For any who had developed relationships with Japanese, the Second World War brought stark confirmation of their power-lessness as their relatives were sent into internment. Visiting Derby in August 1969, a psychiatric team echoed the divisions of thirty years earlier:

> The three races appear to live in separate streams in the town. One is the floating population of whites, staying in the town usually one to two years and very occasionally three years, working in administration offices, banks, business, schools and hospitals. The part-aborigines or 'coloured' are the small business people, clerks, technicians, etc., who are the backbone of the town; many have lived in Derby all their lives. Full-blood natives are mainly doing labouring work in and around the town. . . . The three groups tend to keep separate socially and make friends amongst their own group. (Gault, Krupinski & Stoller 1970 : 175)

Missions

The arrival of missionaries in the Kimberley introduced the most complex of the forces influencing European–Aboriginal relations. While there is disagreement on their impact and consequences, without them some Aboriginal groups would not have survived the turmoil of settlement. Their presence added the third arm of what Rowley identified as the 'triangle of tension' — mission, settler and government (1972b). Tension and ambivalence resulted from an uneasy relationship of necessity. This is not to suggest that direct confrontation did not occur; indeed, J B Gribble, and later his son, were better known in Western Australia for their confrontations than their conversions. However, the mission–pastoralist relationship, friable as it was, involved intersecting interests. The most extensive chronicle of the Roman Catholic church in the north (Durack 1969) was compiled by a direct descendant of the pastoral aristocracy, the 'Kings in Grass Castles'.

Complex motivations brought missionaries to such extraordinary tasks. The histories of the various settlements are as diverse as the individuals involved. However, a common belief informed most early approaches, laying the seeds for one of the most enduring convictions — that the only hope for Aboriginal survival lay in isolation. As Rowley noted, thus assuring survival was not without cost: 'A mission may have spent many decades in one area without bringing its community on to the lines of communication with the outside world' (1972a : 114).

The first mission in the Kimberley was the short-lived Catholic settlement at Disaster Bay on King Sound in 1872. However, following the successful founding of Beagle Bay by Trappist monks in 1890 (taken over by the Pallotines from 1900 to 1981), a variety of religious groups became active. These included: a Church of England mission at Forrest River in 1897, abandoned but later operating from 1913 to 1968; a Benedictine mission at Drysdale River (later Kalumburu, 1907–1983); a Presbyterian mission at Port George IV in 1912 (later moved to Kunmunya from 1916 to 1950, to Wotjulum from 1950 to 1956 and finally to Mowanjum near Derby in 1956); a United Aborigines Mission settlement at Fitzroy Crossing (1952–1979); and a Catholic mission at remote Balgo Hills on the rim of the Great Sandy Desert (1939–1983). Within the Broome region, other than the Beagle Bay settlement, there was a Catholic mission at Lombardina (Pallottine, 1911–1985); and a Catholic mission at La Grange (Pallottine, 1955–1982), which took over from a government feeding station. There was also an independent mission settlement founded on Sunday Island in 1899 by Sydney Hadley, a reformed alcoholic pearler with a long history of arrests in Cossack through the 1880s (Hunt 1986); incorporated into the United Aborigines Mission in 1923, the mission moved to Derby in 1962, with a return by the community to One Arm Point in 1971. Broome itself was the focus of Catholic activity within the Kimberley, including an orphanage from 1912 to 1963, and an Aboriginal boarding school from the mid-1970s.

The diversity of the institutions was matched by varying degrees of acceptance and understanding of Aboriginal communities and customs. At one extreme was rigid intolerance and active prohibition of activities related to traditional lifestyle; at the other, there was the scholarly, methodical work of such figures as the German priest and anthropologist, Ernest Ailred Worms. Regardless, all demanded behaviour that did not conflict with the missions' primary agendas — conversion — which necessarily required an imposed structuring of Aboriginal lives.

While the motivations of pastoralists and missionaries were different, similarities existed on other levels. A major enticement which drew Aborigines towards settlements, whether mission or station, was food (and other commodities, in particular tobacco). Both relied on labour for growth, and at various times and to varying degrees were 'responsible' to the government for Aboriginal welfare. By contrast, a major point of divergence was their respective investment in social change. Pastoralists, requiring a constant supply of labour, benefited from the dependency of Aborigines on the station, who in return were assured a role in station life that provided relative stability. This role required the acquisition of specific skills. However, other than women taken in as domestics, fluency with English and learning European lifestyle skills was often perceived as a threat to the stability of the labour pool (Reynolds 1982). While station owners were relatively unconcerned with traditional life, the situation on missions was different. Despite the isolationist policy: 'The basic intention was to change the socio-cultural system and the individual lives of the people with whom they worked' (Berndt & Berndt 1988 : 45).

Ultimately, this agenda required that Aborigines renounce their traditional identity, which was informed by knowledge of kinship, law and language. To this end some missions segregated the sexes in dormitories. Certain groups were isolated in environments 'uncontaminated' by traditional beliefs, with forced removal of mixed-descent children from throughout the Kimberley to such settlements as Beagle Bay.[4] The use of English was universally promoted, and in some areas aggressive attempts were made to suppress Aboriginal language. However, the inflexibility of the missionaries and the lack of any mutuality of ideas or ideals was not conducive to the internalisation of a mission identity — 'there was no real incentive for such a radical move' (Kolig 1988 : 384).

A more enduring consequence of the missions was education, which even in its limited scope for Aborigines in the Kimberley, ultimately became one of the most important forces for social change. Ironically, through education and the suppression of indigenous languages, the missionaries supported the development of a political voice that was important, *inter alia*, in the decline of the missions. However, there were within the Catholic missions of the Kimberley two quite different experiences. The early coastal missions

(Beagle Bay and Lombardina) contained a large mixed-descent population, who were better educated and had greater contact with the wider society. By contrast, on missions such as Kalumburu, Balgo and La Grange, where there were predominantly full-descent, tradition-oriented Aborigines, control was maintained through isolation. For the less-remote communities, the restricted secular power and relatively limited resources of the missionaries, compared to other Europeans, confronted Aborigines with the reality that 'conversion in the Kimberleys meant accepting commitment to a small ideological and social enclave of little importance to the rest of White society' (Kolig 1988 : 384).

The isolation of Aborigines on remote missions was consistent with early government policies. Limited resources, and the power and position of church organisations, provided the foundations of a relationship that endured the occasional spats (notably with Neville) arising from the government's conflicting roles of Aboriginal protection and European economic development. The gradual change in policy from protection through isolation to assimilation that occurred through the 1940s and 1950s was reflected in the increasing emphasis placed on economic development for both the government-run stations and the missions. The 1950s represented the zenith of missionary expansion in Western Australia, an explicit marriage of secular and sacred interests nurtured under the administration of Commissioner Middleton. La Grange was the last of these cooperative ventures, the Catholic Church taking over the government feeding station (itself born of the wedding of government and pastoral interests) in 1955, subsequently adding an adjoining 200 000 hectare station in 1960.

The political events from the 1960s, and the major changes in Catholic missionary activity worldwide that followed the Second Vatican Council, resulted in a reassessment of the role of the church in the Kimberley. While the Roman Catholic church is still a powerful force in the Broome region, the 1980s have seen the administrative control of all missions pass into the hands of the respective Aboriginal communities and the Department of Aboriginal Affairs. The degree of real change, as noted by Brady and Palmer was less clear: 'Government bureaucracies to some extent were merely substituted for mission control, particularly when it came to issues of community management and the direction of budgets' (1988 : 244).

Late arrivals on the religious scene in northern Australia were a variety of evangelical and fundamentalist groups. There has also been a nativistic revival adapting elements of tradition and Christianity with an anti-white focus (Koepping 1988). Among the former is the Summer Institute of Linguistics, whose extensive work on Aboriginal languages throughout Australia appeals to an investment in heritage and identity. The religious or emotional appeal of other fundamentalist and more strictly evangelical movements rose through the 1970s, occurring during the time of disruption that followed the political changes earlier in that decade. While the rigid posture assumed by some groups may have provided a point of anchorage, there has been a gradual recession of these movements through the mid-1980s, particularly in the more economically privileged areas of the Kimberley.

GOVERNMENT NOMADS

Cathy Clement (1987) has suggested that explorers may have appeared nomadic to Aborigines owing to their transitoriness and lack of discernible impact. The 1970s brought a generation of government workers (to what has at times been referred to as 'the land of the long white socks') who often bore similar characteristics to those earlier 'nomads'.

The complex relationship between the representatives of state authority and various exploration, pastoral and missionary concerns has already been commented on. In the next chapter the development of medical services in the Kimberley will be described. In the remainder of this chapter certain other government agencies influencing the lives of Aborigines will be briefly explored: education and community development.

Education

The Elementary Education Act of 1871 drew no distinction between Aboriginal and non-Aboriginal children. However, an 1897 amendment to the Aborigines Protection Act (1886) passed responsibility for the education of Aborigines to the Aborigines Department. As a consequence, Aborigines were excluded from government schools until the 1940s, only slowly gaining entrance thereafter (Mounsey 1979). The government position can be gauged from the statement

of the member for Beverley in support of the minister for Native
Welfare in 1942:

> Why send these half-castes and natives to school for two or three years?
> Of what use is the schooling to them afterwards? I would rather have
> an uneducated than an educated nigger. A native with some educa-
> tion develops into a bigger scoundrel than does the ordinary native.
> (Cited by Trainor 1973 : 1250)

Missions were designated as the agencies responsible for delivering
education to a population thought capable of only limited achievement. Children from throughout the Kimberley came, or were
sent, to Catholic schools in Broome, Lombardina and Beagle Bay.
Following the Commonwealth Referendum, the phasing out of
the Department of Native Welfare passed the responsibility for
Aboriginal health and education to the respective State departments.
Despite this, the Catholic church retained its primacy in terms of
Aboriginal education, with Broome continuing to act as the major
centre in the Kimberley. It has been suggested that the emphasis on
education is an adaptive compromise to the gradual eroding of the
Catholic power base. Unable to exercise control over Aborigines
themselves, the church shifted its focus to control through education
(Alroe 1988).

Community Development

The 1970s saw the arrival of a new breed of government worker in
the north, intent on social change. While commendably motivated,
in many instances the changed approaches masked fundamental
inflexibilities in terms of relinquishing control. Kolig addressed this
issue in discussing the events affecting the Aborigines of Noonkanbah
prior to their return to their station:

> In this time of Aboriginal 'self-determination', advisers no longer issue
> orders to be obeyed by the Aboriginal clientele. Power has to be wielded
> more subtly and surreptitiously, by careful engineering and exploiting
> existing social trends, rifts, power-struggles and dynamics within a
> community, so as to bring about the desired results, rather than by blunt
> superimposition of will. (1987 : 103)

For the Aboriginal communities the ensuing changes were enormous:

> These were heady days; and the distribution of government funds by
> an enthusiastic Australian government, motivated by a sincere wish

to give a financial impetus to the much-publicised policy of 'self-determination', was often thrust upon groups which were unable to cope administratively with the sudden transition from poverty to comparative riches. . . . The losers in the long run were the Aboriginal communities themselves — not the swollen ranks of consultants and helpers that had mushroomed in the night. (Long 1979 : 363)

As will be explained in the final chapter, administrative considerations resulted in the sudden emergence of supposedly autonomous 'communities' across Aboriginal Australia. The early 1970s also saw concerted efforts to extend the delivery of income maintenance policies to remote Aborigines. The prevailing rhetoric emphasised 'opportunity'.

OPPORTUNITY AND EXCLUSION

Between 1960 and 1966 the Commonwealth extended child endowment and pensioner benefits to Aborigines. In July 1971 the last of the restrictions in the Liquor Act were lifted for Aborigines of the Kimberley and the Aboriginal (Citizenship Rights) Act repealed (Long 1979). The economic unit of Aboriginal society had been (and remains) the primary domestic group. Moves to fringe environments changed the economic balance of this unit as pensioners and child-bearing women became major recipients of cash benefits, and a disparity between the economic potential of males and females emerged. Writing on the effects of these changes in the Alice Springs area, Collmann suggested that the emergent female control of the domestic economy resulted in a shift to a matricentric, matrifocal family constellation, where control of children gives control of resources, 'women are structurally placed, therefore, so as to construct a more satisfactory fringe dwelling identity and existence than men' (1979a : 395). The additional impact of alcohol added to those forces undermining the position and role of males in the domestic arena. Money, advisers, material goods and alcohol, thus, arrived precipitously, and in the context of massive social disruption.

In the late 1970s much of the money and many of the advisers disappeared, along with the heady optimism that had marked their arrival. Emerging from a decade of turmoil, Aboriginal groups in the 1980s had to reformulate approaches to existing problems and confront new ones. Under the umbrella of self-determination are a range of positions, from those advocating traditional values and activities, to others supporting initiatives to empower Aborigines within the wider Australian society. Clearly, it is facile to suggest that, regardless of lifestyle chosen, Aborigines should not want the security and conveniences that Western technology provides. Indeed, the isolated communities arising from the outstation movement depend on motor vehicles, solar powered radio-telephones, and medical services. In 1973, within a few years of citizenship rights, Stanner pragmatically stated:

> I know of no Aborigines anywhere who appear to want to live in a style of life in which there will be no elements of Europeanism. . . . Everywhere I have been in recent years there has been an expressed want for at least pieces of our instrumental culture — goods, money, transport — to be used in a combination of their own choice within their own life-purpose. (1979 : 368)

For Kimberley Aborigines, social change has not been even. The longer history of contact, the presence of a large Aboriginal–Asian population, and earlier access to European education for those in the south-west Kimberley, resulted in groups that have had less difficulty in developing an economic and political base. In Fitzroy Crossing and Halls Creek, more recent arrivals from the east and south re-populate the fringe camps vacated by those moving into town life. They share this setting with those Aborigines blocked in their attempts to pass, and those choosing not to.

For most Aborigines of remote Australia in the post-citizenship rights era, less has been delivered than was offered. The removal of legislative obstacles has not been accompanied by functional access to the benefits of the wider society. Aborigines remain excluded by virtue of limited education, linguistic competence in English and political power. Providing general access for Aborigines to those means for articulating and negotiating grievances presents an as yet unresolved conflict. Self-determination implies the right to reject education based on an assimilationist, Eurocentric model, or to reject it entirely (easy enough to do in the Kimberley). Unfortunately, this also limits the development of skills allowing the individual to choose whether to move within the wider Australian society, or not. Coombs pointed to the difficulties in formulating an educational policy sensitive to such group and personal rights, suggesting it should be:

> an education designed not merely to enable them to live effectively in their own society but also to deal effectively with those aspects of white

society which they must encounter and to give them genuinely effective choice whether or not to become part of white society in preference to their own. (1978 : 232)

During the 1980s, the decade of the Australian Bicentennial (in which Aborigines have become a minority in the Kimberley), tourism and television arrived in the region, introducing powerful images of metropolitan Australia, along with ideals at variance with those traditionally available. At the same time these very agencies are transmitting images of Aboriginal Australians (predominantly images constructed by non-Aborigines) into the international arena, highlighting the asymmetry of resources and opportunities. While the 'Great Australian Silence' that Stanner described as a 'cult of disremembering' (1979 : 214) regarding Aborigines in Euro-Australian consciousness has lifted, it has done so unevenly. Most Aborigines of remote Australia remain powerless and marginal to the political developments in the south and east of the continent.

NOTES

1. This comment on the 'miserablest People in the World' may not have been Dampier's, but added as a 'journalistic summation' (Mulvaney 1989 : 20) in the 1697 manuscript. Philip Jones also indicates a comment to this effect by Rhys Jones (Jones 1989).
2. The treatment of Pigeon by Ion Idriess, in *Outlaw of the Leopolds* (1952) as a cunning villain, may be contrasted to that by Colin Johnson, an Aboriginal writer, who in *Long Live Sandawara* (1979), focuses on Sandawara as hero (Shoemaker 1989). Ironically, a century after Pigeon's death, Leopold Downs station has been returned to the Bunaba people.
3. The securing of Aboriginal labour by kidnapping often involved the collusion of pearlers, pastoralists and government officials. Successful prosecutions were few, the practice continuing until labour shortages were reduced by indentured labour in the 1880s (Hunt 1986).
4. The removal was often arbitrary. During this study I met two elderly women living at opposite ends of the Kimberley. Both had been taken from the same Fitzroy valley station as children — one to Moola Bulla and the other to Beagle Bay — only one ever saw her mother again. The two women met for the first time some 30 years after they had been removed. They were sisters.

Mabarn *and Medicine*

INTRODUCTION

In the mid-1980s, two institutions celebrated 50 years of activity in the Kimberley. The Royal Flying Doctor Service began operations from Wyndham in 1934, and a year later agreement was reached between the State and Commonwealth for the construction of a leprosarium, the *bungaran,* across the marsh from Derby. However, the story of Aboriginal health in the Kimberley is more than the record of such organisations. Health cannot be quantified by the building of clinics or the growth of institutions. While its definition is elusive, it includes at least three components that were identified in the Constitution of the World Health Organization: 'Health is a state of complete physical, mental and social well-being and not merely the absence of disease or infirmity'.

DANGEROUS OCCUPATIONS

The north was, and remains, a dangerous place compared to the rest of Australia. The Europeans who were drawn to the Kimberley were exposed to an unfamiliar and unforgiving environment which was frequently unrewarding and hazardous. Aborigines forced into unfamiliar occupations were particularly vulnerable and often expendable. Workers in the pastoral industry, both European and Aboriginal, experienced high rates of injury and exposure to diseases such as malaria, with little likelihood of medical attention.

While few Aborigines were directly involved in mining, the land around Halls Creek had been traversed by them for millennia. They were able to read its moods and anticipate its vicissitudes. By contrast, it was threatening and inhospitable for many of the thousands of miners who arrived during the goldrush to pursue the elusive lode. The death register from the 1880s is replete with violent deaths, reflecting not only the dangers of the environment itself but also the emotional toll of isolation and hardship.

For non-Aborigines suicide was a not uncommon point of exit from the Kimberley. The first officially recorded such death, on the Halls Creek register, was William Dunkin Cummings, who was last seen alive at 9 pm on 5 November 1898. At that time of the year the wet would have been threatening or would have broken, with daytime temperatures touching 40° Celsius. This 34-year-old son of a clergyman from Colchester had been in the colonies several years. An overdose of laudanum that night secured him official recognition as the first suicide in the east Kimberley.[1] By fateful concurrence 5 November 1898 also saw the death of Leon Dumana in Broome, some 500 kilometres to the west. Dumana, who had come to Western Australia 10 years previously from the Philippines via Queensland, committed 'suicide whilst of an unsound mind by cutting his throat with a knife'. The records reveal that the 'wet' of 1898 claimed two more by suicide (in Broome and again Halls Creek) and in the east as the gold became increasingly elusive there were another nine suicides in Halls Creek alone up to the 1930s, all save one occurring during the 'wet'. While suicide has remained relatively common among Europeans in the Kimberley, until very recently suicide by Aborigines was rare.

The fancy buttons and glamorous jewels which placed Broome on the early financial map of Western Australia were luxuries secured at great risk. No records are available of the number of Aboriginal deaths associated with the pearling industry; clearly, however, there were many. Special legislation (1871, 1873) attempted to address injustices such as 'blackbirding', child and female labour and prostitution; however, abuses continued. The casualties extended beyond the Aboriginal population to the Asian workforce that was employed later. For 1889 the Derby Register of Deaths recorded 30 deaths of males between 18 and 36 years of age. Of these, 18 were listed as from 'beri-beri' (exactly what this meant is unclear), 5 recorded as 'uncertain' and 1 each from drowning, fever, fractured skull, suffocation in a diving suit, exhaustion, rheumatism and neuralgia. The situation in Broome was similar, with 30 deaths in 1897, the average age being 26 years, including 14 Indonesians, 8 Japanese, 5 from the Philippines and 1 each from the Society Islands, Brazil and Thailand. From the turn of the century a separate register of marine deaths was maintained in Broome. In 1915 there were 42 deaths listed on the general register of deaths, but a further 23 deaths occurred at sea, with an average age of 25 years. Of these, 19 died of 'divers' paralysis'. The Asian cemetery in Broome, now a tourist attraction, stands in silent testimony to the sacrifice of young lives in the quest for the pearl.

The influx of European and Asian males also brought demands for women. During the earliest years of settlement the only women in the north were Aboriginal. While there were some white men that lived in long-lasting relationships with Aboriginal women, despite laws which penalised those in long-term relationships rather than those intent only on 'casual' sex (McGrath 1987), Aboriginal women as sexual 'commodities' were frequently degraded and abused. Unlike the Japanese prostitutes in Broome, and the white prostitutes who followed the seasonal meatworkers, Aboriginal women lacked the means to defend themselves through the system (Hunt 1986).

SYSTEMS IN CONFLICT

While differences were significant, for most traditional Aboriginal groups the understanding of 'illness' involved conceptions of intrusion: active intervention by someone or something as a consequence of the sufferer's actions within a social or sacred sphere. Illness was a meaningful experience and had social status. 'Traditional doctors', as healers, enacted socially their role of secular and sacred mediation. With European settlement came a different conceptualisation of illness — as 'disease'. In this view a structural or mechanical 'cause' was sought rather than a social or sacred explanation. The Europeans' positivist paradigms also suggested specific treatments that followed from these theories, and practitioners were frequently intolerant of alternatives that were not amenable to their 'rational' understanding. Such ideas and practices did not arrive in isolation, but as part of the broader social impact of European culture.

For most Europeans the two worldviews and healing systems were incompatible: acknowledgement of the Aboriginal doctor was not only inconsistent with 'scientific' medicine but often offended their religious sensitivities. Consequently, the Aboriginal doctor was undermined by a powerful new 'curative' system, which at times included active suppression of traditional healing practices. The effect of this was to undermine the allied roles of this esteemed figure in maintaining social cohesion through sacred mediation (Cawte 1974) — a further assault on traditional social organisation. It is surprising that traditional healing practices survived at all, as indeed they have. While now more peripheral, the *mabarn* man still exists, fulfilling an important function and occasionally working in conjunction with the European medical system. At times a synthesis of traditional and Christian spirit-healing practices are evident. One practitioner, clearly influenced by both in his work, discussed with great sensitivity his approach to a woman whose grieving process for her baby daughter had been blocked. According to his analysis the baby would not let go, its spirit hanging on to the woman 'from below'. He described his treatment, through verbal and physical means, as taking the woman back down, so that the little girl could let go and allow the mother to come to the surface again. Little could be added by psychiatric expertise.

Becoming a *mabarn* man was usually restricted by sex, age and social standing, but knowledge of readily available 'bush medicines' was for all. Examples can be given of the use of a wide variety of substances: from the earth (an infusion of antbed to treat bowel problems); from animal sources (crushing the nest of the green tree ants to release formic acid, the inhalation of which was used for respiratory problems); and from the plant world, probably the most consistently resorted to.

Confirmation of the effectiveness of a particular traditional treatment was found by Lawson Holman (physician and surgeon in the Kimberley, 1956–1971, personal communication 1988). Patients with lacerations and compound fractures occasionally arrived at the hospital with 'antbed' plasters on their wounds, made from material obtained from specific types of anthill. These were usually promptly replaced with a conventional dressing. Having noticed that there seemed to be more problems with infection following removal, Holman opted in certain cases to leave the antbed plaster on, with good results. Subsequent testing demonstrated antimicrobial properties.

Jack Mulardy, an elder in the Bidyadanga Community (La Grange) explained that not any antbed will do (personal communication 1988):

This one is a particular one you know, the high one we call *marla* [in Karajarri, in Nyangumarta known as *mungkurl*], the little flat one we call *mintipa* in Karajarri, others [including Nyangumarta] call it *kartarra.* That's the one, small flat one. Sometimes big but more flat. Mix them up with water, maybe in a conch shell. Use it when you got a big cut, or some sores, when you scratching like that. Put that one [some gum] on too. Two types [of gum], one is from white gum tree and from bloodwood. Sometimes put them on separate, sometimes mix them up. And it works you know.

Sandy Paddy of the Djarindjin Community (Lombardina) outlined the way in which one tree may be used for a variety of conditions (personal communication 1987). The tree is the 'corkwood tree', *Gyrocarpus americanus* known by its Bardi name *bilangkamar* (Paddy, Paddy & Smith 1987). After easily removing a section of the bark from the trunk of the tree, Sandy explained how it was used for sores, for rheumatism and for snakebite:

> They used to put it on the fires to make it come right through the skin. You boil the skin [bark]. Before they used to put it in the fire until all that liquid stuff between the wood and the skin comes out, then you put it on sores, wash the sores in it. I think it is better if you put it on straight. For rheumatism you can also use the leaves, just put them on the fire, then put them on your rheumatism while they're warm, wherever you've got it. Do it every day, in a few days it is gone. For snakebite you cut the place open and put it inside. Then you squeeze it out and put more in, keep doing that. It's also good for the sting of the devil fish.

To demonstrate the effectiveness of one traditional remedy Sandy took some of the dried gum from a nearby whitegum (*Eucalyptus papuana*) and ground it up. This was used commonly for the treatment of toothache (similarly to oil of cloves). Within seconds of applying the bitter tasting fine red granules, the gum and the tip of the tongue develop a distinct numbness.

Smoking is a process that is used both ritually (after initiation and following a death) and therapeutically, particularly for babies. Susie Gilbert of Broome identified the Conkerberry bush called in Nyangumarta *jima* (*Carissa lanceolata* [Lands 1987]) growing across from her house, and explained some of its applications (personal communication 1987):

> We call it *jima*, it has spikes and little black fruit, comes out in wintertime. When you get a big one you can use the roots. Use the leaves for smoking the baby. Make a big fire and put the leaves on the fire. Put the baby in the smoke just for a little time. Maybe that baby has been crying all night. When the baby is smoked it'll stop crying. Smoke them when they get sick, for diarrhoea or cold sick.

Phyllis Kaberry, working with Aboriginal women in the east Kimberley 50 years earlier related the use of the same bush for smoking the newborn:

> During labour, songs were sung to facilitate delivery and prevent haemorrhage, the umbilical cord was cut and the placenta was buried secretly. The baby was then dusted with charcoal, and string was tied around its wrists to strengthen them. It and the mother were rubbed with conkaberry bushes which had been smoked over a fire and which were applied to ease the pain, prevent bad after-effects and ensure a flow of milk. (1973 [1939] : 242)

This resilience of traditional medicine reflects the fact that, in the Kimberley, contact and adaptation did not occur at a single point in time, but was a continuing process as Aborigines from more isolated and traditional areas moved into the ambit of European influence. With each wave a re-infusion of traditional thought and practice was made available to those who had settled earlier.

PERCEPTIONS AND POLICY

European perceptions of indigenous populations clearly affected intercultural relations and ultimately the health of subject peoples. In Britain science had long been the handmaiden of imperialism, with the Royal Society and the Royal Navy enjoying a distinguished relationship. The navy served as a vehicle for an unprecedented orgy of global information and specimen collection. In turn, scientists addressed the technical needs of the military, and the cultural and ethical issues raised by the expanding empire. It is not surprising that scientific constructions meshed with the requirements of Imperial growth and colonial government. However, those theories have been tenacious; social Darwinism predicted attitudes to Aborigines that have endured.[2] Early anthropologists saw Aboriginal society as a social laboratory to test evolutionary theories. The perspectives of such luminaries as Baldwin Spencer suggested primitive qualities that then became incorporated into popular and political images (Mulvaney 1985).

By 1800, the decline of the Aboriginal population in New South Wales from introduced diseases was obvious. The muted lament that ensued for the supposed passing of the Aborigine reflected an ethnocentric vision of history not unique to Australia. Perceptions of inferiority and vulnerability supported both extreme action, and inaction. The future, it was suggested, was for the strong and vigorous and little could (should?) be done other than to ease their passage to oblivion.

STIGMATISED CONTAGIONS

Infections such as measles and influenza extracted a grave toll among Kimberley Aborigines, not only in the distant past. As late as 1959 an influenza epidemic ravaged the region. The situation in Derby was described by Lawson Holman (personal communication 1987):

> The disease hit the town during Boab week — hit the whole Kimberley — but was particularly bad in Derby because all the Sunday Islanders had come down with it. It was characterised by its ability to mock anything . . . but the worst thing of all was the fact that they would just drop. . . . So many people came to Derby hospital that there were no longer any beds. People were coming with mattresses over their shoulders. . . . Sometimes they just dropped the mattress and fell on it.

However, the hospital was not an option for Aborigines in the 1950s:

> At that time there were 400 on the reserve. For six days without rest Sister Mary Reid managed the reserve all on her own, going from one prostrate Aboriginal to another. There were seventeen deaths on the reserve in the first three days, the children died from adrenal failure.

Medical services in the Kimberley aimed initially at addressing the needs of the European population (there was also a Japanese hospital in Broome from the 1890s to the 1930s). Many Aborigines remained mobile and scattered in small groups; and this, in conjunction with prevailing attitudes, made health care functionally unavailable until comparatively recently. By default it fell upon the missions (and to a more limited extent the pastoralists) to provide basic services. Active government involvement in Aboriginal health was largely a result of the presence of two conditions — venereal diseases and leprosy. The major motivations were concern regarding the spread of these outside the Aboriginal community and the anticipated consequences of that for economic development. Even though it was realised that these afflictions were introduced, by focusing on Aboriginal behaviour and 'morality', Aborigines were soon held responsible.

VENEREAL DISEASES

Non-venereal treponemal diseases existed in pockets of the Aboriginal population prior to European contact. Yaws was found on the coastal fringe of the Northern Territory, and endemic syphilis (*irkintja*) in central and south-central Australia. Lesions suggesting treponemal infection have been identified on osseous remains from Roonka flat on the Murray River in South Australia (Prokopec 1979), those remains having been dated to around 4000 BP (Flood 1983). However, Cecil Hackett has referred to suggestive lesions on a Tasmanian skull, implying the presence of treponemal infection there prior to the flooding of the Bassian Plain some 8000 years ago (Sandison 1980). Paradoxically, the commonly held belief was that venereal syphilis and gonorrhoea were prevalent among Aborigines, which led to the adoption of draconian measures to treat them. In reality, however, those diseases were uncommon in the Kimberley — a point made by Dr Cecil Cook, who completed the first systematic survey in 1924 (Cook 1923; 1974) — and they remained uncommon in the 1950s and 1960s (Lawson Holman, personal communication 1987).

Early confusion with yaws and granuloma inguinale (granuloma) had led to this misconception. In 1907 a medical meeting in Perth resulted in a call for segregation. The following year the Aborigines Department, under the newly appointed Charles Gale, in conjunction with the Department of Health, set up lock hospitals, institutions on Dorre and Bernier Islands off Carnarvon to which Aborigines were forcibly removed to be detained indefinitely. That Dorre and Bernier were hardly habitable had been long known, indeed George Grey had described Dorre in 1838:

> From the top of the cliffs the prospect was not at all inviting; to the westward lay the level and almost desert land of Dorre Island, which we were on; we had the same prospect to the southward; to the northward we looked over a narrow channel, which separated us from the barren isle of Bernier, and was blocked by fearful-looking reefs, on which broke a nasty surf; to the north-eastward lofty bare sand-hills were indistinctly visible. (1983 [1841] : 337)

As honorary protectors, police carried out physical examinations. This situation led Gale to appoint the first female protectors (all in the north), following his tour of 1910. The lock hospitals continued in existence until 1919, some 365 Aboriginals being removed to those desolate isles, 162 dying there (Jebb 1984). This was despite the Australasian Medical Conference recommendation in 1911 that venereal diseases should be treated in general hospitals, not lock hospitals (Lewis 1988). That year the doctor on the island experimented unsuccessfully with samples of a new medicine, Salvarsan. In 1914 the Australasian Medical Congress called for free laboratory testing and treatment for syphilitics, recommendations which were instituted by the States. The 1915 Western Australian Contagious Diseases Act provided for both, as well as professional treatment and adequate accommodation (Lewis 1988). This scheme discriminated against Aborigines, for whom free treatment was not to be provided, ironically fortunate for those languishing off Carnarvon — they did not have venereal syphilis. The nature of these institutions depends on one's point of view. Herbert Basedow, chief medical officer and protector of Aborigines in the Northern Territory, and chairman of the Aborigines' Protection League, reflected:

> The Government responded with commendable promptitude and selected Bernier and Dorre Islands, situated west of Carnarvon, for the purpose of establishing Lock Hospitals. The former island was resumed at a cost of £1,000 and equipped for the women patients, the latter was set apart for the men. Dr F. Lovegrove was appointed to take charge of the establishment, together with an efficient hospital staff. Certain additions were made to the hospitals in 1911. Suitable wards were erected and operating theatres attached to the buildings. During the first three years 353 patients were treated and 125 discharged as cured. A special expedition collected as many natives as possible between the Ashburton River and the Eastern Gold Fields. (1932 : 181)

Such was not the experience of Daisy Bates:

> When the bleak winds blew, the movable huts were turned against them, facing each other, regardless of tribal customs, which meant mistrust and fear. Now and again a dead body would be wrapped in a blanket and carried away to burial in the sands, and the unhappy living could not leave the accursed ground of its spirit. Some became demented, and rambled away and no one of an alien tribe would go to seek them. One day an old man started to 'walk' back over thirty miles of raging waters to the mainland. These shores are infested with sharks, and he was never seen again. Another hid in the thick scrub, and died there, rather than be operated on. A third sat on the crest of a little rise all day long, pouring sand and water over his head, wailing and threatening, in his madness. (in Healy 1978 : 133)

Visiting the island at the same time was E L Grant Watson, who echoed Bates's observations, suggesting that the 'young doctor was more interested, I think, in spirochetes than in suffering men' (1946 : 112). He pointed out how brutal Basedow's 'special expeditions' to find such sufferers could be:

The method of collecting the patients was not either humane or
scientific. A man unqualified except by ruthlessness and daring, helped
by one or two kindred spirits, toured the countryside, raided the native
camps and there, by brute force, 'examined' the natives. Any that were
obviously diseased or were suspected of disease were seized upon. These,
since their hands were so small as to slip through any pair of handcuffs,
were chained together by their necks, and were marched through the
bush, in the further search for syphilitics. (1946 : 112)

The stresses of such an environment, even for those who had the
option of leaving, are reflected in Watson's concluding statements:

Perhaps it should be mentioned, as a comment on the weaknesses and
limitations of our humanity, that the other two white men on the island,
the doctor and the stockman, had been taking shots at each other with
their rifles amongst the sand-dunes. We civilised scientists, though not
quite so crude in our antagonisms, also found island-life a bit of an
ordeal, where two might agree, but three must fall on hatred and
suspicion. (1946 : 122)

All aspects of this dark decade further alienated Aborigines from the
health-care system, which subjected them — but not afflicted
Europeans — to such harsh measures.[3] They were segregated by sex
and expected to work. The limited medical staff, by the nature of
their 'treatments' and moralistic attitudes, defined a punitive
relationship to those in their 'care'. With the ultimate recognition
that those confined were suffering from granuloma, interest in and
admissions to the lock hospitals waned. The last twenty-four
inmates were removed to the 'Depot for Diseased Natives' in Port
Hedland in 1919 (Mulvaney 1989).

With the decline of yaws and *irkintja* (and, thus, of cross-
immunity) due to changes in lifestyle following the Second World
War, and the later introduction of antibiotics, Aboriginal susceptibility to venereal syphilis increased, and cases began to appear at
the end of the 1960s. The numbers escalated rapidly such that the
Kimberley in 1984–1985 constituted 37 per cent of all notifications
for venereal diseases in Western Australia (Randolph Spargo,
personal communication 1987).

LEPROSY

In 1874 the Norwegian, Armauer Hansen, demonstrated that leprosy
was an infective condition due to the *Mycobacterium leprae*. The
international climate at that time had been powerfully influenced

by an outbreak of leprosy in Hawaii, with the death from it of Father Damien of Molokai. Scientific opinion shifted from the view that leprosy was hereditary, to an understanding of it as a contagion. Hansen attended the First International Leprosy Conference in 1897, which designated leprosy as 'virtually incurable', and supported compulsory segregation legislation (Gussow & Tracy 1970). In Australia there was anxious and alarmist speculation with condemnation of those groups (especially Chinese) thought responsible for its transmission. Fears were voiced in the press of 'the ancient scourge', the 'taint of Asia', becoming widespread in the north-west as, for settlers: 'where natives are employed in domestic duties there may be some danger' (*West Australian*, 13 September 1912).

The initial cases in Western Australia were among Asians, the first in the north being a Chinese in Roebourne in 1889. Early cases were transferred to Woodman's Point near Perth, or deported. Leprosy among Aborigines presented problems of a different order. The 1886 Aborigines Protection Act made the Aborigines Protection Board responsible for the health care of Aborigines. Following the initial cases of Hansen's disease, the 1898 amendment of the Health Act provided for special police powers for the control of infectious diseases. However, while the protector had responsibility for Aboriginal health through the Native Hospitals, this did not include those suffering from leprosy, which remained the domain of the Health Department:

> when an Aboriginal was declared to be a leper the Protector either ceased to regard himself as a protector, or he considered the leper to be no longer Aboriginal. For some reason, which is far from clear, as soon as an Aboriginal was diagnosed as having leprosy, the Protector insisted that full responsibility for him was taken by the Health Department and declined to supply him with food, clothes, shelter, hospital or transport. (Davidson 1978 : 53)

Thirty years of confused policy followed. From 1909 lepers were confined on Bezout Island off Roebourne, another desolate spot to which even water had to be delivered by the local policeman once a week (Gerry Benson-Liddon, personal communication 1987). At the outbreak of the First World War an alternative location on a tidal island off Cossack was provided, operating until 1931, at which time a lazaretto was built near the town, provoking predictable outrage from the citizenry. The major government concerns appear to have been financial. The number of cases in the Kimberley increased from

22 between 1900 and 1920, to 161 from 1931 to 1936 (Davidson 1978). The refusal of Native Welfare to look after lepers at the Native Hospitals resulted in expenditure for chartered transportation to centres that could accommodate them. Temporary lazarettos existed at different points in time at Roebourne, Cossack, Beagle Bay and Derby.

In 1930 Bishop Raible offered the services of the Sisters of St John of God to staff a lazaretto at Swan Point on the extreme tip of the Dampier Land peninsula. With the souring relationship between government and church during Neville's tenure, the offer was refused in favour of Commonwealth plans to collect lepers from throughout the north of Australia on the Channel Islands off Darwin (1931–1955). This arrangement rid the State of the responsibility for both the lepers and the financial costs of their care. However, the offer did not include transportation costs. Furthermore, the conditions on the first voyage of the lugger *W.S. Rolland* from Beagle Bay to Darwin, were picked up by Coverley (1933) in his call for the Moseley Royal Commission:

> I ask members to visualise a 13-ton lugger which, when employing an indentured crew, provided for six hands in the hold. Think of 12 leprous aborigines on that lugger, patients who are not supposed to go on deck, but have to remain in the hold throughout the voyage. Those 12 patients are enclosed in a space of about 10 feet square, and included in that space are two sanitary conveniences and all the cooking utensils. There those patients have to exist until they reach Darwin. (1933 : 647)

The trip, which normally took less than one week, because of the unseaworthiness of the vessel lasted 18 days. One of Moseley's earliest recommendations (1934) was the need for a local facility; the leprosarium across the marshes from Derby opened shortly afterwards. The Sisters of St John of God, previously offered by Bishop Raible, began their work in March 1937. However, it was not for another three years that those who had been sent under such harsh conditions to the Channel Islands were to return to the Kimberley.

The consequences of these diseases and the measures taken for their control were enormous. Police patrols of the Kimberley, which continued until 1949, lasted many months, with afflicted Aborigines at times forced to follow the policeman chained to a horse or mule, at night linked about a tree. As the feet are often affected due to nerve damage, forced marches bare-foot across rough country compounded the devastation of the disease. These 'health patrols' were the clearest example of the relationship between the police and medical services.

While there was little else available save isolation to combat infectious diseases, the social impact of forced removal to far distant detention was profound. Furthermore, the legacy of other police actions left little room for trust, thus requiring stealth on the part of the patrol officers. A 1945 report of Sergeant O'Halloran from Derby suggested the fear in which the arrival of a patrol was held:

> The main factors that would make such a Patrol unsuccessful would be (1) Publicity given to the fact that such a Patrol was intended, and the area to be covered. (2) The use of Pedal Wireless Sets for Telegrams or Messages, due to the fact that Station Natives are often aware of the contents of Pedal Telegrams before the recipients. This is not generally the fault of the Station Owner or Manager, but is due to Station House Gins overhearing the conversation on the wireless, and passing the information on to the Native camp. The element of surprise is essential for the apprehension of Sick Natives, and if any Natives in an area have an inkling that a Patrol is approaching the area, they immediately make for the most inaccessible region. (in Davidson 1978 : 172)

An Aboriginal perspective of the process was provided by Nipper Tabagee (personal communication 1988). Through the Second World War Nipper had worked for the military on Noonkanbah station and afterwards with the police, participating in the patrols:

> Constable would go sometimes in front, sometimes behind. Sometimes they'd run off when they see the doctor coming. Come in on horseback, before that tell manager to round up the people because the doctor coming. In those days it was very bad, they had all sorts of sickness in those days. Very important the doctor look at it. Everybody see the doctor and he tell them what to do. See everyone on that station. He give the manager a paper saying that that person got to go to the leprosarium. They wait till they come back with the truck from the leprosarium to pick them up. Sometimes one or two people get away, they don't like to come into the leprosarium. Sometimes they run away and stay in the bush with no medicine. . . . Sometimes they come back. The policeman go round, one from Fitzroy Crossing, one from here [Derby], pick up those people from station and bring that truck. Chain them up first, bring them back to the leprosarium. After they out of their country you can take the chain off, frightened going to that other people's country. Sometimes might be some good people, didn't like it. Sometimes when I didn't know this language, when I come to know what they saying, what they trying to do, what their meaning were, I'd tell them that the medicine make them live, without medicine you dead.

In the 1950s Nipper, himself, noticed a slight weakness; he was discharged from the *bungaran* in 1970.

The setting up of the leprosarium and the introduction of effective drug treatments in the late 1940s (long-acting depot preparations became available in the 1960s) changed the course and social impact of leprosy. Parallels can be drawn between the setting up of the leprosarium and of government stations. Both were in part a response to local white concerns — the loss of cattle on the one hand, and the fear of disease spreading to Europeans on the other. There were also economic implications: the threat to the pastoral industry through falling revenue due to stock loss, or from pastoralists leaving the region to avoid the contagion. However, both were perhaps most powerfully influenced by the considerable costs of transporting Aborigines to distant detention centres.

By the time that the leprosarium opened, the Sisters of St John of God had been nursing in the Kimberley for 30 years. These women worked with little assistance in conditions of extreme hardship, many remaining with this work for decades. While part of their mandate was religious instruction, the realities of their work left little time for that or their own needs. During the war, for instance, there were five sisters for 260 patients and a priest visited to give Mass only once a month.

What of the inmates? Many suffered disfiguring and debilitating complications of the disease that required constant attention unavailable elsewhere. The treatments were often complicated and painful. However, for others there was often scant evidence of the disease and little comprehension of the reasons for treatments. For some the stay was short; for others it was measured in decades, often taking away the most productive years of life. Children born to affected women were removed, families disrupted. There was often no sure knowledge of whether a relative would at some future date be able to leave. Many never did, being remembered in 1985 at the closing ceremonies by the insertion of a capsule containing the names of 357 who died there into a rock on the grounds. A patient who had arrived in his mid-20s recalled his experience:

> I knew I had it, I just found my finger was getting numb. I knew it had something to do with leprosy. I didn't hide it, I knew the doctor from 'the lep'. I was lucky to go otherwise I would have lost it, that's what the doctor told me. I wasn't scared until he told me I'd have to go to the leprosarium, then it was scary. He told me I'd be there for three weeks or so. Then when they took the biopsy, that's when they told me it was positive, that I was infected. That's when they told me

I'd be there for a long time. Then I started to worry, I was twenty-five, I was married. . . .

I stayed out there waiting for three weeks, I trusted them, thought they were going to send me back home. Then the results came back and another doctor came. I felt angry and got angry with them. The only thing that would make me happy was to go to town. Sometimes I had to swim across the creek at night time. . . . They told me that if I kept doing it they'd lock me up, put me in the old gaol. They did lock me up once, then the doctor heard and came and got me out. . . . Then [two years later] the doctor sent the report that I was clear, I could go home. I didn't have to fly back, they run me back all the way in a car. I was very happy. I had an invitation for the last ceremony, when they closed. I was happy to go back and see what it was like. It was really good, all the old people, we were all in a line, we all had an invitation to go back, everyone was there.

Not all patients recall the experience so benignly. A *bungaran* resident of some 20 years reflected bitterly:

I couldn't work out what was happening, I was taken to Derby hospital because of a lump on my arm [soon after the opening of the leprosarium]. I wasn't told why, I lost the best part of my life. . . . I thought I'd never come out, I thought I'd die there, I'd given up hope. . . . [When I left] I was frightened to go look for work, I was frightened to walk in the street. People were scared of me, women were scared of me, I wanted to go back.

As *Mycobacterium leprae* did not recognise age, children were also affected. Looking back at the earliest days of the leprosarium, one man told of his arrival as a child:

I was ten. It was real hard in those days, no treatment like they got now, there weren't many who were discharged in those days, quite a few died there. . . . My brother and sister came there before I did, I remember them leaving on a lugger. My brother died there, my sister got discharged. . . . When I first came there were no visitors, for years. Maybe once every two or three years your parents would come up and they would sit under the tree there. If they had anything they would leave it there and when they went away you would pick it up. Reckon it was pretty bad. . . . Now it's all different. When I went up there they used to have all the women on one side and the men on the other. They had about ten police boys there, some of them were good, some of them were cruel. They were patients who were chosen to do the job. Stop them fighting. They used to fight a lot, all the different tribes there. Most of them were women trouble, you couldn't even look at a girl without getting your face knocked in. . . . Some of the bosses were pretty rough, used to have an exercise place in front of the hospital, used to drill every morning, used to line up. If you got into trouble they used to cut their hair, make them stand there in the sun. The boss would cut it off, the police boys would help them. Call them leaders, never used to call them police boys. The nuns used to go crazy, they were against it. . . . The ones that got discharged in those days didn't have a relapse. Nowadays with the medicine it is quick. Then it took a long time. Needles, and some other stuff they used to rub on. You'd get all white, next thing they'd rub oil after. It would turn into a blister. The injection, I'll never forget, I've got lots of scars from it. Twice a week, they'd give you a needle and you'd wake up all swollen up. Real painful. When they gave it on your buttocks you couldn't sit down.

Although Aboriginal communities have traditionally been accepting of members afflicted by leprosy or other disfiguring diseases, for those who did leave, there were often problems. However, for some the experience provided the opportunity to live with Aborigines from distant regions, and to interact with Europeans on a regular basis without fear of rejection or ridicule. As a result many ex-patients are found in positions of responsibility.

A further consequence of leprosy in the north was legislation introduced in 1941 on the suggestion of Dr Davis of the Health Department. As previously observed, this meant that Aborigines living north of the twentieth parallel were forbidden to travel south of that line (the 'leper line'). The restrictive permit system was modified by amendment to the Native Welfare Act in 1955, but it was not until the 1963 Act that this invisible line also disappeared from the statutes.

HOSPITALS AND BEYOND

Following the Moseley report of 1935 a medical inspector was appointed for the north, and Native Hospitals were subsequently built in Broome and Wyndham. The already existing compound in Derby was described by Hasluck:

> For the reception of the sick natives there was a native hospital at Derby — a small, wooden, three-roomed shed in a big paddock — where the patients (chiefly venereal) who had been brought in from the outback, were treated by a white married couple under the direction of the town doctor. At Broome two or three galvanized iron sheds in the general hospital grounds were available for blacks. (1988 : 61)

By contrast with the Regional Hospital, conditions at the Native Hospital in Derby, staffed from 1952 by the Sisters of St John, were primitive. As one sister recalled, given the abysmal conditions, hygiene was a constant and often losing battle, and basic comfort for the staff or patients a luxury. Without power at night, Aboriginal women delivered their babies by the light of a hurricane lamp into the 1960s. The Native Hospitals themselves were transferred to the Health Department in 1949, the separate systems of health care continuing into the late 1960s, when care of Aboriginal patients was absorbed by the District Hospitals.

The isolationist policies of the Department of Native Welfare not only separated Aborigines from the white population, but effectively prevented information regarding Aboriginal health or welfare reaching the wider Australian society. The silence extended to the medical curriculum of the University of Western Australia, one of the first graduates recalling: 'not one mention of the Aboriginal population's health problems did I hear while at Medical School. I was not aware on coming to Derby [1968] that there was leprosy in Australia' (Randolph Spargo, personal communication 1987). While Native Welfare's involvement with the Native Hospitals had ended, it retained control over access (even for medical staff) to Native Reserves throughout the State until 1972. At that time the Aboriginal Affairs Planning Authority Act abolished the 1963 Native Welfare Act and transferred responsibility for health, education and welfare to the Departments of Health, Education and Child Welfare, which later became the Department of Community Services. It was, thus, only recently that Aborigines were relieved of the restrictions of separate systems of care, and came under the ambit of services available to all citizens of the State.

Through most of these face changes, health care had been focused in District Hospitals. Even in these settings medical practice was not easy. Facilities in the Kimberley hospitals were spartan into the 1960s. Lawson Holman recalled that in order to take an X-ray in the late 1950s, using an archaic machine operated on DC current, the electricity supply to the rest of the town had to be temporarily interrupted. During the 1960s and 1970s hospital and allied public health services were expanded, with a shift in focus to a community orientation. Most notable in this regard was the treatment of leprosy, with surveys initiated in 1968 aimed at case detection through systematic medical examination of the entire Aboriginal population of the region.

The more sensitive of the health professionals arriving in the

Kimberley found that working with Aboriginal patients demanded a re-analysis of procedures and treatments that required little explanation in urban settings. Routine X-rays caused unforeseen anxiety, as described by Ernie King, a doctor in Wyndham in the mid-1960s (personal communication 1988):

> Some of them were absolutely terrified. There was one woman — we thought she had something wrong with her chest — I showed her the X-ray and she began crying, desperately upset. It was even worse with pregnant women when you took a picture of the foetus. After a while I learnt I had to make a point of explaining all about X-rays and bones.

Others were taking medicine to the communities. The Sisters of St John of God were involved in the treatment of leprosy, and the Australian Inland Mission hospitals at Fitzroy Crossing and Halls Creek (handed over in 1980 to the Health Department) were run by nurses. In the late 1960s active attempts were made to interpose nursing staff between the patients in the community and the hospital system. After the successful trial placement of a nurse in the community in Derby in 1968, this approach was extended to Broome, Fitzroy Crossing, Halls Creek and Kununurra with the formation of a new department, Community Health.

The Australian Inland Mission was connected with another of the medical forces important in the history of the north, the Australian Aerial Medical Service. Both had been founded by John Flynn, the Aerial Medical Service opening in Queensland in 1927, being renamed the Flying Doctor Service in 1942 and receiving royal charter in 1954 to become the now familiar Royal Flying Doctor Service. Operations in Western Australia followed a 1933 conference in Perth attended by Flynn, with the Victorian Section accepting responsibility for the Kimberley. While ultimately providing services for all, its origins were clearly a response to the needs of Europeans in remote Australia. As suggested in the constitution framed at that meeting, its aims were: 'To foster, develop and safeguard the health, morale and well being of the pioneer settlers by making readily available medical and nursing facilities' (in Weir 1959 : 8).

The Wyndham base (subscribed to in Melbourne in 1934) was responsible for the entire Kimberley until the Derby base began operations in 1955. The second flight out of Wyndham, to the aid of a sick Aborigine at Forrest River Mission, demonstrated the impact of the new service, even for relatively near communities. Dr R J Cato recorded:

> The Mission is thirty miles from Wyndham by airline across the Cambridge Gulf, but to reach it by land requires fifty miles of rough, stony travelling on foot through the bush. The Mission Superintendent sewed up the message in waterproof cloth and gave it to a native runner, who travelled it in twenty-three hours, swimming two rivers on the way. He was the father of the child that was ill and he spared no effort. The flight across by plane in answer to the call took less than a half hour. (in Behr 1985 : 259)

Ultimately, the consequences of this service for Europeans were far broader than health; it brought communication and education to isolated pastoral holdings. However, regardless of its particular importance to the pastoral industry, the Flying Doctor Service brought benefits to all isolated communities, regular or emergency visits being important events. With the massive social changes and demographic shifts of the 1960s that affected the pastoral industry, the Aboriginal populations on many of the remote leases fell dramatically. This, in conjunction with improved communications and access to transport, has changed the role of the Service; it has increasingly become an emergency service and provides transportation to scheduled clinics by regionally stationed medical officers.

All of the institutions mentioned thus far represent services for or to Aborigines provided by non-Aborigines. The first Kimberley Aboriginal nursing-aide trainees began their courses in Perth in 1954, but it was not until the mid-1960s that training began for nursing-aides in the Kimberley. Of the first group of eight who went through the training in Derby, six passed the competitive State examinations. Having Aborigines in these positions was a significant advance. Additionally, these Aborigines were placed in positions of caring and responsibility towards non-Aborigines, being for many Europeans the first time that they confronted their own preconceptions and the prevailing stereotypes.

However, it was not until the 1970s that Aborigines became significantly involved in health-care policy. Through the 1970s there was a nationwide move towards control of services for Aborigines by Aborigines. Following the establishment of the Aboriginal Legal Service in Sydney in early 1970, the Aboriginal Medical Service (AMS) was inaugurated in July 1971 in Redfern, staffed by Aborigines and volunteer non-Aboriginal health professionals (Fagan 1991).

This initiative resulted from Aboriginal frustration with the inadequacies and functional unavailability of the general health system. The perceived relationship of poor health status to power-lessness and loss of land resulted in a clearly articulated political agenda for the umbrella organisation, the National Aboriginal and Islander Health Organisation (NAIHO):

> NAIHO is an overtly political organisation for the simple reason that we believe the ultimate solution for the disastrous state of Aboriginal health can only be resolved in a situation whereby Aboriginal people have:
> a) total control of their own affairs;
> b) control of resources and facilities to enable them to alleviate ALL contributing factors to their problems;
> c) inalienable Title to Land which can be an economic base. (Foley 1982 : 15)

While there were initially attempts to limit the activities of the Aboriginal Medical Service through funding restrictions, by 1989 there were 64 such services in operation across the country, funded largely by the Department of Aboriginal Affairs (Saggers & Gray 1991). The Aboriginal Medical Service in the Kimberley had its origins in a 1978 meeting held in Broome, attended by local Aborigines, non-Aboriginal community members and Professor Fred Hollows, who had been involved in the National Trachoma and Eye Health Program and in supporting the original one in Redfern. With the experience of the setting up by concerned community members of an Aboriginal alcohol treatment facility (Millya Rumurra) two years previously, a location provided by the Catholic church, doctors from the Central Australian Aboriginal Congress in Alice Springs and the support of the Aboriginal Medical Service in the east, the Broome Regional Aboriginal Medical Service came into being. Funding was initially piecemeal: from a German missionary agency, the Catholic church, and other sources, with a car later being provided by the Lotteries Commission. It was not until 1981 that a small grant from the Commonwealth Department of Aboriginal Affairs opened the way to ongoing predictable funding. Since that time two other regional centres of the Aboriginal Medical Service have opened, in Kununurra in 1983 and Halls Creek in 1987, with plans for a further clinic in Fitzroy Crossing.

Fifteen years after the deficiencies of separate treatment and accountability were overcome by the dissolution of the Department of Native Welfare, with both the State and commonwealth Health Departments moving from the centre stage, a divergent track for Aboriginal Health is again emerging, albeit with the significant difference that Aborigines are now powerfully placed within the administrative structures. The trend was supported by the emphasis of the Health Department of Western Australia in the mid-1980s, which prioritised hospital-based care over public health initiatives. The process of separating off Aboriginal health was consistent with the political changes from isolation and 'protection', through integration and assimilation, to self-determination. However, questions have been raised regarding duplication of services (Saggers and Gray 1991), with Aboriginal health care vulnerable to the economic vicissitudes of Aboriginal Affairs on the wider Australian economic stage.

CHANGING FORTUNES

Throughout Aboriginal Australia, other than the initial arrival of Europeans, the period of greatest social change has been the period of the 1960s–1980s. During this period there have been major and successful programs to combat a wide range of conditions. As a result, through the 1970s there were significant improvements with, for instance, a substantial drop occurring in infant mortality (Thomson 1991). Regardless, Aborigines in the mid-1980s remained at greater risk, with infant mortality rates between two and three times as high as among non-Aborigines. While the standardised mortality ratios (the ratio of observed to expected deaths adjusted for differences in the age structures of the respective populations) for both male and female Kimberley Aborigines were found to be the lowest of five remote regions during the 1980s, they still demonstrated substantial excess mortality, being 1.6 and 2.4 respectively (Thomson 1991). Earlier, Thomson had speculated on a 'mortality gradient' that parallels:

> the extent of social disruption experienced by Aborigines in different regions, and the extent to which the lives of present-day Aborigines are dominated by non-Aborigines. Thus, while it appears that Aboriginal fetal and infant mortality more closely reflects an adverse physical environment and, probably, more limited access to health and medical services, the most reasonable explanation for increases in overall mortality appears to be the adverse social environment experienced by Aborigines in *less remote* parts of Australia. (1985 : S48, my emphasis)

Within the Kimberley an example of this gradient was provided by Kirk (1981), who earlier demonstrated a tenfold difference in the incidence of gastroenteritis between two communities (having high incidences) located close to towns and a third (with low-incidence) that was relatively isolated. However, while isolation in the past may have been protective, the situation is changing, with growth retardation, common among Aboriginal children of the Kimberley, now more pronounced in isolated communities (Hitchcock, Gracey, Maller & Spargo 1987).

In addition to conditions such as chronic ear disease, trachoma, chronic anaemias, respiratory and gastrointestinal infections and low birthweight which still remain common, changed lifestyles have brought new medical problems. From early settlement the arrival of Aborigines at stations, missions and government feeding stations, with a transition to settlement-based life, caused major alterations in diet and activity. Novel foods, unrestricted by indigenous prohibitions (McGrath 1987), and which required a minimum of effort to obtain and prepare, became powerful enticements, at times the means of coercion. Sugar, flour, tea, meat and tobacco were the staples for generations on many cattle and government feeding stations. Over time there has, thus, been a marked increase in obesity, followed by the development of diabetes (Gracey & Spargo 1987), and more recently of hypertension and heart disease. Diabetes is more common among urban Aboriginal groups in the Kimberley (O'Dea, Spargo & Nestel 1982); indeed, it was shown that, with a return to traditional dietary sources and lifestyle, the insulin responses to glucose reverted towards normal in a group of Aboriginal diabetics (O'Dea, Spargo & Akerman 1980).

These conditions have been termed 'lifestyle diseases',[4] with Aboriginal populations perhaps being more vulnerable owing to evolutionary changes that previously favoured survival in environments characterised by 'feast and famine'. The sudden entrance into the cash economy significantly affected health, particularly through factors impacting on nutrition during pregnancy and childhood, including:

> the traditional behaviour pattern of immediate consumption; sharing amongst relatives and clan members; the relative immobility of Aborigines within the social structure; gambling; alcohol abuse; poor prospects for employment; inadequate facilities for food storage . . . electricity and rate payments; etc. (Gracey, Sullivan & Spargo 1988 : 37)

Alcohol use by Aborigines of the Kimberley will be explored in chapter 5. While one cannot quantify the impact, it is clearly massive, and constitutes one of the major direct assaults on Aboriginal health in the 1980s, affecting the individual, the family and the community. However, this situation is further complicated by the stereotyping of Aboriginal drinking. Indeed, as a group often the recipient of stigmatising labels, Aborigines have been understandably sensitive to psychiatry and mental health initiatives. In 1979 a Declaration of Mental Health was formulated by the newly constituted National Aboriginal Mental Health Association. It pointed out that this dimension of Aboriginal ill-health was usually overlooked, and called for the provision of basic mental health services and culturally informed programs of counselling and training (Hennessy 1988). In the ensuing decade there was little movement. In the late 1980s, in the wake of the Royal Commission into Aboriginal Deaths in Custody, the behavioural dimension of health became increasingly recognised, and the lack of appropriate services for Aborigines emphasised. The historical context of these issues has been highlighted by the Royal Commission, and also by the National Aboriginal Health Strategy Working Party, which indicated that 'mental health professionals must understand Aboriginal history — the real life situations of alienation, poverty, and powerlessness' (1989 : 173).

The National Aboriginal Health Strategy was the major development in Aboriginal health during the 1980s, the working party receiving input from professionals and consumers throughout the country. It was conceptualised and directed by Aborigines. Their analyses clearly prioritised the social determinants of Aboriginal ill-health and called for programs based on long-term planning, with inter-sectoral collaboration and Aboriginal control. Thus, in the 1980s, this tumultuous decade that brought unprecedented and often destabilising change to many Aboriginal communities in remote Australia, a growing resource-pool of Aboriginal expertise emerged: included here are the first Aboriginal doctors. Like the Aboriginal nurses who graduated in the mid-1960s, these doctors may powerfully confront tenacious stereotypes and prejudices.

NOTES

Chapter 3 is based in part on previously published material: 'Stains on the caring mantle: Doctors in Aboriginal Australia have a history', *Medical Journal of Australia 155 (11/12)*, 1991, 779–783.

1. While the information in the text was obtained from the death certificate, an interesting connection to the 'Kings in Grass Castles' is provided by one of their descendants, Mary Durack:

   The unfortunate Cummin[g]s who, as reported by the mailman had taken his own life at Hall's Creek, was the young Englishman whose marriage to Bird had been prevented on the eve of the ceremony two years before, when the story of his former association with Oscar Wilde had been brought to their attention. (1975 : 71)

2. Darwin's comments inadvertently contributed to the negative perceptions. In discussing the primitive social structure of the Fuegians he stated 'The Australian, in the simplicity of the arts of life, comes nearest the Fuegian: he can, however, boast of his boomerang, his spear and throwing-stick, his method of climbing trees, of tracking animals, and of hunting. Although the Australian may be superior in acquirements, it by no means follows that he is likewise superior in mental capacity: indeed, from what I saw of the Fuegians when on board, and from what I have read of the Australians, I should think the case was exactly the reverse.' (1988 [1845] : 198).

   Theories linking the cultures of Tierra del Fuego and Aboriginal Australia persisted in different forms (including speculation about a possible land bridge) until the 1920s. Jones (1989) comments on speculations regarding Baldwin Spencer's trip to Tierra del Fuego, where he died in 1929.

3. Mulvaney commented:

   While it seemed appropriate to use the law to regulate the personal lives of alien races, such as wily orientals and savages, nothing was proposed to limit the propensity for spreading disease by randy European bushmen, armed with rifles and grog to ensure their domination. Such was the current attitude to sexuality, that Aboriginal women were blamed as the purveyors of the disease. (1989 : 184)

4. Also noted as major causes of morbidity and mortality elsewhere, including the Northern Territory (Khalidi 1989) and western New South Wales (Gray & Hogg 1989). The latter authors urge caution in the use of the term 'lifestyle disease', suggesting that it should be used only when the condition 'occurs mainly in the same age groups as in affluent societies' (1989 : 34).

Mortality in a Time of Change

Searching through archives may, like a night-backed window, reveal more about the observer than what lies in the darkness beyond. Compiled by Europeans, the early records of the Kimberley focused on their lives — their births, marriages, deaths and deceits. Obscured are the Aborigines who had lived and died unrecorded in the region for millennia. After a century of accommodation and adjustment, these Aborigines are now required to face new dangers accompanying new levels of change. This chapter presents material on Kimberley Aboriginal mortality over 30 years (1957–1986). The period was selected as it covers 15 years before and after the extension of full citizenship rights to Aborigines in the Kimberley.

THE POPULATION

There are two recurring problem areas in the analysis of Aboriginal mortality data: the definition of the denominator (the Aboriginal population) and of the numerator (deaths). Historically, the changing construction of who constituted an Aborigine, and different approaches to collecting data, have led to widely varying population estimates. Consequently, the 1971 census, the first to count Aborigines, reported an increase of 30 000 over national estimates for 1966, mainly due to increases in New South Wales and Queensland. In 1976, following the Referendum, a further 45 000 were added, with the largest proportional growth being in Victoria, Tasmania and the Australian Capital Territory. However, the 1981 census generated a national total 1000 less than that for 1976, with the only areas demonstrating an increase being Western Australia, the Northern Territory and Queensland. It was thus thought at the time that in contrast to earlier counts: 'adequacy of enumeration rather than changing identification seems to be the main factor behind intercensal anomalies' (Gray & Smith 1983 : 8).

The 1986 census counted 227 645 persons of Aboriginal or Torres Strait Islander origin, an increase of 42.4 per cent over the 1981 estimate (Australian Bureau of Statistics 1987). This reversal was attributed to several factors, including increased pre-census publicity and trained field staff. All States and Territories showed an increase, with the greatest proportional growth reported from Victoria and Tasmania (Smyth 1989), suggesting that identification was again the major growth factor. By the 1986 count Queensland had the largest number of Aborigines (61 268, or 26 per cent of the national Aboriginal population), and the Northern Territory had the largest proportion who were of Aboriginal descent (22 per cent of Territorians). Western Australia recorded 37 789 Aborigines, 17 per cent of the national Aboriginal population and 3 per cent of the population of the State. Two-thirds of Australian Aborigines now live in urban or town settings, with 39 per cent under 15 years of age (versus 23 per cent of the Australian population as a whole). The now familiar working definition adopted by the Commonwealth government in October 1978 includes both self-identification and community acceptance:

> An Aboriginal or Torres Strait Islander is a person of Aboriginal or Torres Strait Islander descent who identifies as an Aboriginal or Torres Strait Islander and is accepted as such by the community in which he lives.

The Aboriginal population of the Kimberley is subject to the same vicissitudes. Population estimates by the Department of Native Welfare (which, after 1972, became the Aboriginal Affairs Planning Authority) show a gradual and relatively sustained increase from 5328 in 1957, to 10 092 in 1983 (the peak being 10 384 in 1982). These figures were based on estimates by field officers stationed in the region. After 1984 the figures supplied by the Authority were based on the census, the first being the census of 1981. The Aboriginal population of the Kimberley according to that census was 7933, constituting 41 per cent of the region's total. Thus, the figures for the Kimberley reported by the Aboriginal Affairs Planning Authority *fell* from 10 092 in 1983, to 6186 in 1984 (which for some reason, though stated to be based on the 1981 census, was smaller by 1747). The 1986 census generated a figure of 9511 Aborigines, 38 per cent of the Kimberley population. These figures are widely thought to be significant underestimates.

The most intensive attempt to clarify the Kimberley situation was the work of Boundy (1977),[1] who calculated the population for 31 December 1976, compiled life tables, and estimated the projected distribution by age and sex for 1981 and 1986. His estimate for 1976 was 10 944, with a projected figure for 1981 of 11 811, or 49 per cent higher than the 1981 census. The gap narrowed somewhat in the 1986 census, Boundy's projection (13 180) being 38 per cent higher than the census estimate. Providing support for the contention that the census was under-enumerating, the number of Kimberley Aborigines on the Community Health Register of the Western Australian Department of Health in 1981 was 27 per cent higher than the census figure (Holman, Quadros, Bucens & Reid 1987). In 1986 the Register (used for generating the random sample discussed in the next chapter) contained 12 136 individuals, 28 per cent more than the census (Richard Smith, personal communication 1988). For the purposes of calculations in the latter part of this chapter, Boundy's figures will be used.

Enumerations of Aboriginal deaths are subject to error owing to failures in reporting and, as well, owing to the mis-classification of race. Designation of race was added to the Certificate of Cause of Death only in the 1980s. Mis-classification continued to be a problem at the time of this study.

Problems associated with designation of cause of death are well recognised. Most of these difficulties are compounded in remote areas where, in the past, medical expertise was not available. Coronial idiosyncrasies and changes may influence designation; individuals whose deaths were attributed to 'old age' in one year, may have been classified as 'unknown' in another. As all deaths from external causes are investigated by the coroner, it would seem reasonable to suppose that this designation should be relatively free of mis-registration: that this is not the case, however, is clear.

THE STUDY

The major source of information was the Register of Deaths, copies of which are located in each of four administrative centres in the Kimberley: Broome, Derby, Halls Creek and Kununurra. All registered deaths occurring between 1 January 1957 and 31 December 1986 were included. As there is frequently a delay of several months for coronial findings to be recorded, all deaths registered by 30 June

1987 were examined. Hicks (1985) estimated that in 1983 the Registrar-general identified 74 per cent of Aboriginal deaths occurring within Western Australia, the deficit in part representing mis-registration of race. He concluded that the combination of deaths registered by the Registrar-general, and the records of the Public Health Department (both of which were assumed to be sampling independently from the same universe of events) offered the best opportunity for minimising missed deaths. Accordingly, all files of deceased Kimberley Aboriginal clients stored by Community Health in Derby were examined, and the resulting record compared with the list obtained from the Registrar-general. However, as files were only maintained for deaths occurring from 1980, the cause of death could only be ascertained from that time. Additional deaths emerged in two groups: those that had died within the region and which, for reasons unknown, were not registered; and deaths of Kimberley residents who had died elsewhere, usually after medical evacuation to Perth or Darwin.

Unrecorded local deaths accounted for between 5 per cent and 16 per cent of the discovered deaths, with a prominent increase between 1983 and 1984. Many of these unregistered deaths were accounted for by one particular community. Adding Aboriginal deaths that had occurred out of the region (which could be expected to be more numerous in the 1980s than in previous decades) revealed that missed deaths constituted between 9 per cent and 23 per cent of the resulting total. Also consulted was: a list of deaths that had been the subject of coronial investigation; a list provided by the Registrar-general's office in Perth of deaths that had not been registered owing to incomplete data; and, in certain areas, undertakers' records.

Sources of information were, thus, the Registers of Deaths, coronial reports, and Community Health files, burial records, police records and the use of Aboriginal and non-Aboriginal informants. Information on the Register indicating Aboriginal descent included: an obvious Aboriginal name; the names of parents; place of birth; occupation (earlier under this rubric an Aboriginal was often listed as an 'indigent native'); site of death (such as 'Native Hospital'); place of burial (the 'native section' of the local cemetery); religion (there are very few non-Aborigines associated with the United Aborigines Mission); site of residence; and identified medical conditions, such as Hansen's disease, which when listed could be checked through leprosarium records. A list was compiled of all individuals for whom doubt remained, which was then examined using alternative sources. In approximately five non-infant cases, where it was unclear if the individual had been of Aboriginal descent, informants were asked about lifestyle and how they thought the individual would have identified. While there were difficulties due to limited recorded information for neonatal deaths, the major focus of this study was non-infant deaths.

For the purposes of this study, deaths were classified as from external causes (ICD 9, Class XVII [World Health Organization 1975]), deaths from other causes, and deaths listed as 'unknown' or for whom no cause was ascertainable. Deaths from external causes were further subdivided into: deaths due to motor vehicle accidents (ICD 9, codes 810–829); deaths from other accidents including drowning, burning, aircraft crash, fall, accidental poisoning, work injuries, accidental discharge of firearms, and exposure (codes 830–929); suicide and self-inflicted injury (codes 950–959); and deaths due to injury purposefully inflicted by other persons (codes 960–969). All deaths where the designation seemed unclear or suspect (for example listed as 'subdural haematoma') were further evaluated. This occasionally resulted in reclassification. Two examples will suffice. One non-Aboriginal death listed as a 'gunshot injury to the head' turned out to have been an individual who had shot himself through the roof of the mouth in the presence of a medical practitioner. The death of an Aborigine, of whom it was recorded that he had jumped from a bridge into a stream in flood, was found to be an accidental fall associated with alcohol.

Subsequently, two further lists were compiled. The first contained all deaths from external causes, or listed as unknown, occurring in Broome Shire from 1977 to 1986. The second included all deaths from any cause between the ages of 15 and 30 years occurring throughout the Kimberley during the same period. The coroner's files in Perth were searched and all available reports were reviewed.

FINDINGS

A total of 4372 deaths were identified, of which 689 (16 per cent) were of infants (375 neonatal and 314 post-neonatal deaths). Of the 3682 non-infant deaths (over one year of age), there were 2916 Aboriginal deaths, comprised of 1552 males (mean age: 58 years) and 1364 females (mean age: 59 years). Of 766 non-Aboriginal deaths, there were 655 males (mean age: 51 years) and 111 females (mean age: 52 years). The body of an unidentified adult male found in a state of advanced decomposition could not be classified by race, his age also remaining unknown. The propensity for Aborigines, especially those living in more isolated areas in the past, to depart this life at an age which happens to be a multiple of ten should alert one to the limitations of age data.

The total number identified of deaths by all means demonstrated a peak during the five-year period 1957–1962, representing a real increase in deaths due to the 1959 influenza epidemic mentioned in chapter 3. An apparent sudden increase after 1981 was, by contrast, an artefact, reflecting the inclusion of deaths from Community Health files and missed by the Register in the previous five-year period. Rates were only calculated for this latter period (see table 3). Infant deaths showed a marked fall through the 1970s, with an increase in the 1980s, being an artefact similar to that noted above for adults. The fall in infant mortality was accompanied by a dramatic decrease in hospital admission rates for infants in the Kimberley between 1971 and 1980 (Gracey & Spargo 1987).

The proportions of total Aboriginal deaths recorded as 'unknown' or without cause listed, varied between zero and 8 per cent, save for the 1960s, when the proportion soared to 21 per cent of female and 15 per cent of male deaths, and there was no similar increase evident among non-Aboriginal deaths. That increase fell within the tenure of two magistrates responsible for coronial matters throughout the Kimberley between 1962 and 1970, and probably reflects idiosyncrasies on their part. Most of these deaths came from outlying regions, particularly around Halls Creek, where in one year nearly all deaths were recorded as cause unknown. The age distribution of these deaths revealed clear peaks in the first and eighth decades, suggesting that most were due to natural causes, the elderly deaths having previously been recorded as 'old age' or 'debility'. Because of the prominent changes in infant deaths, subsequent proportions will be calculated as percentages of total non-infant deaths (deaths over one year of age) by five-year periods.

Certain findings emphasise problems arising from comparisons of Aboriginal and non-Aboriginal populations of the north. Through the 30 years the proportions of non-Aborigines in the Kimberley over one year of age dying from external causes was remarkably high, in a range of 25–50 per cent for females and

     Aboriginal health and history

30–48 per cent for males, considerably higher than the proportions for the State as a whole. This reflects the nature of the non-Aboriginal population of the region — younger, transient, and heavy drinking. In addition, many of the long-standing non-Aboriginal residents retired and, thus, died elsewhere, and were also more likely to have been in a financial situation that allowed them to travel south for medical treatment.

Figure 4.1 *Deaths from external causes as a proportion of Kimberley Aboriginal deaths*

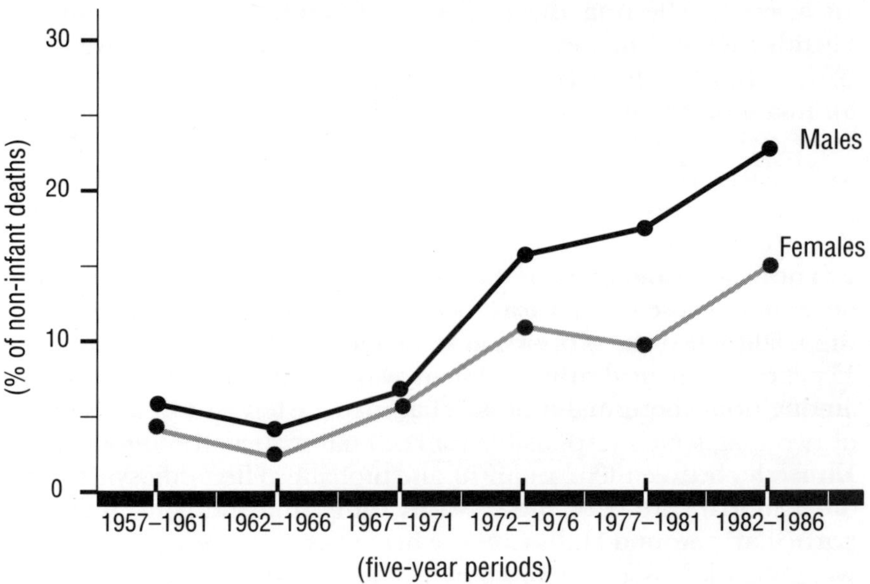

The proportions of Aboriginal non-infant deaths due to external causes are shown in figure 4.1, demonstrating a sustained rise from the early 1970s. In the first 15 years this proportion had been steady in a range of 4–7 per cent of male deaths, and of 2–5 per cent for females. It subsequently increased, to reach 23 per cent of male and 15 per cent of female Aboriginal non-infant deaths between 1982 and 1986. Further dissection (table 1) reveals an increase for both males and females in the proportion of deaths due to motor vehicle accidents, an increase in the proportion of male deaths due to other accidents, and an increase, particularly for women, in the proportions of deaths due to interpersonal violence (the only external cause of death in which Aboriginal women predominate).

Table 1 *Specific external causes (excluding suicide) as proportions of Aboriginal non-infant deaths: 1957–1986*

	Motor vehicle accidents		Other accidents		Interpersonal violence	
	M	F	M	F	M	F
1957–61	0.3	0.7	4.9	2.9	1.4	0.7
1962–66	1.9	0.5	0.9	1.5	0.9	0
1967–71	3.0	2.6	3.4	2.6	0.4	0
1972–76	10.4	4.6	5.0	3.1	0.5	3.1
1977–81	6.4	3.5	8.0	3.5	2.4	2.0
1982–86	9.7	8.3	7.6	2.3	2.3	4.6

Note: M = males; F = females.

Suicide will be the focus of a later chapter; however, the percentages of non-Aboriginal and Aboriginal male deaths due to suicide offers another reminder of the problems of comparisons. Forty-five non-Aboriginal suicides were discovered, distributed relatively evenly throughout the study period. The 10 non-Aboriginal suicides that occurred between 1962 and 1967 (a period of economic downturn in the pastoral industry and rapid growth in the agricultural ventures about Kununurra) constituted 10 per cent of non-infant male deaths. By contrast, the proportion of Aboriginal deaths by suicide increased from essentially zero (there was only one prior to 1972) to 3 per cent (or 10 suicides) of male non-infant deaths for the period 1982–1986. Aboriginal and non-Aboriginal suicides also differed: by age, the modal decade for Aborigines being the third, whereas for non-Aborigines it was the fourth; by location, non-Aboriginal suicides being evenly distributed across the region in proportion to the non-Aboriginal population, whereas Aboriginal suicides clustered in Broome Shire; and by sex, with Aboriginal suicides almost exclusively being of males, while for non-Aborigines the proportion of deaths due to suicide, by sex, was similar.

Thus, there has been a sustained and continuing rise in the proportion of Aboriginal deaths attributed to external causes. The proportion of total Kimberley Aboriginal deaths (including infants) due to external causes, which had earlier been steady between 5 per cent and 6 per cent, in the early 1970s exceeded the proportion for the State as a whole. Examination of the data obtained by Hicks (1985), and mortality figures supplied by the Australian Bureau of Statistics, allows comparison of the proportion of deaths due to external causes found in this study, with proportions for Western Australian Aborigines and the State population as a whole. In order to provide sufficient numbers, figures for the State for 1983 are compared with those for Kimberley Aborigines for the five-year period 1982–1986 (table 2). The overall proportions of Aboriginal deaths for the State and the Kimberley due to external causes are similar, but both are significantly greater than those of the total Western Australian population. A breakdown by age reveals that roughly four-fifths of male and female deaths for both Kimberley and Western Australian Aborigines in the age-range 15–24 years were due to external causes.

Table 2 *Deaths from external causes as a proportion of all deaths: for Kimberley Aborigines, Western Australian Aborigines and the total Western Australian population*

	Deaths from external causes	Total deaths	Percentage of total deaths
	(N)	(N)	(%)
Kimberley Aborigines 1982–1986			
Males	78	378	21
Females	34	252	13
Western Australian Aborigines 1983[a]			
Males	34	200	17
Females	20	123	16
Western Australian total population 1983[b]			
Males	459	4785	10
Females	158	3574	4

Notes: [a] Figures based on Hicks 1985.
[b] Figures provided by the Australian Bureau of Statistics.

The calculation of rates was only possible for deaths occurring after 1980. Using the five-year period 1982–1986, and a population base derived from the 1981 and 1986 projections of Boundy, cause-specific mortality rates for deaths due to external causes for Kimberley Aborigines were calculated. They are compared in table 3 with 1984 rates for the Western Australian population as a whole.

Table 3 *Cause-specific death rates for deaths from external causes:
Kimberley Aborigines, 1982–1986, and total
Western Australian population, 1984*

	Kimberley Aborigines		Western Australia	
	M	F	M	F
All causes	238	110	67	23
Motor vehicle accidents	102	60	23	8
Accidents	80	17	21	8
Violence	25	33	3	1
Suicide	31	0	20	5

Note: 1 M = males; F = females.
2 Death rates are per 100 000 population. Figures have been rounded for
presentation.
3 Figures for Western Australia are for total population, derived from the
Australian Bureau of Statistics.

These crude cause-specific mortality rates for deaths from external
causes demonstrate that the rate of such deaths for Aborigines
exceeds the rates for the general population. Similar findings were
reported during the 1980s for Aboriginal populations from various
Queensland reserve communities (Lincoln, Najman, Wilson &
Matis 1983), Central Australia (Khalidi 1989), rural New South
Wales (Thomson & Smith 1985), and western New South Wales
(Gray & Hogg 1989). Thus, the proportion of deaths due to external
causes and the cause-specific rates for Kimberley Aborigines appear
similar to those found for a number of non-urban regions of
Australia.

The increase in the proportion of deaths due to external causes
that began in the early 1970s coincided with the lifting of the last
restrictions on the sale of alcohol to Aborigines in the Kimberley.
The pattern of increase in the 1970s suggests alcohol-affected male
behaviour: an initial major increase in male deaths from motor
vehicle accidents and other accidents, with a similar increase in the
proportion of females dying as a result of interpersonal violence.
However, in order to better focus on the influence of alcohol, all
coronial reports of deaths that occurred between 15 and 30 years of
age over the last 10-year period of the study were examined. A total
of 57 male deaths and 32 female deaths were discovered; of these,
21 male and 15 female reports implicated alcohol as a factor in the
death. While there may have been some of these deaths in which

alcohol was involved, but not recorded in the coroner's report, the distribution of such deaths remains of interest (table 4).

Table 4 *Deaths of Kimberley Aborigines aged 15–30 years, showing cause and record of alcohol involvement, by proportion: 1977–1986*

Cause	Male		Female	
	Total	Alcohol	Total	Alcohol
	(%)	(%)	(%)	(%)
Motor vehicle accidents	32	43	22	27
Violence	5	10	25	33
Accident	23	33	6	13
Suicide	11	10	3	7
Natural	26	5	41	20
Unknown	4	0	3	0
Sample size (N)	57	21	32	15

Note: Percentages have been rounded for presentation.

For young males, motor vehicle accidents are followed by natural causes and other accidents as the leading causes of death; while in those deaths in which alcohol was incriminated, motor vehicle accidents and other accidents account for over three-quarters. For females, natural causes followed by motor vehicle accidents and interpersonal violence are the leading causes; whereas, when alcohol is considered, violence becomes the leading cause of death and that combined with motor vehicle accidents constituted 60 per cent of deaths. It must be remembered that in deaths from violence, it is the presence of alcohol in the victim, rather than in the perpetrator, that is being recorded. However, it is consistent with the suggestion that in the alcohol-affected environment, additional risk is primarily consequent on the effect of alcohol on male behaviour (motor vehicle accidents, other accidents and homicide of women).

DISCUSSION

This study raised a number of issues. Adequate health planning requires an analysis of trends in mortality and morbidity. However, only recently have reliable Aboriginal population figures become available that allow the calculation of accurate mortality rates. Their absence in the past necessitated reliance on other measures to demonstrate temporal changes, such as the cause-specific proportional mortality used here. In addition, even in recent years, surprising numbers of deaths do not appear on the register of deaths, demanding recourse to other sources of information.

The findings raise questions regarding the nature, timing and location of the changes in mortality patterns for Kimberley Aborigines. Numerous studies have demonstrated that Aborigines are at greater risk of dying as a result of accident or violence. At least within the Kimberley, such vulnerability has not always been the case; the proportions of deaths due to motor vehicle accidents, other accidents and interpersonal violence all appear to begin increasing in the early 1970s and continue to increase to the present. In 1971, the midpoint of this study, full citizenship with drinking rights were extended to all Aborigines of the Kimberley. The social changes of this period have been outlined earlier, and the impact on the construction of identity will be addressed later (see chapter 9). However, it is essential to further locate drinking rights. The 1970s also brought access to money and vehicles, which must be taken into account, for example, when examining deaths from motor vehicle accidents. However, the fact that this increase is in synchrony with increased deaths from other external causes would argue against increased access to means (vehicles) being the sole factor.

Hicks (1985) described the difficulties of assessing alcohol-related mortality from information contained on death certificates, the sequelae of alcohol abuse and dependence ranging over the whole spectrum of medical diagnoses. The psychomotor and behavioural consequences of alcohol are suggested by motor vehicle accidents and other accidents being major causes of young deaths among males. The physical environment becomes increasingly dangerous for a young drinking male in the Kimberley, particularly the road. Writing of the American drinking-driving experience, Gusfield pointed to the 'male character of the behavior and attendant risks' (1985 : 71), indicating that young adults are particularly at risk, even at lower blood alcohol concentrations.

By contrast, the interpersonal environment becomes increasingly dangerous for young drinking Aboriginal women in the Kimberley. In the group activity of drinking, Aboriginal women are exposed to the increased vulnerability of males to the road environment, frequently being passengers of drinking drivers. Drinking also appears to increase their risk of death from homicide. This is in part mediated by exposing the victim to males who are also drinking; indeed, every coronial report used in this study, in which an assailant was known, found both parties had been drinking. Being intoxicated increases aggressive behaviour in males, and in females may also act to increase their vulnerability. As noted by American researchers, 'the increased presence of alcohol in those killed during physical fights is compatible with the hypothesis which posits that alcohol promotes aggressive behaviour and aversive interaction' (Goodman, Mercy, Loya, Rosenberg, Smith, Allen, Vargas & Kolts 1986 : 148).

The relationship of alcohol and violence is emphasised by findings from a review of 20 women who presented to the hospital in Broome over a two-month period following domestic violence. Nineteen of these women were Aboriginal, the modal age group being 25–30 years. In 19 cases, also, the assailant was the woman's partner, with alcohol involved in 18 of them. In only two cases were charges laid. Tuesdays and Wednesdays accounted for 60 per cent of the presentations — Tuesday being pension day, and thus associated with increased availability of alcohol. Interpersonal violence will be examined in detail in chapter 8.

The levelling-off of the proportion of men as victims of violence may reflect the continuing increases due to accidents and motor vehicle accidents; however, this plateau for males occurred in conjunction with an increase in suicides in the late 1980s, almost exclusively confined to men. If one combines deaths from homicide and suicide for Aboriginal males, there is a linear continuation of the early increase due to interpersonal violence. This raises the question of the relationship of homicide and suicide.[2] The intersection of alcohol and rising mortality rates from suicide, accidents and homicide is not unique to Aboriginal Australians. In this regard Kahn (1982; 1986) pointed to similar patterns in Aborigines, American Indians and Eskimos, and suggested that alcohol is also linked to child neglect, domestic violence and family breakup. Alcohol is presented by Kahn in these three cultures as itself a manifestation of cultural disruption.

In this chapter temporal changes in the mortality patterns of Kimberley Aborigines since the 1960s were identified. While the proportion of deaths occurring during the first decade of life has decreased since the early 1970s, Aborigines are not more frequently living to old age. The improvements in infant mortality are offset by the increasing proportion of deaths occurring across young and middle adult years. A similar picture emerges in rural New South Wales, where there has been 'an improvement in infant and early childhood mortality balanced by an increase in adult mortality' (Thomson & Smith 1985 : S52). In a more recent review of Aboriginal mortality, Thomson (1991) notes that while infant mortality has fallen substantially, Aboriginal death rates are still between two and four times those of the wider Australian population, with life expectancies up to two decades shorter. External causes ranks second for Aboriginal males and third for females among causes of death, with diseases of the circulatory system being the leading cause for both. However, the impact of deaths from external causes on younger Aborigines is reflected in the fact that 'the most marked difference between Aboriginal and non-Aboriginal death rates is for young and middle aged adults' (Thomson 1991 : 239). Against the background of these changes in Aboriginal mortality during the last decades, the next chapters will focus on specific emergent patterns of mortality and morbidity in the Kimberley.

NOTES

Chapter 4 is based on published material: 'Changing Aboriginal mortality patterns in the Kimberley region of Western Australia, 1957–86: The impact of deaths from external causes', *Aboriginal Health Information Bulletin 11*, 1989, 27–32.

1. Boundy's figures were based on field contact confirmation of Community Health Services client lists, complemented by mortality and birth records.
2. While seeming to offer support for the Henry and Short model (an inverse relationship between homicide and suicide explained psycho-analytically as equivalent phenomena differentiated by the object of aggressive impulses), numerous studies have called this interpretation into question.

CHAPTER 5

Alcohol

INTRODUCTION

Access to alcohol has long preoccupied those claiming responsibility for the 'welfare' of Aborigines; until the 1960s and 1970s, legal restrictions on sales remained in force. The Licensed Publicans Act (NSW) of 1838 was the first legislation to forbid the supply of alcohol to Aborigines, with all mainland colonies subsequently following suit (McCorquodale 1985). Prohibition legislation was repealed in Victoria in 1957; New South Wales, 1963; Queensland, 1971; South Australia, 1971; Western Australia, 1972; with Aborigines in the Territories being granted drinking rights in 1964.

The subject of Aborigines and alcohol is embedded in the history of intercultural relations. In this context alcohol is not only a substance but a symbol; its prohibition had, and has, meaning. In remote Australia access to alcohol was the most immediate and tangible expression of 'full rights' and for many Aborigines these two things were seen as synonymous (Sansom 1980). Alcohol-affected Aboriginal behaviour, which challenges and confronts Euro-Australian standards and norms, clearly retains this meaning for certain groups (Sackett 1988). Prohibition ensured that alcohol would be a central issue in Aboriginal–police relations, a situation which has continued despite the repeal of restrictive legislation. Aborigines remain the most frequently arrested and incarcerated group in Australia; in August 1988 they were being detained nationally at a rate some twenty times that of non-Aborigines. Almost one-third of these were due to drunkenness, some three times the proportion for such arrests for non-Aborigines (McDonald 1990). In Western Australia the arrest-rate was forty-three times greater than for non-Aborigines, with Halls Creek and Fitzroy Crossing

90

accounting for one-third of all detentions Statewide in 1988–1989 (Midford 1991).

SETTING

In the Kimberley, unrestricted Aboriginal access to alcohol coincided with dislocation from traditional and transitional lands and roles, Aborigines being precipitated into a cash economy and welfare reliance in the often indifferent or threatening environment of town camps. As the focus of economic activity and social life shifted to the domestic arena, social roles, particularly for males, were profoundly altered; their traditional sources of esteem were compromised and there were immense social pressures to drink. Perhaps the most appealing and enduring white role-model in remote Australia was the stockman, whose ability to drink was an affirmation of male frontier values. Alcohol was also frequently used to reward station Aborigines (McGrath 1987), being highly valued as a source of status and esteem. Later pressures to drink included inducements from the beneficiaries of Aboriginal consumption, those involved in the sale and supply of alcohol.

In the decades since the repeal of prohibition, almost all Aboriginal males in the Kimberley have tried drinking. By contrast, the older a woman was at the time of legalisation, the less likely she was to ever become a drinker. Age was a protective factor for Aboriginal women but not men, for whom the early incentives to drink have been subsequently compounded by the social impact of alcohol misuse.

The construction of this problem has changed with time, from a deficiency in self-control (as had also been applied to gambling and sexuality), requiring 'protection'; to deviance, necessitating incarceration; to the manifestation of disadvantage, to be remedied by social interventions (such as the decriminalisation of public intoxication and the provision of 'sobering-up' centres). Only recently has the intercultural context been raised in discussions of Aboriginal drinking; the responses remaining directed *at* Aborigines. The social and historical context was emphasised by the National Aboriginal Health Strategy Working Party: 'there is a consensus in the Aboriginal community that understands the "alcohol problem" from a community perspective, as a symptom (ultimately a symptom of dispossession) of alienation, and discrimination which leads to loss of self esteem' (1989 : 194).

FRAMES

During the past decade cross-cultural studies of alcohol use have generated vigorous debate outside Australia, particularly the relative strengths and weaknesses of ethnographic versus epidemiological approaches, as noted by Heath: 'Anthropologists might wonder why epidemiological methods are so important in alcohol studies; whereas most anthropologists who study alcohol tend to focus on belief and behavior, paying at least as much attention to "normal" as to "deviant" patterns' (1987 : 41).

Heath identified two dominant models: the 'sociocultural model', concerned with attitudes, values and norms; and the 'distribution of consumption model', focusing on 'problem drinking' and attempting to define broad rules governing the prevalence and patterns of drinking across groups. The former orientation privileges a culturally informed experiential (emic) analysis, whereas the latter foregrounds objective comparisons across groups (etic).

ALCOHOL MISUSE: THEORIES AND CONSEQUENCES

IN THE GENERAL POPULATION

Alcohol use and alcoholism have been variously conceptualised. In Western post-Enlightenment theorising, issues of individual responsibility were ascendant, leading to morally-based models. However, in response to the manifest failures of treatments based on such reasoning, disease models evolved during the last century (Room 1984). This conceptualisation was informed both by the medicalisation of what had previously been morally constructed, and by the emergence of biologically based theories, crystallised in the behaviourally defined alcohol-dependence syndrome.[1]

Following the Second World War a sociological critique of the disease model emerged, with context increasingly taken into account. Room (1984) described a shift from a position that presumed alcoholism to be a transculturally valid entity, to a social construction contingent on historical and cultural context. In addition, there was a reformulation of more traditional moral models, including existential analyses ('suspension of control' [Aguilar 1964]), attempts to mediate between the competing constructions ('way of life leading to predicaments' [Drew 1987]), and multi-dimensional integrative models (Donovan 1986).

Those agencies responsible for problematising alcohol consumption among previously alcohol-inexperienced indigenous populations, were the same agencies — government and religious — who controlled public perception and policy. More recent anthropological interest in alcohol use has confronted the prevailing preoccupation with alcoholism and the focus on deviance and pathology. A substantial functionalist literature subsequently emerged examining the normative roles of drinking. It has been argued that this orientation has resulted in a tendency in recent ethnographic literature towards a deflation of problems related to alcohol in tribal societies, in part as a reaction to previous moralistic attitudes (Room 1984). In this sense such approaches are themselves also culturally informed. In contrast to epidemiological approaches that define and measure 'problems', which tend to be uncommon and are thus foregrounded ('problem inflation'), the methodology of ethnography privileges that which is common and 'unproblematic'. As a consequence, Room argues, such depictions underestimate not only problems ('problem deflation'), but abstention.

The issues are timely for the study of Aboriginal alcohol use as epidemiological approaches have only been prominent during the past decade; previously the topic had been located almost entirely within an ethnographic domain. Since the mid-1980s cooperation between Aboriginal alcohol-use researchers has evolved using the differences in focus as complementary approaches to a common goal (Duquemin, d'Abbs & Chalmers 1991). Indeed, Aboriginal alcohol use has attracted more research attention since the mid-1980s than in the preceding five decades, with several comprehensive reviews now available.[2] While there has been a 'historical tendency to attempt single factor explanations' (Healy, Turpin & Hamilton 1985 : 193), most contemporary writers dismiss such approaches and they present 'problem' drinking as complexly overdetermined. While each reflects a particular orientation in suggesting putative causal factors, similarities are apparent. Four broad clusters emerge: biological, including genetic and 'illness' theories of alcoholism; socio-historical, including the history of exposure of Aborigines to alcohol and drinking, and the political forces leading to legislative controls; intercultural, covering the processes of accommodation or adaptation to continuing socio-economic disadvantage; and intracultural, cultural factors supporting patterns of behaviour associated with alcohol use. Before proceeding to examine these areas, the impact of alcohol on Aborigines is briefly reviewed. While this material is correlational, it is frequently invoked to 'prove' that Aborigines have an alcohol problem, and to support stereotypes of Aboriginal drinking.

CORRELATES AND CONSEQUENCES

There can now be no doubt that alcohol use contributes significantly to premature mortality and levels of ill-health in alcohol-consuming populations.[3] Few writers addressing Aboriginal alcohol use would dispute that drinking has had a damaging impact on traditional life, family structure and health. The timing of the increasing proportions of deaths from external causes in the Kimberley strongly suggests the involvement of alcohol. However, it also demonstrates the interplay of alcohol and social change: alcohol functions in this regard dynamically, as both cause and effect: 'alcohol abuse is simultaneously a health problem, a cause of other health problems and a symptom of socio-political related problems' (National Aboriginal Health Strategy Working Party 1989 : 192).

Reports from Western Australia, New South Wales and the Northern Territory support the proposition that alcohol contributes to premature Aboriginal mortality.[4] The available material indicates that 'the proportion of Aboriginal deaths which are considered to be alcohol-related fluctuates around ten per cent (generally higher for men and lower for women): a figure which is three to four times higher than the general Australian population' (Alexander 1990 : 16).

Substantial evidence also exists for the contribution of alcohol to Aboriginal ill-health. In the Kimberley alcohol has been implicated as a major contributor to poor nutrition (Gracey, Sullivan & Spargo 1988) and to associated problems such as diabetes (O'Dea, Spargo & Akerman, 1980). It has also been suggested that low birthweight (and thus neonatal survival) is linked to maternal drinking (Roberts, Gracey & Spargo 1988). The cardiovascular survey, conducted in parallel to the QARK, revealed that for males the major correlate of hypertension was being a current drinker (Smith, Spargo, Hunter, King, Correll, Craig & Nestel 1992).

IN THE ABORIGINAL POPULATION

There are many reasons for problem-drinking; but for Aborigines, as in other cultures, alcohol use is, in the first instance:

very pleasant, its use needs little, if any, organization, it provides a united activity, is non-competitive yet furnishes opportunity to excel. It imitates the white man and indicates equality with him. Moreover, it is readily obtainable and there is time and opportunity to enjoy it. (Bain 1974 : 49)

Convincing theories of Aboriginal alcohol misuse, many of which invoke experiences of social distress such as 'anomie' or 'powerlessness', must acknowledge this socially cohesive and enjoyable starting point. In the typology of intoxication common among Kimberley Aborigines, at the outset, before one is 'sparked up' and on the way to being 'fully drunk', a drinker is 'just happy'.

Genetic theories

'Firewater theories', that presume a genetic (read racial) susceptibility or vulnerability of Aborigines to alcohol, are widespread and often voiced by non-Aborigines in various stages of inebriation. However, they are also heard from those who are more sober and sentient, and from some Aborigines. While there is research evidence from European populations that genetic factors contribute to increased vulnerability to alcohol dependence, at most this is contributory, with environmental factors remaining substantial.[5] Additionally, while there are genetically based racial differences in alcohol metabolism[6], a genetic basis for Aboriginal vulnerability to the direct effects of alcohol is not supported by research evidence. Indeed, with respect to Aborigines there is only one study, which compared a small group of mixed-descent male Aborigines with males of European descent (Marinovich, Larsson & Barber 1976). While the results of that study should be viewed with caution because of the small and heterogeneous sample, the rates of elimination were similar.

However, genetic theories resurfaced following international research (as yet unreplicated) associating the Dopamine D_2 receptor gene with susceptibility to clinical alcoholism (Blum, Noble, Sheridan, Montgomery, Ritchie, Jagadeeswaran, Nogami, Briggs & Cohn 1990). Furthermore, research proposed at the University of Western Australia to examine gene polymorphisms of enzymes responsible for alcohol metabolism in Aborigines (Norman Palmer, personal communication 1990) was rapidly picked up by the local press (for example, Mike Hedge, 'Aborigines show alcohol problems may be genetic', *Australian Dr Weekly* June 1990 : 4; and Cathy O'Leary, 'One man's drink, another's poison', *West*

Australian 12 March 1990 : 4). It is unlikely that genetic theories will be abandoned.

Social theories

Social theorists have generally rejected unitary explanations. Social learning theories emphasise the influence of European, frontier alcohol-use on Aboriginal drinking patterns and the behaviour of drunkenness. Marshall (1983) proposed that in other cultures aboriginal peoples learnt not only 'drunken comportment'[7] but their beliefs about the drunken state itself (including patterns of disinhibition and violent behaviour), from Europeans. Observations in support of this for Australian Aborigines are present from as early as the 1850s, when Flanagan wrote:

> A ludicrous exercise of the disposition to imitate led, in former times, to the general prevalence of an error regarding their inability to withstand the effects of intoxicating drinks, or anything bearing an affinity thereto. It has been proved, however, beyond doubt that the appearances in these instances were only simulated. . . . An aboriginal, coming into a house in the interior where a young man was engaged in making brine by boiling salt, asked the latter if the liquor were rum, to which the only reply received was an invitation jocularly given to drink. The black having responded by swallowing at a draught about a pint of the brine, commenced tossing about his head, arms, and legs, with all the appearances of inebriation. Being taunted with this false display, he replied, with considerable earnestness, 'Me murry drunk, like a gentleman.' (1988 [1888] : 69)

Drinking was a prominent part of colonial life: patterns of consumption were influenced by the hardships and isolation of frontier life, availability of alcohol, social pressures to consume, and legal constraints. European alcohol consumption in remote Australia retains features of frontier drinking, and remains deviant when compared to urban society (for example Brady's [1988] description of Tennant Creek). Exposure was surely an important influence, and probably remains so. As noted earlier, alcohol was also used at times as a reward for station workers, and in payment, or as coercion, for sex.

Prohibition influenced emerging Aboriginal drinking patterns, encouraging patterns of secretive binge-drinking for most who chose to drink. For those mixed-descent Aborigines who hoped to be released from the restrictions of 'the Act', it symbolised their attainment of equal standing with Europeans, and of status with respect to their peers. Thus, not only were whites to be imitated, but the closer one came by virtue of bleaching out the 'taint' of Aboriginal blood, the nearer one was to a spectrum of privileges in which alcohol figured prominently (Tatz 1980). An immediate confirmation of full citizenship was to be able to walk into a pub and drink with, and like, a 'whitefella'.

Socio-environmental theorists have generally proposed a spectrum of causal factors. Most analyses privilege a particular framework, with a caveat frequently offered regarding stereotypes arising from the high visibility of Aboriginal drinking, reflecting both group orientation and the social realities of Aboriginal poverty that restrict access to formal drinking venues as well as private settings. In the Report of the House of Representatives Standing Committee on Aboriginal Affairs (1977) its list of twenty-four causes emphasised issues of social fragmentation. While including a list of nine environmental factors reflecting deprivation, psychosocial issues such as loss of pride and inferiority were perceived as the most potent. Writing several years earlier on his experience with tradition oriented groups, Albrecht had anticipated this tone in a perceptive analysis that included ten social and psychosocial factors:

> 1. No indigenous rules regarding the use of beverage alcohol; 2. The white Australian legal system under which Aborigines must live aggravates the Aboriginal alcohol problem by permitting Aborigines to abuse their social system while remaining part of it; 3. The increasing breakdown of traditional social control mechanisms paralleled the increasing availability of beverage alcohol, and thus added to the problem; 4. The pressures of relationships and gift giving; 5. Status symbol; 6. The use of alcohol by Aborigines to solve their psychosocial problems — boredom, social dysfunctioning, loss of identity; 7. The lack of means to release interpersonal tensions and frustrations predisposes Aborigines to excessive use of beverage alcohol; 8. Kicking back at white staff in charge of institutions; 9. Loss of male identity and self-worth; 10. Loss of traditional expressive outlets. (1974 : 36)

Larsen, studying an urban Aboriginal population, presented a total of twenty-four causal factors, concluding that 'the fundamental cause is obviously differential treatment, i.e. discrimination' (1979 : 146). In a later paper (1980) he developed the theme of discrimination in terms of minority group identification, a position taken up by Healy, Turpin and Hamilton, who contended that: 'the so-called "Aboriginal drinking problem" is more a problem of

black-white race relations' (1985 : 205). As a consequence of discriminatory attitudes, they suggested, drinking became for Aborigines a
mechanism for responding to powerlessness.

Powerlessness became a central theme in the analyses of Brady
and Palmer, and Collmann. Brady and Palmer, examining an outback population, started from the premise that Aborigines are in
a structural relationship to Europeans characterised by powerlessness,
a situation Aborigines wish to rectify. Drunken comportment
signifies a subjective improvement in the imbalance in terms of
increasing boldness in dealing with non-Aborigines, which is
supported by the group perception of drunken behaviour as being
outside the normal constraints of responsibility. According to Brady
and Palmer, access to alcohol provides a means to power within the
community, but in turn is antithetical to corporate controls within
the group, and does not result in structural change:

> Drinking is a positive expression of an alternative to compliance which
> Aborigines use in a vain attempt to rectify their powerlessness. But
> because they act out their expressions within the context of their very
> powerlessness they are ineffective in achieving any change. (1984 : 72)

Sackett also points to the 'popularity of drinking and drunkenness
as modes of Aboriginal non-compliance with the Australian state's
efforts to impose order' (1988 : 73), elaborating that inebriation may
act as a 'handy recusancy tool' (1988 : 75). Barber, Punt & Albers (1988)
examined the conjunction of alcohol and interpersonal violence,
suggesting that inebriation facilitates an experience of 'personalized
power'. Collmann also addressed this issue, presenting drunkenness
for those in the fringe-camps of Alice Springs, as: 'an experience and
expression of their personal power, drinking makes action possible,
that is, it helps create the conditions for people to enact their
images of personal power both among themselves and with others'
(1979b : 220).

Drinking in this construction becomes a means of redressing
powerlessness by emphasising independence: 'what outsiders interpret as degenerate self-destructive behaviour, the Mount Kelly people
interpret as the foremost manifestation of their wealth, independence
and self-control' (Collmann 1988 : 11). Collmann's (1979b) analysis
presented drinking as a mechanism whereby Aborigines construct
social relationships. Alcohol in this interpretation becomes a
medium by which patterns of indebtedness are negotiated. In short,
it is an easily distributable credit resource, the public control of which

becomes a basis for personal esteem. The economic and exchange function of alcohol is supported by the work of Sansom (1980) in the fringe-camps of Darwin, and in Alice Springs by O'Connor (1984), who emphasised issues of exchange and conformity:

> It is a group dependence, which I have termed *contingent drunkenness*. It is contingent in that it depends for its occurrence or character upon some prior occurrence or condition: the correct physical and social environment . . . alcohol has become established as a central object of exchange, and excessive use of this object has become institutionalised as the expected behaviour when people meet together. . . . As members define the group in terms of its drinking behaviour, then those who do not conform cannot, by definition, be part of the group . . . abstention carries a cost and the cost is exclusion. (O'Connor 1984 : 180)

This construction of drinking as a normative aspect of Aboriginal life was supported by Berndt and Berndt, who suggested that drinking 'has become patterned behaviour linked to particular positive values that were or are regarded by many Aborigines as being desirable and part of an expected way of life' (1985 : 521). However, it is a way of life that influences other aspects of Aboriginal society, including ritual and other traditional activities. Sackett (1977) commented on this impact of alcohol, noting that in Wiluna in the 1970s, alcohol had become regularly associated with Aboriginal gatherings for 'Law business'.

These sociological analyses have foregrounded structural and functional interpretations. Since the majority of these have been based on detailed observations of specific groups in which there are substantial numbers of drinkers, the resultant impression created, at times, is of community-wide drinking. Regardless of caveats, this impression is often generalised to the wider Aboriginal population. While these perspectives are non-Aboriginal in origin, they influence the Aboriginal consciousness and perception of alcohol use. Increasingly there are Aborigines who reject imposed labels. However, there are also those confronting the indigenisation and acceptance of alcohol-associated behaviour (Langton 1989; Gibson 1987). Gibson pointed to the distortion of cultural processes such as sharing and reciprocity in the service of individual exploitative demands. Regardless of orientation, quantitative studies are necessary to challenge stereotypes and to complement the depth provided by ethnographic analyses. Before reviewing this field, two additional issues demand mention.

Intercultural factors

Citizenship in the Kimberley brought changes, disappointments and opportunities for Aborigines, and for some Europeans. Both before and subsequently, certain non-Aborigines functioned as intermediaries or brokers, mediating between Aborigines and the wider society. During prohibition, one such group provided alcohol to Aborigines clustered about the towns of the north. Citizenship brought three major changes. First, Aborigines obtained the right to obtain alcohol legally. Second, they gained unprecedented access, at least in terms of previous Aboriginal experience, to the resources of the cash economy. Third, Aborigines were given a new role. For the burgeoning bureaucracy and for a new breed of entrepreneurs, they became an economic resource.

Alcohol is the most direct route through which money entering the Aboriginal community returns to non-Aborigines. In remote Australia many alcohol outlets could not survive without Aboriginal patronage. Taxis, planes and barges are involved in supplying alcohol to remote communities, and Aborigines and non-Aborigines resell alcohol. In one isolated Kimberley community during 1988, a bottle of rum could fetch \$200 around pension-day. Thus, the economic function of Aboriginal drinking must be seen in terms of its wider importance to the non-Aboriginal economy.

In addition, at least within the Kimberley, heavy-drinking Aborigines appropriate the resources of others in their communities. As a consequence, the expenditure on alcohol is greater than the income of drinkers alone could support. As most heavy drinkers are dependent on welfare, the government is involved both in the provision of funds for the purchase of alcohol and as a major financial beneficiary of drinking through taxes on alcohol sales. Aborigines are the intermediaries.

Intracultural factors

At the same time as alcohol and money arrived, demographic shifts brought additional tensions to bear on traditional social structures through the concentration of unrelated and often distant Aboriginal groups on the peripheries of towns. Traditionally, interaction between these groups was limited and clearly structured. Coming from the unknown, strangers constituted a potential threat. Meggitt stated of the Walbiri in the 1950s, that while they may have had an idea of where outlying tribes lay, 'this did not prevent them from imputing to the strangers cannibalism, incest and other practices that the Walbiri deem disgusting' (1962 : 25). Reid indicated that those outside an individual's social universe 'cannot be trusted and are assumed to be sometimes hostile, certainly indifferent to his health and welfare' (1979 : 196). Commenting on the internal forms of identification within the sociocultural system, Berndt and Berndt suggested that they functioned to contrast kin from non-kin — 'those "outside" that range — people from whom one was not always sure what to expect' (1985 : 94).

The intrusion of strangers was, thus, cause for concern and anxiety — stranger wariness — and resulted in attempts to locate the newcomer in a social matrix through questioning about origins and kinship. In this fashion a manner of relating could be defined, structuring subsequent interactions. With the unlocatable stranger there remained a sense of the unknown, the unfamiliar, the potentially dangerous. The options available for dealing with this ominous eventuality included hostility or avoidance.[8]

With the demographic changes of the 1960s and 1970s, Aborigines in the town reserves and fringe-camps of the Kimberley were confronted with having to live alongside groups for whom there was no precedent, no connection. In addition, as traditional prohibitions waned, unions occurred that placed those involved, and their offspring, in positions increasingly difficult to define within the traditional systems. In this setting alcohol functioned in several ways. Gatherings frequently occurred which were focused on drinking, bringing together individuals who would otherwise never have associated, or between whom the relationship was traditionally tense. Then, as now, the undercurrent of anxiety and wariness quickly evaporated in the conviviality and mateship of being 'just happy' or 'sparked up'. In the context of 'grogging' the immediate euphoria of the moment removes suspicion and sanctions prohibited relationships. While the friendliness and euphoria frequently do not survive the inebriated state, for the duration there is 'time out' (Marshall 1983). Jellinek addressed a similar issue in discussing the symbolism of drinking. He noted that in many non-literate societies 'the fear of the stranger is great; the stranger is dangerous and everyone is a stranger who is not of the same ancestry' (1977 : 859).

Consuming alcohol together functions as an act of identification ('we're drinkers'), social networks thus being constituted and reconstituted along traditional group and activity lines (drinkers versus non-drinkers). d'Abbs quoted an informant who had moved to town from a restricted area: 'He's living in Alice; he's drinking man now' (1990:50). Indeed, the drinking identity may become conflated with Aboriginality. As Gibson, writing of the internalisation of certain imposed 'myths' of Aboriginal society, commented: 'For black people, to drink alcohol is to be an aboriginal' (1987:2). Thus, under the confusion and uncertainties of dramatic social transformations lies another dimension of anxiety. Alcohol alleviates this, lubricating social interaction with a wider range of Aboriginal and non-Aboriginal contacts. However, in so doing it acts to further destabilise traditional structures, adding another layer of tension. While this is but a contributory factor to explain its appeal, alcohol again emerges as both cause and resultant in a potent self-reinforcing cycle.

QUANTITATIVE STUDIES

Tenacious pejorative stereotypes variously portray all Aborigines as drinkers, or all Aboriginal drinkers as drunks. These stereotypes have been abetted by the paucity of systematic research. In the absence of quantitative studies a variety of approaches were utilised to estimate alcohol consumption and resultant problems. For instance the House of Representatives Standing Committee on Aboriginal Affairs report on the Alcohol Problems of Aboriginals presented information on expenditure. In the rural Western Australian community of Wiluna it was noted 'that 80% of social security cheques are spent on alcohol and of the total income of the community, the expenditure on alcohol is 55%' (1977:13). Other indirect indicators have included the incidence of alcohol-related events, such as violence. Thus, in discussing violence on Palm Island, 86 per cent of which involved patterns of heavy drinking on the part of the assailants, Wilson stated that 'it is almost deviant not to drink' (1985:54). Similarly, normative domestic violence and widespread consequences for health, finances, incarceration and child-care were associated with drinking in Alice Springs (Lyon 1990). While the picture that emerges suggests widespread and problematic drinking, it is an imprecise image.

Attempts to quantify alcohol use among Aborigines encounter three major obstacles. First, generalisations from studies on particular groups often do not take into account inter-group cultural and social diversity, alcohol consumption varying in prevalence between communities. Furthermore, while the majority of Aborigines now live in urban or town settings, most reported studies are based on remote or rural populations.

A second problem relates to statements of the prevalence of drinking that do not account for intra-group differences. Both the proportion of drinkers and the consequences of drinking vary predictably (and significantly) with age and sex, being generally greatest among young males, as found in a number of other indigenous populations.[9] Consequently, analyses that only provide overall prevalence rates can be misleading.

The third problem arises from the use of aggregate data that do not take into account the diversity of drinking patterns. Episodic heavy drinking also appears to be more frequent among certain indigenous groups, including Aborigines.[10] However, only recently has the pattern of consumption been incorporated into quantitative studies. In the following section research providing estimates of the prevalence and pattern of Aboriginal alcohol use is reviewed.

ALCOHOL 'PROBLEMS' AND IMPRESSIONISTIC REPORTS

In an Adelaide study of Aboriginal 'heads of households' (80 per cent of whom were women), 18 per cent of 108 respondents reported having an 'alcohol problem'. Alcohol problems were also reported to affect 36 per cent of parents or care-givers, 51 per cent of siblings, and 47 per cent of current or former partners (Radford, Harris, Brice, Van der Byl, Monten, Matters, Neeson, Bryan & Hassan 1990). Larsen (1979) presented 'impressionistic results' based on observations by 16 urban community workers in Perth generating the following proportions: 'chronic' drinkers, 11 per cent; 'environmental' drinkers, 29 per cent; 'social' drinkers, 41 per cent; and 'abstainers', 18 per cent. In the same paper, four workers with experience within Perth fringe-camp settings provided figures for the above groups of 34 per cent, 51 per cent, 10 per cent and 5 per cent respectively. Such estimates are of limited use, but certainly convey the impression that non-drinkers are a minority.

CLINICAL STUDIES

The first research providing a quantitative analysis of a discrete region was Kamien's (1978) study of Bourke Shire in rural New South Wales, conducted during the early 1970s. Information was gained from key informants, a structured interview administered to nearly all adults, and his experience over three years as a general practitioner. Kamien attempted to estimate the quantity of alcohol consumed per day, and to identify problem-drinking, defined as alcohol use interfering with family, community or economic life. Of 124 males and 128 females over 20 years of age, 10 per cent of males and 71 per cent of females were recorded as non-drinkers. Heavy drinkers (more than 80 grams of alcohol per day[11]) constituted 53 per cent of males and only 3 per cent of females. An age breakdown showed that for males the proportion of drinkers decreased with age, from all aged 20–29 years, to three-quarters of those aged 50 years and over. Heavy consumption was also an early and sustained pattern for males, decreasing from 71 per cent of the total aged 20–29 years to 46 per cent of those over 50 years old. The proportion of non-drinkers among the women remained relatively stable from age 20 years at 61–81 per cent, with the proportion of heavy drinkers considerably smaller than among the men. Problem-drinkers constituted only 4 per cent of females, but 31 per cent of males (peaking in the fifth decade), including 61 per cent of those living on the Bourke reserve, versus 16 per cent of those living in town. Associated physical problems were discovered in 83 per cent of problem-drinkers, with alcohol-related problems implicated in 40 per cent of all hospital admissions.

In 1985 Harris, Sutherland, Cutter and Ballangarry (1987) reviewed Bourke hospitalisations, finding that one-quarter of Aboriginal admissions were related to alcohol (versus a rather surprisingly low 5 per cent of non-Aboriginal admissions). The sixth decade showed the highest rate of alcohol-related admissions. The authors recorded the results of a quantitative questionnaire of 287 adults. Non-drinkers accounted for 31 per cent of males (versus 10 per cent in Kamien's study) and 55 per cent of females (versus 71 per cent). The proportion of heavy-drinking males had also fallen according to this survey, from 55 per cent to 28 per cent, but there had been an increase in the proportion of teenagers drinking (none in Kamien's study, to 8 per cent of males and 2 per cent of females consuming more than 80 grams per day in 1985). Because there is no information that allows a comparison of the methods for assessing alcohol consumption between the two surveys, and as it is unclear how the 1985 sample was selected, the suggestion of a trend towards younger but less intense drinking must be interpreted cautiously.

Lake (1989) obtained information from 102 subjects over 16 years of age who attended an Aboriginal Medical Service in Adelaide in 1988. Of this clinical sample, 73 per cent of males and 41 per cent of females were drinkers. Of those who were identified as engaging in 'heavy drinking daily or most days' (exceeding an average of 60 grams per day for males and 40 grams per day for females), 37 per cent were males and 8 per cent were females; while 16 per cent of males and 9 per cent of females were classified as 'binge' drinkers (drinking at least 100 grams of alcohol for males and 60 grams for females on one or more occasions during the week).

POPULATION STUDIES

Children

There is limited information available on alcohol consumption by Aboriginal children. A survey of 272 Aboriginal school-children in years six through eleven was conducted in five of ten regions of the New South Wales Department of Education (Williams 1986). In order to minimise informant reticence regarding self-disclosure, the survey questions related to peers' drinking. Of the respondents, 56 per cent knew of large numbers of peers drinking at school; of these, 39 per cent indicated they knew of drinkers less than 12 years of age, with 13 per cent stating they knew of children less than nine years of age drinking. Two-thirds reported that it was easy or very easy to obtain alcohol. Peer-group acceptance was the most commonly identified reason given for drinking. The children surveyed appeared to have a reasonable knowledge of alcohol-related health problems. While the most that can be deduced from this study is that Aboriginal drinking in childhood and adolescence is not uncommon, there is support from the Northern Territory, where Watson, Fleming and Alexander (1988) found that 57 per cent of males and 12 per cent of females aged 15–20 years in the Territory's non-urban Aboriginal population consumed alcohol.[12]

Adults

South of the Kimberley, in the remote Pilbara region, Skowron and Smith (1986) interviewed 162 Aborigines in three locations around Port Hedland where homeless Aborigines gathered. Alcohol-consumption information was obtained for the day prior and a 'typical day'; however, the latter was used for subsequent groupings. Non-drinkers (those who 'usually consumed no alcohol') accounted for 28 per cent of males and 29 per cent of females, with 57 per cent of males and 51 per cent of females drinking in excess of 60 grams on an average day.

Further south, in the rural fringe town of Wiluna, a survey of nearly all Aborigines over 12 years of age was conducted in late 1986 (Smith, Singh & Singh 1987). The authors calculated the alcohol consumption for the day prior to interview for the 121 respondents. In addition, they obtained information on a 'usual day', and from these figures calculated 'average daily consumption'. Of 60 males, 52 (87 per cent) were drinkers, with 4 (7 per cent) ex-drinkers and a similar number (not stated) who presumably had never begun. Of 61 women, 41 (67 per cent) were drinkers, with 11 (18 per cent) ex-drinkers and 9 (15 per cent) who had not started. Very high consumption figures were generated with major differences between 'day prior' and 'usual' amounts (a mean daily intake of 120 versus 411 grams per day). On all measures, males consumed approximately twice the amount that women did, with the greatest proportion of heavy drinkers occurring in the fourth decade.

The largest study to date, in terms of both sample size and the area covered, was the 1986 survey conducted by the Northern Territory Department of Health and Community Services (Watson, Fleming & Alexander 1988), with 1764 individuals interviewed using a standard questionnaire. The sample excluded Aborigines residing in urban households and was based on an attempt to cover three putative demographic factors believed to influence alcohol consumption: community type, liquor status of the community, and geographical location. Individual and group interviews were undertaken in 55 communities, where a quota of individuals were selected by the interviewers walking through the community. Information on quantity was based on a 'usual week', diarising consumption of different alcohol types with the help of a variety of visual aids, the interviews also being used for collecting information on smoking and kava.

Non-drinkers constituted 80 per cent of the female and 35 per cent of male respondents. The proportion of female drinkers increased steadily from 12 per cent between 15 and 20 years of age, to 24 per cent in the fourth decade, remaining around 20 per cent thereafter. The proportion of male drinkers increased from 59 per cent of those aged 15–20 years, to 75 per cent of those in their third decade, decreasing slowly to 47 per cent of those over 60 years of age. Using the guidelines of the National Health and Medical Research Council, at least 68 per cent of female drinkers and 69 per cent of the male drinkers reported consuming at 'harmful' levels. As anticipated, community type was important, the proportion of drinkers decreasing from town camp, to cattle station, to major community, to outstation. Community type also predicted drinking patterns, town campers tending to be daily drinkers, whereas station Aborigines more frequently reported an episodic pattern. Seven designated usual drinking patterns were used, which appear to fall within three broader groups that may be used for comparison with other studies: constant (almost every day); intermittent (with a regular periodicity, usually on weekly or fortnightly cycles); and, episodic (with longer periods between drinking episodes). Using these categories — 40 per cent of those admitting to being drinkers appear to have been constant drinkers; 32 per cent, intermittent drinkers; and 26 per cent episodic drinkers.

Another large survey was performed in Queensland in 1987 and 1988. The researchers set out to enrol 10 per cent of the Aboriginal population above 15 years of age (or 100 individuals in communities with less than 1000 residents) from 17 communities which were chosen to provide a representative mix in terms of alcohol availability and income arrangements. An equal sex distribution was obtained, with recruitment tailored by selecting from individual households to conform with the age distribution derived from national census data. Aboriginal community residents were trained and utilised in conducting the interviews, which involved 1158 respondents (Merrilyn Gascoyne, personal communication, 1990). The proportion of drinkers in this study was larger than reported in the Northern Territory study: 77 per cent of males and 45 per cent of females (males and females overall, 60 per cent), with about half the abstainers indicating that they had previously been drinkers. Identified patterns of consumption conform to the groupings derived (by this writer) from the Northern

Territory study. Preliminary results reported by Harrold (1989) for the drinkers identified in this study suggested that approximately half of both sexes were intermittent drinkers. Of the remainder, females tended to drink episodically, whereas males tended to drink constantly. In this study 85 per cent of the male drinkers and 64 per cent of female drinkers were consuming at least seven alcoholic drinks per drinking day.

In the southern Western Australian town of Esperance, researchers in 1988 surveyed approximately one-third of the Aboriginal population (Sambo 1988). Of 44 males and 54 females interviewed — aged 15–68 years, 80 per cent of whom were 40 years of age or less — 67 per cent were current drinkers, 13 per cent were lifetime abstainers, and 18 per cent had given up alcohol. The only group with a minority of drinkers was the one comprising those over 50 years of age. In all other age-groups the proportion of drinkers varied between 83 per cent (aged 15–17 years) to 53 per cent (aged 31–40 years). The proportion of those who had given up alcohol increased unevenly with age. Having a partner or children did not influence the distribution of drinkers: 61 per cent started drinking between 14 and 18 years of age. Of the 23 drinkers who had imbibed on the day prior to interview, 31 per cent had more than six drinks (more than 60 grams), with average consumption being 61 grams (range 10–180 grams). Information gathered on a 'usual day' for 65 drinkers revealed that one-half reported having consumed over 60 grams of alcohol, the mean being 73 grams (range 5–185 grams). There was a trend (not statistically significant) for males to be over-represented in heavier drinking groups. No difference in quantity consumed was noted with age, 86 per cent indicating that they drank on one to three days per week. A summary of these quantitative reports is presented in table 5.

Thus, contrary to stereotypes suggesting universal drinking among Aborigines, the figures available from various populations indicate a high proportion of non-drinkers, indeed higher than the wider Australian population, among whom approximately 12 per cent of males, and 19–25 per cent of females do not drink (Alexander 1990). However, the research indicates that drinking begins early among Aborigines, with the consumption of alcohol common among young adults, and almost universal for young adult males. It is apparent that those Aborigines who are drinkers are usually consuming more than drinkers in the wider Australian population,

Table 5 *Proportions of current drinkers and of those consuming at 'harmful levels', by sex and identified by study and location*

Study/source			Drinkers				Harmful drinking levels[a]
			Current		At harmful levels[a]		
Author	Location of study	Sample size	M	F	M	F	
		(N)	(% of sample)		(% of sample)		
Kamien (1978)	Bourke: town & camp (New South Wales)	252	90	29	53	3	> 80 g
Watson et al (1988)	Northern Territory non-urban	1764	65	20	46		> 60 g
						14	> 40 g
Harrold (1989)	Queensland communities	1158	77	45	65	29	> 70 g
Skowron & Smith (1986)	Port Hedland: rural & homeless (Western Australia)	162	72	71	57	51	> 60 g
Smith et al (1987)	Wiluna: rural town (Western Australia)	121	87	67	32	18	> 60 g
Sambo (1988)	Esperance: rural town (Western Australia)	105	67[b]		30–49[b]		> 60 g

Note: [a] The definition of what constitutes 'harmful levels' varies; percentages thus depend on the method of calculation adopted by each study.
  [b] Not reported separately by gender.
  M = males; F = females

at levels considered hazardous to health. The emerging picture is similar to that of other indigenous populations in areas of European cultural domination.[13]

ABORIGINAL ALCOHOL CONSUMPTION IN THE KIMBERLEY

An outline of the development of the QARK random sample study has already been presented. A full description of the methodology is available in the technical monograph of the research (Hunter, Hall

& Spargo 1991). Here, the sample will be described, and then the alcohol distribution results will be summarised.

THE SAMPLE

The sample for this survey was generated by the CSIRO Division of Human Nutrition in Adelaide from information furnished by the Health Department of Western Australia. It was based on the Kimberley Region Community Health Register, which provided the best available enumeration of the Kimberley Aboriginal population. From the register, a computer generated random sample was produced stratified by age, sex and location. A total of 638 names resulted, of whom 532 were found to be current residents of the region (all others were accounted for). By the end of the survey 516 (97 per cent) had been located and had consented to the interview and examination, 13 (2.4 per cent) had not been found, and 3 (0.6 per cent) refused to participate. The distribution of the resulting study sample was found to be similar in terms of sex, age and location to the original computer sample.

ASSESSMENTS

Three patterns of consumption were identified during the development of the QARK, informed largely by location and the periodicity of resources (welfare, or the seasonal cycles of the cattle industry). 'Constant drinkers' were identified as individuals who were consuming alcohol almost every day of the week if funds were available. 'Intermittent drinkers' were characterised by a cyclical pattern with drinking occurring for a few days each week or (more usually) fortnight, following pay-day. 'Episodic drinkers' regularly went for prolonged periods (greater than three weeks) without alcohol. Sequential probes providing dichotomous choices were used to identify the subjects' consumption pattern early in the interview.

Each of the three drinking patterns were evaluated differently to generate a quantitative estimate of alcohol consumed. However, all three estimates were based on the mean alcohol consumption of two identified 48-hour periods.[14] In each case the subject was taken systematically through the two days, identifying time, place and company in which drinking occurred. Consumption was recorded in units of beverage type, which were then translated into grams of alcohol and summed.[15] The instrument thus provided two 48-hour records of most recent consumption, which were then converted into an average quantity for 24 hours measured as grams-per-drinking-day (by pattern).

In addition to descriptions of the usual circumstances and company in which alcohol was consumed, information was sought regarding demographics, income, descent[16], language use[17], up-bringing and caretakers during childhood, employment, education, religious affiliation, and family history. For drinkers and ex-drinkers, information was sought on symptoms and experiences consistent with alcohol dependence (histories of amnesic episodes, symptoms of delirium tremens [DTs], an alcohol-related disease or injury, seizures, having been knocked out, admitting that he or she had a 'problem' with drinking, having had specialist treatment for such a problem, and the CAGE screen[18]). For all subjects, lifetime histories were obtained of severe psychological symptoms (severe panic, hallucinations and disorders of ideation), self-harmful impulses and acts, and incarceration. Current anxiety and depression was assessed with the Hopkins Symptom Checklist-25 (HSCL-25).[19] Finally, blood samples were obtained from those consenting. The tests of relevance to this discussion were the mean cell volume (MCV) and gamma-glutamyl transpeptidase (GGT), which have been shown to correlate with self-reported frequency of alcohol consumption[20], and were thus used as one means of validating the alcohol consumption reports.

QUESTIONS

The statistical analysis of the resulting data-base sought to address five related questions:

1 Are social and demographic characteristics related to drinking patterns?

2 Are social and demographic characteristics related to the rate of occurrence of personal and social problems?

3 Are the frequency of drinking and the quantity consumed related to the symptoms of alcohol dependence and biochemical indicators of excessive alcohol consumption?

4 Are the frequency of drinking and the quantity consumed related to the rate of occurrence of personal and social problems?

5 Are social and demographic characteristics and frequency and quantity of alcohol jointly related to the rate of occurrence of personal and social problems. (Hunter, Hall & Spargo 1991)

For a full explanation of the data analytic strategies adopted by Wayne Hall in addressing these questions, the interested reader is again directed to the primary research monograph.[21]

RESULTS

Employment and economic circumstances

This survey demonstrates that the Aboriginal population of the Kimberley is socially and economically disadvantaged. Only 14 per cent of the sample were in paid employment, with the highest proportion being for males between 20 and 50 years old — still less than one-third (27–29 per cent). Among those over 50 years old, at most only 5 per cent were receiving money from paid work.

The median monthly income (cash in hand) was larger for women than for men ($522 and $462 respectively), and for those of mixed-descent compared to full-descent ($543 and $469). The difference by descent reflected not only higher rates of employment (28 per cent versus 6 per cent), but also higher incomes for those working ($1130 for mixed-descent and $520 for full-descent Aborigines). However, a discrepancy still existed by descent among those not employed ($480 for mixed-descent and $460 for full-descent Aborigines). While the difference by descent reflects opportunity (mixed-descent Aborigines being more likely to live in towns where employment is possible, to have been educated and to have had more opportunities for developing skills useful in dealing with bureaucracies), the differences by sex result from the way that the structuring of the welfare system privileges women with children. Indeed, this accounts for the only situation in which full-descent Aborigines receive a greater median monthly income: women 20 years of age or less. This group is more likely to have children (60 per cent for women of full descent versus 40 per cent for those of mixed-descent).

The employment profile for Aborigines is, thus, of late entry into paid employment, of high unemployment rates — unemployment that is often chronic and interspersed by menial work — and of early permanent exit from the workforce. Although our sample did pick a number of quite wealthy individuals, Aborigines of the Kimberley, by and large, are poor.

Social and demographic factors

Age was a predictor of demographic and social characteristics that reflected social changes over time; this was understandable, given a knowledge of Kimberley history. Thus, while 65 per cent of the sample were full-descent Aborigines, the proportion who were mixed-descent increased from 23 per cent of those over 70 years of age, to 56 per cent of those 16–20 years of age. Similarly, while 66 per cent of the sample reported being able to communicate to some degree in a traditional language, the proportion primarily using a traditional language fell with age from 75 per cent of women and 58 per cent of men over 70 years old to 8 per cent of those 20 years of age or less. Among males, the proportion who had undergone traditional initiation also fell with decreasing age, from 91 per cent of those over 70 years old, to 47 per cent of those 20 years of age or less. Clearly, these factors demonstrate the impact of an increasingly urban lifestyle, with the proportion raised in a town increasing from none over 70 years old, to 44 per cent of those 16–20 years of age. Not surprisingly, this was paralleled by an increasing proportion who had had some secondary education — from none of those past their seventh decade, to reach 92 per cent of those aged up to 20 years.

Decreasing formal institutional intrusion into Aboriginal lives since the 1970s is demonstrated in the proportion of Aborigines in the sample who had been brought up by non-Aborigines (generally in missions separated from their parents, differentiated from those who had lived on missions without being separated), which fell from 25 per cent of those over 60 years old, to 2 per cent of the subjects 20 years of age or less. However, there was no accompanying increase in the proportion of the sample who reported having been raised by a biological parent; this proportion remained, for all ages, at around 70 per cent. What did increase was the proportion of the sample raised primarily by a non-parent Aborigine, from 3 per cent of those past their seventieth year, to 27 per cent of Aborigines 16–20 years of age. While this may in part reflect patterns of shared parenting, it paralleled a rising proportion of the sample who indicated that one or both parents had been a heavy drinker; this

 Aboriginal health and history

Figure 5.1 *Current drinking status, for males and females*

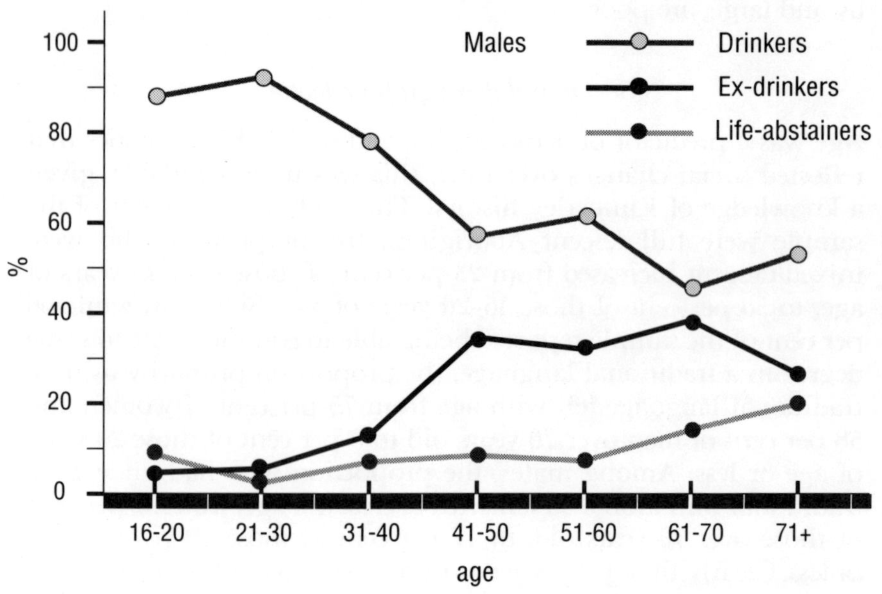

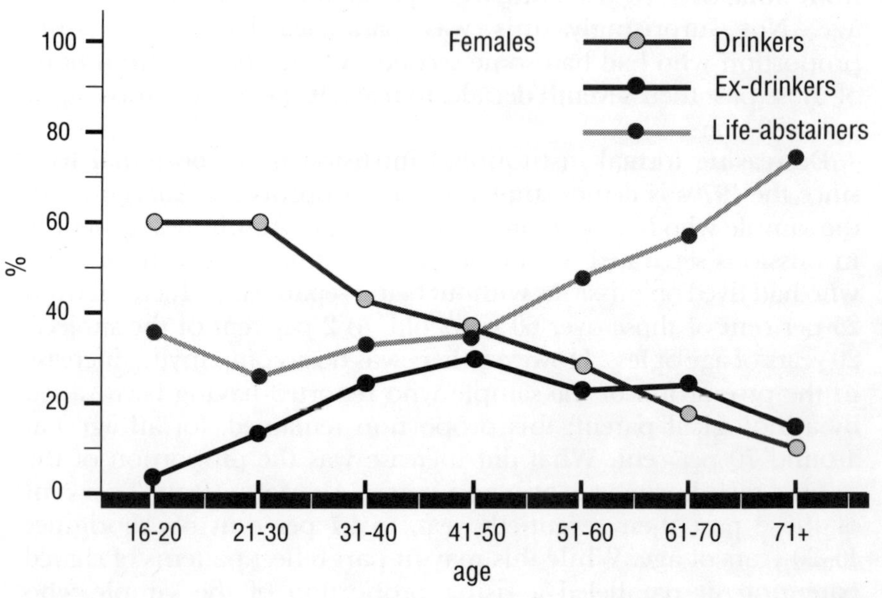

proportion increased steadily from 2 per cent of those over 60 years of age (reflecting prohibition), to reach 60 per cent for the 16–20 age-group.

Alcohol use

Current drinking status was also powerfully related to age and sex (figure 5.1). Clearly, a substantial segment of the Kimberley Aboriginal population does not drink. For women, the older a woman was at the time of interview, the less likely she was ever to have been a drinker; this was not the case, however, for men. Indeed, three-quarters of women over 70 years old had never been drinkers. It is also clear that those who had given up alcohol represented a significant proportion of the sample; for men, this constituted over a third of those aged 41–70 years. Of the ex-drinkers, nearly three-quarters (64 per cent of males and 85 per cent of females) had stopped for more than two years. The major reasons identified for ceasing were personal and family relationships (45 per cent), and health (31 per cent).

From the results of the sample and from knowledge of the Aboriginal population-structure of the region, it was possible to make estimates of the prevalence of drinking and patterns of consumption for the Kimberley Aboriginal population as a whole. This procedure predicted that 76 per cent of adult Aboriginal males are current drinkers, equally divided between constant, intermittent and episodic drinkers. Only 46 per cent of Kimberley Aboriginal women are drinkers, and they are twice as likely to be episodic drinkers as constant drinkers, with intermittent drinkers intermediate. Thus, Kimberley Aboriginal women are both less likely to drink, and less likely to drink frequently, than Aboriginal men.

Age and sex differences persist in the examination of quantity consumed (figure 5.2). Median 24-hour consumption falls progressively with age, being higher for males than females at all ages. The amounts consumed are substantial, the median consumption per-drinking-day for young males being 169 grams, approximately 11 cans of full-strength beer (for young women median consumption was 88 grams). No differences in quantity consumed per-drinking-day were evident on the basis of pattern. However, using the NH & MRC guidelines (see note 11), 74 per cent of episodic drinkers in the sample, 84 per cent of intermittent drinkers, and 94 per cent of constant

Figure 5.2 *Alcohol consumption, by age and sex*

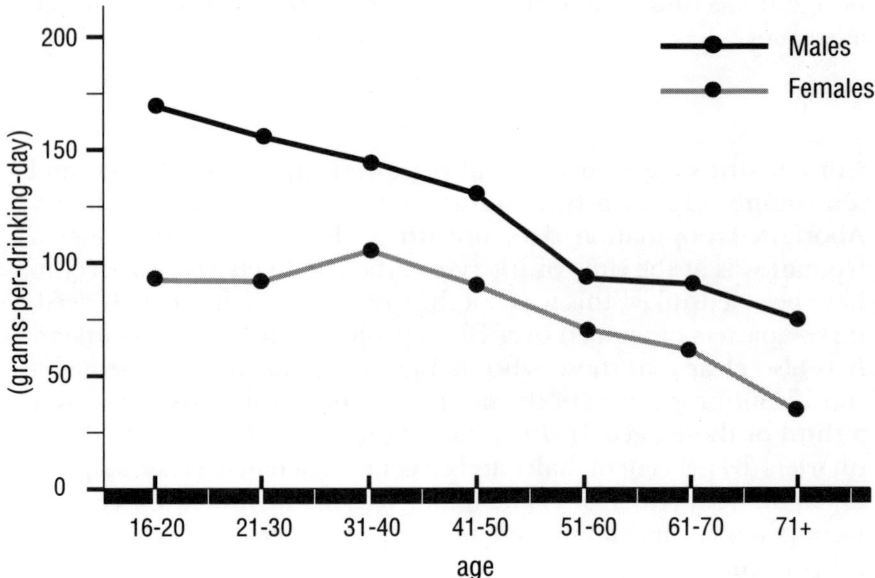

drinkers were shown to be consuming alcohol at 'harmful' levels. These findings are consistent with the earlier summarised material from other studies, which similarly found lower overall prevalences of drinking than in the wider society, but with a higher proportion of drinkers consuming at harmful levels, particularly younger males.

While ease of access did not influence the proportion of Aborigines who were drinkers, it did influence the frequency of consumption, with constant drinkers predictably living within 'easy' access of an alcohol outlet. By contrast, those Aborigines living in very remote settings where access was 'very hard' were invariably episodic drinkers. In table 6 the median alcohol consumption of drinkers is presented by pattern of consumption and ease of access to alcohol. While the median amounts consumed are generally large, there are clearly Aborigines who consume at moderate levels. This is a small group living within easy access to alcohol, but who consume alcohol episodically. The infrequency of consumption and the quantity consumed by these drinkers, thus, appears to be primarily a matter of choice, rather than reflecting the exigencies of access dictated by distance.

Table 6 *Median alcohol consumption by ease of access to alcohol*

Accessibility of alcohol[b]	Drinking Pattern[a]					
	Constant		Intermittent		Episodic	
	g	N	g	N	g	N
Easy	120	75	83	58	29	23
Hard	73	1	143	34	117	23
Very hard	—	0	118	6	132	47

Notes: [a] Alcohol consumption is measured in grams (g) per drinking day (as defined in note 11).

[b] Ease of access was defined by the examiner on the basis of the usual residence of the subject being interviewed: 'easy' — within an hour's journey by road to an alcohol outlet; 'hard' — required a drive of 1–3 hours; 'very hard' — required a drive of more than 3 hours or a plane trip, to obtain alcohol.

Thus, constant drinkers were usually town residents (86 per cent), and drinkers generally were found to be more likely to have been raised in towns; to have had a parent who was a heavy drinker; and if in a relationship, to have as a partner another drinker. The proportion of drinkers in a steady relationship fell with frequency of consumption, from two-thirds of the episodic drinkers, to half of those drinking on an intermittent basis, to just over a third of constant drinkers. Intermittent and constant drinkers were also less likely to identify as Christian.

While there was not a significant difference in median monthly income between drinkers and non-drinkers, there was a difference in the length of time money lasted after pay-day. Among those Aborigines dependent on fortnightly income, the median number of days money was reported to last for non-drinkers was 13.6 days, whereas for drinkers the median was only 7 days. Furthermore, for drinkers, this period was inversely proportional to the frequency of drinking. Thus, for drinkers receiving money fortnightly, the median number of days money lasted reported by those with an episodic pattern of consumption was 13.6 days (most fortnights usually not impacted by alcohol). By contrast, the median number of days with money for intermittent drinkers was 7 days, while for constant drinkers this fell to only 5.1 days. The economic burden of constant drinkers falls on others who are not, themselves, constant drinkers.

In summary, examination to identify social and demographic indicators of alcohol-use revealed that:

- age and sex both predicted drinking, being more common among males and at younger ages.
- sex and ease of access predicted frequency of consumption, being less frequent among women and for those living in areas of 'very hard' access.
- age, sex, and descent predicted quantity consumed per-drinking-day, which was highest among males, younger Aborigines, and those of mixed-descent (who are more likely to be living in towns with easy access to alcohol and, thus, to be constant drinkers).

Consequences of alcohol use

Symptoms of alcohol-dependence

Symptoms of alcohol-dependence were common among drinkers — for instance, two-thirds admitted to more than two CAGE items, and a similar proportion gave a history of blackouts. Using a principal components analysis, a dependence score was generated from nine dependence items (the four CAGE items, and histories of black-outs, fights while intoxicated, alcohol-related illness, DTs, and acknowledging a problem with alcohol). Linear multiple regression was then performed, demonstrating a statistically significant relationship to both quantity and frequency of alcohol consumption. Thus, the more that was consumed and the more frequently an individual was drinking, the higher their dependence score. A similar analysis demonstrated a significant relationship between, on the one hand, GGT and quantity and frequency, and, on the other hand, MCV and frequency of consumption, adding support to the validity of the alcohol measure.

Perceptions of problems

Regardless of the high levels of consumption, and the frequency of symptoms of dependence, a minority of drinkers considered they had an 'alcohol problem' (17 per cent of episodic drinkers, 28 per cent of intermittent drinkers, and 33 per cent of constant drinkers). An even smaller proportion (7 per cent of ex-drinkers and 4 per cent of current drinkers) reported ever having received treatment for an alcohol problem. The small proportion of drinkers acknowledging a personal problem was in contrast to the majority who considered alcohol a community problem (three-quarters of all participants; there were no significant differences by age or drinking status).

The only characteristic predicting a higher proportion perceiving a community problem from alcohol was descent: mixed-descent Aborigines were more likely than full-descent Aborigines to acknowledge alcohol's role. This probably reflects location, as mixed-descent Aborigines, being more likely to live in towns where alcohol is freely available, have greater direct exposure to the immediate social consequences of drinking.

Psychological correlates

Current anxiety and depression scores, as defined by the HSCL-25 were highest among young adults aged 31–40 years, declining with age, and being higher for women than for men throughout. After controlling for age, current depression and anxiety scores were found to increase regularly (and significantly) with increasing frequency of alcohol consumption. A multiple regression analysis confirmed the relationship of these symptoms to frequency of consumption without demonstrating a significant relationship to quantity consumed.

Severe psychological reactions were not uncommon, and were related to both age and gender. For males, histories of all four symptoms (severe panic, auditory hallucinations, visual hallucinations and paranoid ideation) were obtained most frequently from males aged 31–40, falling thereafter with age (figure 5.3). Among all subjects the four severe psychological reactions were found to increase with increasing frequency of alcohol consumption. However, the logistic regression analysis demonstrated that among the drinking subjects, controlling for sex, age and frequency of consumption, the presence of the severe psychological reactions was related to the quantity of alcohol consumed per-drinking-day. Although suggestive, frequency did not make a statistically significant contribution to the prediction of these experiences.

The relationship to alcohol may be explored from a different perspective. Information was also collected on what, for the purposes of the study, were called 'culturally informed paranormal experiences'. These included: having 'seen' a deceased relative in clear consciousness; having extra-corporeal experiences in the course of performing healing activities; and similar experiences or visions in the context of religious ceremonies. The proportion of the sample by age acknowledging such experiences is demonstrated in figure 5.4, along with the proportion who reported having had one or more of the severe psychological reactions.

     Aboriginal health and history

Figure 5.3 *Severe psychological reactions, for males and females*

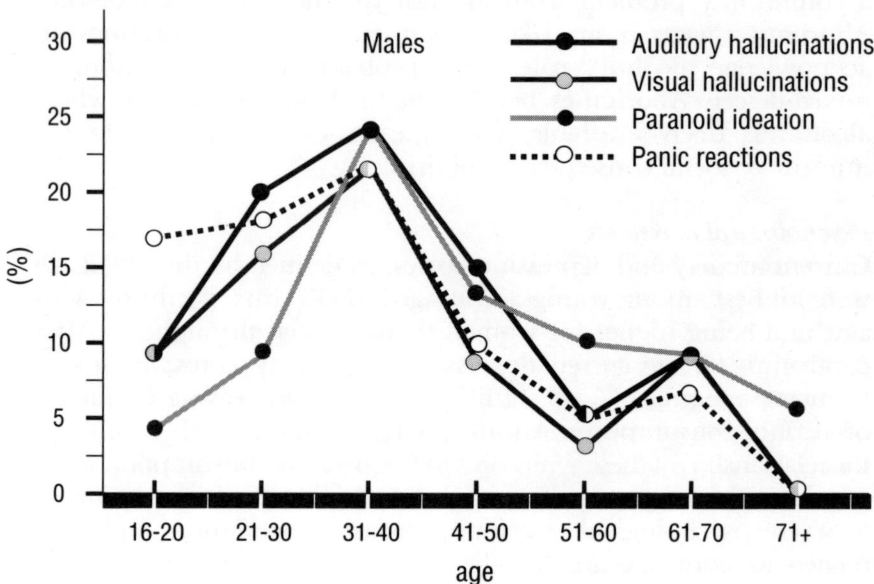

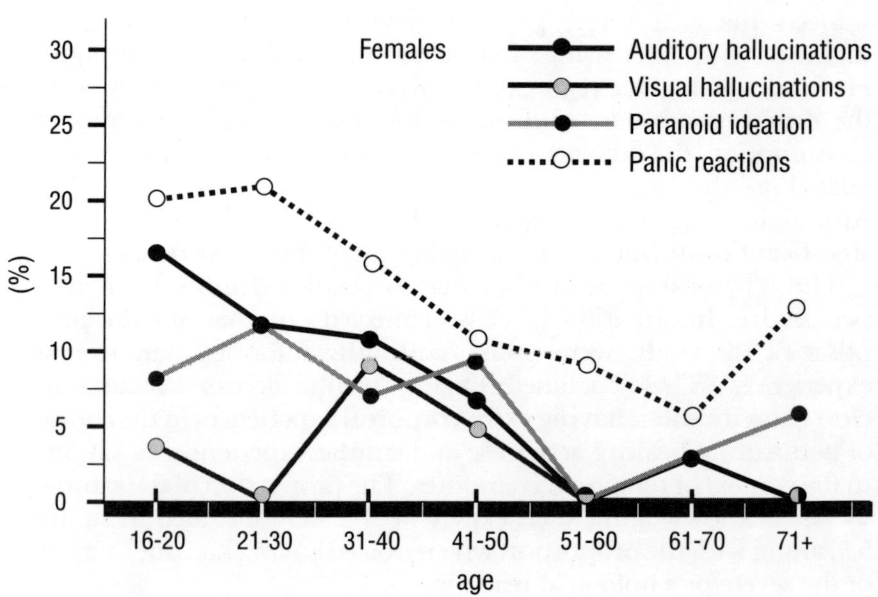

A hypothetical interpretation of the apparent inverse relationship recalls Julian Jaynes's speculations on *The origin of consciousness in the breakdown of the bicameral mind* (1982). According to his theory, consciousness emerged 'historically' as a consequence of the social forces of 'civilization' that resulted in the suppression of an earlier 'bicameral' state in which the individual's subjectivity was embedded in a culturally informed hallucinatory state, interpreted as the mediation of the supernatural — the gods. While this is highly speculative, many older Aborigines had clearly experienced such culturally meaningful phenomena, which were socially integrated in the context of their tradition. These are less common among younger Aborigines, for whom there is an increase in culturally meaningless and frightening ego-alien experiences. Their inability to integrate these experiences may reflect the effect social pressures, compounded by alcohol, have had in undermining traditional practices and explanations. Rather than an increase in 'psychotic' experiences per se among youth, there may instead be a diminution of their capacity to integrate experiences that were previously meaningful, and which, as a consequence, are projected and experienced as threatening and ego-alien.

Figure 5.4 *Severe psychological reactions and culturally informed paranormal experiences*

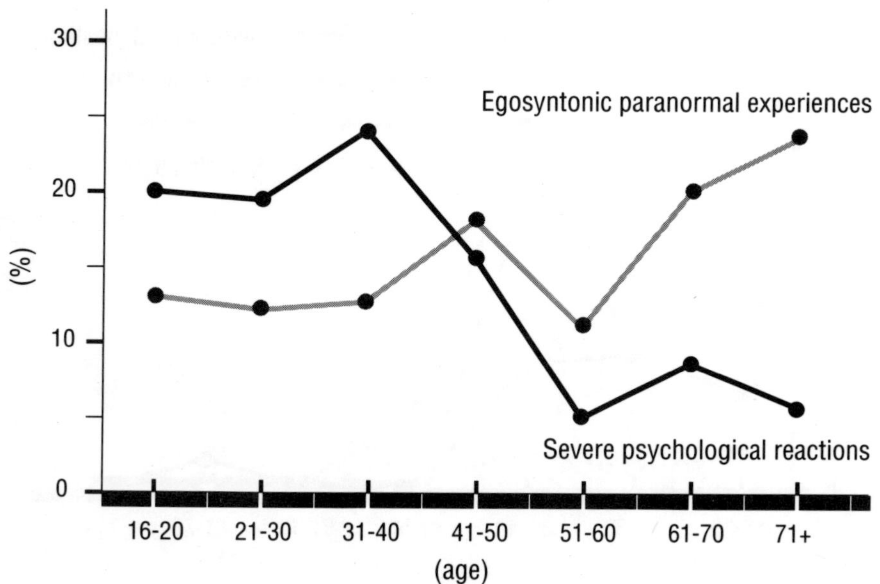

 Aboriginal health and history

Figure 5.5 *Self-harmful ideation, self-mutilation, suicidal ideation and attempts, for males and females*

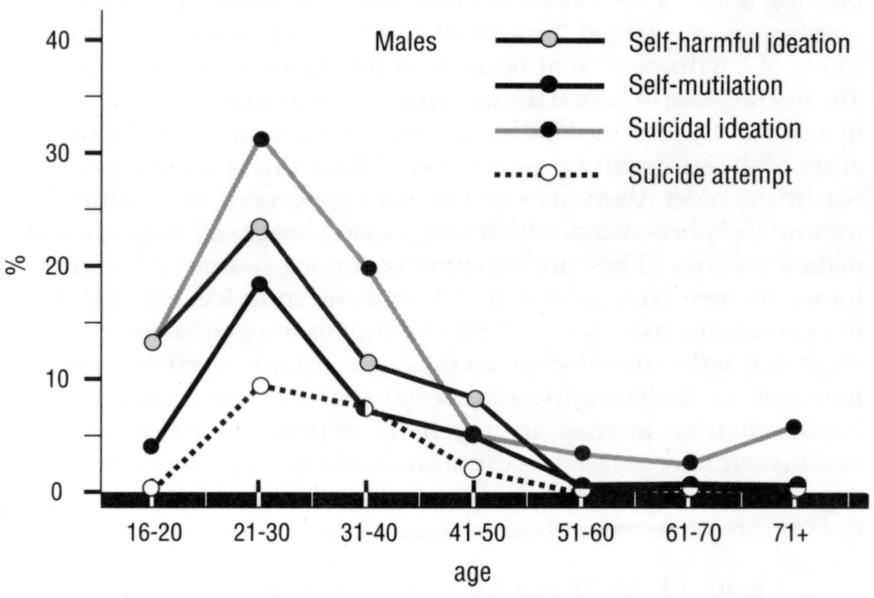

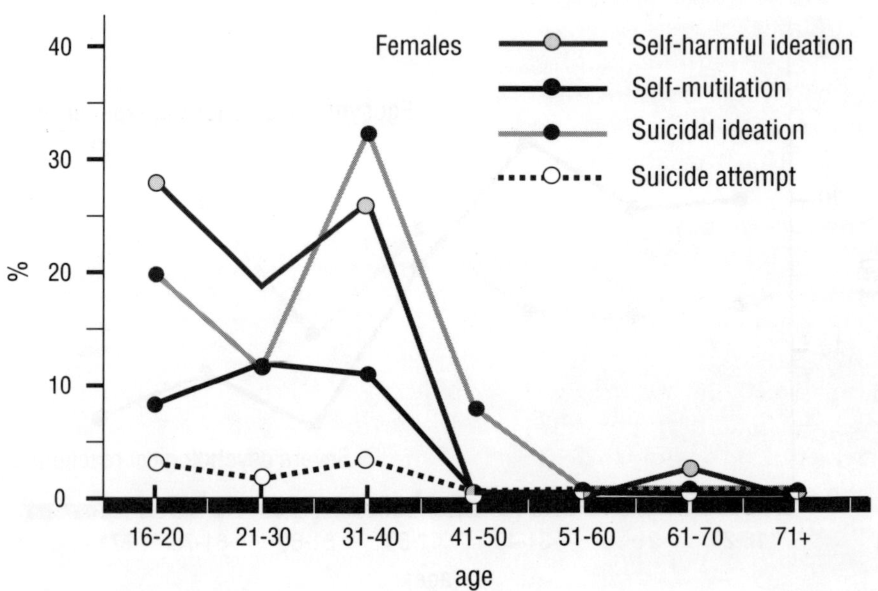

Self-harmful impulses and acts were likewise not uncommon, being strongly related to age, with no significant difference between males and females (figure 5.5).

While no significant relationship was evident between frequency of alcohol consumption and self-harmful (self-mutilatory) ideation, a relationship to a history of having acted on those impulses was found: constant drinkers were 13 times more likely to have self-mutilated than abstainers. The logistic regression analysis performed on the results of those subjects who were drinkers revealed that age was the only significant predictor of impulses to self-harmful and suicidal ideation. Although the number of subjects reporting suicide attempts was small (12), a significant relationship was discovered with frequency of drinking. In addition, a very suggestive relationship emerged (which failed to reach significance because of the small numbers involved) to quantity consumed.

Incarceration

The most impressive relationships were those between the consumption of alcohol and incarceration. Reports of incarceration in a police lock-up, regional or State prison, by age and sex, are demonstrated in figure 5.6.

The message is immediate and alarming. For Aborigines of the Kimberley, especially males, incarceration is to be anticipated at some point in life. Approximately half of the males under 50 years of age have been in prison. For those in the sample reporting incarceration, it was often a frequent event, with 92 per cent indicating that they had been in a police lock-up within the last year, and nearly 20 per cent within the last month. The risk of incarceration was found to increase steadily with frequency of drinking, with the odds ratio for being incarcerated in a police lock-up being 183 times greater for a constant drinker than for a life-time abstainer. Constant drinkers were also found to be significantly more likely to have been imprisoned. The logistic regression performed on those subjects who were drinkers revealed that when entering gender, age, frequency and quantity into the analysis, all save age were found to be predictors of incarceration both in a police lock-up and a regional prison. Thus, for Kimberley Aborigines, being a male and (for both males and females) drinking, both more frequently and more per-drinking-day, were all factors that predicted a substantially higher risk of detention and imprisonment.

 Aboriginal health and history

Figure 5.6 *Lifetime incarceration history, for males and females*

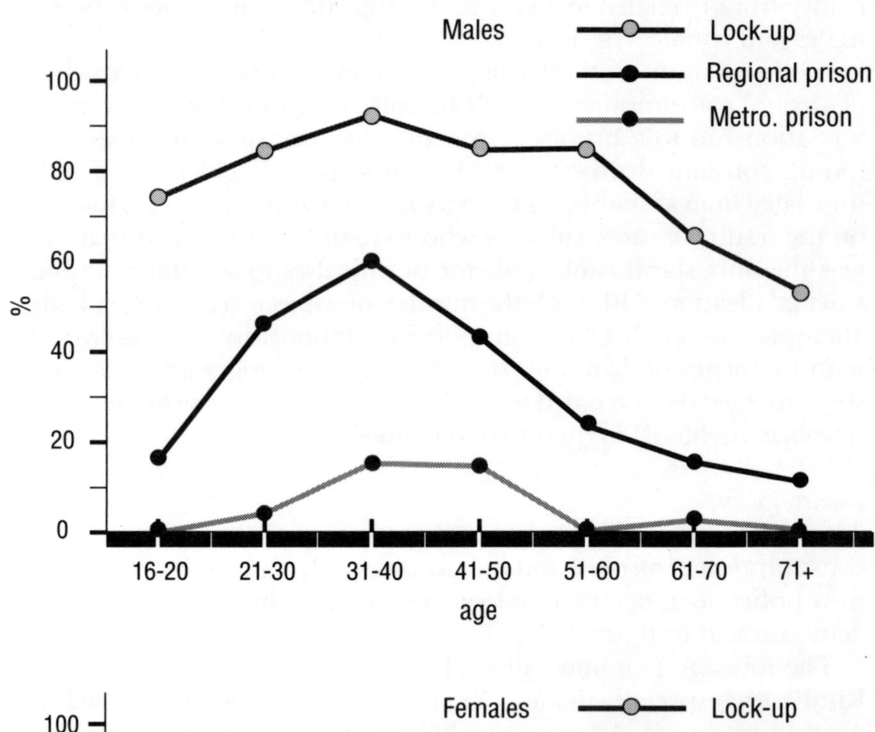

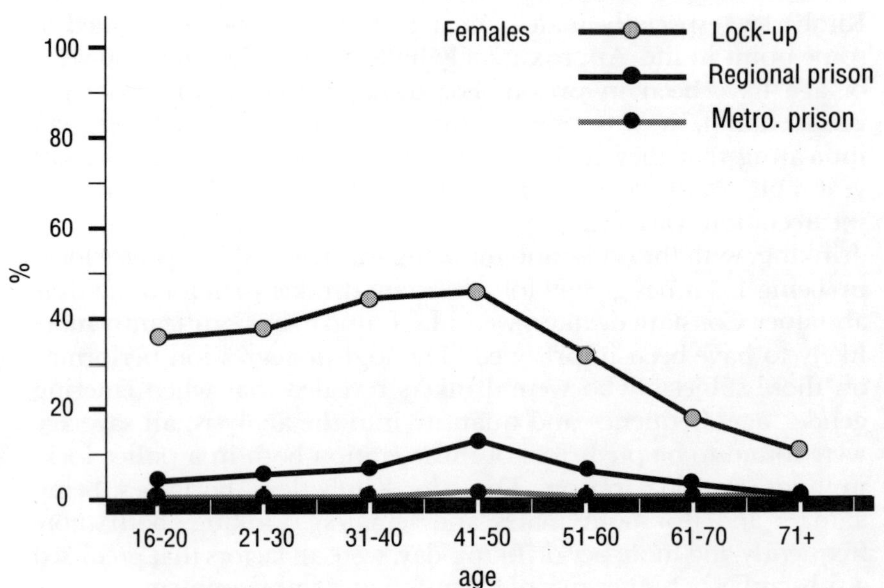

SUMMARY

The QARK survey provides a cross-section to complement the longitudinal picture from the mortality study. Together, they reflect certain aspects of Kimberley Aboriginal society in the last years of the 1980s. It has revealed a population that is, by and large, poor. The welfare system put in place to alleviate disadvantage has set up new asymmetries that are magnified in a setting of limited resources and urgent demands. Aborigines of the Kimberley are entrenched in that system, and appear not to have benefited in terms of employment from the recent economic development of the region.

In this economy of scarcity, alcohol is a substantial diversion of sustenance income, leaving many frequent drinkers without any money for predictable periods. Providing food and shelter for these individuals, supporting their continuing drinking, and often looking after their children, adds to the burden of the community as a whole, most of whose members are striving to cope with scarce resources. The economic impact of alcohol, thus, spills out far beyond the drinking circle.

However, a greater proportion of Kimberley Aborigines are non-drinkers than is found in the wider Australian population, with a substantial group of ex-drinkers among those over 40 years of age, most of whom have given up alcohol without formal assistance. On the other hand, while there is a small group of Aborigines in the region drinking at safe levels, the majority are consuming amounts of alcohol recognised to be harmful to health. This is particularly the case for younger Aborigines, with only a minority at any age admitting to having a personal problem relating to alcohol consumption.

Severe psychological symptoms are not uncommon, and were found to be more frequent among heavy drinkers. Self-harmful and suicidal ideation and behaviour was more common among younger Aborigines, with a weak statistical relationship to alcohol consumption. By contrast, a powerful relationship exists between both frequency of drinking and the amount consumed, and incarceration. The nexus of alcohol–money–arrest is even more blatantly demonstrated by examining the periodicity of detention. Figure 5.7 shows the combined census for the Kimberley's six lock-ups and two prisons for the month of May 1987. While the number in prison remains stable throughout the month, the totals for those in police lock-ups vary between 2 and 100, with an exact two-week periodicity. These peaks coincide with social security payments, which result in an infusion of alcohol into the community. The smaller peaks between represent money entering the community on alternate weeks through old-age and invalid pensions.

Figure 5.7 *Daily combined lock-up and prison censuses, May 1987*

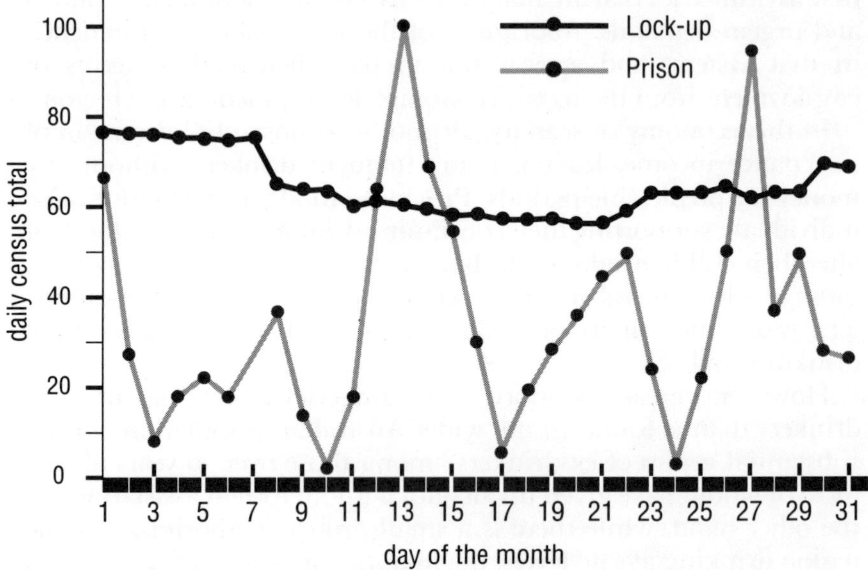

In addition to these predictable variations there are seasonal influences. Thus, in Fitzroy Crossing during the month of May 1987 the mean number incarcerated per day was 5.5. For November of the same year the mean number in the lock-up was 19.3, more than three times that six months earlier. This increase reflects the seasons of the pastoral industry, with those Aborigines employed on stations coming into town as the approaching 'wet' heralds the end of cattle work. Their wages added substantially to the amount of money circulating at that time and, thus, to the amount of alcohol consumed and to rates of incarceration.

Are these findings from the Kimberley representative of Aborigines elsewhere? While this is the only random sample study performed to date, comparison with the prevalence figures presented in table 5 demonstrates similarities with other population studies (all of which are from non-urban settings). Thus, the 76 per cent of males and 46 per cent of females in the Kimberley population who are current drinkers is very close to the 77 per cent and 45 per cent found in Queensland communities, and the combined male and female prevalence of 67 per cent from Esperance. However, while the sex differential persists, the findings from the Northern Territory of 65 per cent and 20 per cent indicate a substantially lower prevalence there of current drinking among women. This may be due to a number of factors, including: the structure of the sample, which excluded urban Aborigines; the consequence of selecting subjects by quota at the site of interview, which may thus have missed Aboriginal drinkers who were in town at the time of the survey; and the impact of the Dry Areas legislation in the Northern Territory, which, it has been suggested by d'Abbs (1990), may have caused demographic changes with drinkers moving from recently designated dry communities to town, at least in the Alice Springs region.

Regardless, all these studies demonstrate the implausibility of the stereotype presenting all Aborigines as drinkers. While also exposing another myth — that all drinkers are drunks — these studies clearly indicate that most Aboriginal drinkers in these regions, when drinking, are doing so in a dangerous fashion. At least within the Kimberley, the impact of such consumption spreads widely through the community, interacting with other consequences of social change. In the following chapters specific behavioural manifestations of these processes will be addressed.

NOTES

1. The essential elements of this syndrome include: 'a narrowing in the repertoire of drinking behaviour; salience of drink-seeking behaviour; increased tolerance to alcohol; repeated withdrawal symptoms; repeated relief or avoidance of withdrawal symptoms by further drinking; subjective awareness of a compulsion to drink; reinstatement of the syndrome after abstinence' (Edwards & Gross 1976 : 1058).
2. The annotated bibliography of Aboriginal health by Thomson and Merrifield (1988) contains 65 citations under the heading 'alcohol abuse' for the period 1970–1984. The increased attention to quantitative studies since the mid-1980s is partly a result of the Royal Commission into Aboriginal Deaths in Custody, under whose auspices two monographs were produced (Greeley & Gladstone 1989; Alexander 1990). There have been several other reviews (Harrold 1989; Kahn,

Hunter, Heather & Tebbutt 1990) and an evaluation by the National Institute of Health of the adequacy of current data sources (Thomson & English 1990).

3. For example, Holman et al (in Thomson & English 1990) have calculated age-specific aetiological fractions to provide a quantification of the effect of alcohol on population-level mortality through a meta-analysis of scientific publications. The aetiological fraction is an index representing the proportion of an outcome (be it disease or death) that can be attributed to the particular agent in question (in this case, alcohol). Thus, an aetiological fraction of 1.00 indicates that all deaths resulting from X (for instance, alcoholic liver cirrhosis) are due to alcohol, whereas a fraction of 0.22 suggests that only 22 per cent of deaths due to Y (males aged 15–34 years in which the cause of death was hypertension) can be attributable to alcohol. Given the earlier focus on deaths from external causes, the aetiological fractions for the contribution of alcohol for males aged 15–34 years are: road injuries, 0.34; fall injuries, 0.35; fire injuries, 0.40; drowning, 0.24; aspiration, 1.00; machine injuries, 0.13; suicide, 0.23; assault, 0.51.

4. Available material includes that of Hunt (1981), who cited published mortality data from country regions of New South Wales for 1978 and 1979 indicating that 53 per cent of male deaths and 21 per cent of female deaths were alcohol related. This appears to be considerably higher than other reports. Thomson and Smith (1985) examined 411 deaths in rural areas of New South Wales during 1980 and 1981, at which time the mortality rate for Aborigines was some four times that of the State as a whole. They found that alcohol was a significant medical problem in 27 per cent of all deaths (34 per cent of male and 15 per cent of female deaths) and 24 per cent of circulatory system deaths. The greatest impact of alcohol was on those aged 35–44 years. Of 323 Aboriginal deaths in Western Australia during 1983, 21 male and 5 female deaths had alcohol mentioned on the death certificates (Hicks 1985). This involved 12 per cent of male deaths and 5 per cent of female deaths over 15 years of age, and 23 per cent of all male deaths in the age-group 20–49 years. For 11 alcohol-related diseases between 1979 and 1983, Northern Territory Aborigines had a higher than expected mortality from all save falls, and suicide and self-inflicted injury (Devanesen, Furber, Hampton, Honari, Kinmonth & Peach 1986).

5. This evidence, mainly from family linkage studies (including twin and adoption studies), suggests that the genetic contribution reflects the interaction of multiple genes (Cloninger, Reich, Sigvardsson, von Knorring & Bohman 1988; Cook & Gurling 1990).

6. An inherited deficiency of a hepatic aldehyde dehydrogenase isoenzyme is common among East-Asian populations, and has been suggested as an inhibitory factor for the development of alcoholism (Goedde & Agarwal 1987). Research regarding the metabolic elimination of

alcohol is complicated by the numerous confounding factors. However, in reviewing the subject, Saunders stated: 'despite the fact that there are racial variations in the composition of both alcohol dehydrogenase and aldehyde dehydrogenase, there are no significant racial differences in the rate of elimination of alcohol' (1989 : 10).

7. MacAndrew and Edgerton's work on this issue is seminal. They suggested that the behaviour associated with alcohol consumption is culturally based and transmitted: 'Over the course of socialization people learn about drunkenness what their society "knows" about drunkenness; and, accepting and acting on the understandings thus imparted to them, they become the living confirmation of their society's teachings' (1969 : 88). They concluded on a chilling note: 'The moral, then, is this. Since societies, like individuals, get the sort of drunken comportment that they allow, they deserve what they get' (1969 : 173).

8. While such wariness is still evident in remote Australia, there is increasingly a strong feeling of relatedness regardless of local group membership, a pan-Aboriginal experience described by Dudgeon and Oxenham (1988) as 'kindredness'.

9. For instance, among alcohol-inexperienced indigenous populations of the Pacific basin descriptions are available from North America (May 1982), Oceania (Marshall 1987), and New Zealand (Awatere, Casswell, Cullen, Gilmore & Kupenga 1984).

10. The above authors also describe patterns of episodic high consumption. Similar patterns have been reported for Aboriginal groups (Kamien 1978), with the association of drinking and its consequences to pension/pay cycles in remote settings commented on (Sackett 1977; Brady 1988; Lyon 1990).

11. Quantities of alcohol are presented as grams consumed. One standard drink (285 ml middy of beer, 120 ml glass of wine, 60 ml glass of fortified wine, or 30 ml nip of spirits) contains approximately 10 grams of alcohol. In remote Australia alcohol is usually consumed by container. The approximate alcohol content of a can of regular beer (375 ml, 5% alcohol by volume) is 15 grams; of a cask of wine (two litre, 11% alcohol by volume), 174 grams; and for a bottle of port (750 ml, 18% alcohol by volume), 107 grams. Unless otherwise stated, the National Health & Medical Research Council (1987) guidelines will be used. Using these criteria, daily consumption is considered 'responsible' if less than 40 grams for males and 20 grams for females; 'hazardous' between 41 and 60 grams for males, and 21 and 40 grams per day for females; and, 'harmful' at levels above that.

12. A similar picture is found among native Americans in the United States (Oetting, Beauvais & Edwards 1988) and Canada (Ministry of National Health and Welfare 1989).

13. Kahn comments on this similarity (1982; 1986). The pattern of low-prevalence figures for current drinking, but excessive rates of

alcohol-related problems due to the high prevalence of heavy drinking by young adults (particularly males), has been reported in surveys of North American Indians (May 1982; Shore & Manson 1983; Watts & Lewis 1988) and Maoris (Awatere, Casswell, Cullen, Gilmore & Kupenga 1984).

14. For constant drinkers this was the 48 hours preceding the interview, and that following the last pay-day. For intermittent drinkers, the estimate was based on the first two days of the last two bouts (generally, after pay-day). For episodic drinkers the estimate was based on the first two days of the last two drinking episodes.

15. Retail alcohol outlets in each centre were visited before the survey to gain familiarity with available beverages. To facilitate accuracy of recall, a number of visual aids were used, including the diagrams from the Northern Territory study and a photo-album containing snapshots of all the various beverage types found in the Kimberley, in their various sizes.

16. Descent is a charged term, often confused with 'Aboriginality' and 'traditionality'. It was recognised that Aboriginality is a social and psychological construction which is independent of descent and tradition. However, it is clear that historical and social factors differentially affected full-descent and mixed-descent Aborigines in the Kimberley (for instance the removal of mixed-descent Aborigines from their parents). Furthermore, these factors are reflected in the differences in contemporary social and psychological issues. Descent is not being used in this work as a biological marker, but as an indicator of the social forces, such as urbanisation and acculturation, which have differentially affected Aborigines of mixed- and full-descent.

17. An index of the retention of traditional language was devised as another indirect measure of acculturation. Many Kimberley Aborigines speak a number of separate Aboriginal languages and dialects, and these were recorded. In addition to traditional languages and standard English, a variety of non-standard forms are encountered in the region. The Sandefurs pointed out that the use of standard English or pidgin frequently reflects social context rather than linguistic preference (Sandefur & Sandefur 1980).

    In the towns the pressure to speak English has been substantially greater than in remote areas. There appears to have been an evolution in the use of languages such that older Aborigines have a traditional language as their primary tongue, and pidgin as a secondary tongue. Younger adults in these settings have pidgin as the primary language. With the increasing availability of education (and the not inconsiderable impact of television), children who often have little or no knowledge of a traditional language use pidgin as a primary, and English as a secondary language. Eagleson (1982) suggested differentiating pidgin (in which the speaker retains a traditional language) from creole, its elaboration and second-generation use as a primary language.

In this study 'English' refers to standard English, non-standard English, pidgin and creole. Three possible experiences of language were tapped to generate a language-retention score. This was derived from the languages that were used most commonly for daily communication, for thinking, and while dreaming. The derived scores fell on a continuum of language experience from predominantly traditional, through functional bilinguality, to the predominant use of a form of English.

18. The CAGE is a simple alcohol screen, the name being a mnemonic derived from four questions. Subjects are asked if they had ever: experienced a need to Cut down; felt Angry or Annoyed at criticism about drinking; felt Guilty about drinking; and had to take an Eye-opener in the morning. Issues of validity are explored in the research monograph (Hunter, Hall & Spargo 1991). It has been administered to homeless Aboriginal men in the Port Hedland area, a score of two or more being used to identify an 'alcohol-related problem' (Skowron & Smith 1986). These authors found that those with high scores consumed significantly more alcohol on the day before the interview, and generally consumed alcohol in greater amounts and more frequently. They were also more likely to have experienced consequences of alcohol — having been hospitalised, incarcerated or staying in the homeless shelter within the last year. For the QARK, the questions were changed to reflect Kimberley Aboriginal idiom — for instance, instead of inquiry about an eye-opener, subjects were asked whether they 'took a reviver for headache'. In this study the CAGE was administered to all drinkers and ex-drinkers.

19. The reasons for choosing the HSCL-25 were described in chapter 1. Providing a measure of anxiety and depression symptoms, it was derived from a 58-item self-administered rating scale developed in the 1950s. The shortened version has been used in a variety of clinical settings and adapted for use with South-east Asian refugees in the United States (Mollica, Wyshak, de Marneffe, Khuon & Lavelle 1987).

20. Although these tests do not demonstrate high sensitivity or specificity when used as screening instruments, both have been shown to correlate with the self-reported frequency and quantity of consumption in clinical (Bernadt, Mumford, Taylor, Smith & Murray 1982), and community samples (Chick, Kreitman & Plant 1981).

21. The strategy involved simplification of the complex data sets on the basis of theoretical relevance, in the service of explanatory parsimony and to reduce the error burden of multiple comparisons. This was achieved through: recognition of a priori combinations predicted by theory; by combining variables on the basis of emerging patterns: and by performing a Principal Components Analysis to define linear

combinations of the variables. Multivariate analysis was then utilised to explore the relationships between two sets of simplified variables. Linear multiple regression was the method of choice when the dependent variable was continuous (for example, quantity of alcohol consumed per day), whereas logistic regression was employed when the dependent variable was categorical (for example, whether the individual had been incarcerated or not).

CHAPTER 6

Suicide

INTRODUCTION

It so happens that in every mental hospital the ingrafting of a neurosis on a psychosis is a daily occurrence. The individual desire for freedom which is accompanied with a dread lest the incarceration should be permanent, results often in a state of anxiety, familiarly termed 'the prison complex'. The medical officer is asked many times a day by patients to be set free. Others react more indirectly by querulousness, abuse or exaggerated emotional traits. An attempt has been made to contrast the number showing this behaviour, taking as control an equal consecutive series of whites.

Behaviour	*Aboriginals*	*Whites*
The prison complex	5%	17.5%
Suicidal trends	0	8%

It is fair to surmise that the aboriginals of the groups under review had practically all come under the influence of civilization. The authority of Totem and Tabu no longer held them bound in the same meshes of inflexible tradition. Thus they might have been expected to produce a few anxiety states, but, of the 5% enumerated, two-thirds were in half-castes and the other a case of senile dementia. . . .

The only feasible explanation to my mind of this immunity is that it depends on the primitive nature of the cerebrum rather than the mode of life. It is not the 'idea' itself, but the structure that matters. The wish to commit suicide is one of the hall marks of the neurotic mind. It is remarkable that the control series of cases show 8% in which this tendency is mentioned, whereas it is absent in the blacks. (Bostock 1924 : 464)

Whatever it was conferring that 'immunity', sixty years after Bostock's remarks, the situation is radically changed. Aboriginal suicide has become highly visible and politically charged, largely as a result of Aboriginal deaths in custody.[1]

133

DEFINITIONS

Camus suggested that 'there is but one truly serious philosophical question and that is suicide' (1975 [1942] : 11). For those remaining, suicide demands explanation or rationalisation. Whether as an act of rage and retribution, or the realisation of hopelessness, helplessness and despair, suicide is a denial of life and the living — the ultimate paradox:

> Suicide may also be regarded as an experiment — a question which man puts to Nature, trying to force her to an answer. The question is this: What change will death produce in a man's existence and in his insight into the nature of things? It is a clumsy experiment to make; for it involves the destruction of the very consciousness which puts the question and awaits the answer. (Schopenhauer 1962 [1851] : 101)

Many illustrious thinkers and theorists have pondered these issues, Emil Durkheim (1858–1917), following in the footsteps of the moral philosophers, worked during a period of interest in the statistical analysis of deviant social phenomena, including suicide, collectively referred to as 'moral statistics'. His seminal study, *Suicide*, was a vehicle for defining sociology as an independent scientific discipline (Douglas 1967).[2] The sociological theories developed by Durkheim and his followers focused on normative social values, underlying which was an assumption of cultural homogeneity that allowed suicide to 'be treated probabilistically and explained in terms of the whole society acting as a unit' (Douglas 1967 : 154). However, cultures are heterogeneous, in addition to which, such assumptions do not take account of suicidal behaviour as a subcultural idiom — as communication.

Grist for the mill of social analysis devolves from anomalous distributions, such as differences by region, age, sex, religion, psychiatric diagnosis, unemployment and access to means. As an intentional act of total self-annihilation, suicide would seem less prone to problems of analysis than the investigations of morbidity or mortality from natural causes. Unfortunately, this is not so. While self-harmful behaviour suggests a wish to die, a wide spectrum of intentions is covered. Indeed, within Western societies there are clear age and sex differences between suicide attempters (para-suicides), who tend to be young and female, and those who successfully kill themselves, who are more commonly older and male. However, over the last two decades there have been increases in suicide rates, especially for young males, reported from a number of industrialised countries including Great Britain, the United States, and Australia.[3] Consequently suicide must be seen in relation to suicidal ideation, para-suicide, ludic suicide equivalents, and deliberate self-harm. Even those who succeed in taking their lives represent more than one population. These complexities are reflected in problems such as how to deal with deaths listed as unknown, suggestive accidents, and the idiosyncrasies of coronial reporting.[4] These problems are magnified in the cross-cultural context.

Such confusion calls for a working definition. Schneidman, while explicitly addressing Euro-American culture, offers the following: 'suicide is the conscious act of self-induced annihilation, best understood as a multidimensional malaise in a needful individual who defines an issue for which the suicide is perceived as the best solution' (cited by Pfeffer 1986 : 342). This avoids the thorny question of whether suicide necessarily implies 'mental illness' or 'derangement' a question arising from altruistic or institutionalised suicides, such as *seppuku* among Japanese.

SUICIDE AND INDIGENOUS POPULATIONS

There is an extensive cross-cultural literature on suicide; the focus of this section, however, is the indigenous populations of the Pacific and Pacific rim. By far the largest and most intensively examined group are native Americans of the United States and Canada, with the annotated bibliography of Peters (1981) listing 65 citations between 1930 and 1980. While suicide appears to have been rare among pre-contact native Americans, it did occur, more frequently among women (Pine 1981). This is no longer the case, with increases particularly among young males between 15 and 25 years old, for whom rates tripled between 1958 and 1982 from 4.5 to 12.1 per 100 000 (May 1987). However, there are wide inter-group differences, with annual rates varying from 8 to 120 per 100 000 (Shore 1975; Shore & Manson 1983). Community concern regarding adolescent Indian suicide was such that suicide prevention centres were set up on various reservations from the early 1970s. Alcohol abuse, presented by Yates (1987) as a normative pattern among youth and young adults, was implicated in 80 per cent of suicides.

Present-day Indian suicides are commonly young males using violent and highly lethal means (May 1987). According to May, higher rates are found in areas with rapid social change, with a tendency to clustering of youth suicide: 'tribes with loose social integration which emphasises a high degree of individuality, generally have higher suicide rates than those with tight integration (which emphasises conformity)' (1987 : 56). In this regard Berlin (1985) proposed that intergenerational tensions resulting from the stress of acculturation and the breakdown of traditional structures may lead to family dysfunction. The resultant parental instability may predispose to suicidal behaviour.

The National Task Force on Suicide in Canada reported that in the early 1980s suicides accounted for 15–20 per cent of all violent deaths of native people, which in turn constituted over a third of all deaths: 'Approximately 60 per cent of the suicides occurred in the 15–24 year age group, with a male/female ratio of 3 to 1' (1987 : 33). Identified characteristics were: frequent use of firearms; soft drug and alcohol abuse; physical signs of depression; single marital status; financial problems; unstable home environment; family history of suicide; occurrence during winter months. Social factors considered contributory included: difficulties in integration; loss of control over individual and collective destiny; deterioration of traditional values and undermining of role models; inadequate education. These factors appear to be consistent with the experience in northern Canada, although there is variation from group to group. Among the Inuit there has been an increase in suicide over the last two decades, again mainly young men (Tsai 1989). Tsai suggested that the contemporary socio-economic realities of Inuit life undermine resiliency to the 'harshness' of life, rendering this group at greater risk through the pressures arising from acculturation and internal colonialism.[5]

In Micronesia, previously the United States Trust Territory of the Pacific, Rubinstein (1983; 1987) examined over 400 suicides, mainly by hanging, occurring over two decades. Annual rates increased from 0 to 4.5 per 100 000 for females, and from 6.4 to 49.5 per 100 000 for males between 1960–1963 and 1976–1979, with Truk (Federated States of Micronesia) and the Republic of the Marshall Islands bearing the brunt of this loss. At a time when the American suicide rates for males aged 15–19 and 20–24 years, were 12.8 and 27.4 per 100 000 respectively, the corresponding rates for the Marshall Islands were 158 and 174, and for Truk 243 and 255 per 100 000. Rubinstein described the emergence of a 'suicide subculture', described as: 'a set of coherent meanings which organise, provide significance for and contribute to the dynamics and frequency of adolescent suicide' (1983 : 658). To hang oneself, for a young male Micronesian, became an increasingly frequent response to personal problems that, on the surface, appeared trivial. On a deeper level this option reflected post-war social changes that disproportionately stressed young males. In particular there was a disruption of the traditional institutions and rituals (such as the lineage men's house), which were important in structuring a period of developmental tension, and which powerfully influenced adolescent socialisation and the culturally informed construction of identity. Furthermore, the economic and political dependence on the United States gave rise to increasing demands for modern consumer goods, profoundly disrupting traditional occupational and social roles. In addition to suicide, alcoholism and violence emerged as consequences of the ensuing role confusion (Marshall 1979).

Exploring the transgenerational impact of destabilising social change in this region, Rubinstein (1987) proposed a cohort effect, involving the generation born following the Second World War. The 1950s and 1960s were a period of tumult as Micronesians adjusted to an American administration following three decades of Japanese control. Neglect was followed by a massive infusion of money and personnel as the administration implemented the 'Solomon report' in the early 1960s, the aims of which were the political annexation of the region through a program calculated to engender dependence. This superficial munificence occurred against a backdrop of military activity, including atomic testing, the consequences of which continue to reverberate. Those most affected in developmental terms, were the children of young adults who began parenting in the post-war period and who continued to have children for the next twenty years (1950–1970). Their children constitute the suicide-vulnerable cohort. Given the age distributions of suicides (mostly between 15 and 24 years of age), this predicted an increase in suicides through the late 1960s and 1970s, peaking in the early 1980s and perhaps falling towards the mid-1990s. As far as the mid-1980s Rubinstein's predictions were holding.

Hezel (1984) investigated the 129 suicides that occurred on Truk between 1971 and 1983. Half of all the suicides had consumed alcohol prior to death. Both he and Rubinstein (1983; 1987) identified the peri-urban or rural fringe — areas of rapid social change — as having the highest suicide rates. Most were associated with a disruption of a significant relationship, usually with family members. In this regard Hezel enlisted a traditional concept, *amwunumwun*, in which self-abasement, withdrawal, or a self-injurious act is used to communicate a dysphoric emotion in the hope that the situation will be rectified. In this process the self is perceived as having been wronged, and *amwunumwun*, as a transformation of anger, communicates both protest and despair. Suicide, in this construction, represents a recourse to an extreme form of *amwunumwun*. A reverse of this process was also postulated, in which the self is experienced as the offender. These 'shame' suicides, or 'reverse *amwunumwun*', aim at the restoration of family homeostasis, status and esteem.

An investigation of 31 of 61 suicides occurring since the Second World War on the island of Palau in the south-west of Micronesia also focused on the breakdown of traditional bonds (Polloi 1985). All bar one were male, three-quarters were single, and most had grown up during the period of American administration. One-third of these suicides had been drinking prior to their suicide.

Contemporaneous with the dramatic Micronesian increases, a similar picture was developing in Western Samoa. In a population of around 160 000 there were 237 suicides from 1970 to 1981 (Oliver 1985), and 106 between 1981 and 1983 (Bowles 1985). These were largely young males who died as a result of paraquat ingestion. A 'blocked opportunity model' (MacPherson & MacPherson 1985) focused on youth who were alienated from the traditional values of the society and yet still constrained by the traditional power structure. Increased desires and expectations among young Samoans, during several decades of social change orchestrated by New Zealand and the United States, were not accompanied by opportunities for social mobility. Intergenerational conflict was also presented as an explanation in a model utilising the Samoan concept of *musu*, which like *amwunumwun*, 'represents a culturally defined way of feeling and acting in response to conflict with someone in authority, especially parents, towards whom one owes love and respect and should not express anger' (White 1985 : 6).

Melanesia's cultural diversity precludes generalisations. In some areas a traditional pattern of female suicide predominated (White 1985); in others, such as the Kandrian peoples of New Britain, males were most vulnerable, interpreted by Hoskin, Friedman and Cawte (1969) in terms of stress resulting from social fragmentation due to chronic tribal conflict, coupled with a paradoxical emphasis on close interpersonal ties. Among the Bimin-Kuskusmin of Papua New Guinea the traditional female preponderance has given way to increasing rates among socially isolated young males experiencing a sense of failure in a group context where male roles were previously clearly defined (Poole 1985). In a comment relevant to Aboriginal suicide, White stated that the increases among indigenous populations across the Pacific:

> are only one part of a broad change which is occurring in patterns of mortality and morbidity in the Pacific and developing world generally. . . . The specter of infectious diseases as the most serious threat to health is rapidly being replaced by lifestyle-related disorders such as diabetes, hypertension, malnutrition, alcoholism and death or injury resulting from violence. (1985 : 1)

SUICIDE AND ABORIGINES

Most information on Aboriginal suicide prior to the Royal Commission into Aboriginal Deaths in Custody is anecdotal, often informed, as in the quotation opening this chapter, by the prejudices of the time. Cleland (1962) recorded a possible suicide attempt in the Northern Territory in the 1940s and a suicide of an Aboriginal prisoner some 20 years earlier in South Australia. Cawte (1972) described one suicide, and a number of attempts, among the Kaiadilt people who had been transferred from Bentinck to Mornington Island in the Gulf of Carpentaria following a period of devastating environmental pressures.

Soon after the Referendum, surveys were conducted in the Kimberley among tradition-oriented populations (Jones 1972; Jones and Horne 1973). While no suicides were discovered, they commented on reports of three suicides and one attempted suicide during the previous 40 years among Aborigines who had given up tribal life. Their proposition that death from 'boning' may be a suicide equivalent was also suggested by Berndt and Berndt (1985) to explain the loss of will observed among Aborigines selected as victims of sorcery. The potent fatalism thus engendered by sorcery appears to involve both an acceptance of the inevitability of death by the victim, and the withdrawal of support by the social network (Eastwell 1982). Forty-five years earlier, in 1937, Warner had made a similar observation in Arnhem Land:

> The society itself creates a situation which, if unchanged, makes it impossible for the individual to adjust himself to it even though he tried; and in addition he usually not only makes no effort to live and to remain

> part of his group but actually, through the multiple suggestions from
> it, cooperates in his withdrawal therefrom. He becomes what his society's
> attitudes make him, committing a kind of suicide. (1969 [1937] : 230)

Reid (1983) listed several suicide attempts precipitated by loss among the Yolngu of Arnhem Land and suggested that risk taking behaviour may represent a ludic suicide equivalent. Eastwell (1988) reported two suicides over a 30-year period in the same region. Both were males: one occurred during recovery from delirium tremens and the other, while considering himself to have been the victim of sorcery, appeared to suffer from episodes of alcohol-induced jealousy. Eastwell speculated on the relationship of suicide to alcohol-related instances of males placing themselves in harm's way. Brady (1988) recorded one alcohol-associated Aboriginal suicide in Tennant Creek in the context of increasing rates of alcohol-related deaths from external causes.

The role of alcohol was also explored by Reser, who commented on the relationship of suicide to the disinhibition of 'socialised "drunken behaviour"' (1989a : 19). Elsewhere, Reser explored alcohol's particular impact in a changing cultural context:

> The at-risk character of many young Aboriginal men in contemporary
> Australia derives in part from a cultural context in which self-
> construction, and emotional experience and coping appear to result
> in a particularly vulnerable and at-risk emotional state, especially
> when intoxicated and experiencing conflict and/or social isolation.
> (1989b : 338)

A detailed case description of an Aboriginal suicide on Melville Island provided a vehicle for a psychoanalytic exploration of local myth and mourning ceremonies. Robinson (1990) interpreted a central myth of the Tiwi as suggesting that 'some form of suicide is, at least unconsciously, an element of traditional Tiwi psychology' (1990 : 164). He focused on the vulnerability of young males to intentional self-harm, pointing to social forces that had destabilised adolescent male development, and led to intergenerational conflict and problems of social differentiation. Responding to this paper, Reser (1990a) criticised both the failure to provide any alternative to the psychoanalytic orientation, and the suggestion that suicide may have been 'an element of traditional Tiwi psychology'. He also noted the remarkable similarity (uncommented on by Robinson) of the social explanation for adolescent male Aboriginal suicidal behaviour, to that provided for Micronesian suicides by Rubinstein.

Reports of Aboriginal para-suicide are also few in number. Burvill (1975) documented four males and fourteen females hospitalised in Perth in 1971–1972, three of the four males being less than 25 years of age. Kamien (1978) described four serious suicide attempts in Bourke in the early 1970s, all of which were associated with alcohol. A questionnaire study of 88 heads of households was carried out in Adelaide during 1988 and 1989; of the 72 women interviewed, one-third reported past suicidal thoughts, and one-fifth admitted to at least one attempt (Radford, Harris, Brice, Van der Byl, Monten, Matters, Neeson, Bryan & Hassan 1990). The following associations with suicidal behaviour emerged:

> employment instability of partner or care giver, lack of knowledge of at least 1 parent and foster home (but not institutional) experience by age 12, being in receipt of a pension or benefit, in receipt of past emergency aid, living in rented housing which was deemed unsatisfactory, personal mobility, lack of access to a private vehicle, frequent changes in employment, unemployment, a present major health problem in self or partner, drug abuse not including alcohol, number of police calls to the house, being bashed or sexually assaulted, a personal perception of non-acceptance by the rest of society, that 'minor violations of the law' bring major distress, frequent feelings of anger and that one did not have 'reasonable control' of one's life. (1990 : 2)

In a study from north Queensland, 44 male and 21 female Aborigines were identified as having attempted suicide in the 15 years up to 1988 (Reser 1991a); of these, 71 per cent were aged between 15 and 25 years. There was, also, a dramatic increase in attempts from 1986. Forty-five attempters were interviewed, with nearly all males and half of the females indicating that alcohol had been involved:

> It is clear that in the north Queensland data the pattern of alcohol use by a number of heavy regular and binge drinkers is placing them at a much higher risk of attempting suicide. Indeed this risk is over 18 times higher than that for those who drink only lightly, occasionally or not at all. (1991a : 272)

ABORIGINES: INCARCERATION AND SUICIDE

THE ROYAL COMMISSION

Concern regarding the treatment of Aborigines within the criminal justice system has had a long history[6], and in the late 1980s became the focus of national attention. Soon after the Human Rights

Commission was established in December 1986, an inquiry was initiated under Marcus Einfeld to examine the administration of the criminal justice system as it affected Aborigines. However, between December 1986 and June 1987, a series of six hangings of Aborigines in custody in Queensland occurred, leading to the announcement in early 1987 of an inquiry by the House of Representatives Standing Committee on Aboriginal Affairs (put on hold due to the dissolution of the federal parliament). As reports accumulated from across the nation of other Aboriginal deaths in custody, pressure for a Royal Commission mounted, which was subsequently announced in August 1987 under Commissioner James H Muirhead, a Federal Court judge and former justice of the Supreme Court of the Northern Territory. His letters patent and terms of reference instructed him to inquire into the deaths since 1 January 1980 of Aborigines and Torres Strait Islanders in custody or detention, and subsequent actions taken in respect of those deaths.

Through 1988, as the enormity of the task became evident, four other Commissioners were appointed, and an extension obtained. Under pressure and in anticipation of the Commission's scrutiny, the Western Australian government released the results of an interim State inquiry in January 1988, with 32 recommendations. Throughout 1988 the issue retained national prominence, with the first formal report from the Commission, containing 56 recommendations, released just after Christmas. Soon thereafter Commissioner Muirhead resigned, his position taken in April 1989 by Elliott Johnston. The interim report demonstrated that the excess of Aboriginal deaths in custody was accounted for by the massive over-representation of Aborigines in custody. Accordingly, the scope of the Commission was broadened to examine the legal, social and cultural factors predisposing to this asymmetry. To this end, the full complement of five Commissioners was restored with the appointment in June 1989 of the only Commissioner of Aboriginal descent, Patrick Dodson, who was based in the Kimberley to specifically examine the underlying issues. Ultimately, the Commission also resulted in the setting up of a research division in Canberra, and Aboriginal Issues Units in each State.

After several delays, the Commission delivered its mammoth 11-volume report in April 1991. The inquiries into the 99 deaths did not support accusations of foul play, but did point to failures in the duty of care of those responsible for Aborigines in custody.

However, the main thrust focused on the broader issues of social disadvantage, with history foregrounded: 'The view propounded by this report is that the most significant contributing factor is the disadvantaged and unequal position in which Aboriginal people find themselves in the society — socially, economically and culturally' (Royal Commission into Aboriginal Deaths in Custody 1991 : I : 15).

The 339 recommendations were consistent with this orientation: 'The principal thrust of the recommendations, as of the report, is directed towards the prime objectives — historically linked — of the elimination of disadvantage and the growth of empowerment and self-determination of Aboriginal society' (1991 : I : 27). Given the attention to the underlying social issues, health was foregrounded, with the implementation of the National Aboriginal Health Strategy recommended. As noted in the previous chapter, alcohol was given particular attention, which, 'is in the final analysis, in its general form, linked to the health of the society and can only be overcome as part of a policy of renewing and strengthening Aboriginal community and family life' (1991 : I : 27).

The investigated deaths in this enormous and detailed report were summarised as follows:

the 99 deceased Aboriginal people comprised 88 males and 11 females;
their mean age at the time of death was 32 years;
nearly twice as many deaths occurred in police custody (63) as in prisons (33);
Western Australia and Queensland had the highest numbers;
abnormally high numbers occurred in calendar year 1987;
more of the deaths resulted from natural causes (37) than from hanging (30), with much smaller numbers being associated with head injuries (12), gun shot (4), other external trauma (7), alcohol poisoning or withdrawal (5), and drug use (4); and
the average time in custody before death was much shorter in police custody (12 hours) than in prison custody (15 months). (1991 : I : 55)

Of the deaths due to hanging in police cells, four dominant characteristics emerged: the shortness of time since arrest, most being within two hours; the pervasive involvement of alcohol, the only one who had not been drinking was suffering severe withdrawal; youthfulness, only one being over 30 years old; and being confined alone. The possibility that publicity could have been a factor in the sudden increase in 1987 was suggested in the Commission's first research report, which stated that while the epidemiological analysis 'cannot prove that media coverage and public concern about

Aboriginal deaths caused an increase in those deaths, that hypothesis cannot be discounted' (Biles 1988 : 5).[7]

Substantial media interest was initially aroused by the suicides in custody of two Aborigines in Yarrabah (Queensland) in December 1986, with another six in Queensland during the following year constituting half of the Aboriginal hangings in custody nationwide for 1987. In 1988 Western Australia became a focus of media attention as it emerged as the State with the greatest number of deaths, and owing to the attempts by the Police Officers Union to halt the Commission. While between 1980 and November 1987 there were three Aboriginal hangings in custody, in the following year there were four further suicides in custody in Western Australia. Such evidence is at best only suggestive, and the question was left open in the final report. However, it was not reflected on by the media, whose language at times compounded the issue, with terms such as killings, deaths and suicides used without clarity, and often interchangeably.

That the issue should have become politicised is hardly surprising. Indeed, Beckett (1988), the editor of a volume on the construction of Aboriginality written during the early days of the Commission, stated therein that 'urban Aborigines have made police killings in custody their issue for 1988' (1988 : 211). At an extreme was the presentation of Aborigines dying in custody as 'heroes', such as in November 1987, when at the height of public attention (and suicides), the Aboriginal and Islander Dance Company staged *Survival* in Sydney. Brian Hood, reviewing this production, stated of the depicted hangings: 'The full company of dancers, holding candles, slowly gathers to mourn, yet also to celebrate their growing band of heroes, as well as their own survival' (*Bulletin* 24 November 1987, p. 125).

INTERNATIONAL EXPERIENCE

A review carried out for the Royal Commission of the international deaths in custody literature revealed that the Australian rates, while not the highest, were higher than in most of the countries examined (Biles 1990). Even a brief perusal reveals that concern extends beyond Australia. While comparisons are complicated by the differences in the systems involved, police custody consistently emerges as the location posing the greatest risk for completed suicide in custody. Factors associated with increased vulnerability include: being a young adult male; arrest for a relatively minor offence; confinement in a lock-up; being alone in the cell; with the suicidal behaviour occurring within hours of arrest. However, perhaps the most important feature, almost invariably mentioned, is alcohol, in particular being intoxicated at the time of arrest.[8]

KIMBERLEY SUICIDES IN CUSTODY

The Royal Commission investigated five Aboriginal deaths in custody in the Kimberley, all occurring in Broome (in May and November 1987 Broome accounted for only 10.7 per cent and 8.4 per cent respectively of the daily police lock-up census totals for the Kimberley, and it had 65 per cent of the region's prison population — personal communication, Police Department of Western Australia). With all the region's Aboriginal deaths in custody, Broome stands out in these grim statistics. Of these five deaths investigated by the Royal Commission, two died of heart attack in the regional prison and two died in the police cells, both by hanging. The fifth died after transfer from the police cells to the hospital as a result of a head injury that had been missed at the time of arrest, his state of consciousness being attributed to intoxication.

The two suicides in Broome (1983 and 1987) were both full-descent Aborigines, a 28-year-old from the Kimberley and a 42-year-old from outside the region (O'Dea 1989; 1990). Both had many previous arrests, were heavy drinkers with symptoms of alcohol dependence, and had histories of disorders of ideation and perception associated with alcohol withdrawal in the past (one had been given a diagnosis of 'alcoholic hallucinosis' by a medical practitioner). Both men were arrested for public drunkenness, one at 3:30 pm on a Saturday and the other at 6:30 pm on a Tuesday. They were found dead within three hours of incarceration, being the only inmates in the lock-up, both hanging themselves by attaching makeshift cords to the cell door. Post-mortem blood alcohol levels were similar and high, being 0.264 and 0.279. Both had been seen within two days by medical personnel, one just prior to his death, and both had sought help from a local alcohol treatment facility in the past, one within days of his demise. Finally, both had histories of problems with interpersonal relationships and one had had a recent altercation with his partner, having been arrested repeatedly and imprisoned as a result of past violence to her. The circumstances of the Broome lock-up are of note: it has two heavy doors, a five-metre corridor and a breezeway between the police working area and the cells. There was no means of communication, the police station itself being virtually soundproofed from the cells, and unattended between 2:00 am and 6:00 am.

Suicides in custody constitute an important and highly visible subgroup of Aboriginal deaths in custody, and of Aboriginal suicides (in 1988 there were nine Aboriginal suicides in Western Australia out of a total of 183 for the State as a whole [5 per cent], four being in custody [Police Department of Western Australia, personal communication]). Alcohol is implicated at every level, with heavy drinkers at greater risk of being arrested, and over-represented among those who commit suicide. At least until the decriminalisation of public intoxication in late 1990, lock-ups in the Kimberley were largely filled with heavy drinkers on 'drunk' charges. During August 1988, out of a total Kimberley lock-up population of 1391, 1288 (93 per cent) were Aboriginal (though constituting just under half the Kimberley population), with 686 (49 per cent) being there for simple intoxication (Police Department of Western Australia). Thus, at least half (probably much more including alcohol-related offences) are intoxicated at the time of incarceration.

The vulnerability of Kimberley Aborigines to suicide in custody must be located in the wider context of suicide within the Aboriginal population generally, and in the changing patterns of mortality identified earlier. One example will suffice to make the point. During the same period covered by the Commission when there were these five Aboriginal deaths in custody in the Kimberley, the following deaths occurred, too, immediately outside one Broome camp (see table 7).

Table 7 *Deaths outside one Aboriginal residential camp,*
Broome: 1979–1987

	Sex	Age (years)	Circumstances	Blood alcohol level
1.	M	24	lying on road	0.189
2.	M	50	pedestrian	0.264
3.	F	19	pushed	0.326
4.	M	38	pedestrian	(untested, suspect)
5.	M	69	pedestrian	0.181
6.	M	37	pedestrian	0.133
7.	M	37	pedestrian	0.162
8.	M	18	lying on road	0.140

Source: from information supplied by the Police Department of Western Australia.
M = males; F = females.

As can be seen, the involvement of alcohol in the deaths of these Aborigines, all of whom were within yards of their home, is ubiquitous. In assessing the additional vulnerability of intoxicated Aborigines to self-harmful behaviour as a result of incarceration, which may be compounded by a failure of adequate care on the part of custodial authorities, account must be taken of the increasing vulnerability of this same group out of custody.

LOCK-UP STUDY

In December 1987 and January 1988 the Broome lock-up was visited at 8:00 am daily, and 100 consenting Aborigines who had not been seen previously were interviewed in private (the number in the cells varied from none to thirty-one, averaging about four). During the two months of the study police records in Broome revealed that there were 365 charges, of which 300 (82 per cent) involved Aborigines (78 per cent of male detainees and 93 per cent of female detainees were Aborigines). These 300 charges against Aborigines included 43 against juveniles (14 per cent) and involved 210 individuals; 63 people were charged more than once, of whom 5 were charged four times and 2, five times, and 1 had been arrested eight times.

The age range in the sample was 12–65 years, the mean for both sexes being 32 years. Over one-quarter came from elsewhere in the Kimberley, and one-fifth from outside the region. Only one person had no previous arrest history and 89 had had multiple arrests; the current arrest being related to alcohol in 92 cases. A history of hospitalisation for alcohol-related conditions was obtained from 46 individuals, with 15 having histories of seizures, and 27 describing delirium tremens. All bar one of the 99 respondents to the CAGE had at least one affirmative response; a score of two or more was found in 80 individuals, of three or more in 53, and of all four in 17. Blackouts were described by 80 individuals. Thus, a substantial majority of this sample were experiencing significant problems from drinking.

Nineteen individuals described having experienced hallucinations in association with alcohol, 27 indicated episodes of paranoid ideation, and 28 gave histories of panic sufficient for them to seek aid. At least one of these experiences was reported by 16 males (26 per cent of males) and 15 females (50 per cent). A further 28 individuals had had impulses to self-mutilate (21 per cent of males,

43 per cent of females), with 17 having at some time acted on those impulses (13 per cent of males, 27 per cent of females). Past suicidal ideation was reported by 25 individuals (20 per cent of males, 37 per cent of females) and a previous suicide attempt was described by 15 individuals (12 per cent of males, 30 per cent of females). From 57 individuals (50 per cent of males, 73 per cent of females) a history of at least one of these experiences or impulses was obtained.

All prisoners were alert save two (who were easily roused), with five individuals not fully oriented, and immediate recall obviously deficient for only two individuals. Three admitted to paranoid ideation, two of whom provided descriptions of current hallucinations — all reporting symptoms preceding their arrest (one had been diagnosed as schizophrenic).

Nine individuals described suicidal impulses in the previous 24 hours, including four males (6 per cent of males) and five females (17 per cent). Seven of these individuals gave histories of attempts and all nine reported previous suicidal ideation, two of whom had been chronically suicidal, four indicating their feelings related to events preceding arrest, and three relating that their ideation had followed their arrest (one female and two males). These two males both described frustration and rage, and included the only individual to attempt suicide during the course of the study, being found with a sock around his neck soon after arrest. He was in his late teens and from another State, and had a past history of substance- and alcohol-abuse, alcohol-induced panic states, interpersonal violence, multiple suicide attempts, and a family history strongly positive for psychiatric disorder and para-suicide. Five months later he was found hanged (not in custody) following an altercation with his partner; his post-mortem blood alcohol level was 0.128.

From the interviews and examinations there, a picture emerged of a group detained in police custody with a very high prevalence of alcohol-related problems; a group among whom, in keeping with the high mobility of the Aboriginal population, are many individuals from outside the region.[9] Recent or current suicidal ideation was common, particularly among younger prisoners, and was usually associated with a past history of suicidal ideation and attempts, lending weight to the proposition that police lock-ups concentrate a suicide-vulnerable population. Isolation (intentional or not) was anecdotally identified as exacerbating anxiety, and thus identified as a likely contributor to the propensity for self-harm. A reformed (and previously frequently arrested) Aboriginal alcoholic gave this description of his earlier experiences:

> After heavy drinking, you know, you get paralytic drunk and get the shakes, you can hear voices, voices saying 'I'll kill you'. I've been through that, hearing voices and things. It makes you feel you want to commit suicide. Makes you think people coming to get you, makes you think that before they get you you'll kill yourself, commit suicide. . . . When you're locked up and going through that thing you need people around, you should have the lights on. In the light you're safe, but in the darkness you think that person going to come and kill you.

Thus, there are four interrelated issues: incarceration in police cells; alcoholism and acute intoxication; alcohol-precipitated disorders of ideation and perception; and suicide. Alcohol can be seen to be related to each of these. From the previous chapter it is evident that Kimberley Aboriginal drinkers:

- are more likely to be heavy consumers of alcohol than drinkers in the wider Australian population;
- have almost invariably been arrested, often numerous times;
- are at greater risk of developing symptoms of psychological distress than their non-drinking peers, and;
- more frequently report histories of self-harmful thoughts and actions.

Those in the lock-up described exacerbation of their distressing experiences when secluded. Detention of Aboriginal drinkers, thus, appears to compound the risk of suicide in a group whose vulnerability, regardless of arrest, is already greater.

KIMBERLEY ABORIGINAL SUICIDES: 1957–1989

The Royal Commission brought attention to Aboriginal suicide at a time when, in the Kimberley, the number of suicides in the wider Aboriginal community was increasing dramatically and the pattern changing. For the decade of the 1960s only one Kimberley Aboriginal suicide was discovered; during the 1970s there were three; and in the 1980s 21 Aborigines died by their own hands. The changing patterns in Kimberley Aboriginal suicide only became obvious well after the initial work had been completed. In order to demonstrate this point, those suicides occurring up to 1987 will be examined first, followed by suicides in 1988 and 1989.

SUICIDES: 1957–1987

Suicide emerged only in the 1980s as a contributor to the increase in the proportion of deaths from external causes among Kimberley Aborigines, constituting 3 per cent of male non-infant deaths between 1982 and 1986. For the three decades examined during that part of the study (1957–1986) 14 suicides were identified from the registers of deaths. In addition to these 14 suicides, the initial analysis also included the suicide of one Kimberley resident who died elsewhere, and two in 1987, one of whom also died outside the region. Sources of information included certificates of death, coronial reports, records from local medical services, and various informants.

These 17 suicides were comprised of 15 males (mean age, 30 years; range 17–42) and 2 females, (aged 20 and 21 years). Twelve of the suicides (71 per cent) occurred in Broome Shire; the two deaths occurring outside the Kimberley were of individuals also from Broome. One of the females died by hanging, the other by overdose. The means used by male suicides were uniformly violent; hanging (10), gunshot (3), a knife wound to the heart (1), and laceration of the ulnar artery (1). Deaths occurred in all months save March and November without seasonal predilection.

The only two who were not of mixed-descent were also the only suicides in custody. The two females had had difficulties in interpersonal relationships, one having just experienced a major loss. Both females had family histories of alcohol-related problems and had been heavy drinkers: post-mortem blood alcohol level in one was 0.247, with THC (cannabis) detected in the other (but no alcohol). As Aboriginal men are clearly at greatest risk, this discussion focuses on male suicide. For reasons of confidentiality neither the year of death nor age will be linked to specific cases, and histories presented have minor distortions which do not, however, alter the substance of the clinical or historical material.

Little information was obtained for one of the 15 males. Aged in his twenties, he came from inter-State and died in a remote setting. He was wanted as a witness in a murder trial and his suicide is believed to have been related to events surrounding that case. Of the remaining 14 suicides, 11 (79 per cent) had histories of problem drinking, with family histories of heavy alcohol consumption in seven of 11 (64 per cent). Eight of twelve (67 per cent) for whom information was available, had been drinking prior to the suicide, with post-mortem blood alcohol levels available for five, ranging between 0.164 and 0.279.

A history of a previous attempt was provided for four (possibly five) of 12. One ingested a toxic substance and was taken to the local hospital, where his stomach was pumped, following which he returned home and successfully suicided. Another, several years before his death, had been hospitalised after jumping off a boat in dangerous conditions. A third stabbed himself on several occasions and required medical attention for self-inflicted lacerations to his abdomen only hours before his suicide. The fourth had slashed his abdomen two years earlier. Eight of the 12 males had either sought help from relatives, medical workers, clergy or friends, or made explicit statements of their intention. In two cases these statements had been made repeatedly over a number of years. One additional male had been trying unsuccessfully to contact his family just before his death. Neither of the women are known to have made such statements or sought aid.

While the proportion of heavy drinkers may seem high, given the prevalence figures presented earlier, the figures are not dissimilar to those for the wider population of young Kimberley males. However, histories were obtained of episodes of disordered ideation and perception (frightening paranoid ideation and hallucinations), that were either precipitated or worsened by alcohol, from seven of 14 individuals (mean age, 33 years). Two of these had repeated episodes of delirium tremens (alcohol withdrawal), while the other five were reported, in addition, to have had prolonged periods of disturbed behaviour in which they appeared to be hallucinating and fearful. The following histories provide examples.

Case 1 had a long history of heavy drinking and had attended the hospital one month before death complaining of 'hearing voices and seeing things'. At that visit the hospital notes record that he 'appeared normal and did not appear to be affected by alcohol'. Relatives and friends described him as having been shy and withdrawn, but always careful of his appearance. He was drinking wine heavily before his death and had become accusatory, described by a close acquaintance as having been 'off his head, blaming people for trying to kill him'.

Case 2 died in custody. He had previously been admitted with other family members to an alcohol-treatment facility, where he was noted to be experiencing visual hallucinations, and was treated with chlormethiazole (used in the management of alcohol withdrawal). A month before his death he was diagnosed as suffering from 'alcoholic hallucinosis' at the local hospital. He had been drinking heavily at the time of his arrest.

Case 3 had a six-year history of hallucinations and paranoid ideation, which focused on his belief that he had been 'sung', which usually manifested itself after he began drinking. At other times he was quiet and withdrawn. He often presented to the hospital, and was referred to Perth for psychiatric evaluation, where a diagnosis of delirium tremens was made (it is unlikely that this is sufficient to account for the longitudinal picture). The night before his death he absconded from hospital and visited relatives, complaining of threatening voices and accusing those supposed malefactors of conspiring to kill him.

Case 4 was a daily drinker for many years, but owing to illness he had been abstinent for several days. By the evening of the third day he was tremulous, agitated and began talking in his tribal tongue to unseen interlocutors, later insisting that they were intent on harm. Despite close attention and the entreaties of relatives, he managed in an unobserved moment to sever his left ulnar artery. No other psychotic features were apparent.

Case 5 had longstanding contacts with the health system and alcohol-treatment facilities. He had had 'the horrors' (delirium tremens) on several occasions and experienced hallucinations when drinking, insisting that people were observing him and planning his demise. He had stabbed himself in the chest while drinking a month earlier, and several hours before he successfully suicided he had cut his stomach, again while intoxicated.

Case 6 frequently sought help from a variety of institutions, including the police and hospital, because of fears that he was being pursued for having broken certain tribal laws. However, the onset of his panic was predictably linked to drinking. Both medical assistance and a traditional healer had been enlisted with temporary amelioration of his fear, which promptly returned when he again drank. He had been treated with chlormethiazole and chlorpromazine (an antipsychotic) and subsequently received a diagnosis of paranoid schizophrenia. Alcohol was not detected at autopsy.

Case 7 was often seen by local medical officers. The hospital notes recorded 'disorders of ideation and perception' following drinking, involving a preoccupation with sexually transmitted diseases and accusations against those he supposed had infected him. In the three days before his suicide he was arrested twice while drunk; on the second occasion he was taken to the hospital, where his intoxicated state was commented on several hours before he was found hanged in his cell.

Ten of the 15 male suicides (67 per cent; mean age, 28 years) had experienced a real or threatened disruption to an important inter-personal relationship (including the man who suicided while avoiding involvement in a trial in another State and was, consequently, separated from his family and friends). Other loss events included: a partner and child(ren) leaving (3 cases); the breakup of a longstanding relationship (1); the death of a close relative or partner (2); and a major altercation with a partner (2). Four of the five suicides for whom no history of a loss was obtained had experienced disorders of ideation and perception. Only one individual, the youngest in the group, had neither; his suicide occurred following what, on the surface, appeared to be a minor accident resulting from reckless bravado while his relatives were absent.

As noted earlier, all save two of the males were of mixed-descent. Non-Aboriginal ancestry included Chinese, Filipino, Malay, Japanese, Maori and European. From the random sample survey, approximately half of those between 15 and 30 years old were of mixed-descent, suggesting an over-representation of suicide among those of mixed-descent. Furthermore, among the males, seven had ancestry from one particular Aboriginal linguistic descent group and four of these were related, being a great-grandson and three great-great-grandsons (cousins) of the same European male. All four were alcoholic, and three demonstrated a pattern of paranoid and hallucinatory experiences associated with drinking, all being apparently free from such experiences when abstinent.

The 10 male suicides from Broome to 1986 for whom most information was gathered were compared with two sets of age-matched controls. This comparison confirmed that of nine variables (history of heavy drinking, family history of heavy drinking, disorders of perception and ideation, being in a current relationship, having children, having experienced a recent loss, a history of institutionalisation, a history of parental institutionalisation, and mixed versus full Aboriginal descent), three occurred with greater than expected frequency: mixed-descent; a history of disorders of ideation and perception; and a recent disruption to an interpersonal relationship.[10]

SUICIDES: 1988–1989

In the last two years of the decade there were eight male suicides in the Kimberley. None were at the time of their death receiving earned income, although one was involved with the Community Development and Employment Program (CDEP). One of the others was an old age pensioner and two received invalid pensions. Five died as a result of hanging and one each by self-immolation, shooting, and jumping from a moving vehicle. All save two were 20 years of age or less, the others being 32 and 70 years of age. Three were full-descent; all, however, resided in urban areas. A comparison to the 15 male suicides occurring up to 1987 (see table 8) revealed that the proportion of the suicides who were 20 years of age or less had increased from one of 15 (7 per cent), to six of 8 (75 per cent), with those of full-descent increasing from two of 15 (13 per cent), to three of 8 (38 per cent).

Four suicides had histories of recent interpersonal conflicts or losses. All four of these were 20 years of age or less, and all had been drinking before their suicide (the four post-mortem blood alcohol levels ranged from 0.117 to 0.260, with a mean of 0.174). Six of the eight were, or had been, heavy drinkers; however, only one of these (diagnosed as schizophrenic) had a clear history of disordered ideation or perception. One other was receiving treatment for a psychotic disorder, and a third, who had not been psychiatrically evaluated, was a past heavy drinker who was relatively socially isolated, with a history of auditory hallucinosis and religiosity preceding his death.

The only individual without either a history of recent loss, or of disordered ideation or perception, was the 70-year-old, whose suicide appears in sharp contrast to the others. Previous attempts were documented for two, with seven making statements about their intent prior to their death. These recent suicides are compared in table 8 to the those male suicides occurring in the period 1957–1987.

Aboriginal suicide in the Kimberley, thus, continues to occur primarily (in these last two years exclusively) among males, with the proportion of younger suicides increasing. While the proportion

Table 8 *Comparison of Kimberley Aboriginal male suicides:*
1957–1987 and 1988–1989

	Suicides 1957–1987 (ages 17–42)			Suicides 1988–1989 (ages 17–70)		
	Reports	Sample size[a]	Percent-age	Reports	Sample size[a]	Percent-age
	N	(N)		N	(N)	
Aged 20 years or less	1	(15)	7%	6	(8)	75%
Disorder of ideation/ perception	7	(14)	50%	3	(8)	38%
Recent loss/disruption	10	(15)	67%	4	(8)	50%
History of heavy drinking	11	(14)	79%	6	(8)	75%
Family history of heavy drinking	7	(11)	64%	7	(8)	88%
Previous attempts	4	(12)	33%	2	(8)	25%
Prior warnings	8	(12)	67%	7	(8)	88%
Drinking before suicide	8	(12)	67%	4	(8)	50%

Note: [a] Number of sample size varies with availability of information for each case.

of full-descent Aborigines has also increased, it remains less than would be expected in the general Kimberley Aboriginal population. Furthermore, the suicides have continued to occur among town-oriented Aborigines, suggesting social rather than descent issues. Among younger males, a fight with a partner in the context of heavy drinking was a common precursor.

The QARK allows comparison of the six recent young suicides (mean age, 18.3 years) with the 23 randomly selected male subjects aged 16–23 years (mean age, 18.4 years). See table 9.

The differences in the methods of information collection and small sample sizes, with consequent wide confidence intervals, make caution mandatory in interpretation. However, compared to the wider Kimberley population, those who suicided in these two years were: more likely to have been town residents; to have past histories of suicidal ideation and past attempts; and to have come from families in which there was heavy drinking. While all the suicides were drinkers, it is evident from the previous chapter that, not only is consuming alcohol normative for Aboriginal males in this age-group (20 years old and less) in the Kimberley, but levels of consumption

Table 9 *Comparison of two groups of Aboriginal males
aged 20 years or less: from QARK random sample and
from suicides 1988–1989*

	QARK random sample [a]		suicides[b]		p
	N	%	N	%	
Full descent	16	70	2	33	n.s.
Town residence	6	26	6	100	< .01
Work:					
independently employed	2	9	0	—	n.s.
CDEP[c]	10	43	1	17	n.s.
Current drinkers	19	83	6	100	n.s.
Past suicidal ideation	3	13	6	100	< .01
Past suicide attempts	0	—	2	33	< .005
Past psychotic symptoms	4	17	3	50	n.s.
Family heavy drinking	13	57	6	100	< .05

Notes: [a] sample size = 23.

    [b] sample size = 6.

    [c] CDEP = Community Development and Employment Program.

are high. Trends suggesting an over-representation of mixed-descent Aborigines and for histories of disorders of ideation and perception were present, but did not reach statistical significance.[11]

THE PARENTAL GENERATION

A family history of heavy drinking was obtained for all young adults who committed suicide in 1988 and 1989, compared with just over half of the subjects in the random sample. For all the suicides paternal relationships were problematic, with inconstant paternal figures, and in three cases reports of severe violence. The fathers of two had never been present, one had left when the child was five years old, and one had himself committed suicide.

The QARK also provides a window on the parental generation. In the previous chapter it was pointed out that reports of heavy parental drinking increased with decreasing age (as does the proportion of the sample raised by an Aboriginal person other than a parent). The parental generation of the young men who suicided in 1988 and 1989 were aged between approximately 38 and 58 years at the time of the QARK study, there being 79 males and 75 females identified in this age-range. Almost two-thirds of the males and one-quarter of the females were current drinkers, just over a quarter of each being past drinkers. Thus, 91 per cent of males and 61 per cent of females in the parental generation were, or had been, drinkers. From the 48 male and female subjects in the QARK sample aged 20 years or less, reports were obtained of *heavy* parental drinking involving 54 per cent of their fathers and 19 per cent of their mothers (including reports by 12.5 per cent that both were heavy drinkers).

Of the 79 males, who were aged 38–58 years, 67 (85 per cent) had been arrested, 60 (76 per cent) more than once. Of these, 30 (38 per cent) had been imprisoned, 16 (20 per cent) more than once, with 8 (10 per cent) being sent to detention in Perth or Darwin. Of the 75 females in the same age-group, 31 (41 per cent) stated they had been arrested, 22 (29 per cent) more than once. Seven (9 per cent) had spent time in prison, three (4 per cent) on more than one occasion, with one having been sent to detention outside the region. Thus, in the Kimberley, the parental generation of the group of young adult Aboriginal males at greatest risk of suicide is characterised by histories of widespread drinking, particularly affecting men; high rates of arrest and imprisonment, again primarily males; and increasing reliance among drinkers on other Aborigines as caretakers for children — factors which are embedded in the wider social transformations that confronted this generation as young adults.

RELATED ISSUES

There can no longer be any question that suicide among Aborigines is increasing. The group at greatest risk in the Kimberley are young adult males. The over-representation of town-oriented and mixed-descent Aborigines emphasises the importance of social factors. Recent disturbances of interpersonal relationships remain typical of the younger group, with intoxication in the context of conflicts with a partner being a common antecedent. The relationship to disorders of ideation and perception is less clear, perhaps because of the younger age of these suicides compared to those who died before 1988. Regardless, the involvement of alcohol is pervasive.

ALCOHOL AND SUICIDE

The relationship of alcohol and suicide, although clear, is complex as there are a number of clinical conditions in which both occur with frequency. Indeed, Menninger (1938) suggested that alcoholism is itself a form of suicide. An analysis of the relationship of suicide and alcohol must therefore take into account depressive disorders, impulsivity, disruption of interpersonal relationships, and disorders of ideation and perception.

And depression

The increased risk of death by suicide for alcoholics is, at least in part, mediated through the development of an affective (depressive) disorder that is usually secondary to the alcoholism itself.[12] Indeed, depressive symptoms tend to abate quickly with cessation of drinking and improvements are generally maintained with abstinence. In contrast to depression, in which suicide is most likely at the height of an acute depressive episode, suicide among alcoholics tends to be a late event, reflecting the chronicity of the process. As will be discussed below, interpersonal loss is a vulnerability factor, particularly for alcoholic males, and is related to depression, with the group at highest risk being alcoholic males who are concurrently depressed and have experienced a recent loss.

And interpersonal loss

Of 202 suicides reviewed as part of the San Diego Suicide Study, 97 per cent had one or more life stresses (Rich, Warsradt, Nemiroff, Fowler & Young 1991). The most prominent pattern, particularly for younger suicides, was 'conflict-separation-rejection', with interpersonal loss appearing to confer particular vulnerability for male drinkers. In another investigation of 50 alcoholic suicides, over half were found to have a history of depression, and just over a quarter were found to have experienced a significant loss within six weeks of their deaths (Murphy, Armstrong, Hermele, Fischer & Clendenin 1979). Clearly, the relationship between suicide and interpersonal loss, especially in the context of alcoholism, is complex.

And disorders of ideation and perception

It is well known that alcohol withdrawal — either total withdrawal or a substantial reduction by intake — can cause disorientation and experiences of disordered ideation and perception. Patterns of acute and chronic auditory hallucinosis, often with paranoid elements, may occur with prolonged drinking, and may proceed to a chronic form (alcoholic hallucinosis) indistinguishable from schizophrenia (Alpert 1985). However, to further complicate the picture, suicidal ideation is not uncommon in schizophrenia, particularly in conjunction with depression and substance abuse.[13]

Despite prohibition, Aboriginal alcohol-related psychoses have been long recognised. There is, for instance, the case of 'Tommy', a 40-year-old Aborigine who died after almost a year as a patient in the Claremont Psychiatric Hospital (Western Australia) in the early 1920s. He had been:

> admitted in a state of acute alcoholic mania with vivid auditory hallucinations, great excitability, dirty and destructive habits. It is remarkable how the alcoholic psychoses run true to type, that is the combination of hallucinosis and delusions of persecution associated with sex. (Bostock 1924 : 461)

Brady and Palmer commented on alcohol-induced misperceptions and paranoid ideation associated with panic in their study of isolated Aboriginal communities, stating that 'sometimes drinkers claim they have seen spirits in the night and cry out hysterically in alarm, demanding help and rescue' (1984 : 25). Such alcohol-related experiences appear to be common among heavy drinkers in the Kimberley. In addition, the Northern Territory Department of Health (Devanesen, Furber, Hampton, Honari, Kinmonth & Peach 1986) reported that between 1977 and 1982 the hospital separation rates for alcohol-related disorders for Aboriginal males and non-Aboriginal males were roughly similar and remained steady. However, over the same time there was a sixfold increase in the standardised hospital separation rates for the diagnosis of 'alcoholic psychosis' among Aboriginal males. While the numbers are relatively small (5–31 separations for Aboriginal males with this diagnosis), and while it may in part reflect changed diagnostic practices, other groups (non-Aborigines and Aboriginal females) did not show the same sustained increases. In addition, those being so labelled were younger than their non-Aboriginal counterparts.

And other conditions

Diagnostic confusion likewise occurs in other psychiatric conditions associated with impulsivity, recklessness, unstable relationships and drinking, in which suicidal behaviour is not uncommon. While there appear to be patterns of familial transmission for some of the personality disorders with these characteristics, and for the propensity to problems with alcohol, they appear to be overlapping conditions with an additive effect in predisposing to violent behaviour, including suicide.[14]

Summary

From the international literature there, thus, appears to be a relationship between alcohol and suicide which is, at least in part, mediated through the development of depression as a consequence of drinking. The immediate effect of alcohol on emotion is worse with both chronicity of drinking and increasing intoxication. Suicide is generally a late event among primary alcoholics, with those at greatest risk being male alcoholics who are concurrently depressed and who have experienced recent losses. Certain personality patterns characterised by impulsivity and unstable interpersonal relationships have a higher likelihood of suicidal behaviour with alcohol, particularly if depressive symptoms are also present.

In addition, alcohol is capable of producing disordered ideation and perception, and within the Aboriginal population of northern Australia this picture appears to be becoming more common, with males particularly vulnerable to alcohol's psychologically intrusive and behaviourally destabilising effects. Such pictures were found in the histories of older Aborigines who suicided in the Kimberley; the recent, younger suicides more frequently took their lives while acutely intoxicated following an interpersonal dispute.

SUICIDE AND ABORIGINAL SOCIAL INTEGRATION

These findings do not explain why suicides emerged in this Aboriginal population only in the last decade. Despite the contemporaneous lifting of prohibition, it is clear that alcohol is not the sole causal factor. Any explanations must also address the disproportionate representation of one group — town-oriented, young adult males.

Reser and Eastwell (1981) pointed to a similar group being susceptible to the 'fear of sorcery syndrome'. Their analysis presented personal psychological security as contingent on social integration, thus rendering isolated or extruded individuals psychologically and physically vulnerable (a similar situation was described for traditional Arnhem Land Aborigines by Warner 1969 [1937]). The impact of chronic alcohol abuse on the capacity for meaningful integration within the social network may function similarly, thus contributing to suicide vulnerability. These networks of interpersonal relationships necessary for the construction and maintenance of personal identity are of particular importance in Aboriginal societies. Reid made this point with respect to the Yolngu of Arnhem Land, for whom 'it is rather like being at the centre of a series of concentric circles' (1983 : 86). Myers identified a similar dynamic in the Central Desert: 'Pintupi ethnopsychology seems to view an individual's internal states as extensively connected with a web of significant others or with "objects" that Western observers would describe as external to the self' (1986 : 107).

Myers elaborated on the interpersonal definition of emotion and its importance in maintaining and making safe relationships and relatedness. As a corollary, threats to relatedness — if significant, widespread, or persistent — may represent an assault on the very fabric of identity and self. The frequency of active help-seeking or warnings among the heavy drinking male suicides may represent desperate attempts at reintegration by generating a social (caring or protective, thus self-affirming) response.

Several authors have alluded to the role of anomie (to be discussed in chapter 8) within Aboriginal societies as a result of Western contact and domination. This, in itself, does not explain why Aborigines, who have been the subjects of European domination and subjugation for generations, are killing themselves now when their access to economic and political means — and thus to power — has theoretically never been greater. However, as already suggested, the changes were frequently illusory; as Bandler has pointed out, 'the problem of unequal wages was only partially solved during this period [of citizenship]; it evolved into the present problem of unequal opportunity' (1989 : 33). To understand this phenomenon requires an interrogation of the real consequences of these social and political transformations for the distribution and articulation of power and its impact on the construction of identity. Powerlessness is most blatantly manifest, and extremely felt, by those deprived of their liberty. It is, thus, telling that Aboriginal suicide has emerged and received systematic attention primarily as a consequence of Aboriginal deaths in the silence and bitter seclusion of police and prison cells.

NOTES

Chapter 6 is based on previously published papers: 'On Gordian knots and nooses: Aboriginal suicide in the Kimberley'. *Australian and New Zealand Journal of Psychiatry 22*, 1988, 264–271; 'Aboriginal suicides in custody: A view from the Kimberley'. *Australian and New Zealand Journal of Psychiatry 22*, 1988, 273–282; 'Suicide, alcohol, incarceration and indigenous populations: A review'. In J. Greeley & W. Gladstone (eds), *The effects of alcohol on cognitive, psychomotor and affective functioning* (pp. 96–118). Monograph No. 8, National Drug and Alcohol Research Centre, Sydney, 1989; 'An examination of recent suicides in remote Australia: Further information from the Kimberley'. *Australian and New Zealand Journal of Psychiatry 25*, 1991, 197–202; 'The social and family context of Aboriginal self-harmful behaviour in remote Australia'. *Australian and New Zealand Journal of Psychiatry 25*, 1991, 203–209.

1. Ironically, the investigations of the Royal Commission into Aboriginal Deaths in Custody spanned both the Australian Bicentennial celebrations, and the 200th anniversary of Australia's first recorded suicide in custody:

   > The oldest female convict [on the first fleet] was Dorothy Handland, a dealer in rags and old clothes who was eighty-two years old in 1787. She had drawn seven years for perjury. In 1789, in a fit of befuddled despair, she was to hang herself from a gum tree at Sydney Cove, thus becoming Australia's first recorded suicide. (Hughes 1987 : 73)

2. According to Berrios and Mohanna (1990), in using suicide as the arena for defining the role and boundaries of French sociology, Durkheim ignored texts exploring the issue at the individual level and systematically distorted existing moderate psychiatric views.

3. Information on international patterns from the World Health Organization was presented by Diekstra (1989); from Great Britain by McClure (1984a; 1984b) and Murphy, Lindesay and Grundy (1986); from the United States by Murphy and Wetzel (1980); and from Australia by Dorsch and Roder (1983), Goldney and Katsikitis (1983), Kosky (1987) and Hassan & Carr (1989). Differences in the socio-economic correlates of suicide in the United States and Australia were explored by Lester and Yang (1991).

4. The influence of deaths listed as unknown, or suggestive accidents, has been explored by McClure (1984a) and Sainsbury and Jenkins (1982). The idiosyncrasies of coronial reporting are not uniform across different societies (McCarthy & Walsh 1975), being influenced by method of suicide and by age (Walsh, Walsh & Whelan 1975). Errors appear to consistently favour under-reporting. While within Australia there have also been, and remain, changes in the use of the 'undetermined' death category, it is unlikely that this explains the substantial increase in suicides among young males (Cantor & Dunne 1990).

5. Drawing on the work of Berry, Tsai (1989) presents acculturation as a bilateral process of adjustment. When inter-group asymmetries exist

such that the adjustment burden of acculturation falls largely on one group, 'acculturative stress' results, manifest in social and emotional problems. Tsai contrasts this process to 'internal colonialism', in which there is a vested interest in maintaining an asymmetry between the periphery (frontier/colonised) and the centre (metropolis/colonisers) in the service of exploitation. Stress arises as a consequence of exclusion of the colonised from equitable participation in the dominant society.

6. The Forrest Commission of 1884 examined, among other things, the conditions under which Aborigines were detained on Rottnest Island.

7. The question of the role of suggestion is vexed. A century ago Durkheim stated that 'the idea of suicide may undoubtedly be communicated by contagion', but qualified that such individual effects were not reflected in changes in suicide rates. However, he pointed out that 'the contagious events so often noticed in the army or prisons' were 'easily explicable once it is acknowledged that the suicidal tendency can be created by the social environment' (Durkheim 1970 [1897]: 131–140). In a review of the influence of media coverage of suicide Goldney (1989) reported that, of 13 studies in the last two decades, 10 supported the hypothesis that there was a significant relationship between reporting and subsequent suicides. He gave considerable attention to a study of teenage suicide in the United States between 1973 and 1979, which demonstrated increasing rates of teen suicide (particularly female) following television coverage of suicides of prominent figures (Phillips & Carstensen 1986). A subsequent reconsideration of this article extended the period under investigation to 1984 (Kessler, Downey, Milavsky & Stipp 1988). While a significant association was found between 1977 and 1980, this reversed in the period 1981 to 1984. The authors found no relationship to the dissemination of the stories, in contrast to a suggestion by Phillips and Carstensen. To explain the reversal around 1980, two alternatives were considered: that the nature of reporting may have changed; and that a change had occurred in the public perception of suicide.

8. The international literature is reviewed in E. Hunter, 'Aboriginal suicides in custody: A view from the Kimberley'. *Australian and New Zealand Journal of Psychiatry 22*, 1988, pp. 273–282. A special area for concern is juvenile suicide in custody. A series from the United States by Hayes (1983) included 15 juveniles, of whom 12 died in isolation, with only 5 of the total charged with serious crimes. The paradox that isolation is used for the 'protection' of juveniles in adult detention centres was noted by Hayes, and also by Flaherty (1983), who compared 21 suicides of minors in adult detention centres across the United States with 6 occurring in juvenile centres during 1978. The suicide rate for those dying in adult centres was some 3.5 times that of the general population; a rate, itself, twice as high as the rate in the juvenile centres. Seventeen of these minors died while held in isolation.

9. Research on Aboriginal imprisonment in northern Western Australia revealed that there 'seemed to be a tendency for those away from their usual tribal area to be particularly liable to arrest' (Duckworth, Foley-Jones, Lowe & Maller 1982 : 33).

10. These 10 male Broome suicides were compared to two matched groups of controls. The first control group consisted of 35 Aboriginal males appearing on the Broome Register of deaths, whose age at the time of their death was within ten years of the index case, and who died within five years of that suicide. The second group of 40 was obtained from hospital admission records, four controls being selected for each of the index cases, two being the first age-matched Aborigines admitted to hospital prior to the date of suicide, and the first two admitted subsequently. The mean age for these ten Broome suicides was 31.3 years (S.D. = 7.5); for the dead controls, 37.3 years (S.D. = 8.3); and for the hospital controls, 30.6 years (S.D. = 7.4). Information was gathered on the nine issues identified in the text. Two cells in the table are empty, as hospital admissions reflected the disproportionate mixed-descent town population, and as information regarding a recent loss for the live controls was compromised: for this group, in contrast to the suicides and the deceased controls, there was no clear temporal point of reference.

Suicides, live controls and dead controls, by nine psychosocial variables

Psychosocial variable	Suicide		Live control		Dead control	
	N	%	N	%	N	%
Heavy drinker	7	70	33	83	25	71
Family history of heavy drinking	6[a]	67	33[b]	85	16[c]	49
Disorders of ideation/ perception	7	70	12[d]	32*	9[c]	27*
Relationship	7	70	26	65	21	60
Children	5	50	20	50	22	63
Recent loss	8	80	—	—	5[e]	17**
Institution	4	40	20	50	21	60
Full-descent	2	20	—	—	23	66**
Parent in institution	4	40	17	43	17	49
Sample Size (N)	10		40		35	

Notes: * p < .05   ** p < .01

Sample sizes in some instances varied, according to the availability of information — as indicated below:

[a] Sample size = 9.   [d] Sample size = 38.
[b] Sample size = 39.   [e] Sample size = 30.
[c] Sample size = 33.

11. All four reporting past experiences of disordered ideation or perception from the random sample indicated that their experiences occurred in conjunction with alcohol. None had received psychiatric treatment. Of these four, two described past impulses to self-harm, compared to only two of 19 (11 per cent) among those from the sample without a history of ideational or perceptual disturbance. Nearly three-quarters of the random sample young males had been incarcerated, including all four with histories of disorders of ideation or perception (100 per cent) compared to 13 of the 19 (68 per cent) without such histories.

12. The research on suicide and alcoholism has taken two courses: examination of the rate at which individuals identified as alcoholic subsequently suicide; and the determination of what proportion of suicides were alcoholic. The direct effect of alcohol on mood is complex, influenced by numerous contingent and interacting factors (Chesher and Greeley 1989). In a review of the research, Frances, Franklin and Flavin stated that:

> alcohol has been found to be associated with 50% of suicides and to increase the risk of suicidal behavior both for alcoholic and non-alcoholic populations. Between 5% and 27% of all deaths of alcoholics are caused by suicide. The incidence of alcoholism among persons who commit suicide ranges from 6% to 30% in different studies with approximately 20% most frequently cited. Lifetime risk for suicide is 1% in the general population, 15% for major affective illness, and 15% for alcoholism. (1986 : 316)

Diagnostic confusion arising from co-morbidity was addressed by Schuckit (1986); he noted that while depression is common in the lives of alcoholics, the alcoholism is usually primary, particularly for men. In addition, affective symptoms usually remit following cessation of drinking (Brown & Schuckit 1988), with improvements maintained among those remaining abstinent (Pettinati, Sugerman & Maurer 1982).

13. Suicidal ideation has been reported in one-third of a series of 801 schizophrenics, with suicidal patients tending to show depression, aggressiveness and substance abuse (Dassori, Mezzich, Keshavan 1990). In a comparison of depressed and non-depressed hospitalised alcoholics, Cadoret and Winokur (1974) found an excess of alcoholic paranoia in the non-depressed males. In the same study the depressed males were reported to have both more frequent and more serious suicide attempts. The authors speculated on the internalisation (depression) versus projection (paranoia) of aggression and guilt. The relationship of suicide to psychosis was also examined among 134 suicides in St Louis, in which 25 (19 per cent) were psychotic, and 33 (25 per cent) alcoholic. Five (15 per cent) of the alcoholic suicides were psychotic, all male (Robins 1986).

14. There appears to be a subgroup of male alcoholics who demonstrate particularly severe alcoholism associated with sociopathic behaviour in which patrilineal familial transmission occurs (Cloninger, Bohman & Sigvardsson 1981).

CHAPTER 7

Bloodlines: Violence to Self and Others

My girlfriend and I had an argument. I went to the liquor store and she came behind in a Toyota, a Hilux. I bought two flagons and went back to the reserve. A big mob of blokes were bludging off her. I went and bust the flagons and went home. She was jealousing me and started abusing me saying her brothers could belt me and all that. I grabbed a broken flagon and stabbed myself. I didn't want to kill myself. I stabbed it and threw it away. When I got up to try and hit her I saw my gut sticking out.

25-year-old Aboriginal male from southern Kimberley, 1987

My husband is always drinking — he gets drunk, comes home, then there's an argument and he start to hit me. He talks rubbish. He hits me with a broomstick, with a cup — anything he can pick up. Last time he bashed me up and knocked my teeth out. He hit my little girl too — she help herself, open door and run to uncle place. He promise to shoot me with gun — me and the children are frightened of him. He told me 'you go to your father and mother — get out of my house'.

Quoted in Bolger 1990 : 25

Premeditated self-annihilation occurs at an extreme of the spectrum of violent behaviours, which includes the different experiences described above. In this chapter non-suicidal intentional self-harm and interpersonal violence among Kimberley Aborigines is explored, and a historical paradigm developed to explain the changing patterns of violence.

SELF-MUTILATION

These rituals then come to appear as attempts to promote personal integration in a difficult, transitional period of life . . . as efforts to resolve some of the ambivalences about becoming adult and to express others, their purpose seems to be to help the child accept and succeed in living henceforth in accordance with the adult role of his sex. Thus these ceremonies . . . seem to foster personal and social integration. They

166

should be understood as efforts of the young or of society, to resolve the antitheses between child and adult, between male and female and between polymorphous-perverse and genital tendencies. Whether or not they succeed is another question.

Bruno Bettelheim 1955 : 44

There appears little to connect Bettelheim's analysis of self-mutilation with the experience of the Aboriginal man recovering in hospital. Bettelheim was drawn to his work by observations of disturbed youth in Chicago. His analysis of 'Australian rites' was based on Spencer and Gillen's work in Central Australia between 1894 and 1898. According to Bettelheim, these male rites were attempts to gain access to the power of women, the rituals being an affirmation of male power that excluded females. While there is no suggestion of empowerment in the Kimberley vignette, the intercultural and intracultural dynamics of power are central to this examination of non-traditional self-mutilation, defined by Favazza as the 'deliberate destruction or alteration of body tissue without suicidal intent' (1989 : 113).

RITUAL MUTILATION

Early accounts of male dominance of the sacred (as distinct from the economic) domain of power have led to accusations of sexist ethnographic bias (Bell, 1983). This will be explored in the next chapter. Regardless, social change has clearly undermined the salience of traditional ritual in the lives of contemporary Aborigines. New rites of passage have emerged, informed by different power relations. Only a brief note will be made on one ritual form of bodily mutilation, subincision.

Reflecting the attitudes of the wider society, psychiatrists have historically foregrounded the 'exotic' in their writings about Aborigines. Predictably, interest in self-mutilation focused on male rites, in particular subincision, found throughout the Centre and extending into some areas of the Kimberley. Genital self-mutilation is rare among Europeans, and generally associated with psychosis.[1] Various explanations for the origins of the Aboriginal rite have been offered including: hygiene, a form of 'preventative medicine' (Morrison 1976); contraception, sexual pleasure, symbolic functions (in terms of a vagina or menstruation equivalent), and for easy access to blood for ritual purposes; and totemic, in terms of producing a similarity to the bifid marsupial penis (Cawte 1973). Cawte was wisely circumspect in stating that he believed 'subincision to be complexly overdetermined' (1973 : 390).

NON-TRADITIONAL SELF-MUTILATION

In 1982 the trial of Alwyn Peter brought the issue into the public domain, later highlighted by David Bradbury's controversial and brutally frank 1989 film *State of Shock*. Peter, while intoxicated, had killed his de facto wife on the Weipa reserve. Defence barristers presented Peter as the victim of history and circumstance, documenting paternal alcoholism and chronic domestic instability, ill-health, school problems, incarceration, alcoholism — and recurrent self-mutilation (Sturgess & Brennan 1982). They described him as being controlled by his mother and grandmother. Alienated from land, tradition and tribal elders, the authors suggested that 'the evidence of self-mutilation and violence to loved ones is a clear statement that Alwyn and his contemporaries often see life as it is lived on reserves as worthless' (1982 : 46).

This case was examined by Paul Wilson, who indicated that self-mutilation was common among males of south Weipa. According to Wilson, Peter displayed major changes with alcohol, resulting in fights with family and spouse. Indeed, the women of the family were portrayed as both the precipitators and restrainers: 'Often, when he and Deidre fought, Alwyn would slash himself with a razor blade or knife. . . . He does know that he was very drunk and furious with Deidre, and he remembers cutting his left arm with a razor. . . . A few weeks later Alwyn committed the same act again. On this occasion he was angry at both Deidre and his mother' (1985 : 23).

For Peter, self-mutilation or violence seemed an inevitable expression of frustration, for which he had no other coping mechanisms. There appeared to Wilson a confusion of violence to self and others. Indeed, it was Deidre's attempts to prevent him mutilating himself once again that led to the homicide. Throughout the accounts, the tension between Peter, and his mother and spouse is central. His father was a heavy drinker, and Peter's mother was the stable figure in the family, at times using the police to control her son's outbursts. Wilson concluded that in that area of Queensland, where self-mutilation was largely a male behaviour: 'frustration, aggression and alcohol are the hallmarks of contemporary self-mutilation' (1985 : 31).

Self-mutilation in the Kimberley

Early in the research a number of repetitive self-mutilators were encountered, and conversations with them and other informants suggested that this was a phenomenon of the 1980s — 'cutters' were recognised but without being stigmatised. Four male and six female self-mutilators were later contacted and interviewed. Subsequently, questions regarding deliberate self-harm were incorporated into the QARK.

Clinical sample

While among the first group contacted most information was collected on the six women, certain sex differences were noted. The wounds of the females were generally restricted to spiral cuts of the non-dominant arm, often inflicted with broken glass. By contrast, males tended to involve the body widely and seriously, the torso of one (the partner of a cutter) being covered by a grid of scars. All were town oriented, with only one male employed. All of the females knew of peers who were cutters, and groups were subsequently contacted in which several members bore scars.

The six females, all of whom had begun self-mutilating in the 1980s, were aged between 19 and 31 years. Extensive medical histories were universal, with frequent hospital attendances, often for abdominal and pelvic complaints. All had been involved in violence, with serious assaults (murder or rape) having occurred in the families of three of these women. The fathers of all five for whom information was obtained had alcohol problems, and the partners of the three women in relationships were heavy drinkers, one having assaulted his partner and another with a history of repeated self-mutilation. Incidentally noted (a point that will be returned to later), three of these women were without children, having requested medical help for their infertility. One other woman had one child, but was subsequently unable to conceive, and the oldest woman in the group had only two children.

Random sample (QARK)

Within the QARK sample 22 males and 28 females admitted to having experienced impulses to self-mutilate, ranging in age from 16 to 63 years — only one being over 50 years old, and over three-quarters being less than 35 years of age. There were 14 males and

12 females aged between 18 and 46 years who reported having acted on those impulses, 81 per cent of those giving arrest histories, and 47 per cent having been in prison (compared to 60 per cent and 37 per cent respectively of the random sample less than 35 years of age). Similar proportions of ideators, self-mutilators and the general sample aged less than 35 years had been raised by their biological parents. However, the proportion of those relating that one or both parents had been a heavy drinker increased from 52 per cent of the sample less than 35 years old, to 62 per cent of those who had ever considered self-mutilation (including the mutilators), and to 73 per cent of those who had actually harmed themselves.

More symptoms of anxiety and depression were reported by sample subjects having previously had impulses, and by those who had acted on those impulses, than by those in the sample less than 35 years of age (table 10). While not statistically significant, the higher scores for ideators (which includes those who had actually self-mutilated) compared to those who acted on their impulses, suggests that self-mutilation may function to dissipate distressing emotions through acting out.

Table 10 *HSCL-25 anxiety and depression scores for 3 groups from the QARK*

| | | HSCL-25 scores | | | |
| | | Anxiety | | Depression | |
	N	mean	SD	mean	SD
A. Subjects less than 35 years of age	182	1.519	.523	1.454	.432
B. Ideators	50[a]	1.792**	.629	1.763***	.563
C. Self-mutilators	26	1.765	.66	1.737*	.576

Notes: *   p < .05 (compared to sample A)
      **   p < .01 (compared to sample A)
     *** p < .001 (compared to sample A)
      [a]   Ideators also includes Group C (those who self-mutilated).

Among the 50 ideators, 38 (76 per cent) were current or past drinkers, as were 24 of the 26 who had acted on their impulses (92 per cent).[2] Closer examination of alcohol consumption revealed that, while no relationship was demonstrated between drinking status and impulses to self-harm, a relationship was demonstrated between drinking status and the odds of acting upon such impulses: after adjustment for age and gender, constant drinkers were 13 times more likely to have engaged in self-mutilation than were abstainers. Among drinkers the only significant predictor of self-harmful impulses and acts, was (younger) age.

Self-mutilation in context

Ritual mutilation is a process of great antiquity; tooth avulsion has been found in Aboriginal skulls dated to 7000 BP (Flood 1983). There is no way of giving estimates for ritual self-mutilation, but it is likely that it is ancient. However, there are fundamental differences between such practices and contemporary self-mutilation. As noted by Favazza (1987), ritual practices are culturally sanctioned, reflecting the tradition, history and symbolism of society, and are woven into the fabric of social life. He contrasted this to the 'deviant' self-mutilation of the 'mentally ill', which is innovative, impulsive, idiosyncratic, and of no socially integrative consequence. However, he later suggested that culturally sanctioned and 'pathological' self-mutilation share similar purposes as they 'acknowledge disruptions within the individual and the social body, and provide mechanisms for the reestablishment of harmony and equilibrium' (1989 : 124).

In general clinical practice, self-mutilation is usually encountered in association with a limited set of psychiatric conditions. Historical factors reported by Favazza include: childhood sexual or physical abuse; violence at home, with prohibition of verbal expressions of anger; a hypercritical or absent father, or protective or dominant mother; loss of a parent; parental discord; a family history of mental illness (especially alcoholism); and a sense of abandonment and unlovability in childhood. According to Favazza, current factors include: alcohol and drug abuse; a restrictive environment; real or perceived rejection by others; and psychotic religious preoccupation. As with research on violent suicide, the neurotransmitter serotonin has received recent attention (Winchel & Stanley 1991). Imitation or 'contagion' among peer networks of clinical adolescent populations has been described by Walsh and Rosen, who suggested that it: 'is best understood as an interaction of individual psychopathology with dysfunctional relationships in a given social context' (1985 : 656).

The clustering of Aboriginal self-mutilation in certain groups (geographically and by age) suggests it may be meaningful as a subcultural communication. It must, thus, be considered in terms of the social forces affecting these groups within the Kimberley, and in relation to the other patterns of harmful behaviour. Just as there was often a history of interpersonal loss among the suicides, unstable and violent relationships, usually involving partners who are drinkers, were frequent among the self-mutilators.

Indeed, self-mutilation often occurs in conjunction with 'jealousing', a term used throughout the Kimberley to describe a relationship in which there is a conviction of the partner's infidelity. Brady (1992a) notes that 'jealous fights' are a common cause of violence in remote communities, and in discussing violence to women, Bolger suggests that such jealousy commonly reflects 'a guilty conscience on the part of the man' (1990 : 28). However, just as jealousy has long fascinated and horrified European observers, redefined variously between the poles of normalcy and pathology (Mullen 1991), 'jealousing' among Aboriginal groups is not new, existing well before Roheim (1974) described Aboriginal children at Hermannsburg imitating adults by playing at jealousy half a century ago. In present-day 'jealousing' there are repetitive accusations, intrusive behaviour, and persistent attempts to impose restrictions, such that the individual being 'jealoused' will identify himself or herself as 'a prisoner'. This involves both sexes and is common, occurring with and without alcohol. However, drinking clearly accentuates the process, the ensuing violence often involving others in the community.

Alcohol, thus, appears to be facilitatory rather than causal; while impulses to self-mutilation occur among drinkers and non-drinkers, those who act out those impulses are usually drinkers. However, alcohol is also involved indirectly, with self-mutilators frequently relating that their parents had been heavy drinkers. In the previous chapter it was demonstrated that such histories were also obtained for those young Aboriginal males who had committed suicide. Self-mutilation and suicide have, therefore, emerged as significant behavioural problems in the 1980s among a group of young adult Aborigines exposed to one of the consequences of social change in the last decade — the impact of alcohol on the family. In the Kimberley their generation is the first to have reached adulthood in environments in which parental heavy drinking is common. In such settings children's exposure to violence is often normative. In the next section intentional interpersonal violence will be discussed, and a historical model developed to provide an explanatory frame for violence generally.

INTENTIONAL PERSONAL VIOLENCE

The black woman's arms rise helplessly to protect her head as the blows rain down on her. It doesn't matter that tomorrow her man will hardly remember the reasons for the argument or the beating that followed. Today, inflamed by cheap grog, he is incensed enough to maim, rape, or even murder.

Margaret Harris *Sydney Morning Herald* Spectrum 16 February 1991, p. 37.

The half-page photograph accompanying the article to which this was the opening statement captured the described act with just enough precision to leave no questions about identity or intent. Rorschach-like, its shadows left room for projection and fantasy around the issue identified in bold type immediately below — 'BLACK VIOLENCE'. The subtitle — 'why whites shouldn't feel guilty' — was echoed in the abstract, which summarised the content to follow: 'Brutality is part of black culture, and it's time whites shed their guilt for Aboriginal violence'.

This article was about Aboriginal violence in the Kimberley. The argument, attributed to a Kimberley psychiatrist, proceeded from the premise that violence was a feature of traditional Aboriginal societies, to the conclusion that Aborigines must be allowed to take responsibility for their own problems, and that policies guided by guilt on the part of non-Aborigines are unhelpful. While neither proposition is unreasonable, the connecting reasoning certainly is: this suggested that, as violence was present before the arrival of Europeans, present-day violence is simply a continuation of pre-existing patterns. The possibility that Aboriginal experiences of colonisation and dispossession (white violence was not mentioned) may be an issue — the 'conventional view', or ' "white guilt" theory' — was mentioned to be dismissed. There is no possibility of avoiding the implicit conclusion that, as non-Aborigines are not responsible for 'Black violence', Aborigines are. This view does not acknowledge that Aboriginal violence is changing. To 'discover' violence in traditional society says little save that violence is a feature of all societies. Theories of Aboriginal violence must explain its manifestations and transformations, and take into account the relevant intervening social factors, central among which are Aboriginal-European relations.

At the time of Harris's article media coverage was in transition, its constructions shifting from Aborigines as 'victims', to 'criminals' — a point made by the Human Rights and Equal Opportunity Commission Enquiry into Racist Violence. This reflects broader attitudinal changes in which: 'the portrayal of Aboriginal people as a law and order problem, as a group to be feared, or as a group outside of assumed socially homogeneous values provides legitimacy for acts of racist violence' (1991 : 121). The sociohistorical paradigm that follows seeks to explain the changing form of Aboriginal violence by foregrounding the intercultural context.[3]

PRESENT-DAY ABORIGINAL VIOLENCE

As with alcohol use, Aboriginal violence received little systematic attention until the last five years. There have subsequently been many articles and reviews, including works in 1990 alone by Edmunds, Atkinson, Bolger, Brady (a), Lyon, Reser (b) and myself. While orientations differ, there is general agreement on certain issues.

Present-day Aboriginal violence is primarily directed at other Aborigines, with women being the most frequent victims[4], young men most commonly the assailants, and the precipitants often jealousy and arguments over food and money in the context of intoxication. The conjunction of heavy drinking and male violence towards women has led to suggestions that both represent assertions of male identity in an intercultural context in which they are relatively powerless, and an intracultural field of increasing marginalisation. In the opinion of Edmunds (1990) violence, vandalism and imprisonment have become subcultural identity and status referents in some remote communities. The association of alcohol and violence is so glaringly apparent as to invite simplistic causal ascriptions. Compelling as the connection is (not only among Aborigines), such analyses do little to clarify the association unless one assumes (unwisely) that alcohol *directly causes* violence. However, this ignores context and fails to explain the particular expressions of violence.

For the purpose of this discussion, violence refers to behaviour causing or intending to cause harm. By focusing on personal violence, the discussion is restricted to physical harm which may include as its object others, or the self. While this analysis proceeds primarily on a social level, the interrelatedness of forces on social, interpersonal and personal psychological levels is recognised. Indeed, it is the ultimate consequences of historically located social forces for child development and the construction of identity that is central. In summarising the cross-cultural psychology literature on aggression, Goldstein and Segall emphasised the importance of this issue:

> An overwhelming impression . . . is that child-rearing antecedents must loom large in any framework that attempts to explain human aggressive behaviour. It cannot be understood except as a complex product of the experiences that human beings have while growing up, wherever in the world they happen to be born. (1983 : 475)

ABORIGINAL PERSONAL VIOLENCE: A PARADIGM

In table 11 the changing patterns of violence in the Kimberley are placed in an intercultural and sociohistorical context. The phases do not represent discrete historical periods, dates indicating how recently the dynamics characterising that stage persisted in *some* areas. Clearly, the chronology will not necessarily be relevant elsewhere. Furthermore, elements of early stages persist, the paradigm in this sense being synchronic rather than defining historical events.

Table 11 *Aboriginal personal violence in the Kimberley: an intercultural/sociological paradigm*

Period	Form of violence	Interpretation by whites	Role of whites	Structure of violence
presettlement up to 1860s *ca.*	ritualised	savagery	speculator	structured B ↔ B
'pacification' up to 1920s *ca.*	frontier	treachery	instigator	structured W → B
'pastoral' quiet up to 1950s *ca.*	suppressed	innocence/ 'happiness'	'protector'	covertly structured W → B
reaching out up to 1980s *ca.*	intracultural 'appealing'	inherent 'weakness'	spectator	unstructured B ↔ B
breaking out from 1980s *ca.*	1. normative	deviance	moraliser	unstructured B ↔ B
	2. intercultural 'coercive'	defiance	reactionary	unstructured B ↔ W

Note: B = Black; W = White.

Presettlement

Aboriginal dispossession relied on the exercise of European power through the calculated use of force. Explorers and settlers anticipated and not infrequently provoked intercultural conflict. They brought with them preconceptions of primitive savagery and treachery to support their violence. Thus, while early observations on the 'ways of the natives' are numerous, they are hardly objective. However, the role of violence in pre-contact societies is an important issue. While it was suggested in Harris's article on 'Black Violence' that little information was available, this is not the case.

Information from three sources exists: the paleopathology of skeletal remains, the observations of early ethnographers, and the refracted vision of the past available through cultural artefacts such as pre-contact Aboriginal rock art. While such material is open to a wide range of interpretation, the depiction of interpersonal violence is not, in my experience, a conspicuous theme. With respect to the paleopathology, Prokopec, discussing studies of the remains discovered at Roonka Flat in 1969, stated that the evidence of traumatic changes 'shows that the way of life in the hunter-gatherer society was a tough and dangerous one; this is also seen from the mean span of life' (1979:21). Skull and forearm fractures in these ancient remains is suggestive of interpersonal violence rather than the environmental risks of a hunter-gatherer existence. Brady (1990a) has identified similar patterns of injuries among Aboriginal women in a contemporary alcohol-affected remote setting.

Numerous early ethnographers — including Spencer and Gillen (1968 [1899]) and Strehlow (1970) from central Australia, and, in particular, Lloyd Warner (1969 [1937]) from Arnhem Land — described ritual executions and deaths from 'warfare' (which Warner linked to the sexual economics of polygyny). Examining economic activities of traditional Aborigines, Rose (1987) discussed violence, raising some questions about Warner's interpretations, but supporting the considerable scale of homicide. He emphasised that such killings usually resulted from conflict between, rather than within, local groups, once again related to the control of women as an economic resource.

In succeeding periods such activities were suppressed by religious and government agents. However, ritual killings continued, and concern about them remains among tradition-oriented Aborigines.

While pre-contact life may have been short, and violence not uncommon, such violence was contained and structured. There also existed alternative ceremonial means to conflict resolution (Peterson 1970). While violence was, thus, meaningful and consistent with social cohesion, for the early Europeans it was simply 'savage barbarity' (Tench 1979 [1793]; this from a First Fleet officer of Marines involved in supervising the inhuman treatment of fellow Europeans).

Pacification

The bloodshed accompanying the European expansion into Aboriginal Australia has, until recently, been more evident on the map than the historical record. At Cape Grim in Tasmania, 'Mount Victory' overlooks one of Australia's numerous massacre sites which, as Mulvaney noted, signified 'a victory for terrorism and a Pyrrhic victory for European colonists' (1989 : 52). Battle Mountain, Skull Creek, Nigger Creek, Murdering Creek — each tells of Aboriginal worlds violently torn apart. For Aborigines, the unpredictable violence of the frontier meant that 'survival was to be found either far away from Whites, in the inhospitable lands of the desert, or in the immediate and continuing proximity to Whites, in the settlement' (Kolig 1978 : 66). As an enduring signifier, Aboriginal rock-art of the frontier clearly shows rifles and pistols in the rendering of whites, and McKelson (1979) noted that, borrowing from English, the Garadyari (of the southern Kimberley) word for 'gun was *dyilaman*, meaning "kill a man", a tragic linguistic relic from the past' (1979 : 215). While 'quiet' had descended much earlier in south-east Australia (and near silence in Tasmania), the reality of frontier violence continued in remote Australia well into the twentieth century, with Reynolds (1982) estimating that some 10 000 Aborigines were killed in frontier skirmishes between the 1860s and 1930s in northern Australia. The 1926 'Onmalmeri massacre' in the Kimberley, which precipitated the Wood Royal Commission, is located at this level; it also reflects the collusion of pastoralists and police, and the hopelessly compromised role of the latter as 'honorary protectors'.

Pastoral quiet

Aborigines accommodated, adjusted and adapted — survival demanding acquiescence to the overt demands of Europeans. When 'pacification' had been completed, 'civilising' began. The law of the gun was supplemented by legislation enacted successively by all States for the 'protection' of Aborigines. Throughout the north, be it on missions or stations, a period of 'pastoral' quiet ensued. Especially on missions, less so on stations, attempts were made to minimise the role of Aboriginal custom and language. Traditional patterns of conflict resolution and punishment were, for the priests and pastoralists, both onerous and threatening, their suppression compromising the existing Aboriginal social structures. Nevertheless, traditional practices continued, often covertly.

The suppression of such activities and the system to which they belonged relied on authoritarian controls affecting every aspect of Aboriginal life. The isolation of Aborigines in remote Australia was matched by the segregation of those living in closer proximity to European centres, who were induced to live in settlements, concentrating groups and tensions. Infringements of tribal law still demanded a response, but were ill-recognised by non-Aborigines, and were incapable of being addressed by the conventional legal system. As a consequence, when the pressure for response became critical and conflict erupted, the ensuing violence was frequently less structured or contained by the system of which it had previously been an integral part. This is exemplified by a report from the Western Desert area of Western Australia (Jones 1971). In the late 1960s it was noted that, where still practised, traditional thigh spearing infrequently led to severe wounding, as the process conformed to a mutually understood and accepted pattern. However:

> in an area where spearing is proscribed (Jigalong) an aberrant type of spearing is seen, suggesting that a rather delicate balance between an aggressive drive and its controlled release exists, and that when attempts are made to prevent traditional spearing a new type of dangerous, unstereotyped spearing occurs, which is more damaging to the group as a whole. (1971 : 264)

Thus, the precipitants of conflict remained and the consequences, when rupturing through the imposed prohibitions, were less likely to be structured and, thus, more frequently hazardous. During this period behaviour that challenged non-Aboriginal authority was of necessity uncommon, and was promptly responded to with measures unique to the treatment of Aborigines. Out of sight of the majority of Australians, restrained and restricted by draconian legislation, Aborigines were conveniently silent — eclipsed from history and the white Australian consciousness. Stanner (1979) referred to this era as the 'Great Australian Silence'. Most Europeans were confronted by sanitised depictions of 'Our Aborigines'.[5] Submission necessitated by survival became confused with passivity; acquiescence with contentment; obedience with respect.

Regardless, a latent disposition to savagery remained suspect. The conflicted European attitudes were reflected in the appeal of the boxing troupe, which, thinly disguised as sport, regularly drew large crowds. Drum and bell pierced the festive chaos, drawing attention to the 'stable' paraded before faded depictions of past 'heroes'. Aboriginal boxers were a predictable attraction at such macabre festivals of violence and racism. If the blackfellow should lose, it satisfied aggressive white impulses; if he should win, it confirmed suspected innate violent propensities. In the heavily sweat-ridden and beer-laden tent air, white crowds could also indulge themselves in the spectacle of two 'darkies' doing violence to each other in the name of entertainment.

However, boxing also allowed some Aborigines a degree (usually fleeting) of social mobility. Aborigines, as gladiators and entertainers, were given temporary reprieve from some of the controls over their lives. Tatz (1987) has documented the disproportionate representation of Aborigines among Australian title-winners, and noted the pride and motivation that these fighters provided for other Aborigines. To so succeed was not without cost: some Aborigines, respected and acclaimed while winners, were persecuted and abandoned after their inevitable fall. During this period overt Aboriginal violence was, thus, suppressed and given vent in narrow white-controlled avenues that served to reinforce suspicions of latent racial characteristics.

Reaching out

The political pressures culminating in the 1967 Referendum were followed by decades of unprecedented social change on a national level, with Aborigines of remote Australia experiencing the greatest relative transformations. In the Kimberley, Aborigines were precipitated into a town-oriented, welfare-dependent cash economy, with unrestricted access to alcohol. The preceding chapters have demonstrated that here began a sustained rise in the proportion of Kimberley Aborigines dying of external causes. The early pattern suggested alcohol-affected behaviour, with males increasingly vulnerable to the consequences of their own disinhibited and reckless behaviour, and females more frequently the victims of others' behaviour (possibly themselves alcohol-affected). The increase in male suicide in the 1980s occurred concurrently with the emergence of self-mutilation and a further increase in female homicide.

Thus, as the pastoral quiet receded, patterns of intentional harm, to others and to the self, became prominent, with three common features. First, alcohol is frequently associated. Second, intended violence (as opposed to accidents) appears to be usually male-initiated, and directed at the two major relational objects — self and partner. Third, the violence is almost entirely confined to the intracultural domain. That alcohol is not a sole causal factor is again clear. Aborigines had been drinking and becoming drunk in Australia since Baneelon (Benelong) was introduced to alcohol (Tench 1979 [1793]). However, earlier Aboriginal alcohol use was structured by legislation and its summary enforcement, and the restrictions of limited resources. By contrast, patterns of consumption that developed from the 1970s are not similarly constrained.

During this period Europeans were increasingly intolerant of Aboriginal aggression, as were many older Aborigines who had been required for decades to suppress such impulses. Among younger Aborigines, frustrations were compounded by the sudden arrival of information about the wider society, from which their continuing exclusion was evident. The drunken state resolved this bind; the intercultural and intracultural injunctions of sober behaviour were replaced by expectations of a drunken role that allowed behaviour otherwise prohibited: 'in many Aboriginal contexts the social expectations for "being drunk" is that you will become angry and possibly violent' (Reser 1989a : 19). In addition to such subcultural expectations, individual responsibility for otherwise unacceptable behaviour while intoxicated is diminished. 'Deviance disavowal' (Collins 1988) deflects blame, which is then ascribed to drinking itself, as suggested by Sackett's (1988) observations in Wiluna:

> Drunks, in marked contrast to their sober fellows, are said to 'look for trouble' and 'always have to have a fight'. That drunken people often do just this proves that they are 'away'. It also means their transgressions are explained and received as being completely involuntary and, consequently, non-culpable. (1988 : 70)

As MacAndrew and Edgerton noted of 'drunken comportment', during inebriation there may be a suspension of responsibility for an individual's action as he is 'removed from the accountability nexus in which he normally operates' (1969 : 90). Brady (1992b) has suggested that this 'removal' may be consciously sought as a 'deliberate enabling mechanism' allowing violent behaviour. In this sense of 'time out', Marshall suggested that alcohol acts as 'an enabler or a facilitator of certain culturally given inebriate states' (1983 : 200), which in the Aboriginal context owes much to their experience of drunken Europeans.

The dichotomisation of drinking and dry behaviour has become more clearly defined with the development of outstations and communities where alcohol is (theoretically) banned, and excessive behaviour frowned on. This is in contrast to town settings and certain well known drinking communities where drinking and drunkenness are, if not accepted, tolerated. Vulnerability in these settings is compounded by the disinhibition of those constrained from such behaviour in more remote areas, who come to town to drink, and be drunk. In an examination of alcohol, violence and power on Palm Island (Queensland), Barber, Punt and Albers (1988) proposed that alcohol functions, particularly for men, to provide a sense of personal empowerment. For Aboriginal males, contemporary experiences of powerlessness are most sharply defined in the intercultural context and reinforced by the asymmetry of intercultural sexual relations.

The objects of male violence, self and partner, suggest the importance of power relations. In traditional society power devolved onto two interrelated arenas: the economic and the sacred (Mol 1982). While women provided the greater portion of regular sustenance in traditional societies, the control of the economic domain rested with men, articulated through the control of women as a vital economic resource (Rose 1987). Likewise, although women certainly had their own rituals and sacred life, the Law, as defining and regulating the daily pulse of life, was controlled by initiated men. Indeed, Laughlin and Brady (1978) suggested that ritual may be conceptualised as a power resource.

The permanent presence of Europeans massively disrupted the existing power relations, devaluing and undermining the centrality of ritual. Dislocation from traditional lands and activities denied older men access to the source of their sacred power, at times disrupting the process of transmitting those aspects of culture to younger generations. Discouragement or prohibition of traditional patterns of partner choice restricted older men's access to young women and further compromised their power (Burbank 1988).

The traditional economic domain in the Kimberley was transformed on missions and stations. The institutional dependency engendered by the missions' paternalistic policies was incompatible with autonomy. As the traditional means of production and the objects of desire changed, Aboriginal autonomy was further undermined

> The missionary short-circuits the cultural process that gives an Aborigine status and power in traditional society. The reality of missionaries' status and power is their control over the economic goods Aborigines need (food, tobacco, alcohol, access to social security benefits), their ownership of lands (chiefly in the form of government grants) and their ability to call on police support. (Alroe 1988 : 39)

Aboriginal males' expertise in the pastoral industry ensured that they remained the central economic figures in that Aboriginal domestic arena (in spite of the women's access to the homestead). For Aborigines on both missions and stations, the changes since the 1960s have resulted in a further shift from institutional dependency to welfare dependency, entrenching the male loss of power. Further destabilisation occurred as many Aboriginal males were forced from important roles on stations. From the 1960s, as women with children and pensioners gained access to the welfare resources of the wider society, they emerged as the largest per capita recipients of predictable resources in remote Aboriginal Australia. Indeed, as demonstrated by the QARK, throughout their lifespans Kimberley Aboriginal women are in receipt of more money than men.

For most young men, regardless of talent or education, economic options remain limited. By contrast, pregnancy may be protective for young Aboriginal females (the fertility rate for Western Australian Aborigines aged 15–19 in 1987 was eight-and-a-half times greater than for non-Aborigines [Gee, Webb & Holman 1989]) — a point made by Brady (1992a) in relation to drug use and associated behaviour. Such protection may be afforded by the access it provides to the economic resources of maternal benefits, and through an ego-ideal valued by the majority culture — motherhood.

Fertility also provides an insight into an earlier mentioned feature of self-mutilation. In contrast to suicide, women are at least equally represented among self-mutilators. However, among the first group of self-mutilators encountered — an observation supported by subsequent meetings — childlessness or infertility was a recurrent concern. While a child is of paramount importance to an Aboriginal woman's sense of self and self-esteem, the intrapsychic conflicts associated with infertility are compounded by significant financial disadvantages and the corollary social implications. For some men, the relative security of regular and non-contingent income requires controlling the assets of a woman. As it exists, the system frequently not only entrenches dependency but creates an asymmetry of resources that predisposes to conflict. These circumstances serve to undermine male avenues to self-esteem, and encourages hostile dependent relationships (indeed, double dependence, on the welfare bureaucracy and frequently on Aboriginal women). Such is the apparent reversal to the distribution of power traditionally, or in white society even, that Roberta Sykes observed:

> White women struggle to reach the place and gain the benefits of the power and position of white men. However, I do not know of any Black woman who aspires to be in the place of the Black man. (1989 : 16)

Why was violence directed primarily against other Aborigines? Brody introduced the term 'cultural exclusion' to describe the functional exclusion of politically, racially and socio-economically disadvantaged groups from the ideals and resources of their respective disempowering groups through restrictions on their access to the means to achieving those ends. This may occur despite the renunciation of discrimination by the dominant group, and is accentuated by 'the unprecedented transmission of information and desires by pictorial and auditory means to semi-literate peoples without the techniques for satisfying their newly acquired wishes' (1966 : 852). The dominant group controls both the avenues to political communication and negotiation (literacy, education, political and professional access, etc.) and the prevailing value systems. Excluded individuals are defined in terms of deficits and weaknesses, their actions 'described by the dominant system as characterological inadequacy or defective impulse control: they are formulated conventionally in terms of a value judgement' (1966 : 855). That which excludes one, one's very identity (in this case Aboriginality) may be denied — or attacked. Paradoxically, where there is extended the possibility of conditional access, exclusion may have the greatest impact:

> from the self esteem view-point, the effect of dissonant cultural context may be even more insidious than that of direct prejudice. The reason is that if others attack us directly, it is possible to mobilize our

psychological defences — to conclude that the other is stupid, bigoted, and ignorant, to counter-attack with our own epithets, and so on. If on the other hand, we accept and internalize the general standards and values of the dissonant context then we come to despise ourselves — to believe that we are strange and different, that we are inept at the skills and talents valued in the new environment, that we are ignorant of the things that count. This kind of attack is particularly devastating, for it is an attack from within. (Rosenberg 1979 : 113)

Dudgeon and Oxenham (1988) identified these processes among Aborigines who internalise the negative expectations and assumptions of the dominant culture. The intercultural construction of inadequacy is compounded by failing role models and family instability. In the Aboriginal communities of the Kimberley where heavy drinking is common, households may be constantly in flux. In such 'concertina households' Sansom contrasted 'enduring ties between mothers and their children . . . with what might be called "contingent fatherhood"' (1982 : 125). In these increasingly matri-centric and matrifocal family structures the impact of paternal unavailability is most detrimental for the development of boys (Nurcombe 1976). Likewise, boys appear most vulnerable in settings of prolonged instability and discord, where self-esteem and self-efficacy are compromised. The resulting role-uncertainties for young males support the development of negative self-evaluations and conflicted relationships to women, the nexus of intracultural aggression — toward self and partner.

Aborigines of remote Australia remained largely unaware through the 1970s of the international movements against racial discrimination involving civil disobedience and violence, and were further restricted in collective action by their local-group orientation. Nevertheless, as Aborigines became capable of confronting their unequal status — which included the history of drastic and summary 'justice', without retribution — resistance emerged. Reactance theory, invoked by Reser (1989b) in the context of Aboriginal deaths in custody, offers insights into the forms of Aboriginal resistance. According to this hypothesis, resistance is motivated by both actual or threatened loss of freedom, or conditions of high dependency, unless control is lost entirely, as was the case previously for Aborigines, at which time helplessness ensues (Brehm & Brehm 1981). In the face of overwhelming social power, reactance results in the indirect expression of resistance.

With the gradual relaxation of controls over Aborigines in remote regions, 'unacceptable' behaviour, often involving alcohol, became a means for rejecting white expectations and resisting bureaucratic demands, a 'handy recusancy tool' (Sackett 1988 : 75). Vandalism and 'delinquency', while frequently destroying 'community' property, was directed at the broader system generating dependency and 'ambiguity'. Indeed, as Tatz noted early in the 1970s, the pervasive ambiguity of Aboriginal life may appear as a syndrome: 'first, a feeling of *frustration*; then a sense of *alienation* from society, or of not belonging, of foreignness; then *withdrawal* from that society, no longer caring about membership, a separation from that world; then *violence*' (1979 : 94).

The intracultural containment of interpersonal violence may be construed, not only as a consequence of these social factors, but also as a message termed by Marx 'appealing violence'. This is resorted to when someone has: 'reached the end of his tether, and feels unable to achieve a social aim unaided by others. It is a cry for help' (1976 : 2). Such an appeal is made where there is a high degree of dependence, and when other avenues are exhausted or unavailable. In Australia non-Aborigines remained spectators, detached from Aboriginal violence to other Aborigines. Rather than responding to this violence as a message and appeal, the institutional response was initially a retreat to avoid accusations of authoritarianism or paternalism. This has accentuated the issue; it is a confusion of authoritarianism with structure, which (I argue), is needed by every human to ensure predictability and safety. Consequently, moralistic denunciations have subsequently been accompanied by calls for a return to the previous 'harmony' of authoritarian controls and a further withdrawal of services and support that, under the thin veil of self-determination and self-help is, in essence, punitive.

> Whites, through accepting such acts as Aborigines screaming obscenities, sleeping on the footpath, fighting, etc., as products of diminished responsibility, are able to write them off as mindless rather than appreciate them as meaningful. Indeed, by defining drunken deeds in and of themselves as problematic Whites establish the conditions and justifications for further intervention: for more advisers, more police and harsher corrective measures. (Sackett 1988 : 76)

Breaking out

The changing mortality patterns of the 1970s were but one manifestation of destabilising change affecting an unprepared population.

Young adult and adolescent Aborigines of today grew up in that environment. It is among this group that self-violence is most prominent. Their parents represented a watershed. They were the generation exposed to the 'bran nue dae' as young adults, and were the first generation to be able to drink at the legal drinking age. Their parents did not have free access to alcohol until well into adult life, and their children are the first generation to have grown up with widespread parental drinking.

Aboriginal children in such environments are more likely to experience the behavioural concomitants of heavy drinking, including violence. Discussing 'wife beating', Kahn (Kahn & The Behavioural Health Team: 1980) presented data collected by Aboriginal health workers, who reported that this was an almost universal occurrence in the Queensland community under study, usually associated with male drinking and not considered unusual. While directly involving a minority, these 'domestic' disputes engage community attention. The acceptance of such violence is conveyed to children, reflected in an uncommented-on vignette from a study of alcohol and power:

> On one occasion we were drinking with a group of Palm Islanders when a distraught child burst into the room to tell her mother that her sister was being beaten by her man outside the [beer] canteen. The mother's reaction was to calm the child down and reassure her that this sort of thing was bound to happen from time to time. (Barber, Punt & Albers 1988 : 99)

In this last period, heavy drinking and violence (particularly to women) have become normative experiences in the lifescape of many young Aborigines living in remote Aboriginal Australia. However, remote Australia is no longer isolated Australia, with communications and mobility dramatically increasing the transmission of information (including issues affecting Aborigines) to Aboriginal communities nationwide. The development of a *national* consciousness for Aborigines, focused in urban Australia, gained particular momentum during the 1970s. With the growing recognition of solidarity between Aboriginal groups on certain issues, Aborigines have recognised that they may exert pressure to change the manifest inequalities of status and opportunity. Aboriginality has evolved from a static construction emphasising persistence, to Aboriginality as resistance (Keeffe 1988). The sophistication of Aboriginal initiatives for social change is determined by those factors (education, experience, funding) previously withheld from Aborigines — factors which remain functionally unavailable for most Aborigines of remote Australia. In these areas many young adults were raised in environments of normative violence. They are now exploring their newfound capacity to make demands of, and confront non-Aborigines without necessarily precipitating harsh retribution. Thus, the potential for a level of violence involving non-Aborigines.

In addition to identifying 'appealing violence', Marx defined 'coercive violence', in which an individual uses violence 'rationally and in a premeditated and controlled manner, as an extreme but often effective means towards achieving a social objective' (1976:2). In contrast to appealing and normative violence, this other form of violence ruptures the intracultural containment that had earlier characterised Aboriginal violence. So long as the victims were Aborigines, whites interpreted appealing and normative violence in terms of inherent deficit, and maintained a detached or moralistic stance. However, the subsequent direct involvement in this violence of whites (although largely restricted to violence against their property) has resulted in their stance becoming increasingly reactionary.

To exemplify this process, an Aboriginal community that in a short period has experienced all the aforementioned dynamics will be described. Although isolated, their experiences are firmly located in the intercultural context of Aborigines throughout remote Australia. In a short space of time these young adult males have gone from being identified as 'mission boys' to defining themselves as 'warriors'; from evoking benevolent platitudes, to focusing reactionary rhetoric.

'MISSION BOYS' AND 'WARRIORS'

Balgo is home to some 400 Aborigines. On the edge of the Great Sandy Desert, it is over 300 kilometres from the nearest town, Halls Creek. Balgo Hills had been founded as a Catholic mission in 1939, concentrating Gugadja (Kukatja) speakers from the desert to the south and east. It was run under strict and, by most accounts, authoritarian control until the 1970s. 'Un-Christian' impulses, such as aggression, were suppressed. The people of this isolated settlement were, and remain, tradition-oriented. The mission also attracted Aborigines from other groups, such as the Walbiri from across the Northern Territory border. Gugadja (Kukatja) traditional life, including relations with the Walbiri, appears to have been interspersed with confrontation and violence (Meggitt 1962) and, certainly, the mission did little to alter the underlying tensions.

The 1970s brought increasing pressure on the mission to relinquish its authority to the Department of Aboriginal Affairs (DAA), control being handed over in 1983. As the community was entering the welfare system, there was a withdrawal of occupational and other structures that had previously been rigidly enforced. Little was provided to redress the vacuum. Alcohol became available, and binge drinking increased despite the difficulties, dangers and costs of long journeys on dirt roads to Halls Creek or Rabbit Flat. Visiting the community in the 1970s, Jones (1977) encountered conflict that he related to the pressures of population density, sexual and marital problems, inactivity, and personality/psychiatric factors, specifically alcohol. Trying to curb violence among younger men, elders had attempted to impose sanctions, including confinement. Regardless, binge drinking continued, and 'aimless' vandalism spread. Despite the influx of government money, there was little improvement in living standards, with persistent squalid camp conditions. Much money was diverted back to non-Aboriginal hands, with one community adviser convicted of fraud. The DAA refrained from attempts to provide structure, perhaps as it may have been interpreted as a return to 'mission-like' paternalism.

Whites increasingly developed a siege mentality. When I first arrived in 1987, an administrator's house was surrounded by high wire fences, inside which prowled a German Shepherd dog. Bars across the windows testified to the need for 'protection', and I was regaled with stories of attacks on the office with spears and boomerangs. The imminent danger suggested by discussions with several of the non-Aboriginal government workers was supplemented by allusions to an Aboriginal cache of weapons in the desert. As bizarre as this scenario would appear, I was to hear it several times in different settings across the Kimberley.

At that time the community was receiving Community Development and Employment Program (CDEP) funding in lieu of social security. It was the responsibility of the community to arrange payment and to supervise work. Men were paid $4 an hour for working, and women $2 per hour. However, all women with children were independently provided with supporting-parent benefits and, in addition, each Tuesday received $72, called locally 'Tuesday money'. Pensioners were also paid separately. At the bottom of the economic ladder were childless women, who missed out on supporting-parent benefits and 'Tuesday money', and received only half the CDEP rate of pay as men. Poverty in this harsh environment was, thus, compounded by a system taking little account of either the nature or meaning of work, or the tensions resulting from the economic asymmetries inherent in the system.

In April of 1988 the Health Department withdrew its personnel following a series of break-ins and vandalism of the new clinic, destruction of clinic vehicles, and fears that the milk had been 'poisoned'. The staff subsequently returned, but by Christmas they were once again withdrawn. Unfortunately, an outbreak of meningitis in the Northern Territory spread to Balgo, and it was instructive to find, on arriving at the community, that the only person providing medical care was an elderly nun. At this point the community had also been deserted by the Department of Aboriginal Affairs because of similar fears and the destruction of their office; it had withdrawn the administration of Balgo to Kununurra, some 600 kilometres distant, and limited contact to a weekly delivery of money. Violence and vandalism in the community continued. The reactions of the bureaucracies had been, in essence, punitive.

About this time a truck driver, who had parked his beer-laden rig at the local hotel in Halls Creek, emerged to find Aborigines attempting to lighten the load. His response was to produce a rifle from the cab, following which Aborigines 'attacked' the pub and the police station. It is telling that these two institutions were the focus of Aboriginal violence, as they have been elsewhere, in Western Australia including Laverton, Wiluna and Geraldton. The media labelled the disturbance a 'riot', and Aborigines from Balgo were identified. The feeling among whites of the Kimberley may be gauged by the 19 December edition of the *Kimberley Echo* (from Kununurra, all page 1). Under banner headlines proclaiming 'HALLS CREEK A TOWN OF FEAR' and beside a photograph of a bloodied policeman, the story opened:

Blacks from Balgo Hills Mission Station, approximately 300 kms south of Halls Creek, having forced all administrative staff off, have turned their attention to the township. On 'sit-down' money pay days, Halls Creek residents, including aborigines, live in fear of the groups of drunken desert blacks who roam the town and frequent the local hotel.

Brief mention of the 'riot' was supplemented by descriptions of past Aboriginal violence. The next article, under the heading 'Good Samaritans Bashed', related the experience of a young couple who, while apparently trying to render assistance to an injured Aborigine, were 'recently attacked by a car load of aboriginals on the Tanami Road near Halls Creek' (in fact, their car had hit this man in the first place). The general feeling was captured in the letter to the Editor (p. 4) of M E Scott, of Broome, who wrote:

> Sir,
> How much longer will the Police force allow themselves to be the targets of systematic bashings by gangs of blacks? These bashings are obviously a well orchestrated assault on the police. It's time our guardians of the law adopted South African tactics and started using dogs and riot guns. That would put a stop to this ridiculous situation.

Arriving at Balgo shortly after, I noticed new graffiti. Children had been painting 'WARRIORS' on walls about the settlement. Clearly, being identified as violent, as 'bad blackfellows', was a greater source of esteem than the void that had preceded it. At each point when the stakes were increased, as the community flailed about seeking limits to define an internal structure, the response of the various bureaucracies was to back off. In the absence of permanent medical staff the Health Department subsequently began flying nurses in daily from Halls Creek and advertised for the running of the clinic to be contracted out. The Department of Aboriginal Affairs remained absent for much of 1989, and negotiations were entered into to ensure a permanent police presence in the community. Thus, after nearly a decade of retreating, covert punitive abandonment was followed by a call for a return to authoritarian controls. In 1990 the continuing medical services were finally contracted — to the Sisters of Mercy. *Plus ça change, plus c'est la même chose.*

CONVERGENCES

On 25 September 1988, a young Aboriginal male, Dennis Dumbiri Rostron, shot and killed his de facto wife, father-in-law, mother-in-law, and his two children at remote Mulgawo outstation near the Liverpool River in Arnhem Land. The shootings occurred in the area of Australia least intruded into by non-Aborigines, 'Aboriginal land', where tradition remains highly valued. Alcohol played no direct part in this tragedy. Attempting to understand these events, survivors searched for traditional explanations, reaching back to events of past decades. As noted by a relative of the deceased:

> Date back long time now. That mob, he killed this person long ago and that's why they pay $500 to kill us mob — but they got our uncle. Our uncle maybe got shot because of $500. We want that $500 to come back and break it into half to buy some tucker and ceremony. If the $500 still away, could be that someone gonna get shot or get killed. . . . We want bundle of spears to pay us because of what happened at Mulgawo, and *maraian* ceremony, and we want some female to be paid [to us]. And if not, we'll carry on and kill them. We just don't go and shoot them like he did. We do it secret way. Someone will do it for us. If it is paid, that's enough.
>
> (*Sydney Morning Herald* 'Good Weekend' 4 February 1989 : 33)

It might be suggested that this violence is independent of the intercultural variables elaborated above. However, it is as firmly located in an intercultural context as the brutal murder of a Florida woman by an adopted-away Aborigine, who was abandoned as an adolescent in the United States and subsequently sentenced to death. While the circumstances and crimes seem worlds apart, there is more in common than the killing of a woman by a young adult Aboriginal male. James Savage was torn from his culture at an early age; Dennis Rostron was required to pursue a shadow of a 'traditional life' on a white-designated remote Aboriginal reserve. Both experiences reflected the legacy of white legislation and the asymmetry of intercultural power that functionally limited their ability to negotiate their grievances (indeed, perhaps even to conceive them) with the majority culture. Their issues are Aboriginal issues, cutting across designations of traditionality, descent, and region. Both in their own way were statements of hopelessness, helplessness, despair — and rage.

It is, as previously observed, among the most disadvantaged and powerless that these phenomena, violence to others and to the self, are increasing — among unemployed heavy-drinking males, and similarly vulnerable, childless women living at the periphery of the dominant culture. They are members of the first generation to grow up in communities with widespread drinking and welfare dependence. The conflicts over resources occur in an environment that is increasingly dangerous, particularly for Aboriginal women. One hypothetical explanation for the concurrent increase in male violence to women and to themselves is that, in this male subgroup, both behaviours are responses to perceived powerlessness:

> In these post-traditional communities the status of women increased whilst that of men declined. It is therefore not surprising, today, to find Aboriginal women in positions of dominance in the family and leadership in the community. By contrast many Aboriginal men have lost both their status and their self-respect. The path now followed by so many of the men, from hotel to gaol, is but an inevitable consequence of their loss of status and purpose in society. (Gale 1978 : 2)

In this statement Gale juxtaposes the disempowerment of men relative to women, with a corollary decline in their position and status in society as a whole. Intracultural and intercultural contexts are inextricably linked, and tied to the experience of Aborigines as a colonised people. A similar dynamic, though in a vastly different setting, is discussed by Nandy; in examining the psychology of colonialism in India, he pointed to a homology between the sexual and political dominance of Western colonising powers. As a legitimisation of dominance and exploitation: 'it produced a cultural consensus in which political and socioeconomic dominance symbolised the dominance of men and masculinity over women and femininity' (1983 : 4). In such a setting, for the victims — the colonised, the male subjects — their position was: 'a product of one's own emasculation and defeat in legitimate power politics' (1983 : 10).

The denial of masculinity within a subjugated population is relevant to this discussion. John Newfong commented on the character Sweet William's attempts to break free from the 'black matriarchy' which had contributed to his powerlessness, in Robert Merritt's play *The Cake Man*:

> When one society is dominated by another society and the dominating matrix of society is male-dominated, the men of the *dominated* society will be emasculated. And it's almost a subconscious thing, you see. You notice that in *The Cake Man* the mission superintendent and inspector . . . defer to Ruby — this is to further undermine William's standing, simply by not addressing themselves to him. And this is what is always done. (in Shoemaker 1989 : 243)

Aboriginal violence is a statement of the compromised position of men in their communities, and their powerlessness as Aborigines in contemporary Australia. Male attacks on women and themselves reflect the consequent profound deficits in self-esteem. The restricted means to redressing the intercultural power asymmetry (cultural exclusion) supports the ultimate intracultural expression of this conflict through violence, be it directed against the self or significant others.

Thus, while there is little similarity between traditional rites and contemporary non-traditional self-mutilation, they are related — through power. The former was a cooperative process of social integration and empowerment, necessitating the coordinated participation of socially powerful initiated elders. By contrast, contemporary self-mutilation occurs among a subgroup poorly integrated into a minority culture, itself functionally excluded from the mainstream of Australian society. Violence is the idiom of this exclusion. Indeed, as demonstrated by the vignette opening this chapter, the object of violence may, to a certain extent, be chosen arbitrarily. The enraged young man in question gouged his abdomen with a broken flagon, and then immediately attempted to strike his girlfriend's face. It could as easily have been reversed. The conjunction and confusion of violence to self and partner points not only to a period of significance developmentally — early childhood — but to the self and other as signifiers of powerlessness: the self, that which identifies one's excluded and emasculated status; the significant other, reinforcing the post-colonial inversion in the Aboriginal dynamics of power. Aboriginal male violence towards women, thus, represents a displacement of rage from the perceived oppression of a dominant and excluding culture, to the perceived beneficiaries intraculturally, encouraged and enabled by alcohol's brief, illusory empowerment.

While suicide, self-mutilation and interpersonal violence have emerged only in the last decade, they occur in parallel to other increases including deaths from external causes generally and, by extension from the QARK sample, the proportion of drinkers in the population and of families with parental heavy drinking. For both of these latter their point of departure from earlier steady levels is that period of social change that extended from the 1960s to the 1970s. Note was earlier made of Rubinstein's analysis (1987) of Micronesian suicide, which posited a cohort effect, with the vulnerable subgroup being those belonging to the birth cohort spanning a period of unprecedented and unplanned change. A similar analysis may be used to integrate the changing patterns among Kimberley Aborigines (figure 7.1).

Figure 7.1 *Hypothetical cohort effect among Kimberley Aborigines*

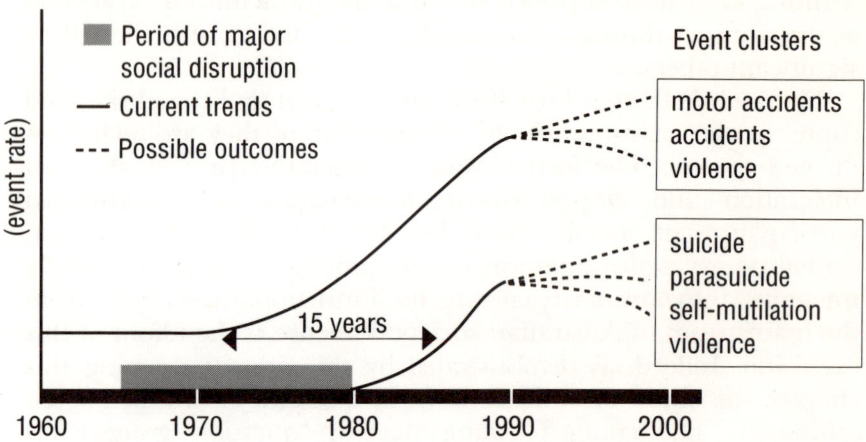

The period of major social change in the Kimberley that has been identified throughout this book was from the mid-1960s to the end of the 1970s. It was around the mid-point, in the early 1970s, that the restrictions on the sale of alcohol to Aborigines in the region were lifted. There was subsequently a sustained increase in the proportion of deaths from external causes — primarily accidents, motor vehicle accidents and interpersonal violence — consistent with the direct impact of alcohol on male behaviour. This earlier curve in figure 7.1 also represents the proportion of drinkers in the population and thus, as well, the proportion of families in which there were heavy-drinking parents. The increase in self-harmful behaviour, and another increase in the proportion of females dying by homicide, occurred though the mid-1980s, delayed some 15 years. Those in this group are primarily teenagers and young adults. They were yet to be born, infants, or children at the time that the earlier increases occurred, the period of most rapid social change, consistent with the cohort model developed by Rubinstein. They belong to the generation who were the children of those young adult Aborigines who were most dramatically affected by dislocation, dispossession and disempowerment during that period of turmoil, and who suffered the losses demonstrated by the first curve. These young adults of the 1980s and 1990s are the first generation to grow up with widespread drinking, and its family and social consequences. While the earlier curve represents the direct impact of alcohol in the context of social upheaval, the increases in self-harm and violence occurring in the 1980s represent the delayed consequences, refracted through the impact of disturbances in family and social functioning on psychological development and the construction of identity.

Figure 7.2 *Predisposing factors for current Aboriginal violence in the Kimberley: a hypothetical schema*

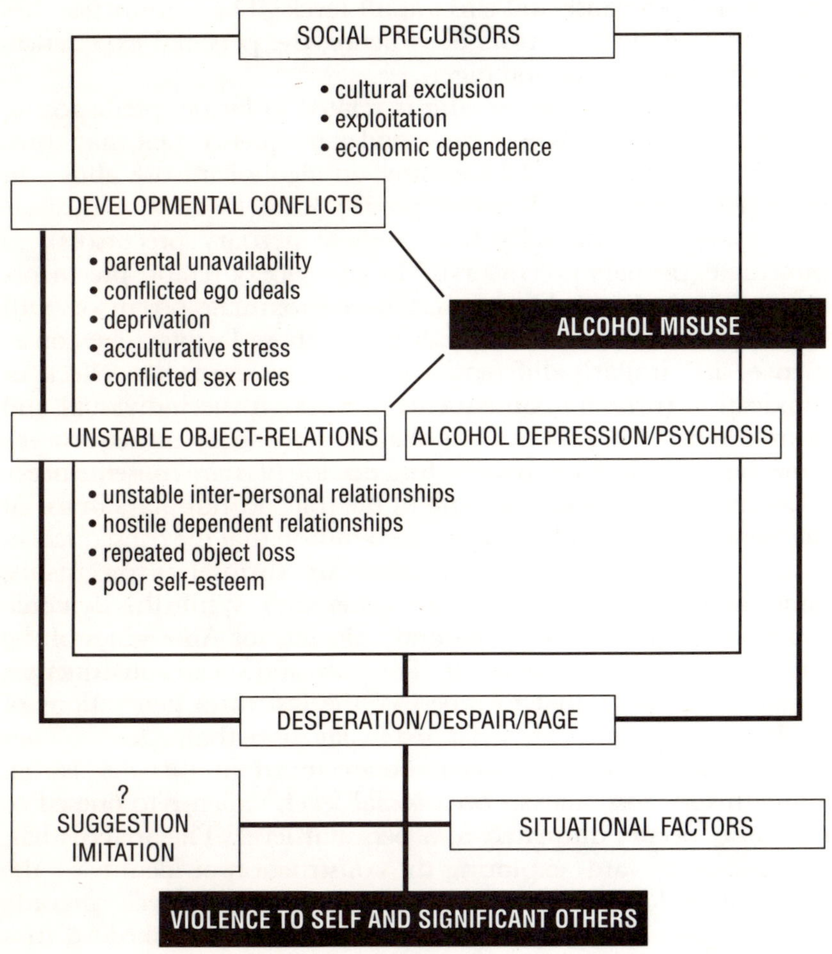

A central theme in the discussions of alcohol use, violence, suicide and other self-harmful behaviours, has been the historical and intercultural context. To conclude this chapter two models are presented that provide a theoretical integration of these issues. In the first (see figure 7.2), those factors predisposing to violent behaviours are identified. The left side of the diagram demonstrates the influence of social (intercultural) factors on child development and, subsequently, on psychological functioning, particularly the capacity for stable interpersonal relationships and self-esteem. On the right-hand side alcohol is located centrally, to emphasise its relation as both cause and effect at all levels. The conjunction lies in the immediate precursors of violence, the personal experiences of desperation, despair and rage.

Alcohol misuse in this setting is related to factors predisposing to violent behaviours as both cause and consequence. One may, thus, construct a parallel model focusing on alcohol misuse/abuse. In figure 7.3 factors are identified predisposing to alcohol misuse/ abuse, varying temporally from remote (tertiary precursors), to immediate (primary precursors). The presence of remote precursors increases both the likelihood that more proximate precursors will also be present, and the vulnerability to those factors. The consequences are similarly differentiated, from the immediate effects of intoxication (primary consequences), through the individual and group impact of persistent alcohol abuse (secondary consequences), to the long-term impact on social functioning (tertiary consequences).

Essential for an understanding of the role alcohol plays in social fragmentation and violence is the recognition that the consequences of alcohol misuse on a social level are themselves precursors, rendering vulnerable the following generation. While this dynamic also operates in other societies and cultures, for Aborigines of the Kimberley there is no precedent. The pace and social consequences of change are such that members of the last three generations of Kimberley Aborigines are separated by far more than age.

Historical factors have been foregrounded in this discussion. While this focuses analysis on a social level, violence to oneself or to another occurs ultimately at a personal level. The analysis has, thus, moved towards exploring the construction of identity — the subject of the following chapter. However, these two levels can only by artifice be separated, as personal experience is embedded in a complex of social relations that is constantly evolving. Conflicts of identity at the intrapersonal level in this section of the Kimberley Aboriginal community frequently involve a sustained experience of oppression and powerlessness on the interpersonal and intercultural

Figure 7.3 *Precursors and consequences of Aboriginal alcohol misuse in the Kimberley: a hypothetical schema*

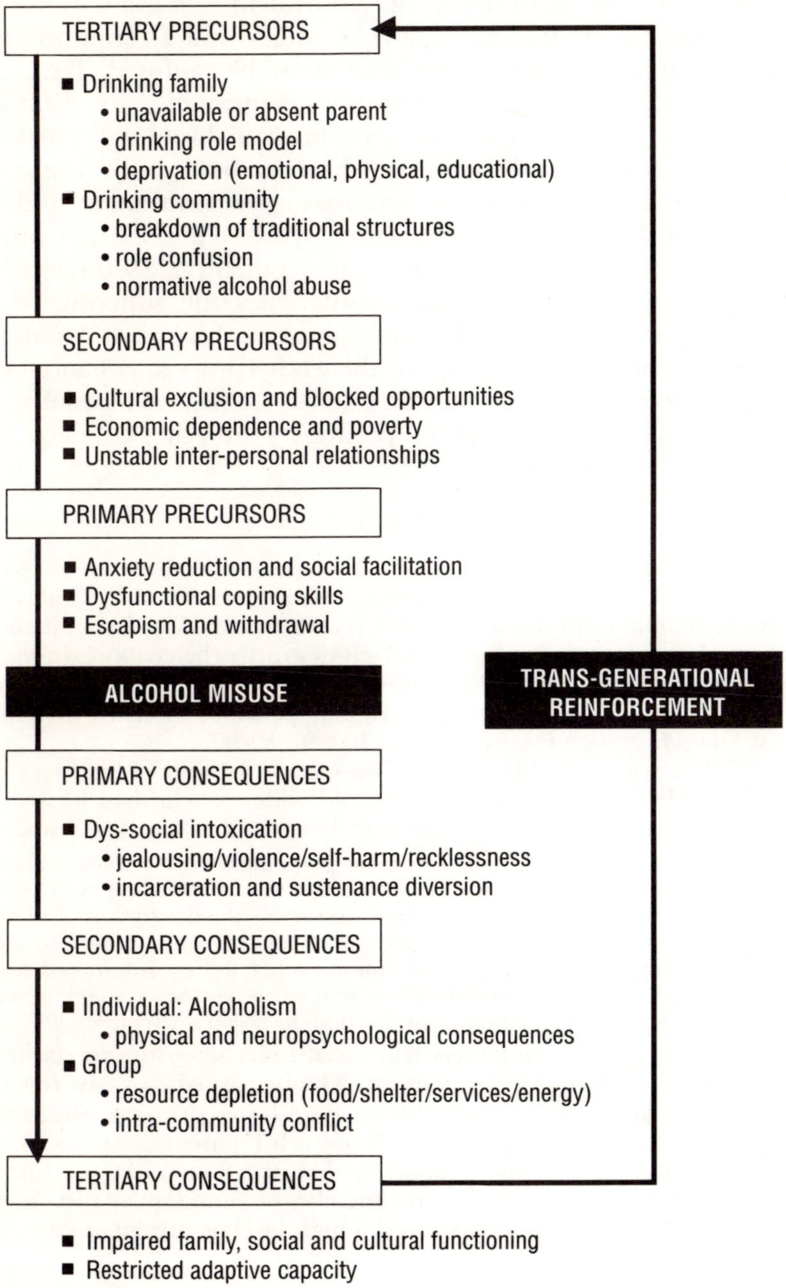

TERTIARY PRECURSORS

- Drinking family
  - unavailable or absent parent
  - drinking role model
  - deprivation (emotional, physical, educational)
- Drinking community
  - breakdown of traditional structures
  - role confusion
  - normative alcohol abuse

SECONDARY PRECURSORS

- Cultural exclusion and blocked opportunities
- Economic dependence and poverty
- Unstable inter-personal relationships

PRIMARY PRECURSORS

- Anxiety reduction and social facilitation
- Dysfunctional coping skills
- Escapism and withdrawal

ALCOHOL MISUSE

TRANS-GENERATIONAL REINFORCEMENT

PRIMARY CONSEQUENCES

- Dys-social intoxication
  - jealousing/violence/self-harm/recklessness
  - incarceration and sustenance diversion

SECONDARY CONSEQUENCES

- Individual: Alcoholism
  - physical and neuropsychological consequences
- Group
  - resource depletion (food/shelter/services/energy)
  - intra-community conflict

TERTIARY CONSEQUENCES

- Impaired family, social and cultural functioning
- Restricted adaptive capacity

level. This is aggravated and entrenched by alcohol, and frequently articulated through violence. In attempting to confront power-lessness and its accompanying ambivalent self-evaluation, the externalisation or internalisation of anger and frustration may, particularly in the context of intoxication, be confused. Tenacious and enduring stereotypes of Aborigines contribute to the dismissal of such statements and acts as 'grog talk' or 'humbug'. However, alcohol misuse and self-harmful behaviour have motivations and meanings that go beyond the immediacy of inebriation and the confines of the drinking circle. Those involved are not only angry, but experience sadness and anxiety, and contemplate self-harm and suicide. Their idiom of distress articulates the suffering of an excluded minority. In the party atmosphere, exuberance and transient social integration of 'grogging on', there is fleeting ego-enhancement. Like the bottle, the alcohol-exalted self is fragile, and unstable. Its shattered shards are painful and perilous — and they cut deep.

NOTES

Chapter 7 is based on previously published papers: 'A question of power: Contemporary self-mutilation among Aborigines in the Kimberley'. *Australian Journal of Social Issues 25 (4)*, 1990, 261–277; 'Using a socio-historical frame to analyse Aboriginal self-destructive behaviour'. *Australian and New Zealand Journal of Psychiatry 24*, 1990, 191–198; 'The intercultural and sociohistorical context of Aboriginal personal violence in remote Australia'. *Australian Psychologist 26 (2)*, 1991, 89–99.

1. This is not invariably the case. Wan, Soderdahl and Blight reported from Hawaii on a 'stable' 64-year-old widower who had incised the entire ventral surface of his penis in 17 operations over five years:

    > Prior to his wife's death, they were planning to move to Australia for retirement. They had studied much about Australia, including its aborigines, in preparation for the move. He came across the description of urethral incision, coined subincision, a common practice among the Australian aborigines. . . . This practice, among other things, heightened sexual pleasure. He was fascinated and saw in it an avenue for sexual release. After some hesitation and much consideration, he began his venture. (1985 : 287)

2. The two lifetime abstainers had certain characteristics in common, both being town-oriented women. The first, aged 36 years, reported that her father and all her siblings were heavy drinkers. She viewed her mother as being the most powerful parent, responsible for providing most of the support within the family. At the time of interview she was married and a member of a fundamentalist church. Her HSCL-25 score (1.9) revealed a high level of current anxiety. The

second woman, aged 20 years, reported that both parents and her siblings were heavy drinkers, and she was, herself, married to a drinker. While her current anxiety and depression scores were not particularly high, she reported past experiences of panic, and indicated that her cutting occurred when she was depressed.

3. Reser (1991b) provides an extensive, though polemical, critique of the article on which this section was based.

4. Convictions of Aboriginal males for sexual assault in Western Australia increased from 48 to 490 per 100 000 between 1961 and 1981 (Broadhurst 1987).

5. This was the title of a small brochure prepared by the Commonwealth Government for National Aborigines' Day in 1957, and revised and reissued in 1962. Tellingly, it is suggested on the title page that: 'This publication should be read in conjunction with "Assimilation of Our Aborigines" (1958), "Fringe Dwellers" (1959), "The Skills of Our Aborigines" (1960) and "One People" (1961)'.

CHAPTER 8

Issues of Identity

INTRODUCTION

When I was young they sent me to school
to read and write and be nobody's fool
they taught me the white ways and bugger the rest
cos everything white was right and the best.

So I grew up in a white man's sense
and I found belief and I gained confidence
no doubts were apparent in my little world
so I sailed on to big things with my wings unfurled.

My world was so rosy until I saw
that nothing that I did could open the door
cos when you reach somewhere no matter how soon
you're nothing more than an acceptable coon.
'Acceptable Coon', by Jimmy Chi and Stephen Pigram

Jimmy Chi's musical *Bran Nue Dae,* based on his youth in Broome and in a Catholic boarding school in Perth, opens with the musings of the adolescent Aboriginal hero and prodigal son, Willy. He is reflecting resignedly on the futility of striving to meet white expectations, and on the contradictions of their values, realising that Aborigines are, regardless of effort, relegated by those defining and imposing the standards, to marginal status — at best he could be an 'acceptable coon'. Having rejected, or fled, the rigours of an authoritarian Catholic school system, Willy returns home to Broome with his 'uncle', Tadpole, a wily drifter who had lived on the fringes of white society. Both are travelling north to renew connections, to become whole. Willy's is an odyssey of personal exploration and growth — to discover sexuality, rediscover family, and realise the hypocrisy of political and social systems, captured by the theme song, sung by Tadpole:

200

Now this man longa Canberra, he bin talkin' about a Bran New Dae
— us people bin waiting for dijwun for two hundred years now. Don'
know how much longer we gotta wait, and boy it's makin' me slack.

> Here I live in this tin shack
> Nothing here worth coming back
> To drunken fights and awful sights
> People drunk most every night.
> 'Bran Nue Dae', by Jimmy Chi and Michael Manolis

Jimmy Chi is well qualified to reflect on these issues. The ideas that
were finally distilled into *Bran Nue Dae* began to take shape in the
late 1960s. Having dropped out of university, and sensing that he
had failed to realise the internalised expectations inculcated through
his own Catholic upbringing, he was admitted to a psychiatric
hospital. Two decades later, out of that 'failure' emerged a production
performed nationally and internationally. The issues raised in the
play are germane to this work. The main character (and the author)
are from the Kimberley. They had experienced the pressures and
demands of different cultures, and were in a critical phase of identity
development and consolidation (adolescence and young adulthood)
during that period of rapid social change from the mid-1960s
through the 1970s.

DEFINITIONS AND USAGE

In earlier chapters various behavioural outcomes (deaths from
external causes, suicide, violence, self-mutilation, alcohol use)
among Aborigines of the Kimberley over the last 30 years were
examined. Hypotheses have been presented which draw on historical
correlates operating on a social level. Mediating between social forces
and changes in behaviours at a population-level is the individual.
However, these levels of analysis are not separable. Individual
identity formation is contingent on the way the group(s) to which
the individual belongs constructs and articulates its defining
characteristics. It is also influenced by the occurrence and understanding of a constellation of personal, family, community and
social events experienced during the course of life, particularly
childhood.

For the purpose of this chapter the following definitions have
been adopted: 'identity' is defined as 'The sense of self, providing

a unity of personality over time'; personality being 'Deeply ingrained patterns of behavior, which include the way one relates to, perceives, and thinks about the environment and oneself' (American Psychiatric Association 1987 : 399; 403). While unlikely to be universally accepted, these definitions have the benefit of simplicity, the essential elements being: that they define a personal experience (both sensory and cognitive) of oneself in relation to a wider system, which is manifest through sustained, and hence relatively predictable patterns of behaviour. Individual experience, the social context, and time, are thus all involved.

However, Aboriginal 'identity' is invoked and used in multifarious ways. For instance, at times it is conflated with the concept of 'Aboriginality'. Further dissection provides for 'traditional', and 'acculturated' identities, even a 'political' identity. Such concepts are generally imposed, non-Aboriginal, descriptive labels. Indeed, even analysis and discussion by Aborigines is more likely to proceed to formulation and political praxis among those who have, pragmatically, adopted contemporary avenues of expression that unavoidably incorporate the values and standards of the wider society. While traditional languages and Aboriginal attempts at standard English were long devalued by the wider Australian community (Donaldson 1985), Aborigines must of necessity now use the forms and constructions of English to reach a substantial audience (Ariss 1988). These linguistic tools (metaphor, simile, etc.) are themselves transformative, constraining and subtly altering the objects of description (Gergen 1986). Additionally, Aboriginal writers and researchers are often required to consult European-compiled and -controlled archival and archaeological sources — with the result that, as Jordan (1988) suggested, within the domain of Aboriginal studies the past is mediated by non-Aborigines.

ABORIGINES AND ABORIGINALITY

RESILIENCE OR STAGNATION?

Identity and culture are inseparable. Pre-contact Aboriginal societies, to the extent that it is possible to speculate from early records of contact and from groups that have remained isolated until recently, demonstrated remarkable 'cultural conservatism' (Gould 1970). However, this should not be understood as stagnation. Indeed, given the substantial climatic and ecological changes over the millennia of Aboriginal presence, the persistence of cultural forms speaks of astounding resilience.[1]

Aboriginal culture was, and is, adaptive. Warner (1969 [1937]) commented on the material conservatism of traditional Murngin (Arnhem Land) society in the 1930s, while at the same time describing how aspects of Macassan ritual were incorporated.[2] Conservative in terms of possessions yet rich in terms of ritual life, Aboriginal Australia was a culture of diversity unseen by intruders from a world of objects and time. Under later and more sensitive scrutiny a rich religious life emerged, with the elements of group and personal identity embedded within it. Transcending and linking, lay the Dreaming, providing a cosmic context that structured the relationship of those journeying in the present to each other and to a mythical 'past' manifest in the land. Land and ritual may have changed, but the primacy of the Dreaming did not. However, while the relative pace of social change was less than among the peoples of Europe and Asia who arrived over the last two centuries, Aboriginal societies, as with cultures anywhere, were dynamic and responsive social entities. The upheavals accompanying European colonisation transformed their physical and interpersonal environments, demanding a new level of adaptation. What was introduced was time — historical time. An examination of emerging constructions of self, of personal and group identity, necessarily requires both longitudinal and horizontal perspectives: 'the development of society is both synchronic and diachronic. . . . We have to think of societies in terms of both a set of simultaneous institutions (synchronism) and a process of historical transformation (diachronism)' (Ricoeur 1984 : 38).

'The European view of the Australian Aboriginal has never been neutral and has never been innocent' noted Donaldson (1985 : 15). Nor has the perception of adaptation — away from the primitive integrity of real 'bush' Aborigines. Confronting this narrow view of cultural change, which is in contrast to the emphasis on 'progress' in Western cultures, von Sturmer highlighted the need for a changed position that moves:

> significantly away from the habitual stance which treats Aboriginality as a fixed quantity or entity, mutable only in the direction of loss — that is, towards less Aboriginality. In other words, it does not treat it as axiomatic that any transformation in Aboriginal lifestyle is away from

> the truly Aboriginal — towards either total immersion in or assimilation into the national lifestyle, however that may be characterised; or into a dissolute and sordid caricature found at the fringes of national life. (1984 : 262)

A basic premise of the following discussion is that Aboriginal cultures, embedded in changing physical and social environments, continue to adapt and evolve. This process may lead towards greater uniformity, but this does not imply an inexorable cultural loss. The forces and events that impact this evolution involve all who have participated in the post-contact history of Australia. While in most of the source materials Aborigines are in 'synchronic suspension' in an 'ethnographic present' (Clifford 1986 : 111), the frame for this examination of how identity is constructed and reconstructed, is historical.

LEVELS OF CONTINUITY

Speculation informs much theorising about the non-material aspects of pre-contact Aboriginal societies. The available material indicates the central importance of group identification, the bonds locating the individual interpersonally, linked to a specific tract of land which served to manifest a mythical past in a present reality.[3] This social matrix extended not only horizontally, but vertically through the generations: the exclusivity of membership is demonstrated in the Kimberley by an enormous linguistic richness, including speech enclaves that survived with less than 100 speakers. Within the group lay structure and safety, defined through a predictable ordering of interpersonal space. The encompassing social categories functioned not only to locate individuals but to provide a template for interaction:

> There was no form of category or unit in traditional Aboriginal Australia which was 'open' or to which one could belong voluntarily through purely individual choice. Religiously and economically, people were placed quite firmly within the total system — no room was left for an uncommitted, floating population. (Berndt 1977 : 2)

The basic social category was kinship (Berndt & Berndt 1985), which in complex but predictable ways structured interpersonal space, weaving the individual into a sustaining social fabric. Myers (1979) suggested that Pintupi emotions were interpersonally defined, the self and the fabric of the group being coextensive, such that elements of shared identity with important others became incorporated as part of the self. The resultant integrity provided reinforcement and support for the individual, with traditional mechanisms such as healing practices facilitating reintegration and reaffirmation of group identity. As noted in the discussion of suicide, denial of relatedness thus constituted a threat to shared identity.

Gender and economic roles

Group and kinship systems were woven into the fabric of religious and economic life and articulated through mytho-ritual practices, and patterns of reciprocity and obligation. The economic and the sacred represented the fundamental domains of power within Aboriginal societies. In both the most clear division was that between the sexes. Throughout Australia the basic economic unit was the domestic unit, within which roles were clearly defined. As earlier described, Aboriginal women were by and large responsible for the greater part of the predictable food supply and were, thus, an economic resource (Rose 1987); Kaberry (1973 [1939]) suggested that women used their economic indispensability as a power tool. However, the food collected by women went 'mostly to their own families. What men hunted and caught was mainly utilized, firstly, to cement specific social relations and to fulfil ritual obligations' (Berndt & Berndt 1985 : 149). Social prestige accrued to the food of the hunt and, although women could eat while foraging, men had the prerogative of distribution within the camp. The availability of food was inextricably entwined with the sacred, human intercession necessary to ensure sufficiency in an ecology of limited resources. Religion thus constituted the other empowering domain, the 'normative basis of power' (Howard 1982 : 2) manifested through the all-encompassing scope of the Law.

The sexual division of power in the domain of the sacred has been contentious. Early ethnography consigned women to the realm of the secular, Montagu (1974 [1937]) stating in the early 1930s that in Aboriginal societies, women's generative role was perceived as being a 'medium'. This construction reached its zenith later in the same decade with Warner suggesting that, in contrast to the lifelong sacred progress of Aboriginal males, women demonstrated little such movement: 'a man's social value is correspondingly more important, and his place in the rituals is partly due to and partly expresses this' (1969 [1937]: 7). This did not go unchallenged; Phyllis Kaberry confronted Warner's position on the putative lack of sacred progress in the lives of Aboriginal women. For Kaberry, religion and social organisation (such as patrilocality) entrenched the 'political subordination' of women (1973 [1939]: 185). Bell's later (1983) analysis not only emphasised the important role of Warrabri women's ritual life, but supported Kaberry's contention of past ethnographic sexist bias.

Examples of sexist bias are easily found, for instance in Abbie's work of the 1950s and 1960s. Writing on the status of Aboriginal women, he began by questioning (with reference to Kaberry) the general interpretation of their life as one of 'oppression, hardship and slavery', but suggested that though hard, it was probably no less harsh than that of socio-economically underprivileged women in European society. This included being 'knocked about or even killed . . . passed on by their husbands . . . prostituted' and having their husbands 'bring other women into the home'. He continued that they had the 'same emotional capriciousness as other women and the same capacity for expressing their feelings vocally in what can become an endless vituperative tirade', but insisted that he did not want 'to leave the impression that every Aboriginal woman is a virago'. Finally, the Aboriginal woman, on the march like a 'beast of burden' was compared to 'a white woman on a hot shopping day', leading to the conclusion that 'a woman's lot in any community is, in sum, about the same' (1970 : 207–209).

Authority of the sacred

Nevertheless, the power conferred through the 'secret-sacred' (Berndt 1979) was controlled by men, the sequestration of ritual power manifest in the asymmetry of sanctions for intrusion into the ritual domain of the other sex (Merlan 1988). Religion gave knowledge and, consequently, power, which was withheld from the profane world of the uninitiated. In assuming sacred roles, Aboriginal elders were manifesting the social order and affirming the society itself:

> Some roles symbolically represent the order in its totality more than others. Such roles are of great strategic importance in a society since they represent not only this or that institution, but the integration of all institutions in a meaningful world. (Berger & Luckmann 1979 : 93)

Access to sacred power required transformative rituals enacted by initiated men. Through subordination to their authority the initiate ascended in social status, gaining access to a range of privileges, including wives. The ultimate guardians of the Law were older men who had demonstrated their social responsibility through their knowledge of ritual. Age was necessary but not sufficient. The rites of passage (birth, marriage, initiation, death) were the major social transitions in male life (Mol 1982) — ceremonies that for Roheim in the 1920s constituted the 'backbone of the whole social organization' (1974 : 55). Social identity was, thus, 'sacralized' (Mol 1982), and power sequestered. Myers, pointing to a paradoxical coexistence of hierarchy and egalitarianism in Pintupi life, indicated that, while there was an overlap of sacred and secular life:

> The social order and the prevailing power relations are accrued through presenting the political order as the social organization of esoteric knowledge, presenting the power and domination of males as a result and mainstay of the cosmic order. This view of authority depicts as natural and necessary the protracted immaturity of younger males while they pass through the ritual cycle, allowing the older men to keep the women for themselves while providing them with a domain in which to exercise their authority. (1982 : 97)

In this system young men constituted a potential threat to the hegemony of older men. Indeed, as touched on in the discussion of violence, according to Warner (1974 [1937]) the killing of young Murngin men was necessary to maintain the system of polygyny. Access to the sacred power conferred through ritual was, therefore, largely restricted to men, whose mediation ensured the bounty of the land and gave meaning to the social framework. Those thus privileged were shaped by, and instrumental in shaping, culture (Kolig 1989).

Domain of childhood

The domain of childhood before European settlement may also only be speculated on. With a child's father frequently much older than his or her mother (or mothers), the matriline (great-grandmother, grandmother, sister, niece) was generally more extensive than the patriline. Family size and the number of immediate contacts of the child would have been substantially smaller than is the case today. The most comprehensive examination of tradition-oriented child development is Annette Hamilton's (1981) study at Maningrida in northern Arnhem Land. She explored the works of earlier writers and elaborated an Anbarra model of child development. A common theme of most descriptions is an indulged childhood with less imposition of adult discipline than would be the case in most Western settings. According to Hamilton, a relative absence of controls over the child's emotions, especially anger, was typical, described by Myers as 'autonomy of desire' (1986 : 110). Physical discipline appears to have been minimal. Roheim's (1974) description of a reaction to the punishment of a child at Hermannsburg in the 1920s is telling: 'the children at the Mission were influenced by the white school methods and it is the deliberate infliction of pain, the sadistic pedagogy of the white man, which so scandalized the natives that they attacked the Missionary' (1974 : 75). Roheim was impressed with the use by mothers of threats associated with the supernatural in controlling children: 'If we consider the four major techniques of pedagogy — erection of an ego-ideal, use of a bogey to create fear, corporal punishment, and preaching — the first two predominate, while the third and fourth are nearly absent in the Central Australian nursery' (1974 : 76).

Jimmy Chi, discussing the confluence of Aboriginal, Asian and Irish Catholic superstition in his childhood half a century later, pointed to similar processes:

> When you are a child they tell you ghost stories so you will stay at home. When you are a kid they will say 'look out *Badi-badi* there, look out, this is dangerous!'. So you get this fear of snakes and things. They will say 'look out devil dog out there'. It also makes you very receptive to spiritual conditions. Fear is part of psychic development. (personal communication, 1987)

Invoking malign spirits that threatened beyond the arena of safety controlled by the mother was also commented on by Hamilton (1981). However, the general experience appears to have been one of relative under-regulation of early childhood with few external controls imposed by adults and, thus, 'little to prepare the individual for the subjection to authority of others' (Kaberry, 1973 [1939] : 70). With development, girls were gradually introduced into their adult roles, remaining close to their maternal figures and participating in women's activities and responsibilities. For males the situation was different. Although there was increasing time spent with adult males, they were excluded from the important domain of male sacred life. In contrast to girls, the period of under-regulation ended abruptly. The boy considered ready for initiation experienced a sudden stripping of old attachments and an affirmation of new relationships. The transformation was dependent on the cooperation of the entire community, but particularly of older males, into whose world he was receiving induction. Merlan (1988) has pointed out that the development of an adult identity was different for each sex; for males it was socially constructed, whereas for females it was primarily physiologically determined.

This description has only briefly focused on the intricacies of traditional Aboriginal religious life and child development. Certain forces have been introduced that will be of importance in examining change over time. The use of the past tense does not imply that the foregoing no longer obtains.

ELEMENTS OF CHANGE

Aboriginal cultures, resilient in the face of pre-contact ecological transformations, have had to adapt to unprecedented social and ecological change brought about by the recent intrusion of Europeans. In the following discussion those social forces impacting Aborigines since settlement (where possible the Kimberley will remain the focus) will be examined from the perspective of their possible effects on the construction of identity. Three broad epochs will be dealt with in turn which, as with earlier discussions, are not discrete periods. These are: contact and conflict — the upheavals of European intrusion, ending with the 'pacification' of the region following permanent settlement; adaptation and survival — accommodation to permanent non-Aboriginal settlement and its demands on Aborigines; assimilation and self-determination — the continuing process of adaptation to the social transformations following the Second World War.

CONTACT AND CONFLICT

The permanent European settlement of the Kimberley resulted in a confrontation between two worlds. As with tradition-oriented societies generally, that of the Aborigines was characterised by stability: hierarchical structuring (of sacred life), personal integration, role definition, predictability, mutual dependence, limited exploration of the unknown and suppression of internal tendencies to change

(Born 1970). By contrast, the settlers came from a society that valued change, growth, individualism and initiative. To the balanced but often perilous existence of the indigenous hunter-gatherers, they introduced a new dimension of danger. The settlers came for land, and were to appropriate and use it in ways that were ultimately incompatible with a continuation of Aboriginal traditional life.

The assault on the traditional construction of identity thus began with the introduction of the unknown — of people and things that challenged the stable order of the native cosmos. It was their very source of stability, order and continuity that the strangers wanted — the land. There was no way that such an assault on the fabric of social and personal identity could be anything but bloody — and it was. Regardless of intermittent retaliation, the conflict was one-sided. To control the land required the pacification of its inhabitants (land before labour). Suddenly, a new dimension of order had entered the equation of Aboriginal lives. Old men drawing authority from the realm of the sacred confronted superior technology.

For most Aborigines at the contact interface, disease and violence shattered social and kinship networks. Movement was necessary from zones of danger, either to collection points around already settled stations or missions, or further out 'beyond the limits of civilisation'. It was often safer to be in a close and dependent relationship to Europeans, than free but vulnerable in the bush (Kolig 1987). The predictability and ordering of life as it had been known was in turmoil and the traditional means to power undermined:

> Above all, Aborigines realized that the power that accrued from their cosmological assumptions was weak, in fact may never have existed as more than an illusion. It withered away before the bludgeoning power that Western society wielded. (Kolig 1982 : 27)

ADAPTATION AND SURVIVAL

For Aborigines who survived the initial confrontations, and those others who arrived later, there were limited avenues for adaptation. Born presented four modes of adaptation to rapid social change, based on Merton's theories, which will be returned to later (see table 8.2, below):

1. Retreatism: a return to, or conscious preservation of, the traditional patterns of behavior with a corresponding resistance to new patterns.

2. Reconciliation: a combination of the traditional and the new; an attempt to 'co-exist' or to 'strike a happy medium'.
3. Innovation: as complete as possible an acceptance of the new patterns of behavior with a conscious rejection of tradition.
4. Withdrawal: an overt rejection of both the traditional and the new; tradition continues to influence behavior, but there will be little value placed on such influence and it will generally be denied as much as possible. (1970 : 538)

Elements of all these adaptive styles may be found among Aboriginal groups in post-pacification Kimberley. However, common to all settings was the primacy of European cultural values and demands. Aborigines could stay and work — or leave. However, for tribal Aborigines the 'empty' areas of 'desolate' country were already occupied. That country clearly now 'belonged' to another group, whose exploitation of its bounty, particularly during the dry months of the year, left little margin for sustaining a larger population. Thus, the possibility of leaving the ambit of European activity, of physical retreat,. was limited, safety being the trade-off for a superficial rejection of Aboriginal culture.

Despite this, personal and group identification with traditional culture remained strong. Innovation and withdrawal were, therefore, not typical, innovation being additionally limited by the restricted opportunities for Aborigines. This phase corresponded to the formulation and institutionalisation of protection policies that effectively separated Aborigines or dictated the forms of adaptation possible within areas of European occupancy.

Reconciliation, then, in Born's sense, was most typical — Aborigines moving into a variety of structured relationships with Europeans. Given the enormity of what had preceded, the Aboriginal capacity for survival and adaptation was remarkable. What emerged were transitional identity structures adapted to the realities of European demands and expectations. Identification with the aggressors brought a level of safety, which was fuelled by the fury of pacification: 'the absurd desire of the vanquished to identify with the victor, notwithstanding his cruelty, existed in the Kimberley long before terrorism brought to us the expression "Stockholm syndrome"' (Kolig 1987 : 39). For the majority of Aborigines the dynamics of adaptation evolved in mission and station settings, the nature of adaptation in each being different.

Imposed and internalised structures

Station life provided perhaps the most powerful transitional identity, as Aborigines remained close to their traditional land. These Aborigines also frequently came from a common descent group and were able to maintain a seasonal return to a traditional lifestyle during the 'wet', when station work came to a halt. Station owners were primarily interested in Aboriginal work-performance, and intruded less into Aboriginal life outside work. The stations also allowed entry into an economic domain that valued (if not paid) Aboriginal labour and expertise. A station hierarchy evolved that conferred prestige and supported self-esteem. While women were also involved in cattle work, Aboriginal males were dominant in this arena, thus maintaining male esteem and power. The importance of living and working in the cattle industry cannot be overstated:

> Aboriginal men used cattle work to regain or maintain their pride as men, in a colonial context. Their use of this work to continue ritual ties with land challenged colonial ownership and the domination of white Australian culture. (McGrath 1987 : 46)

Aborigines in this context were resources. Life was structured and predictable, the self-esteem of a tangibly purposeful activity contributing to an enduring identification with station life and an internalisation of its values. By contrast, the missions generally provided only external and frequently authoritarian structure. They did not support the development of elements of identity linked to self esteem, or an enduring internalisation of values: 'missionary Christianity has succeeded neither in instilling in Aboriginal people a distinctly Christian view of human existence and morality, nor in gaining admittance to their social life to a noticeable degree' (Kolig 1988 : 376). Missions tended to concentrate groups from diverse regions with consequent inter-group rivalry and conflict. There were clear guidelines about what a mission Aborigine should be like, which were incompatible with traditional identity, and frequently included attempts to suppress Aboriginal language. Traditional lifestyle was discouraged (Berndt and Berndt [1988] suggested that it is only recently that, through necessity, the response to traditionalism has changed from suppression to syncretism, 'indigenization') and, by contrast to stations, there were fewer means to self-esteem through valued activity or support for the traditional power structure. This is a point of particular importance; indeed, the low incidence of 'psychiatric illness' found among Aborigines on Northern Territory cattle stations during the 1960s was attributed in large part to the self-esteem benefits of employment (Cowdy 1970). As Maggie Brady has also noted, in relation to the relative absence of petrol sniffing[4] in communities with station backgrounds: 'The cattle industry was significant, not because it was "work" (there are countless menial, repetitive and mundane opportunities for Aborigines to work) but because it was productive — an economic enterprise' (1992a : 189).

The benefits of a mission lifestyle were primarily protection and food, 'pacification by feeding' (Kolig 1987), for which Aborigines were required to demonstrate a superficial deference to mission routine. The cost included greater interference with family life, as missions tended to focus on children and to separate them in dormitories from their parents. Thus, while stations provided external structure and supported a transitional identity (internalised structure), missions provided only external (imposed) structure.

By the end of this period, Aborigines in the Kimberley (excluding the 'coloured' urban populations that will be returned to later) may be considered to have grown to adulthood in one of four social environments that may be differentiated on the basis of the two above constructs — order (imposed structure) and identity (internalised structure). In addition to the Aborigines on missions and stations, there were those who had grown up in the bush, and a fringe-dwelling population which later increased dramatically, and whose adaptation was consistent with Born's concept of withdrawal. However, these two groups may also be conceptualised in terms of internalised and imposed structure. Those Aborigines who had reached maturity in the bush clearly maintained a strong and enduring traditional identity. They were relatively unaffected by (or resisted) the destabilisation of contact and had thus avoided the imposition of European external controls and structuring of their lives. By contrast, fringe-dwellers had frequently experienced enormous disruption in their lives (including access to alcohol), with greater difficulty in maintaining traditional links. However, as Collmann (1988) noted, the fringe-dwellers' environment allowed them to resist the imposition of European controls. Figure 8.1 demonstrates the relationship of these two variables in the transition-phase social environments.

Figure 8.1 *Socioenvironmental characteristics of transition-phase communities: order vs identity*

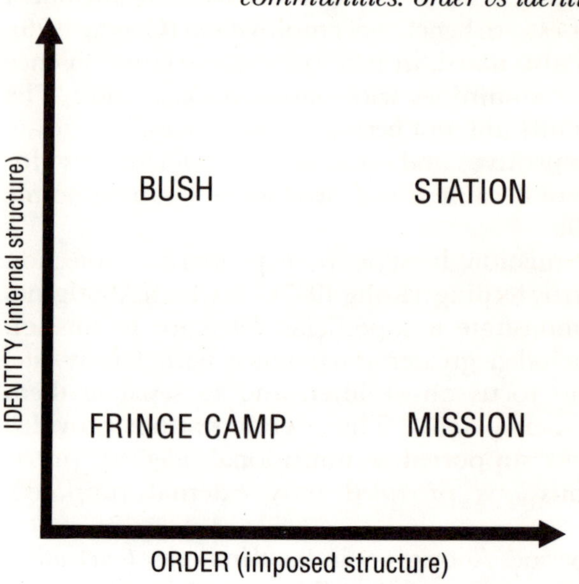

This schema will be returned to in discussing the consequences of the withdrawal of imposed controls that accompanied the transition from policies of protection to assimilation and self-determination. However, several specific developments of the period of adaptation will be addressed first.

Changing role of women

The position of Aboriginal women in this period reflected the imbalance of power, not only between the sexes, but between whites and Aborigines:

> It was the superordinate position of these men in relation to the Aboriginal women that is important. These women were blamed for their part in the affair, but the absence of sexual relations between Aboriginal men and white women indicates that it was a question of the powerful and the White, using the powerless and the Black. Exploitative sexual relationships depend primarily on power for their success. (Palmer & McKenna 1978 : x)

The division of labour on the stations brought Aboriginal women into the homestead and into relationships with Europeans, as workers who were able to observe them and develop social and linguistic tools, and as sexual partners. This afforded them a degree of social mobility not available to Aboriginal men (McGrath 1987). Bell (1983) disagreed with this interpretation of 'privileged access', but suggested that the ability to attract white men changed the balance of power, in addition to which, the shift to settlement life increased women's opportunities for other relationships. While it was relatively less common in mission settings to find Europeans appropriating Aboriginal women for partners, the hostility of Europeans to the power of older males, and opposition to the practice of promise-brides and polygyny, also challenged traditional sexual power differentials.

Intracultural differentiations

As the population of mixed-descent Aborigines grew in the Kimberley, many of whom in the south-west were descended from Asian indentured labourers, new levels were added to the European-Aboriginal dichotomy of power. There emerged on East Kimberley stations what Shaw (1981) equated to a caste system. The situation appears to have been similar among the nearby Walbiri as described by Meggitt in the 1950s:

> The Walbiri are aware that, in terms of material possessions, power and prestige, they rank low in the hierarchy of social statuses in contemporary Northern Territory society.
>
> At the top they see the 'Whitefellow', who, they believe, commands almost unlimited wealth and power. This power has many expressions. The Whitefellow has policemen ready to enforce his commands, he has complete freedom of movement, he can manipulate symbols on paper so that other people (especially Aborigines) are made to act in ways often uncongenial to them. A long way below stand the 'Yellowfellows' — half-caste Aborigines, so-called Afghans and other Asians. They are thought to have fewer material possessions and less money; they have much less power, and Aborigines often have claims over them arising out of consanguineal and affinal ties. Whitefellows who through marriage or consorting with Aboriginal women are liable to the same sorts of claims tend to be placed in the Yellowfellow category. At the bottom of the scale is the 'Blackfellow', with few possessions and little money, prestige, or power. (1962 : 34)

The growth of the mixed-descent population was regarded by many Europeans with alarm. Much of the early legislation regarding

Aborigines in Western Australia was directed towards increasing European control over this group. The emergence of a relatively empowered, literate, 'half-caste' population in the south constituted a threat, dealt with by legislatively grouping all people of Aboriginal descent, regardless of 'quanta' of descent or education, as natives. Aboriginality was, thus, defined in terms of ambilineal descent (Beckett 1988). European paranoia persisted, fuelled by various vested interests, and is typified by Royal Commissioner Moseley's comment, 'time is not distant when these half-castes, or a great majority of them, will become a positive menace to the community: the men useless and vicious, the women a tribe of harlots' (1935 : 8). Prior to the eugenic theories characterising the latter days of Commissioner Neville's tenure, the particular evils of the half-caste were defined in terms of inheritance (the worst of both black and white), and morality (born of sinful unions), producing consequent expectations of limited capacities, untrustworthiness and immorality. Such perceptions were communicated to those aspiring to citizenship, who were required to exorcise any atavistic racial remnants. Even so, they only infrequently crossed the legislative threshold, constantly having reaffirmed their separateness and inferiority. As Palmer and McKenna stated of this double bind: 'part-Aboriginal people not only lack a true sense of identity, but the opportunity to develop such an identity is consistently denied to them' (1978 : viii).

In the Kimberley, an urban coloured population formed the mid-level of a tripartite society. Robinson (1973) described the situation in Derby of the 1950s and 1960s:

> Part-Aboriginal people consider themselves to be culturally sophisticated in relation to the 'bush-people' of the Reserves. Many of them have Citizenship Rights and drink at the town's two hotels, while Reserve people have to acquire their liquor surreptitiously, and drink it away from European observation. A few people of part-Aboriginal descent may even deny their Aboriginal background and attempt to 'pass' in European society. Most are disinterested in traditional life, or in the organization of life on the Reserves. Reserve people resent the superior attitude of part-Aborigines, the 'yellow-fellows'. They are 'rubbish people', whom they see caught between two cultures. An old Bunaba man from Fitzroy Crossing summed up the Aboriginal view of part-Aborigines: 'White-fellows have got a country. Black fellows have got a country. Coloured People have no country. They just come from a jack donkey and a good mare.' (1973 : 214)

However, a stable subgroup ultimately emerged. Indeed, by the time of a psychiatric survey conducted in Derby in 1969, mixed-descent adolescents were found to be the best adjusted compared to both those of full-descent and non-Aboriginal background, the authors considering that this was owing to 'sound socioeconomic and familial backgrounds' (Gault, Krupinski & Stoller 1970 : 180).

Not reflected in their assessment of this Kimberley urban mixed-descent population is the history of family disruption and dislocation that resulted from government policy towards 'half-castes'. As part-Europeans they could not stay with Aborigines: as part-Aborigines they were denied the rights accorded to Europeans. Mixed-descent children were, therefore, removed from across the region to be reared in missions — many only decades later, or never, meeting their parents.[5] While this group was a minority compared to the full-descent population in the hinterland, their relatively better education and opportunities further differentiated them. Additionally, the requirements of citizenship, which provided an escape from the onerous restrictions of 'the Act', were such as to discourage identification with tribal characteristics.

Intergenerational impact

European intrusion into the Aboriginal family did not impact solely on mixed-descent Aborigines. In all mission settings and on many stations Europeans claimed jurisdiction over Aboriginal children, separating them from their parents, either entirely through removal, or in dormitory life that created separate domains of responsibility for the family and European authority. Even on stations, separations occurred as cattle work took fathers away for protracted periods. Institutional life and schooling introduced a new dimension of discipline to Aboriginal childhood.

Based on experiences at Jigalong, a mission settlement just south of the Kimberley, Tonkinson (1982) suggested that Aborigines adapted to these demands by discriminating two domains of authority — that of the mission ('whitefellow business'), and that of the camp ('blackfellow business'). He suggested that parents could see the benefits of education and learning 'whitefellow ways', but, being unwilling to take responsibility for the discipline entailed, they allowed the missionaries to assume that role. This arrangement maintained order until the mandate for controlling Aboriginal communities passed out of the hands of the missionaries. For some communities the passage from traditional child-rearing, through the rigid discipline of missionary life to its unstructured aftermath, occurred within the span of a lifetime. In discussions with her Aboriginal informant Elsie Roughsey on Mornington Island in the 1970s, Huffer touched on the intergenerational conflicts of the transition:

> mothers like Elsie growled and fussed and threatened, but failed to follow through with suitable action, with the result that their children quickly learned that talk was meaningless. Confrontation was avoided, even when unacceptable activity was obvious. This was well illustrated by Elsie's failure to challenge her sons when money was missing from her purse.
>
> This lack of confrontation and control of offspring was in direct contrast to what the middle-aged parents experienced in the dormitory. Perhaps it reflected attitudes from pre-Mission times. As reported to me, in the old days if parents severely punished a child, the grand-parents or other relatives might take the child away. Elsie said, 'Children are more spoiled now than when we lived in the Mission: it's the softness of the parents'. Yet she also reported that her father told her, 'Don't hit the children, be kind to them'. In these two statements Elsie revealed the disparate parental models that she experienced. Neither model was sufficiently internalized to allow her to be without conflict in her role as a mother. (1980 : 138)

Regardless, during this period Aborigines experienced relative stability in comparison to the violent years of early settlement, but at a price — institutional dependence. Within the constraints of the policies of protection, Aborigines conforming to expectations had restricted, but relatively stable and predictable, life options on missions and stations. Children, who increasingly had access to a language that often remained foreign to their parents, encountered new and seductive ideals. Tonkinson noted that children came to 'possess powers they never had traditionally — the power to abandon Aboriginal culture in favour of that of whites' (1982 : 126).

ASSIMILATION AND SELF-DETERMINATION

The momentum of social change for Kimberley Aborigines since the 1960s has been a landslide compared to any period since settle-ment. Slowly following the Second World War, gaining momentum during the 1960s and most profoundly felt since the 1970s, the most important change impacting on the construction of identity was the withdrawal of the overt, imposed controls over Aboriginal lives. While covert control remains, the leverage does not rely on legislation or force, but on economic dependence. The mechanisms are more subtle, the agents transformed and at times unaware:

> In this time of Aboriginal 'self-determination', advisers no longer issue orders to be obeyed by the Aboriginal clientele. Power has to be wielded more subtly and surreptitiously, by careful engineering and exploiting existing social trends, rifts, power struggles and dynamics within a community, so as to bring about the desired results, rather than by blunt superimposition of will. (Kolig 1987 : 103)

Economic roles

Prior to citizenship rights, pensions were made available to the aged, infirm and to women with children. Their sudden access to reliable sources of funding occurred at the same time that Aboriginal males were being displaced from their jobs on stations, and forced with their families into fringe-camp settings. Economically, a shift in dependency occurred, from the paternalism of stations and missions to reliance on government funding and services. As the 'privileged' recipients, women with children frequently became the major providers; this asymmetry was not redressed by later access to unemployment benefits for males — a fact confirmed by the income findings of the QARK.

Guidelines determining who was eligible constructed a new 'ideal welfare recipient' (Collmann 1988), — usually a woman with children living in a settled situation (with or without a male). Because of the requirement to maintain children in school, fringe-dwelling women were separated from their partners employed in the pastoral industry, who were absent through work for long periods. Collmann suggested that the 'conditions under which women acquire welfare benefits . . . encourages them to minimize their relationships with men' (1988 : 105). Men were, thus, economically vulnerable in a system that not only privileged mothers, but imposed relatively greater restrictions on a group often poorly equipped to understand and deal with bureaucratic systems. Not only was there increasing financial dependence, there was also an increasing reliance on intermediaries to negotiate the complexities of the system. Jimmy Chi has Tadpole comment sardonically:

> Other day I bin longa to social security, I bin ask longa job — they bin
> say, 'Hey, what's your work experience?' I bin tell 'em, 'I got nothing.'
> They say, 'How come?' I say, 'Cause I can't find a job.'
>
> *Bran Nue Dae*, by Jimmy Chi and Michael Manolis

Sacred roles

Aborigines moving into towns experienced a further erosion of
sacred roles through separation from their land and as their children
learnt English as their first language. This is not to suggest that
losing contact with traditional land and reduced fluency in an
Aboriginal language has resulted in the demise of law and culture.
It does, however, mean a difference in the way in which law and
culture are articulated, impact on daily life, and hence are internalised. This is exemplified by changing patterns of partner choice.
Writing on Aboriginal adolescence in Arnhem Land, Burbank
alluded to tensions between the sexes and between generations
arising from contemporary practices of partner choice: 'Today when
young girls choose a man to marry, they are choosing a male who
is not only chronologically younger than husbands generally were
in the past, but one who is less socially mature according to
Aboriginal standards' (1988 : 33), and: 'the substance of the battle over
marriage: adults want to arrange their children's marriages,
adolescents want to choose for themselves, and the criteria for mate
selection is different for each generation' (1988 : 114).

Such secular social adaptations had a direct impact on the role of
the sacred in everyday life. However, changes are not uniform. Indeed,
an increase in male ritual activity was noted in the mid-1970s in the
Kimberley, attributed by Akerman (1979) to factors including: a spiri-
tual revitalisation associated with the land-rights movement; involvement of greater numbers of part-Aborigines seeking to redefine their
Aboriginal identity; and increasing interest of non-Aborigines in
aspects of traditional Aboriginal culture. Another factor may have
been an attempt to reassert male sacred power through female-
exclusive rituals. Similarly, Allen (1967) interpreted a re-emergence
of male rites such as circumcision in Melanesia as countering
threatening female dominance, and Barwick suggested that a
resurgence of male rituals among mission Aborigines in Victoria in
the 1890s may have been because 'they found the women ready to take
advantage of their new religious equality' (1978 : 62).

The erosion of the male power-base accelerated through the periods of assimilation and self-determination. As described during the discussion of suicide, 'transitional role conflict' leaving men 'emasculated and powerless' was noted in Inuit culture in association with both male suicide and violence to women (Tsai 1989). Similarly, the process of social change and adaptation clearly impacts on Aboriginal male attitudes to women. Suggestive of the ambivalence and unconscious determinants of such attitudes is the following account from a description of nativistic movements that arose in the north-west in the 1960s, combining elements of traditional beliefs and Christianity. In discussing the work of earlier researchers, Koepping related the following transformations in a traditional myth:

> It appears in summary that the women who travel in the *kurangara* period of creation time, when it was still dark, were originally benevolent beings full of creative essence, as were men. They lost their Dreaming power at their final destination, where the young men accompanying them were initiated, the secret traditions laid down, and the festive ceremonial meal held. The women then went into the ground, handing over their Dreaming power to the men. These are the *traditional* versions. In the 'new' *wandji* traditions, however, these women while accompanying Dreaming heroes are dangerous: they look like 'half-castes', are more powerful than men, and live on today as ghost-like beings (called *djurawin*). They are unable to have sexual intercourse and can use black magic (*imbal*) against anybody disturbing them. They had acquired this magical power on their travels through the land of the medicine men (supposedly located south of Port Hedland for Pilbara informants, in Roebourne and Onslow for informants from La Grange and Anna Plains). The women also send forward from their vaginas snakes, scorpions and millipedes who could make their victims sick or kill them. These women travelled to Dingari, went into the ground, and will return in our time with the help of the great red kangaroo. (1988 : 406)

Certain aspects of this symbolic progression are striking. Women traditionally had power, which was relinquished to men at the time of initiation. In the traditional account the women and their powers are benevolent. In the new version they are potentially dangerous. There is a suggestion that this relates to their capacity for relationships with non-Aborigines (they are 'half-castes', arising from such unions) and thus undermining Aboriginal male power: female sexuality is dangerous. In addition, the power sources are perceived in terms of European locales, in the 'south', or in certain towns. Threatening and potentially lethal snakes emanating from their vaginas suggests concerns regarding their appropriation of male phallic power. The transformation in the myth may be seen as an expression of increasing male concerns regarding female independence and empowerment.[6]

A corollary is that certain settings that are largely male preserves may be a focus of investment in tradition-oriented practices. Paradoxically, one such area is prison, where in the Kimberley the population is predominantly Aboriginal, and male. In this regard Duckworth, Foley-Jones, Lowe and Maller stated:

> The usual speculative assumption is that prison has a destructive and generally negative effect on the maintenance of a vibrant traditional culture. Less often voiced is the alternative possibility that prisons may act as centres for the reinforcement and dissemination of traditional beliefs and ritual, perhaps encouraging the spread of cults or rituals over very large areas because of the wide catchment of Northern prison populations. (1982 : 36)

Many of those in prison are there as a result of violence to women. There have been attempts to claim mitigating circumstances by ascribing such violence, which is often associated with alcohol, to traditional practice and customary law. Aboriginal women have become vocal in resisting this expedient distortion, with Bolger (1990) quoting an Aboriginal informant who remarked that women are now the victims of 'three kinds of violence in Aboriginal society, alcoholic violence, traditional violence, and bullshit traditional violence' (1990 : 53). Tensions are thus ultimately manifest most clearly between men and those women closest to the conflict — their partners and mothers. Violence against partners has been well covered in the material presented in chapter 7. This writer has had numerous anecdotal reports suggesting that aggressive behaviour and violence to mothers is also increasing. The wife of one community chairperson related instances of young men physically attacking their mothers while intoxicated. She went on to contrast this to the same young men 'cowering' before older women in public when not drinking.

Opportunity or exclusion?

The political transitions from protection, to assimilation, to self-determination/self-management, entailed not only shifts in intra-cultural power but a broadening of the range of individuals identifying as Aborigine as the oppressive restrictions were lifted and attitudes within the European population changed. The policies of assimilation appeared to present Aborigines with an opportunity to identify with the dominant culture. However, this was a unilateral and unidirectional process; it was Aborigines who were expected to change. These dynamics are demonstrated by Rack's paradigm (in Littlewood and Lipsedge 1989) for examining the mental health problems of immigrants, in which two sets of hypothetical questions are posed. The immigrants are asked: Is the new culture valued and to be adopted? and: Is the old culture valued and to be retained? The questions to the host community are: Are newcomers helped and encouraged to adopt the host culture and rewarded for doing so? and: Are racial differences and alternative lifestyles respected?

Figure 8.2 *Rack's paradigm for the social differentiation of immigrant groups*

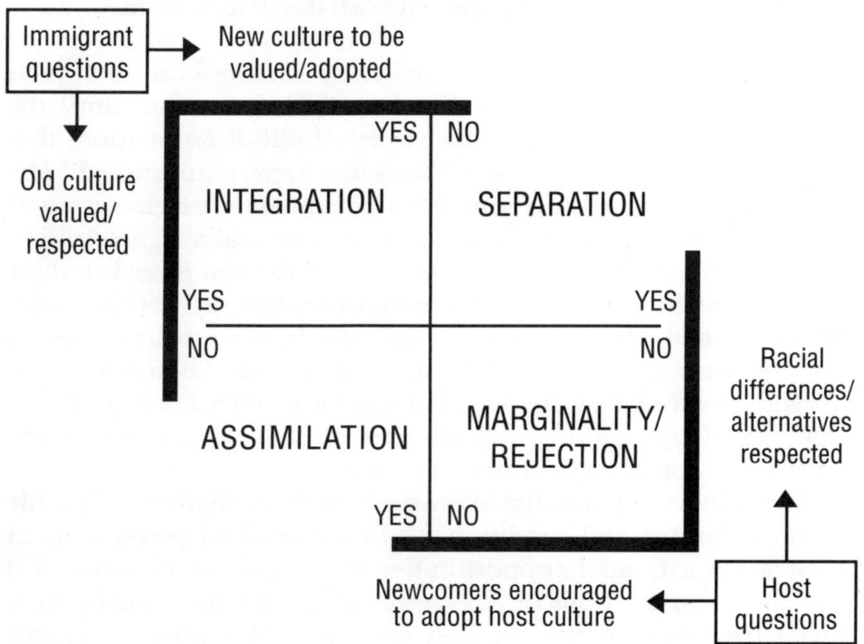

By substituting the indigenous minority for the immigrant group, and Euro-Australian society for the host community, this paradigm may be used to explore Aboriginal adaptation, with marginality or rejection best describing the situation before the adoption of assimilation. Non-Aboriginal acceptance and respect for Aboriginal culture and lifestyle was not substantially changed as a result of the policies of assimilation, a process requiring only unilateral (Aboriginal) change, and which failed for bilateral reasons: Aborigines did not disavow their Aboriginality and, regardless of formal policies, they remained functionally excluded. By contrast, the subsequent policies of integration and self-determination demanded bilateral adaptation (Sommerlad & Berry 1970). The goals and survival of these policies depended on increasing opportunity for Aborigines. However, in reality the doors remained functionally closed. During the previous decades they had been told what they could be, where they could be, who they could be: it was all limited and, thus, attainable. The message conveyed by the optimistic rhetoric of the early 1970s to many Aboriginal communities of the Kimberley was that they could now be whatever they willed, go wherever they wished, perhaps have whatever they wanted. They could not.

While the last of the federal legislative restrictions on Aboriginal access to social security were lifted in 1966, it was not until the 1970s, after the adoption of the policy of self-determination, that state controls over Kimberley Aborigines were relinquished. The mechanisms for implementing income-maintenance legislation and delivering services to Aborigines of remote Australia lagged behind (Smith 1990). Nevertheless, by contrast to what had preceded, there was relative abundance to reinforce the optimistic expectations, with education and television offering new ideals, powerfully presented and seductively packaged to appeal to young Aborigines. The absence of effective means for attaining the proffered benefits of the new era of opportunity, indeed even of articulating consequent grievances, constitutes cultural exclusion.

Aboriginal entry into the mainstream of Australian economic life remains limited and conditional. Non-Aboriginal perceptions of their failure to grasp the opportunities offered have been incorporated into new constructions of Aborigines that emphasise inadequacy, characterological deficiency and deviance. Aboriginal economic failure became a self-fulfilling prophecy, mismanagement and opportunism on the part of non-Aborigines compounding the lack of resources and skills, often under an illusion of Aboriginal control. For instance, following the Western Australian government's rejection of land rights, certain Aboriginal groups in the Kimberley were granted cattle leases. Through overgrazing and erosion, most leases had long been economically marginal, even if each one had provided some livelihood for a single European family. But, with many leases already in financial crisis, the opportunities they provided for a whole Aboriginal community were limited, thus confirming widely held beliefs that 'it's no good giving Aborigines land, they can't use it properly'. Such assessments, which use the single and limited yardstick of profit as a measure of success, do not take account of the important social and cultural benefits that Aboriginal control of stations (and land rights generally) has brought.

An 'Aboriginal' consciousness

The intracultural tensions associated with the blocked opportunities of cultural exclusion supported the development of 'pan-Aboriginality', Keeffe suggesting that: 'Aboriginality, in the fullest and dialectical sense of the word, has emerged from the active response of Aborigines to their unequal status in Australian society' (1988 : 79). However, pan-Aboriginality is frequently portrayed as 'un-Aboriginal', a reaction based on conceptions of culture that reject any possibility of cultural adaptation. While there are problems with Aboriginality as an encompassing category, it has become a cultural and political reality of Aboriginal Australia: 'Aboriginality, as a word of significance for Aboriginal people, belongs in a semantic complex with the keywords, education, culture and power' (Keeffe 1988 : 79). It is a complex and dynamic concept, informed by numerous forces, including: increasing numbers of mixed-descent Aborigines identifying as Aboriginal and attempting to reconstitute or consolidate their links with tradition (Akerman 1979); a reaffirmation of tradition among marginalised Aborigines (Berry 1970); the need for collective action and representation in the political arena, especially land rights; the growth of the discipline of 'Aboriginal studies' and such institutions as the Australian Institute of Aboriginal Studies, that validate Aboriginal culture and Aboriginality in European terms (Jordan 1988); the emergence of a recognised Aboriginal cultural voice through literature; the movement in the 1980s to incorporate and aestheticise traditional Aboriginal culture as part of the national heritage in a multicultural collective history (Morris 1988).

Within the Kimberley the process is most noticeable in urban areas experiencing rapid social change where intercultural conflict is most pronounced. A further stereotype of Aborigines has since emerged, as activists or 'stirrers', again leading to reflections on 'real Aborigines' versus 'pseudo-Aborigines', which in turn reinforce the historical non-Aboriginal preoccupation with both descent and tradition as the only valid indices of Aboriginality.

For the individual the process of identification demands both recognition and confrontation. Dudgeon and Oxenham describe a 'sequence of what happens to some Aboriginal people in the path of self awareness' (1988 : 10). In their paradigm the individual passes through successive stages of:

- 'internalisation and shame' involving the internalisation of dominant culture values and attitudes to Aborigines;
- 'resistance, active and passive' to those internalised negative views;
- 'acceptance' of positive views of Aborigines, with questioning of dominant culture stereotypes of Aborigines;
- 'hostility' and rejection of those views with an appropriate emotional response (anger) to those that hold them;
- 'consolidation' of the newly emergent referents of Aboriginality, and active and open demonstration of these referents;
- and 'self-actualised Aboriginality', a rapprochement in which 'the individual has accepted their Aboriginality and also there has been an acknowledgment and working through of those parts of themselves that reflect dominant society values, with some retained and some rejected' (1988 : 11).

Autonomy and controls

Nationwide, the major verbalised demand of Aboriginal groups in the post-assimilation period has been for autonomous control (of land and services). In the Kimberley the transition from direct administration by the Department, stations and missions, to administration by Aboriginal organisations occurred in the 1970s. Regardless, most remained dependent on government sources for funding and, hence, subject to external controls. In order to facilitate the delivery of services to the substantial, and now theoretically autonomous Aboriginal population that had earlier been administered through missions and stations, a new political structure was necessary. As a consequence: 'Since the early 1970s the term "community" began to replace terms such as settlement, mission, and pastoral properties, often without any more than a tautological definition' (Smith 1989 : 3). Community, as an imposed structure, will be discussed in the next chapter. However, while the term suggests social organisation, communities were generally defined by locality; this meant that, given the population movements of the time in the Kimberley, they frequently contained groups in conflict and competition for resources.

For some isolated communities the new political structures required the demonstration and exercise of authority in ways alien to their previous experience. The removal of overt external controls occurred precipitously. At the same time, problems and confrontations resulting from alcohol were emerging or increasing, further compromising the tenuous authority of the older generations. In some communities an authority vacuum emerged, with ambivalently perceived non-Aboriginal community advisers reluctant to take responsibility.

Predictors of adaptation

The particular history and experiences of various communities resulted in different responses to this new political order. Within the towns, the long-established and most acculturated 'coloured' population were least obviously influenced. For the other four groups previously identified (see figure 8.1), the reduction in external 'order' (imposed structure) had what, in retrospect, may seem obvious consequences. For Aborigines raised in the bush, or for those coming into settlements most recently (1960s and 1970s), the consequences have been profound. They had no interim period to develop adaptive coping strategies (within the transitional settings of European-controlled stations and missions), and encountered a majority culture that did not value their traditional identity (internalised structure). The impact of alcohol on this group has been devastating.

For the population who had grown up and lived in fringe camps the situation has not changed substantially. This group continued to minimise the impact of external controls on their way of life which, however, involved a relatively greater exposure to the acculturative stresses that are part of fringe-camp existence. Compared to the more recent arrivals, they have developed considerable 'street sense' and ability to work the system within a limited field of power.

Station Aborigines have fared relatively better than other groups, their adaptive transitional identity facilitating the development of an enduring internal structure. Continuing identification with the pastoral industry is clearly evident, even among many who left the stations a decade earlier. Those that have been able to remain on their stations (either working for non-Aborigines or part of the nascent Aboriginal pastoral concerns) stand out in the experience of this writer, demonstrating confidence and self-esteem not evident to such a degree in the other groups (save for the long-term, relatively acculturated, town population identified above).

By sharp contrast, Aborigines from mission settings have experienced more difficulty. By the mid-1980s all missions in the Kimberley had ceded responsibility to local control through the Department of Aboriginal Affairs. Prior to this, the smooth running of these establishments reflected almost total control of day-to-day life by mission staff, with minimal delegation of responsibility. At greatest disadvantage were the isolated communities containing greater proportions of tradition-oriented Aborigines, specifically La Grange, Balgo, Kalumburu and Forrest River (the special circumstances of mission populations removed to town reserves will be dealt with below). There seems to have been little attempt to adapt the existing, albeit problematic, mission structures. Their removal was not accompanied by the development of alternatives, with the absence of authority and leadership for some communities compounded by the disruptive consequences of heavy drinking.

A separate mission group had been precipitated into fringe-camp life several decades earlier. The entire Presbyterian mission at Port George (later Kunmunya) had been moved to Mowanjum just outside Derby in 1956, and the Sunday Island mission population transported to the Derby reserve in 1962. The former (predominantly full-descent Aborigines) developed into the now permanent settlement of Mowanjum community whereas the Sunday Islanders (with a large proportion of mixed-descent Aborigines), after a decade languishing in the reserve environment, themselves organised a return to One Arm Point near Sunday Island in 1971 to set up a new community. Mowanjum is, thus, more typical of fringe-camp adaptation. Sunday Islanders represent a special instance, with a history of longer contact with non-Aborigines and involvement in the pearling industry. They remained relatively separate from other Aboriginal groups during their decade in Derby and, with advocates from inside and from outside of the community, were better placed to deal with Europeans (Robinson 1973). So, they are perhaps closer (in terms of internalised structure) to the situation of station Aborigines.

CONSEQUENCES FOR CHILDREN

The shift to fringe-camps from stations and missions concentrated groups, resulting in higher population densities. Additionally, reductions in infant mortality increased the proportion of children by comparison to earlier times. It was anticipated that Aboriginal adults would reassert their role in the discipline and control of children. As noted earlier in discussing Tonkinson's (1982) Jigalong study, Aborigines in that remote Pilbara community had relinquished a significant dimension of that function to European mission control, defining it as 'whitefellow business'. When it became redefined as 'blackfellow business' a conflict arose, with some among the older residents hankering after the predictable structure of the past:

> What they miss is the kind of paternalism that was unflinchingly applied in the social field of 'the settlement' — that which absolved them of tasks they did not want, or feel any need, to assume. The present problem stems from several major sources: continuities in Aboriginal understandings about power and its locus as external to the self; traditional attitudes to children, whose non-problematic status in the precontact society was transformed by the settlement situation and a new social field that demanded new rules; and a legacy of missionary paternalism that masked emerging problems and left Aborigines ill-prepared to assume necessary responsibilities associated with community self-management. (1982 : 124)

The demands of reasserting control over the behaviour of children was also affected by structural changes in child-care. Problem drinking, early mortality from non-natural causes, and incarceration — all disproportionately directly involve young adult to middle-aged Aboriginal males, often, as described previously, withdrawing them from their families. A major consequence is the disruption of paternal roles, with an increasing emphasis on the mother-grandmother axis in terms of stability in the child's environment. However, with alcohol-use also now increasing among younger women, the burden of responsibility for their children is frequently passed on to older women, leading to what Brady (1991) has called the 'stressed out granny syndrome'.

Aboriginal children are still more likely to develop within an environment of scarcity and adversity compared to the non-Aboriginal population. Gracey (1991), reviewing information on the Kimberley, pointed out that this is the case from intra-uterine development, through infancy to childhood; it results in low birthweight, increased foetal mortality, failure to thrive, and deficits in later childhood growth. Environmental factors identified in the reviewed research included inadequate housing, hygiene and feeding practices, compounded by repeated infections throughout childhood. Nutrition research has demonstrated that, while the diet of Kimberley Aboriginal children is deficient in a range of essential nutrients — including calcium, retinol, vitamin D, and certain trace elements — the primary cause of decreased growth is a lack of calories (Smith 1991). Remote communities are doubly disadvantaged in terms of nutrition, with substantially increased costs for basic foodstuffs. The understandable appeal of expensive consumer items in the context of limited budgeting skills has further impacts on sustenance income. In a prospective study of 49 infants from birth to two years from Fitzroy valley communities, it was found that: 'Families of children who grew adequately had fewer consumer goods such as televisions and refrigerators than those whose growth was worse' (Gracey, Sullivan, Burke & Gracey 1989 : 323).

In the relentless topography of poverty, Aboriginal children in unstable environments are, thus, exposed to physical, psychosocial and sociocultural deprivation (Nurcombe 1976). Their environments are frequently lacking, not only in terms of cultural/psychological stimulation (increasingly being television-based), but in terms of what would be considered basic to the surroundings of non-Aboriginal children and the development of fundamental 'life-skills'. While life-skills are clearly culturally informed, and while such skills may not be relevant to the lifestyle of many Kimberley Aborigines, their importance to the majority culture does impact on Aborigines. For example, in the report of the Mining and Exploration Working Group participating in the 1987 Kimberley Regional Planning Study, the importance of training programs for Aborigines was emphasised at the outset. However, soon thereafter it was noted that: 'Aborigines entering training programmes sometimes need additional "life" skills to enable them to understand the requirements of working' (Griffiths 1987 : 4), these skills being then defined in terms of such things as hygiene, punctuality, responsibility. While the lack of such skills did not preclude the building of a viable cattle industry, which was reliant on Aboriginal effort and responsibility, the new economic developments of the region make different demands. Accordingly, the absence of such skills becomes a marker of, and at times a pretext for exclusion.

This may be illustrated by the results of a house-to-house survey by the community nurse in a stable community on the main road through the region, which in 1987 revealed the following for a population of 247. A total of 36 dwellings, of which 14 had greater than nine people and 10 had septic systems. There were: 13 refrigerators; 3 washing machines; 14 tables; 35 chairs; 60 beds; 10 built-in cupboards; 2 food cupboards; 4 clothes cupboards with no clothes hangers. For cooking facilities, 4 used gas sometimes (Margaret Stott, personal communication 1988). Children reared in such environments are disadvantaged should they wish to gain access to the benefits of the wider society not only by underdeveloped educational and linguistic tools but also by deprivation of experiences basic to children in the majority culture — and valued by those who control access.

Gender differences

As pointed out earlier, children in drinking environments are likely to have to contend with parental — usually paternal — absence. These forces have a significant impact on child development. For Aboriginal boys, the compromise of traditional and contemporary role models resulting from the father's absence or functional unavailability has a damaging impact on the development of male identity (Edmunds 1990). The conflict of adult ideals was reflected in an observation recounted by a schoolteacher at a remote Catholic school. Boys and girls at the same primary level had been asked what they would like to do when they left school. The girls gave answers reflecting identification with roles and ideals that they encountered in their experience of the world — teacher's aide, health worker, mother. The boys, by contrast, had derived their ideals from television — karate or boxing champion (kung-fu movies being very popular[7]) — or had stated that 'they'd pick up their cheque at the office'.

The experience of cultural exclusion can also differentially impact on male development. In describing psychopathological reactions to elements of cultural exclusion among American Blacks, Brody identified issues stemming from problems in masculine identification:

> These patients came from a matricentric family structure . . . of a submissive or remote father and a controlling mother without respect for her spouse because he cannot act according to white, i.e., dominant, ideals or prototypes. This family structure contributes to further identity confusion because it does not provide adequate role definition for its growing sons; it does not provide the contributions under which a boy can learn effectively how to become an adult male. (1966 : 857)

Systematic information regarding sex differences affecting children was not collected during this research. However, several incidental findings will be described, the interpretations being entirely speculative.

During the course of work at One Arm Point on the Dampier Land peninsula, the headmaster of the school noted that the boys at that school seemed to have more difficulty with achievement than the girls, and also that they seemed to be smaller. From a casual observation of the children lined up during a break, his suspicion regarding size appeared to be well-founded. Coincidentally, a child anthropometric survey had been conducted in the area by the CSIRO Division of Human Nutrition. Growth charts, based on measurements of children at seven Kimberley communities including One Arm Point, were thus available. The data indeed indicated that boys at One Arm Point fell lower on the percentile charts than boys from other communities, whereas girls showed no such difference. Measurements of circulating growth hormone carried out in 1983 and 1984 showed no significant difference between the communities. However, growth hormone levels from samples taken in 1986 showed One Arm Point boys to be significantly lower ($p < .05$) than boys from any other community, whereas girls again showed no such difference (Richard Smith, personal communication 1988).

These differences were not seen among children from Lombardina, a community 15 kilometres distant, with a similar ethnic background and similar nutrition sources. The most significant difference between the communities lies in their history. As noted previously, the Sunday Island population had been uprooted in the early 1960s and transferred to Derby prior to citizenship rights, returning to nearby One Arm Point a decade later. Those experiencing the most disruptive consequences of the changes are the group now parents of adolescents. Lombardina, by contrast, has had a relatively more stable continuous history as a Catholic mission. The question that arose (and must remain speculation) is: Could the social disruptions experienced by the Bardi of One Arm Point, which impacted most profoundly on the social roles of males in the generation who are now parents of children and adolescents, result in stresses differentially affecting their sons and daughters and thus their growth rates? As Green, Campbell and David (1984) noted, most research on psychogenic failure to thrive has focused on maternal psychopathology, although alcoholism and father-absence have been mentioned.

At the same time a brief ad hoc questionnaire was distributed to the teachers at the One Arm Point school, asking them to rate boys' and girls' performance in their classes on each of eight dimensions scored from 1 (very poorly) to 5 (very well). This was later circulated to teachers at predominantly Aboriginal schools throughout the region. The results are recorded in table 12.

Table 12 *Mean teacher perception scores for Kimberley Aboriginal children, by sex*

	No. of children	Mean scores	
		Boys	Girls
	N		
Oral comprehension	26	3.23	3.27
Written comprehension	24	3.04	3.17
Mathematical concepts	25	3.36	3.24
Constructional ability	26	3.88	3.54
Coordinated skills	26	3.85	3.62
Self-motivation	26	2.96	3.35*
Self-discipline	26	3.12	3.62*
Acceptance of direction	26	3.19	3.65**

Notes: * $p < .05$
** $p < .01$
Score for each dimension was given on a range of 1–5.

The limitations of these data are obvious. It is recognised that the survey is affected by numerous confounding variables, including sex and ethnicity of the teachers, differential maturity for boys and girls, which may operate across cultures and setting. At most it suggests that teachers tend to see little difference between boys and girls in their comprehension and mathematical capabilities, a tendency to perceive slightly better functioning of boys in motor activities, with the most prominent differences being in the dimensions which relate to the internalisation of controls, in all of which girls are perceived as performing better. One cannot extrapolate to actual functionality of these children, but it does reinforce the suggestion that Aboriginal boys in the Kimberley are perceived (at least by their teachers) as demonstrating less self-control.

The third incidental finding arose from a request related to the earlier study of Kimberley mortality. A school in the Broome region with students from throughout the region, requested help to identify deceased ex-students. The school had been graduating for only 11 years; 23 male deaths were identified (around 9 per cent of the male graduates) and 5 female deaths. This led to an examination of the same age-group from the mortality study (see chapter 4). Among those individuals 15–30 years of age at the time of death, the ratio of male to female deaths for the region as a whole was 2 : 1. It was not possible to directly compare ratios to those deaths from the school (as many students had attended only briefly and there had initially been somewhat fewer girls at the school); however, the ratio for males to females appeared to be considerably higher than one would have expected based on the ratio in the general population.

While this social experience may be protective for females, it seems more likely that, for some reason, it tends to heighten male vulnerability. A possible mechanism may be that boys have more difficulty adapting to the change: moving from community to town life and, then, their later return. They may experience more acutely the conflict arising from proffered ideals and goals that are subsequently found to be unrealisable — the experience of which becomes internalised as self-deprecation resulting in deficits in self-esteem, possibly manifest by recklessness and self-destructive behaviour. By contrast, as earlier noted, motherhood has significant psychological, social and economic implications and may also act as a protective factor for young Aboriginal females.

The cycle of vulnerability

The environment of Aboriginal childhood — whether for females or for males — is often harsh. In a graphic description of late 1960s fringe-camp life Nurcombe alluded to the entrapment of Aboriginal children by their circumstances. His observations could apply to children in some Kimberley Aboriginal communities nearly two decades later:

> The individual who grows up in this environment is trapped by strong feelings of fatalism, helplessness, dependence and inferiority. He lives for the present, from day to day. He grows to have children who are also trapped, and who are aware of the increasing gap between them and their dominant neighbours. He sees his inability to close the gap as due to discrimination, whereas Europeans stereotype him as hopeless, shiftless and unemployable.
>
> The range of work he can do is, in fact, limited, and this is a direct consequence of his educational background. He enters primary school with a receptive verbal capacity at least 18 months below the mean for his age group and about six months below the mean for his rural European neighbours. Unfortunately he does not catch up; he falls farther and farther behind. He reaches his limit of educability in a conventional setting by about the fourth year of primary school, around the time when hypothetical arithmetical concepts are introduced. The deficits are cumulative. He is advanced class by class until the first or second year of secondary school, when he drops out at the statutory leaving age. (1970:6)

Many Kimberley Aboriginal children must contend with socio-environmental factors to which most non-Aboriginal children are not exposed, and which have significant consequences for self-esteem. They are further disadvantaged by the health consequences of those environments. In addition to sub-optimal growth, there are specific problems that are relevant to education, such as the continuing high levels of ear disease. Thus, while the Australian Bureau of Statistics estimates that 2 per cent of the national population have hearing loss sufficient to interfere with communication, hearing loss was found in approximately 20 per cent of an urban Western Australian Aboriginal population (Kwinana, 20 kilometres from the capital), and 40 per cent of two remote communities, one of which was La Grange in the Kimberley (Kelly & Weeks 1991).

High rates of school absenteeism among Aborigines are both cause and consequence of the influence of these factors on self-esteem, also reflecting the failure of existing systems to deliver education in a culturally informed and appropriate manner. However, the existing systems can only deliver services to children who attend. They are caught in the dilemma of either enforcing demands for attendance, and thus being perceived as authoritarian or paternalistic; or presuming that non-attendance is a matter of Aboriginal choice, and 'respecting' that. In one Broome Catholic school absenteeism is negligible, a result of an active program requiring staff follow-up of those missing. In Derby the 1987 absentee rate at the Catholic primary school (90 per cent Aboriginal) was about 30 per cent. The high school had an Aboriginal absentee rate for years one to seven of 28 per cent, compared to a white rate of 6 per cent. An examination of the 37 most consistent absentees at the primary school demonstrated that 26 (70 per cent) came from families in which there was heavy drinking or gambling. There is an overflow of consequences from drinking and gambling that affects everyone in communities where they are prevalent. Most vulnerable in the long term are children. Unfortunately, certain aspects of such environments perpetuate a transgenerational cycle of vulnerability:

> Children and adolescents who grow up without their home base providing the necessary support and encouragement are likely to be less cheerful, to find life — especially intimate relationships — difficult, and to be vulnerable in conditions of adversity. In addition they are likely to have difficulties when they come to marry and have children of their own. (Bowlby 1988 : 9)

The most significant recent issues affecting Aboriginal childhood have, thus, been a breakdown of the processes (both traditional, and on stations and missions) that structured and made safe periods of developmental transition. The rituals, social controls and expectations that guided males through adolescence, from the under-regulated world of a matrifocal boyhood, to the social expectations of manhood, have become less salient. The 'freedom' of childhood gives way to the constraints of poverty, dependence, and continuing rejection by the dominant society. Traditional, culturally constituted defences are inadequate to the demands of a new and rapidly changing social situation. Deprived of the social symbols and structures that ground coping and adaptive processes in the wider society, there is frustration and anger — externalised towards non-Aboriginal authority, or internalised towards their culture, their partners and themselves.

ANOMIE, EXCLUSION AND POWERLESSNESS

Any work that includes suicide within its ambit must consider anomie. It has repeatedly been invoked in relation to Aborigines.

Warner suggested that a Murngin Aborigine anticipating death experienced a withdrawal of social supports: 'The social configuration in which he finds himself operating at this time is one of anomia for him' (1969 [1937]: 230). Cawte interpreted Kaiadilt vulnerability to depression as due to 'difficulties in the area of human ecology, their history of recent disaster, forced migration and poor social integration or "anomie"' (1972: 79). In discussing the compromised role of religion in structuring Aboriginal social order, Mol (1982) indicated that 'alienation, anomie and lack of motivation are the backlash of rudderless communication — a not uncommon phenomenon amongst Aboriginals affected by the West' (1982: 50). Kolig presented the association with powerlessness:

> Barely alive after the first Western onslaught had subsided, Aborigines have since found themselves almost totally powerless vis-a-vis the wider, white dominated Australian society. They have shrunk to an uninfluential and rather inconsequential remote minority without power and prestige. Internally the disruption of the traditional power process has widely resulted in anarchical conditions festering within Aboriginal sub-society, and often one feels distinctly reminded of Durkheim's anomia. (1982: 15)

Of Greek etymology, the first known use of the word *anomy* in English characters was that of William Lambarde, an Elizabethan jurist who, true to its classical sense, utilised it in 1591 in terms of 'the lack of normative standards, the absence of shared norms from which disorder, doubt and uncertainty would ensue' (Orru 1986: 183). The sociological use of the term dates from Durkheim's study of suicide. His was a social usage to describe an environment in which a relative absence of norms predisposed to increasing *rates* of suicide. However, it has often come to be used to describe an opposite situation in which there is pervasive overcontrol and prohibitions, a situation in its extreme described by Durkheim as fatalism, also predisposing to increasing rates of suicide.

Subsequently, the use of the concept has been confused, with the individualisation of anomie, which has come to be associated with a personal psychological experience of marginality and maladjustment (Munch 1974). Srole and others attempted to quantify this, with Cole and Zuckerman (1971) providing an inventory of 98 empirical studies up to 1964. Ultimately, 'anomie' came to refer to a social condition, and 'anomia' to describe a psychological experience. Certain theories integrate social and psychological usages, Merton hypothesising, rather tautologically, that 'anomic individuals are more apt to engage in deviant behavior, the higher the degree of anomie in the social system' (1971 : 230).

Returning to the uses of the terms opening this section, Kolig and Cawte appear to use the term in its social sense, Warner and Mol suggesting an individual experience. It is the social use that is relevant to this discussion, offering an avenue for a more detailed examination of exclusion and powerlessness. Merton provided a clear connection with Brody's concept of cultural exclusion in his definition of anomie as 'a breakdown in the cultural structure, occurring particularly when there is an acute disjunction between cultural norms and goals and the social structured capacities of members of the group to act in accord with them' (in Clinard 1971 : 12). The process of acculturation necessitates adoption of the norms and goals of the dominant group. This is mandatory where the pressures are to assimilate; it is less obvious, but still present, where the process involves integration and self-determination.

To merge into the current of non-Aboriginal life — assimilation — requires re-socialisation. Berger and Luckmann (1979) pointed out that re-socialisation is at odds with primary socialisation (infant and childhood internalisation of basic roles) and secondary socialisation (based on subsequent social experiences). These latter socialisation forces are particularly powerful in societies of limited complexity, as the pressures to conform are correspondingly greater. The failure of assimilation, thus, reflects Aboriginal (rejection of re-socialisation) and non-Aboriginal (cultural exclusion) factors. While assimilation policies have been renounced, these forces continue — the material and status benefits of the wider society still requiring negotiation in non-Aboriginal terms. Aborigines, like other excluded groups, continue to experience a dissonance between goals and means. Merton (in Clinard 1971) provided a schema for examining adaptations to this disjunction on which Born's (1970) typology, outlined previously, was based (see table 13).

To clarify this schema in terms of the experience of Aborigines as an excluded group, 'cultural goals' should be understood as the incorporated norms and values of the majority culture — re-socialisation. 'Rejection' of institutionalised means should be read as the denial of those means by the dominant culture — cultural exclusion. Thus, ritualism per Merton (Born's retreatism) represents a rejection of dominant culture norms and an affirmation of

Table 13 *Merton's typology of modes of adaptation:
a comparison with Born*

Merton	Born	Cultural goals	Institutionalised means
Conformity	Reconciliation	+	+
Innovation	Innovation	+	−
Ritualism	Retreatism	−	+
Retreatism	Withdrawal	−	−
Rebellion		±	±

Notes: + signifies acceptance.
       − signifies rejection.
       ± signifies rejection of prevailing values and substitution of new values.

'tradition' as a *consequence* of exclusion; a denial of access to the means of the dominant society. Rebellion may, thus, be conceptualised as the reaffirmation of Aboriginality in the political arena, which requires rejecting European values, with delineation of new goals (for instance, land rights, autonomous control), combined with devising new means (political praxis). Ironically, this entails an apparent rejection of the norms of the dominant society while appropriating its means.

Aboriginal groups in the Kimberley have experienced up to a century of accelerating change, in which the process of equilibrative adaptation to environmental demands (referred to by Laughlin and Brady [1978] as 'homeorhesis') has been incomplete. In a setting of unremitting deprivation, adaptive potential is compromised, with orientation increasingly towards the short term, a day-to-day existence. Such activities as gambling and drinking are powerfully reinforced among a group with little to lose.

In the areas of most rapid social change, adaptive capacities are maximally compromised. Such settings, which predispose individuals to responses characterised by Merton as ritualism or retreatism, appear most closely to approximate the social configuration of anomie. A self-reinforcing disintegrative cycle develops and, with the breakdown of sociocultural integration, personal distress increases. This was presented by de Figueiredo (1983) as the 'law of sociocultural demoralization', which states that 'at a given rate of sociocultural change, the prevalence of demoralization in a community is inversely associated with the sociocultural integration in that community' (1983 : 77).

Demoralisation is also referred to repeatedly in descriptions of

Aborigines. As used by de Figueiredo, the term describes a state of distress combined with a subjective sense of incompetence. That seems to be consistent with the general usage. This presents difficulties for those with experience of Aboriginal communities as, even in those materially deprived settings, Aborigines often do not seem to be manifestly distressed or troubled by their lot. Such superficial examinations often suggest, to those wanting to see it that way, that 'they don't care', or that 'that's how they want it'. However, as was demonstrated by the HSCL-25 section of the QARK, specific inquiry clearly reveals admissions of psychological distress.

The confusion stems from culture-bound expectations of the communication of distress. The European articulation of personal distress is as a psychological experience, usually in response to a defined precipitant, with set emotional manifestations. There is generally no difficulty in interpreting Aboriginal mourning rites as, other than being extreme by European standards, they have a defined cause and clearly understood affective response. However, the issues that have been discussed above are pervasive and unremitting for certain segments of Kimberley Aboriginal society. No discrete event or point in time is identifiable, and the manifestations can only be understood by recognising the 'idiom of distress' (Nichter 1981). Throughout this work we have, in fact, been discussing this idiom — suicide, violence, problem drinking, and so on.

Compounding Aboriginal vulnerability (particularly that of young males) is the paucity of protective mechanisms subserving psychosocial resilience in the face of adversity. Rutter identified four components to this process:

> protective processes include those that reduce the risk impact by virtue of effects on the riskiness itself or through alteration of exposure to or involvement in the risk; those that reduce the likelihood of negative chain reactions stemming from the risk encounter; those that promote self-esteem and self-efficacy through the availability of secure and supportive personal relationships or successful task accomplishment; and those that open up opportunities. Protection does not reside in the psychological chemistry of the moment but in the ways in which people deal with life changes and in what they do about their stressful or disadvantageous circumstances. (1987 : 329)

The ability of Aborigines in the highest risk groups — children living in environments with frequent heavy drinking, inconstant caretakers and insufficient or intermittent sustenance — to take advantage of these protective mechanisms is limited. Aborigines in such settings are:

- in a culturally informed setting that does not encourage constructive confrontation, thus limiting their capacity to alter exposure to risk in the interpersonal setting;
- restrained by poverty, which reduces the options in terms of physical alternatives;
- restricted in their range of coping mechanisms, with experience favouring avoidance or acting out;
- confronted by a devaluing of traditional sources of self-esteem by a society that also demeans conventional Aboriginal initiatives;
- ensnared in a legacy of inadequate life-skills, poor academic experience and discrimination, with opportunities for social mobility functionally blocked.

Resignation and fatalism might appear reasonable responses to such a situation. Fortunately, however, personal factors are also of critical importance in the development of resiliency (Felsman 1989). Indeed, studies of other underprivileged groups demonstrate that resiliency may develop regardless of the severity of adverse childhood environmental circumstances, particularly if means are provided to confront discrimination and exclusion, as noted by Long and Vaillant in their discussion of disadvantaged urban children in the United States:

> The overwhelming impression . . . is that early, continuous, and improving work opportunities enable most people to overcome even the worst starts to life. If deprived family backgrounds do not necessarily permanently disable the majority of urban children, the intervention and concerted provision of economic opportunity becomes a less hopeless and more urgent task. (1989 : 212)

LIVING ON THE EDGE: GAMBLING AND ABORIGINES

During the Bicentennial year, the annual revenue of the federal government amounted to some $60 billion (*Bulletin* 5 July 1988, p. 132). It was estimated that, during the same year, Australians would risk the equivalent of a third of this total in gambling, translating into $1200 per man, woman and child, of which almost $200 would be lost (*Weekend Australian* 11–12 June 1988, p. 1). In recent decades attitudes towards gambling have changed, with the transformation of the dubious social status of *nouveau riche* bookies into the respectability of the gaming 'industry'. The first Tuesday in November allows the bootless and unhorsed across the continent to participate in the patrician rites of Flemington. From the image of a wily digger playing two-up, to a prime minister at the track or the tables, the construction of gambling is as an activity quintessentially Australian. Its idiom percolates through our language; it has entered our national soul.[8]

What is not captured, even in such startling figures, is the disproportionate impact of gambling on certain sections of the Australian population. Not surprisingly, the poorest in society stand to lose most, even when losing less. At the bottom of the Australian economic ladder, Aborigines attract little contemporary attention to their gambling, and it is their poverty that fuels the absorption, paradoxically often most intense when resources are leanest (Sansom 1980).

White folk wisdom suggests that Aborigines are keen gamblers. Historically, gambling was linked to a spectrum of predispositions including alcoholism and promiscuity, that required legislation in order to protect them from temptations, and by extension, from internal moral weaknesses. Such attitudes were often internalised. For instance, Haebich records a set of 'rules' arrived at, under some pressure, by Aborigines in the Katanning region of southern Western Australia. Following an initial injunction that: 'They must be good', the list went on to include that there should be: 'No gambling in the way of cards and 2-up allowed, they can have a game of cards at night when their work is done but not play for clothes or money' (1988 : 146). Economic expediency was frequently the covert motivation for European indignation, the Moseley Royal Commission capturing this attitude:

> The objection to payment is based on the assertion made by many pastoralists that the native has no idea of the value of money, that he is an easy victim for unscrupulous itinerant hawkers and that it encourages him in his gambling desires, which are firmly fixed. He will, of course, gamble without money; for a game of cards he will, if losing, divest himself piece by piece of his clothing to enable him to continue the game; but, with money, his gambling instincts are aroused to the fullest extent. It may be that, with closer supervision and by taking a greater interest in this attribute of the native, his squandering habits might be checked. The fact remains, however, that as things are at present the money he earns is not of the slightest use to him. (Moseley 1935 : 6)

Attitudes have changed, as have the stakes. Aboriginal gambling is tolerated by non-Aborigines, and remains an important social activity, Robinson observing that:

the winning and losing of money or material possessions is not necessarily the most important aspect of the game . . . card-schools substitute a forum for interaction between people and groups where traditional ceremonial activities have been abandoned, or receive less emphasis in the camp situations of towns and missions. To treat card-playing as 'gambling' is to introduce an immediate bias in its description, and there is a strong possibility that its positive role in interpersonal relations will be underplayed. (1973 : 209)

In the intervening twenty years the social function of gambling has continued. However, as the socioeconomic circumstances of Kimberley Aborigines and the stakes have changed, so have the consequences.

ABORIGINAL GAMBLING IN THE KIMBERLEY

The games

Other than legal gambling, such as TAB (Totalizator Agency Board) and Lotto, there are four major games played in the Kimberley — gambling outside of towns being synonymous with cards. *Kuns*[9] is by far the most common and widespread card game played throughout the region (Robinson 1973; Robinson & Yu 1975). There are a maximum of eight players, dealt five cards (face cards are removed), with rotating dealership. In the late 1980s the fill-in would typically start at $5–10 and progress up to $100 or more by the end of a game, with the winner nominating the amount of the next fill-in. In addition to the main pot (the 'middle'), side bets (the 'up') are made and claimed after the second, fourth and the last card are dealt. At each of these points the hand is summed, a winning hand being divisible by ten — '*kuns*'. If nobody has *kuns*, then the hand with the largest leftover above kuns wins (thus, twenty-seven beats sixteen and thirty-six, but not eighteen).

In some areas a cut is taken for the house (the '*tong*') amounting to one hand from the 'middle' (12.5 per cent) of each round. This probably has an Asian origin, and has been traditionally the practice of small-time gambling entrepreneurs, usually mixed-descent town Aborigines. Part of the attraction of games that 'cut *tong*' is the relatively controlled environment that allows gamblers to get down to the business at hand. Drunks are discouraged from these settings, and players may receive a cup of tea and perhaps some biscuits. A recent wider interest in cutting *tong* appears to reflect the entrepreneurial aspirations accompanying the growing financial sophistication in towns. In more isolated communities cutting *tong* remains rare. If all eight players bet $10 at each point in the game, and in the unlikely event one individual wins at each of the three possible claim points, the total won is $270 for a $20 outlay, with $10 being 'cut for *tong*'. All bets are laid before dealing, thus winning is entirely dependent on chance.

Cuncan (*kunkan*) is played in the same region, though it is less popular. This game involves five players dealt seven cards (if less than five players, eight cards are dealt; and if only two players, ten cards), and resembles rummy. *Tong* is also cut in certain settings, and all bets are laid prior to cards being dealt; thus, the turnover of money is less rapid than *kuns*, but is likewise determined almost entirely by luck.

The last major card game, played in the east and central Kimberley and into the Northern Territory, is two-three-card or *cabul*-card. Less common, this is played with thirteen players dealt two cards initially, then a third. Here *kuns* (ten) itself loses, with scores closest to nine winning. Otherwise, the game is similar to *kuns* with face cards included.

Finally, confined to Broome, there is the game of sticks, a more complicated game of Chinese origin. This was introduced by indentured labour around the turn of the century when, as a world pearling centre, fortunes were made and lost. There are reports of thousands of pounds passing across the tables in a single hand (Hunt 1986). Sticks is the most formalised of the local games, conducted at well patronised venues.

Variants of these games are found. In the south central areas the rules of 'one-take-em' may be in action among young men to prevent money being removed before all is in the hands of one player. Participants are, thus, prohibited from handing out of the ring any money from their winnings until they have either won all the money available, or no longer have anything to lose.

The players

There are no restrictions on who can play. In one very remote community of approximately 200 individuals, less than ten residents other than young children and the infirm elderly could be counted as non-gamblers. While the high visibility, big winner/big spender gamblers tend to be men, women throughout the Kimberley are the constant players. Children as young as eight years old are given change to gamble with, and adolescents are able to join adult circles. Differences in terms of mixed-descent versus full-descent are subtle. There is a larger mixed-descent population involved in playing sticks, reflecting the Broome population structure and because of historical associations with the game. As a result of reduced literacy, full-descent Aborigines somewhat less frequently use legal gambling facilities, although a literate 'broker' may be called on to 'pick one' at the TAB. However, literacy is no obstacle to cards, and the rapidity of calculation involved in the games refutes assumptions of Aboriginal computational ineptness (Robinson & Yu 1975).

The various churches in the Kimberley have at different times all frowned on gambling, and on certain missions gamblers were punished. The decline in the influence of the missions throughout the region in the last decade has been accompanied by an increase in visible gambling. Some fundamentalist groups (such as Children of God, People's Church, Family Church) have taken an active stand against alcohol and gambling. However, in communities where these groups are involved, even if their effect on drinking has been significant, their impact on gambling has been insubstantial.

Alcohol itself has a complicated relationship to gambling, as serious gamblers tend not to drink while gambling, and to frown on drinkers who are disruptive to the game. Drinking is reserved for the aftermath of the game, and is then frequently pursued with enthusiasm. From another perspective, those individuals who are constant heavy drinkers tend not to gamble, as their resources are consumed by alcohol. In addition, the credit of this group is understandably poor. Certain remote communities where alcohol is actively prohibited attract gamblers from outside, as resources there are undiminished by the draining-off of funds for alcohol.

In games based almost entirely on luck, advantages are hard to come by but vigorously sought. Indeed, 'luck' itself may be more than fortuitous, as noted by Robinson in his discussion of Bardi gambling:

> A person wins at cards because he has good luck, and luck is considered to be tangible. Luck is something which is linked with the spirit-world and can be given to men by the *raija*; according to some players, by the major culture heroes themselves. Bad fortune may be attributed to the malevolent *nari*. (1973 : 211)

Abetting luck may involve cheating (which occasionally leads to fights, but is not in itself a source of 'big shame'); however, magic is more commonly resorted to. There are numerous highly esteemed talismans and rituals that are frequently adaptations of traditional magical practices (particularly women's love magic). *Jirri* (Kimberley-wide term of uncertain origin) may be swallowed, rubbed on, or worn, to enhance luck at cards. A powder made from the root of the Leichhardt Pine (*Nauclea orientalis*) found near Timber Creek in the Northern Territory reputedly offers the greatest surety of success, and may be used in a variety of ways. The author was told of young men in one area who rub Bundaberg rum onto their hands before playing (a rum deal?). There appears to be no limit to the substances involved, or the desire to obtain powerful *jirri*, which may consequently be sold at high prices, or exchanged. A full-descent Aborigine, as much at home by the race-tracks and in the casinos of Perth and Darwin as in the card-circles of the Kimberley, described an exchange with a man from distant parts whom he met in his northern travels. The stranger coveted a powerful pearlshell *jirri*, and in exchange offered a stone, an *umbul* (Wunambal, the 'eye' of a river snake — rare *jirri*). These two men meeting secretively to exchange the objects of power from their respective 'countries' conjures an image spanning the millennia.

The stakes

Stakes vary enormously. The single factor that clearly correlates with the amount in the ring is the time since pay-day. As communities tend to have the majority of their residents on one or two payment schedules, money is infused in blocks. There is, thus, a cyclical pattern of funds available to players, although the funds do not necessarily have to be those of the players themselves. For instance, pensioners (who are paid on alternate weeks to unemployment benefits) may be prevailed on to provide money to enter a game during the 'slack-week' ('give us a start'), whilst players may be cajoled by those hovering on the periphery of the ring to 'put me in'.

As previously mentioned, from a $5–10 starting point in a game of *kuns*, the fill-in at the end of the evening can reach $100 and more, thus giving between $200 and $800 riding on the main bets (the 'middle'). Money will circulate until sequestered in one or a few hands, with wins of several thousand dollars not uncommon, and wins up to $5000 being known. While these amounts may seem small by comparison to major gamblers in urban Australia, the stakes are in reality of a different order, as they reflect a major diversion of community sustenance income. Indeed, what may be riding on the cards is the quality of family nutrition for the next fortnight.

The losers

Certain individuals identify and are identified as consistent losers. Those people who regularly part with their money are understandably welcome to the circle; indeed, in certain respects their losses count as credit. In return, they may be invited to share alcohol afterwards, or be credited with a new stake to re-enter the game. However, the elderly and pensioners are the most commonly acknowledged consistent losers. Old-age and invalid pensions generally provide the largest per capita infusions of money into communities, arriving at a time when those settlements are depleted of funds. Peterson (1977), writing about the Central Reserve in 1970 when old-age and invalid pensions were essentially the only predictable sources of income in many communities, suggested that gambling acted to redress the asymmetry in income between pensions and the inconstancy of other sources. In one Kimberley community the games had for a time been structured so that the pensioners could only play amongst themselves to afford them some protection.

The consequences

The consequences must be seen in the broader context of the social and economic realities of Aboriginal Australia. In those Kimberley communities where gambling is common, it is impossible to avoid the direct or indirect repercussions. The fallout from gambling involves the entire community. The sole restriction is the supply of money; its consequences affect physical, psychological and social health.

Physical

The poor nutritional status of Kimberley Aboriginal children has been commented on. An association was made in Western Australia between gambling in Aboriginal communities and under-nutrition, and used by the Western Australian Liberal opposition spokesman on Aboriginal Affairs to support a call for the substitution of food vouchers for welfare payments (*Sunday Times* 12 June 1988).

While this is a contentious position, it is clear that gambling adversely affects nutrition. Given the substantially greater costs of food in remote Aboriginal communities, the line between subsistence and under-nutrition thins. Gambling is a direct competitor for sustenance resources. While the losers forfeit their subsistence income, the winners themselves may jeopardise their food outlay as the winnings are frequently spent on capital and luxury items or alcohol (in very remote communities planes may be chartered to fly the winner and his friends out 'to bust the money' in town, or to fly alcohol in). For some, an option in the face of a week or more without money, is to go hunting or fishing. While this provides highly nutritious food, it again needs to be shared around, and often the responsibilities for supply and preparation fall on a subgroup, usually women. This is further complicated as certain game, particularly kangaroos, have been massively depleted in the central and south Kimberley over the last two decades. To such marginal communities losing money is tantamount to restricting the flexibility and predictability of nutritional sources.

In any setting of compromise, those at greatest risk belong to the group least able to fend for themselves; the children, the aged, and the infirm. Individuals do not need to be directly involved in gambling to be affected. The nutrition of children whose parents or caretakers are heavy players may be neglected while games are in progress. For those whose losses have been substantial, the spectrum of available foods is severely restricted through the remainder of the families' pay period. The general hygiene of households may also be compromised when gambling debts result in electricity and water bills being neglected.

Psychological
The resistance to extinction of intermittently reinforced behaviours such as gambling increases their tenacious appeal in the face of protracted runs of 'bad luck', which is compounded by poverty. Aboriginal life in many communities is such that saving for 'luxury' items is essentially impossible, both because of the negligible margin between costs for essential foods and income, and the vulnerability of retained funds to the demands of others. For many, the only way

in which an accumulation of money at one point in time is foreseeable is the prospect of a big win. With such a hand-to-mouth existence the potential, unlikely or not, of a big win is a far greater motivation than the threat of loss, which at worst throws one on the largesse of the group ('freedom's just another word for nothing left to lose'). However, this pattern is also inimical to the accumulation of resources necessary for any form of planned economic or domestic improvement.

There is a significant difference to the non-Aboriginal psychological sequelae of problem gambling. This usually presents as a result of the social fallout from mounting losses and debts, with agitated depression characterising the desperation phase of the loser. By contrast, for Aborigines in the Kimberley the constraints of poverty limit the degree of indebtedness, which is socially negotiated in a very different way. Furthermore, subjective distress is generally not a feature of indebtedness per se. It is not the actual losing of money that causes problems, but the desire for more in order to continue. The dogged demands to 'put me in', or to 'give me a start' are frequently accompanied by anxious, persistent pestering.

This may be exemplified with information from the QARK random sample. The respondents were almost equally divided between current gamblers and non-gamblers. For both males and females the mean age of gamblers (41 years each) was somewhat less than for non-gamblers (49 years), though similar by sex. For males, just over two-thirds of both gamblers and non-gamblers were drinkers. By contrast, for women, drinkers constituted one-half of the gamblers and only a quarter of the non-gamblers. The HSCL-25 anxiety and depression scores were obtained for 466 subjects (table 14).

Table 14 *HSCL-25 anxiety and depression scores for Kimberley Aborigines, by sex and gambling status*

| | | | HSCL-25 scores | | | |
| | | | Anxiety | | Depression | |
		N	mean	SD	mean	SD
Males	Gamblers	115	1.429	.506	1.287	.335
	Non-gamblers	123	1.275*	.409	1.267	.32
Females	Gamblers	112	1.468	.498	1.432	.428
	Non-gamblers	116	1.367	.414	1.398	.419

Note: * $p < .05$ (just fails to reach $p < .01$).

There is a tendency for higher anxiety scores among gamblers, which reaches statistical significance only for males. By contrast, the depression scores show only minimal differences. The significant difference in anxiety scores among males but not females may relate to a reduced sense of security regarding predictable income among males compared to females. Additionally, for some, securing the means to continue gambling leads to involvement in illegal activities.

For the child, parental gambling may mean a care-giver who is only intermittently available to provide both the nutritional and emotional nurturing required for phase-appropriate development. Children of regular heavy gamblers are at times both physically and emotionally neglected for variable periods. Wins on the part of their parents become linked to the sudden appearance of luxury items, food, and indulgence. From well prior to the age at which a child can gamble, the game itself is associated powerfully with temporary (and frequently lavish) relief from deprivation, which in turn is a powerful reinforcer for gambling later in life. The spillover of consequences also impacts on schooling, as games pursued late into the night leave children exhausted, and parents poorly motivated in the morning to prepare them for school. Lack of money for lunch at school is often cited as a reason for non-attendance.

Social
Gambling in many Kimberley communities is a major focus of socialisation and discourse. Many other activities have become organised around it, such as drinking, and the patterns of re-distribution of credit and obligation within the community. It is a *social* activity, and as such has powerful integrative functions for certain subgroups. It has been suggested that restrictions enforced against gamblers on reserves in previous decades contributed to the movement from those settings to squatters' camps (Rowley 1972c). It may also act as a powerful competitor for other social pursuits, such as investment and involvement in traditional pursuits and ritual performances (Maddock 1977).

The credit function of gambling within Kimberley Aboriginal communities extends widely. Indeed, winners may at the end of the evening be playing against their own money, having funded others to enter or re-enter the game. Credit is a central theme in the social organisation of Aboriginal communities (Sansom 1980), Aborigines being, by and large, excluded from the credit resources of the wider society. The ebb and flow of funding that accompanies gambling, thus, allows maintenance of a potential line of credit. However, as a corollary, in such situations the holding of funds becomes extremely difficult. Money ungambled or unspent is vulnerable to the predations and demands of others, since all gamblers are in a circle of reciprocal indebtedness. There is, accordingly, a pressure to gamble just as there is to consume among drinkers — the rate of these activities contributing to social standing (Collmann 1979b; Sansom 1977). Such demands militate against thrift, and those attempting to conserve funds may be compelled to resort to various devices, such as hiding money, or investing in external agents. These agents in isolated communities may be Europeans (teachers, advisers, health workers) who are outside the credit system. For Aborigines who have non-welfare income, these patterns of rapid expenditure undermine the tangible benefits of employment as, practically, the fruits of labour evaporate leaving only the prospect of more labour. The line between welfare and 'king for a day' thins.

This is not to suggest that gamblers, themselves, fail to recognise gambling as causing problems. Numerous devices are resorted to in an attempt to minimise the negative consequences. For instance, many gamblers reported that they will try to buy all their provisions immediately after being paid, and before heading off to the card circle, recognising that their capacity to hold onto money when the gambling starts is limited. And the relationship with alcohol has been touched on earlier. While drinking is not typical during games, and drunks discouraged, the community as a whole may suffer in the wake of a large win. Alcohol is almost invariably involved, and may result in the sudden infusion of large amounts into otherwise dry, remote communities.

SUMMARY

Gambling is here to stay, for non-Aborigines and Aborigines, and its profitability (for both government and private enterprise) will ensure that it flourishes. Other than a small group of 'pathological' gamblers in the wider society, most non-Aboriginal gambling involves expenditure from surplus income. Here lies a fundamental difference: there is no surplus income for most Aborigines in remote Australia. For those communities where gambling is pervasive, it is the conduit for a major drain on resources and energy, contributing to patterns of indebtedness and rapid expenditure that undermine personal and community development. As such it must be seen to be contributing to the climate of dependency in the economically marginal Aboriginal communities of remote Australia.

Thus, the appeal of gambling will remain undiminished. The topography of poverty, broken fleetingly by the dreams of a big win, will ensure that. Anticipation, and the excitement of the unanticipated, enliven the dulled rhythms of daily life. In such a landscape gambling may appear a not unreasonable pastime — a tension breaker — or at most perhaps a minor vice to be overlooked, given the harsh socio-economic conditions of Aboriginal life. This is not to suggest that gambling has caused this situation, just as alcohol is not *the* cause of Aboriginal 'problems'. Both are epiphenomena reflecting intracultural and intercultural forces and conflicts at a profoundly deeper strata of Aboriginal experience.

While gambling has significant medical consequences in the Aboriginal communities of the Kimberley, its intensity and form is a result of social and economic forces acting in a particular cultural setting. However, the potency of gambling lies, in part, in its ability to undermine not only the economic means of advancement but also the means of subsistence. Gambling contributes to the stagnation of plans for the future in order to sustain desperate hopes in the present. Gambling in this area of Aboriginal Australia is quintessentially the foreshortening of desire.

NOTES

1. Rhys Jones made this point at the plenary session of the 1990 ANZAAS conference in Hobart.
2. From the East Kimberley through into the Northern Territory the Indonesian word *balanda* is used by Aborigines to denote a European.
3. According to Bell (1983), Aranda kinship relationships were 'mapped' onto country.
4. Brady's (1991a) comprehensive review demonstrates that petrol sniffing is most prevalent in three regions; in Arnhem Land, Central Australia, and the eastern goldfields region of Western Australia. Until 1991 it had not been considered a problem in the Kimberley, at which time it emerged in a remote ex-mission community with contacts to the Centre.
5. From the QARK sample it emerged that about one in seven of the Aborigines in their fourth and fifth decade, and one in four of those older, had been raised by non-Aborigines and were, thus, in one way

or another subjects of removal. The process in the eastern States was of a different order. As recently as the 1960s, Aboriginal children (particularly those of mixed-descent) were removed from their parents for their 'moral protection', to be raised in state and mission custody. In New South Wales it is estimated that some 5625 children were removed between 1883 and 1969 (Read 1981). Massacres and murders aside, this systematic forced transfer of children from one group to another is sufficient to support accusations of genocide as defined under the United Nations' 'Principles of International Law', to which Australia is a signatory (Tatz 1983). The psychological consequences for those removed, and their families, are only now being explored, and scattered families re-united through the organisation 'Link-Up' (Edwards & Read 1989).

6. The salience of the sacred in the lives of Kimberley Aborigines appears to vary predictably by age, but also by sex. During the random sample study all male informants were asked if they had been through initiation law, and both males and females were asked whether they would wish this for their children or grandchildren. Among older males and females the proportion answering affirmatively to the latter was high, some three-quarters of females and over four-fifths of males. For middle-aged and younger adult males this fell to a plateau of around half. However, for similarly aged females the proportion answering positively continued to fall, to less than a third of those below 30 years of age.

7. In a discussion of petrol sniffing in Arnhem Land, Brady commented on the television and videos in the context of gang identification:

    The supremely masculine ambience of the gangs has been partly inspired by the burgeoning popularity of videos, which are particularly prevalent in Arnhem Land. Virtually every house has a video machine; one I visited had three T.V. sets. Kung Fu movies have an ongoing fascination; although the Rambo films have superseded them. (1991)

8. This section is based on a paper I wrote in conjunction with my brother; E. M. Hunter & R. M. Spargo, 'What's the big deal? Aboriginal gambling in the Kimberley region'. *Medical Journal of Australia 149*, 1988, 668–672.

9. I am indebted to Peter Randolph of the Western Australian Museum, who, after reading my original paper, provided a copy of the Robinson and Yu (1975) paper on *kuns*. The spelling of this word varies somewhat, previously being rendered by me as *'cunce'* and by Robinson (1973) as *'guns'*.

Structures and Change

Several years ago I was talking to Ginger, a hard-living European Kimberley resident. He had been in the region for many years and had lived with Aborigines, more by default than by choice. Regardless, he was at pains to emphasise how tolerant he was of Aboriginal ways, how he tried to treat 'blackfellows just like they were white'. As if to underline this he added that he'd 'always give a blackfellow a smoke'. Here lay his recent gripe. He explained that he had always been a careful drinker ('not like the blacks, they can't hold the grog, once they get the flagon . . .'). Unfortunately, on this occasion he had been arrested for public intoxication, sharing the cell with a group of about 15 Aborigines who were in various stages of intoxication and recovery. While for them this was a familiar experience, for Ginger (rather surprisingly) it was the first time. By morning he was in considerable distress, seeking relief where he could find it: 'there was this bloke that I kind of knew who was pacing up and down. I was burning for a smoke and I see he had one going. So I went up to him and said "hey mate, how about a smoke?" Then the bastard turns around and tells me to go get a job!'

Ginger was in no condition to appreciate the humour of the ironic inversion. His anger stemmed from having interpreted the response to his request as an affront to him personally — despite his being the sort of individual who, in his own eyes, could treat 'a blackfellow like a whitefellow'. However, the Aboriginal riposte was based on a lifetime of such experiences, of denials of his individuality as a result of his racial identity. This episode contributed to Ginger's conviction that 'you can't understand 'em'. Indeed, he couldn't.

SOCIOCULTURAL IMPOSITIONS

Attempts to 'understand them' have a long history. Early explorers, settlers, legislators, and anthropologists saw Aborigines refracted through the lenses of then current racial 'theories'. Aborigines were quickly incorporated into an expedient worldview based on a hierarchy of primitiveness (Jones 1989). Their all too obvious susceptibility to the consequences of contact is clear in the melancholy-suffused portrayals current during the last century, reflecting an all too obvious ambivalence about the anticipated racial and cultural loss (Maynard 1985). The vanishing 'sable nomad' was a recurrent symbol in a European mythical Australian landscape. On some metaphysical level the 'passing of the Aborigines' suggested the pain necessary to the birth of a new society. It also, of course, legitimised the appropriation of land, and minimised the moral discomfort associated with facilitating their passage.

Thus, in addition to being either obstacles (to settlement) or resources (labour), Aborigines had a symbolic function for Europeans. To so function as signifiers, they had to conform to European expectations rather than be understood in their own terms — a task which was, anyhow, complicated by the changing sociopolitical milieu and an uncompromising 'otherness'. As described early in this book, depictions of Aborigines by early writers generally catered to preconceived ideas, be they of savagery or simplicity. Those observers were generally not sensitive to the nuances of the contact situation. Aborigines in literature only gradually began to be treated as real people, albeit romanticised, with serious attempts to address Aboriginal subjectivity emerging in the works of writers such as Xavier Herbert and Patrick White. In these (and other) portrayals, the intercultural distance is articulated through an 'otherness' which has remained elusive, reflecting a history which is 'different from that of white Australia. It comes from a different beginning; it occupies a different space in the present; it is moving towards a different future' (Healy 1978 : 293).

The exploration of Aboriginality by Aborigines has only recently had an audience, which remains predominantly white. Black writers such as Jack Davis, Oodgeroo Noonuccal (Kath Walker) and Mudrooroo Narogin (Colin Johnson) are challenging these readers with language that consciously excludes (Shoemaker 1989). Where white writers had struggled to understand the divide in white terms, black authors have focused on this as a central theme in their exploration of Aboriginal identity, both as continuity and opposition.

While certain symbols of Aboriginal Australia are increasingly and widely recognised, for non-Aborigines their meaning is informed by the needs of a changing sociopolitical climate. A construction

     Aboriginal health and history

of traditional or 'authentic' Aboriginal culture has been valorised in the service of defining an 'Australian' prehistory (Morris 1988). Guilt and concern for atonement is reflected in images privileging Aborigines as victims, contributing to a political climate characterised as 'goodwill guilt' (Tatz 1983 : 299). Deviance has been recently foregrounded in portrayals of Aborigines as alcoholic, violent and uncontrollable — a rhetoric, as shown earlier, that appeals to an increasingly reactionary segment of the general public. As Shoemaker noted, the difficulties with symbols continues: 'White Australian administrators, politicians, anthropologists and writers have experienced profound difficulties in proceeding from a conception of black Australians as indigenous symbols to an appreciation of Aborigines as people' (1989 : 188). Despite the rhetoric of self-determination, Aborigines remain largely dependent on, and thus controlled by, European institutions, with Europeans central in terms of controlling access to the records and artefacts of the past, adjudicating claims to land, defining standards by which Aborigines are judged, and determining the very definition of who constitutes an Aborigine.

During the last decade the Australian public has had unprecedented exposure to Aboriginal issues through the media. This has been largely through coverage of 'problems', either between Aborigines and non-Aborigines such as confrontations over sacred sites, or within Aboriginal groups (health status, housing, deaths in custody, violence, child-abuse). However, while there have been dramatic social changes, Aborigines continue to have only limited control over them. Constructions of Aboriginality, the structuring of social life, the nature of problems, and their solutions, remain primarily imposed.

IMPOSED CONSTRUCTIONS

The long history of European concern with identifying and quantifying Aboriginal 'blood' has been discussed, as have the draconian restrictions for those 'coming under the Act'. Across Australia the removal of mixed-descent Aboriginal children from their parents was an accepted practice into the second half of this century, supposedly for their 'protection'. At the same time, mixed-descent Aborigines remained functionally (and legislatively) excluded by the majority culture and were portrayed as manifesting the worst characteristics of both cultures. The preoccupation with colour, with 'degrees' or 'quanta' of Aboriginal blood was in this sense irrelevant. Designations such as 'full-blood', 'half-caste', 'quadroon', or 'octoroon', made little functional difference in this 'arithmetic of colour' (Tatz 1980).

Present-day popular interest in Aborigines reflects, in part, non-Aboriginal needs that are realised in two expedient images of Aborigines. The first is of an articulate, vocal, usually urban-oriented, apparently politically empowered and engaging individual, whose sophistication appeals to non-Aboriginal self-perceptions of progress and tolerance. The second is a romanticised construction, drawing either from ideals of traditional (the 'culture guardian') or transitional (the 'born stockman') themes. However, in most of the fringe-camps and Aboriginal 'communities' of remote Australia, Aborigines are not empowered, and life is not romantic. The images have more to do with European needs than Aboriginal realities.

In remote regions such as the Kimberley Europeans may be heard talking of the 'real blackfellow' of the past, elevating this inaccessible artefact and drawing a comparison with contemporary Aborigines who, by extension, are not 'real'. The dichotomy of traditional and non-traditional (Merlan 1989) suggests an authentic identity versus a pseudo-identity. This was reflected in early ethnography and is inherent in land-rights legislation, which privileges the claims of those with 'tribal' characteristics (Collmann 1988). Implicit is an inversion of values; from the historical concern with quantifications of 'blackness' (implying primitiveness), which rewarded approximations to 'whiteness' or to white standards, to more recent attitudes that elevate the 'uncontaminated'. In this later construction tradition and Aboriginality are conflated as a fixed entity.

However, for non-Aborigines Aboriginality is contingent, both on racial characteristics and on behaviour. This is certainly not new, as the legislative acceptance of Aborigines as citizens was long contingent on behaviour which demanded a denial or suppression of identification as an Aborigine. The Western Australian Natives (Citizenship Rights) Act 1944 gave adult natives the right to apply for State citizenship but, as McCorquodale noted, the transition was both prohibitive and conditional:

> With the application he had to furnish a statutory declaration that he wished to become a citizen of the state and two recent references from reputable citizens certifying his good habits and industrious habits. The

magistrate had to be satisfied as to the fact and duration of adoption by the applicant of 'the manner and habits of civilized life', that citizenship would conduce to the applicant's welfare, that the applicant could speak and understand the English language, was not suffering from active leprosy, syphilis, granuloma or yaws; was of industrious habits, good behaviour and reputation, and was reasonably capable of managing his own affairs. Should he subsequently contract any of the diseases described, twice be convicted of an offence under the Native Administration Act 1905 or of habitual drunkenness, or fail to adopt the manner and habits of civilized life, the Certificate could be suspended indefinitely or cancelled. (1985 : 89–90)

Even now acceptance remains conditional. While no longer contingent on a process of 'de-Aboriginalisation', it still requires conformity to non-Aboriginal expectations — if not to one of the prevailing constructions of the 'authentic Aborigine', then on achieving success in white terms, be it in sport, professionally, or through other 'acceptable' channels.

IMPOSED STRUCTURES

The European structuring of Aboriginal societies began in 1788, and has since influenced every facet of Aboriginal lifestyle, including language, clothing, settlement, housing, food, economy, work, religion, education, law, and health. The imposition of non-Aboriginal social structures such as missions, stations, orphanages and the bureaucracies of adoption, has been largely utilitarian, facilitating either the control of Aboriginal access to resources, or the availability of Aborigines, themselves, as a resource. The mechanisms have ranged from coercion by force to control through sustentation. With the wisdom of hindsight, the rationalisations supporting policies of protection and assimilation are easily questioned. However, as enlightened, by contrast, as the policy of self-determination may appear, it also represents an imposed form with its own norms and standards. Indeed, Gajdusek pointed out that the democratic parliamentary system is itself an imposed structure that was instrumental in depriving indigenous populations of their land, and which: 'serves best those who created it and brought it in by religious and political proselytization in the name of humanitarianism to counteract the "barbarism" they encountered in tribal life' (1990 : S61).

For most Aborigines, the changes brought about through this system were largely cosmetic, as noted by Brady and Palmer:

While the switch in Government policy to self-determination and later self-management allowed for a loosening of the bonds of dependency, Government bureaucracies to some extent were merely substituted for mission control, particularly when it came to issues of community management and the direction of budgets' (1988 : 244).

While most of the earlier imposed policies and processes have left their mark in contemporary Aboriginal social structures, in this section three particular issues with enduring consequences will be addressed: centralisation, social organisation, and economy.

Centralisation

In Anderson's view centralisation, presented as the hallmark of government policy since contact, was: 'one of the processes which brings about sedentism in which groups are brought together, often by external force, to live in one place with other groups' (1989 : 67). Centralisation proceeded despite the small-group orientation of traditional Aboriginal societies, the resulting settlements usually being situated to expedite concentration. Self-reliant through supervised and enforced subsistence activities, their economies were infrequently integrated into the wider economic system. As a consequence, the later relinquishing of authoritarian controls by Europeans left such settlements without a viable economic base. According to Anderson, in the subsequent competition for authority and limited resources, the primacy of family or 'mob' loyalties became manifest, with resulting inter-group inequalities.

Social organisation

From these policies of centralisation in the post-assimilation era has developed a new social administrative unit — the 'community'. At the time of the 1967 Commonwealth Referendum, Stanner voiced his concern regarding such structures, suggesting that there was current the belief that the joint enterprises of community development or cooperatives were:

> especially suited to Aborigines. I do not discount these ideas but some theorists are not at all troubled by the known facts that the record of experiment with such schemes is not impressive, and that Aboriginal groups, for all their ideals, are usually made up of factions. This divisiveness is supposed, somehow, to be certain to vanish within any joint enterprise. (1979 : 243)

Despite such caveats, as pressure for social change in the 1970s mounted, governments and agencies were called on to provide a system which was culturally sensitive to Aboriginal needs, functional (bureaucratically expedient), and acceptable to the sensitivities of the wider Australian population. However, the constructions of Aboriginal culture which informed the bureaucratic decisions were not Aboriginal:

> The cultural traditions and practices considered 'typically Aboriginal' . . . were based on stereotypes of group-orientation, decision-making by consensus and 'community' affiliation. Not surprisingly, these stereotypes fitted well with existing non-Aboriginal systems. (Eckermann & Dowd 1988 : 62)

The concept of the community appealed to ideals of self-management and democratic process. Having recognised the need for improvement, planners and policy-makers were influenced by the concept of 'community development' that was cause for optimism at that time among development planners internationally. It was clear that there was an urgent need for development in Aboriginal Australia; such development was apparently obtainable through 'community development'; thus it followed that the focus of such activity must be the 'community' (Colin Tatz, personal communication 1990). Through the 1970s communities appeared on the map across Australia, suggesting to the unwary a fundamental social transformation. In reality, little had changed save the designation and the appearance that Aborigines were in charge. 'Community' emerged as an administrative entity serving primarily the needs of the Department of Aboriginal Affairs in the 1970s. To that end, it was geographic and demographic considerations, rather than social ones, that determined definition. Unrealistic economic projections for these ventures were not realised, leading to the inevitable corollary that the communities, rather than the bureaucrats and administrators, were responsible (Smith 1989).

Economy

This is not to suggest that there have been no benefits from the administrative and social changes. It is simply to state that this structure, functional or not, is imposed. For some, perhaps many or most, the ambiguity of the term and the lack of consideration for either traditional groupings or economic viability, rather than easing disadvantage, entrenches asymmetries: 'many Aboriginal geographic communities/towns are not "self-governing social units", but can often be collections of families, language groups, or clans who can be in competition for resources' (Smith 1989 : 19).

Twenty per cent of Aborigines live in such settings. Their economic and social prospects are particularly poor, having the lowest income of Aborigines nationally, with three-quarters being dependent on social security (Fisk 1985). In remote Australia, reliance on social security has been entrenched by the limited opportunities available owing to low levels of skill, education and experience, compounded by consequences of poverty such as ill-health, alcoholism and self-destructive behaviours.

Entrepreneurial potential and economic independence are further compromised as Aborigines also do not (by and large) have access to either inherited wealth, or the credit resources of the wider society. The welfare system structures contemporary Aboriginal life. One need only visit towns in remote Australia on successive weeks to see the difference between 'pension week' and 'slack week'. The social impact is unavoidable, reflected in the periodicity of resources and behaviours such as drinking and its social consequences. As emerged from the QARK sample, the welfare structuring of the Aboriginal economy has also resulted in asymmetries that may predispose to patterns of conflict over scarce resources. Introduced to replace previously discriminatory and paternalistic systems, social security is, thus, clearly not unproblematic; DeMaria has suggested that public welfare has 'acted as a vector for nothing less than cultural destruction'. (1986 : 37).

IMPOSED PROBLEMS

Aborigines are a 'problemed' people. The discourse of Aboriginal affairs is replete with problems, which can all be subsumed under 'the Aboriginal problem'. These terms serve in part to locate and confine such issues within the domain of the 'other'. They support the projections of the majority society and encourage 'blaming the victim' (Ryan 1971). This is not to suggest that Aborigines do not have problems; there are many, and a number of these issues — alcohol misuse, self-harm and violence — have been addressed. One further related example which has recently been extensively covered by the media will be examined — delinquency.

As already noted, the removal of Aboriginal children by the state has a long history. Goodall pointed out that in New South Wales the removal was historically gendered, with a shift from policies that saw Aboriginal girls more frequently removed, to the current excess of boys in the welfare and juvenile justice systems. She suggested that earlier policies reflected an: 'interaction between prevailing anxieties about race *and* gender, labour market needs and pre-existing administrative precedents' (1990 : 8). Following the Second World War, environmental and psychological factors gained favour over genetic theories as explanations of behaviour, including 'criminality'. The dramatic reversal of the Aboriginal population decline, and the rural economic recession of the 1970s, have served to heighten white sensitivities and anxieties, with responses which 'invariably target Aboriginal male adolescents as a group threatening white citizens' persons and [mainly] property and so requiring punishment and restraint' (1990 : 9). The change in gender of removed Aboriginal youth reflects a construction of Aboriginal children (particularly mixed-descent) *as problems*. From a focus on racial inferiority and immorality (mixed-descent girls, thus, needing to be 'protected' from Aboriginal males, and by extension themselves), attention shifted to a preoccupation with deviance and delinquency — 'badness'.

Aboriginal youth is over-represented at every level of the juvenile justice system. Research from South Australia in the 1980s confirmed the excessive and early involvement of Aboriginal youth, who were found to be more likely to be drawn into the system (that is, more frequently arrested rather than reported, and more likely to be referred to the children's court rather than a Children's Aid Panel), and with a greater probability of being sentenced to detention (Wundersitz, Bailey-Harris & Gale 1990). However, while Aborigines appeared disadvantaged by decisions at each level of the system:

> Aboriginality per se did not prove to be a factor which independently influenced that decision. In other words, there was no statistical evidence of racial discrimination against Aborigines at this point. There was, however, clear evidence of what could be referred to as a class bias. (1990 : 13)

Decisions at each level were significantly influenced by offence-independent social variables (such as unemployment or having left school, and being in a single parent or foster home) that were in conflict with the norms of the mainstream society. In this sense

Aboriginal youth is disadvantaged in the legal system primarily because of their disadvantage within the social system. While earlier chapters have demonstrated that violent crime among Aboriginal males does appear to be increasing, most of the offences involving Aboriginal youth are minor, and often compounded by the system:

> a kid is apprehended for riding a bicycle while drunk. We then have a drunk in charge of said machine, riding a defective machine, refusing to give an address, offensive language and, inevitably, resisting arrest. Convicted, the same youth appears before another magistrate on another charge. Asked about priors, the youth has a sheet of five previous convictions. . . . In the end, if the practice continues, we become guilty of, or party to, the manufacture of a class of juvenile criminals — whereas, in truth, the original behaviour was hardly inimical to either the local Aboriginal, let alone wider society. (Tatz 1989 : 8)

IMPOSED SOLUTIONS

Evolving constructions of Aboriginal problems have necessitated revised solutions. Throughout, the common denominator has been that, as with the definition of problems, the determination of solutions lies largely with non-Aborigines. This is not to devalue or demean contemporary initiatives and programs that have been implemented with good intentions and often with consultation. However, historically, the systematic killings and programs aimed at restricting births or transferring children suggests far less benign 'solutions' that aimed to remove the problem permanently. For many Australians well into this century, perhaps unaware or unwilling to acknowledge European complicity in the 'passing of the Aborigine', the decline of the Aboriginal population was reassurance that the problem would solve itself.

On State and federal levels in Aboriginal Affairs most interventions have had a problem-oriented focus. The wider socio-economic improvements that provide skills and opportunities, which ultimately form the basis of changes in health and social well-being, have not flowed on. The situation is compounded by the confusion of assimilation and empowerment in conventional economic terms. However, fundamentally it is an issue of providing real choice — be it to enter the stream of the wider Australian society, or to reject it — which ultimately requires providing the means to examine, evaluate and execute such choices. Aboriginal culture is not stagnant, and suggestions that thus empowering Aborigines undermines their Aboriginality, are myopic. Whether guided by self-determination, self-management, or their successors, the promulgation of policy and development of programs requires a wider understanding of social change that acknowledges both traditional and conventional needs of Aborigines, in a society that contains both Aborigines and non-Aborigines. Without addressing the wider issues, solutions have the unfortunate potential of contributing to, or becoming, problems in their own right. Some examples relate to areas covered earlier: economic dependency and health.

Economic dependency

Concern over welfare dependence, or perhaps resentment at Aborigines' (belated) access to social security and their choice to spend it in particular ways, has been longstanding. In 1976 the Community Development and Employment Program was initiated as a substitute for the individual payment of unemployment benefits. Under this scheme communities are paid benefits in block with additional on-costs for administrative and other expenses: the communities themselves then organise work projects.

While this scheme theoretically gave considerable power to the Aboriginal community council, ultimate control rested with the Department of Aboriginal Affairs. Inter-group rivalries and problems in asserting authority frequently compromised the smooth operation of the system. Furthermore, the program was not easily responsive to the fluid nature of community membership among highly mobile Aborigines in remote Australia. There might frequently be a significant hiatus before the complex bureaucratic process of transferring benefits for an Aborigine leaving a community could be completed, during which time he or she would be dependent on the largesse of others, or hungry. Perhaps of greatest concern, this approach to administering welfare has for many communities become an end in itself. As such, it has contributed to entrenching welfare reliance. At the same time there is understandable resentment at being required to work for the dole. Regardless of the particular programs involved, the long-term costs of economic dependence are recognised by Aborigines:

> We are still the stereotyped welfare class of people as viewed by the Australian public. Sadly, deep down we view ourselves in a similar way.

However, as a nation within a nation, as Aboriginal and Islander Australians, we are more dependent than ever. We are, with some exceptions, in every demeaning sense, largely dependent on our annual welfare handout. We live from budgetary year to the next, living off the conscience and the goodwill of the general Australian public, and the fantasies of often poor quality and opportunist politicians. (Perkins 1991a : 20)

Health

Fundamental to liberation from the limitations and controls of welfare reliance is socio-economic efficacy. Along with inter-sectoral collaboration and long-term planning, this was identified as essential for Aboriginal health improvement by the National Aboriginal Health Strategy Working Party (1989). The call for long term planning is not new, but has not been a feature of Aboriginal health initiatives to date. A national plan for Aboriginal health with ill-defined goals was proposed in 1973 by the Commonwealth Department of Health, but was not endorsed by State or Territory governments. The 1979 report on Aboriginal health by the House of Representatives Standing Committee on Aboriginal Affairs gave rise to the Aboriginal Health Improvement Program (1981–1985), with more limited, but no less ambiguously identified goals. In December of 1987 the Commonwealth, State and Territory Ministers for Health and Aboriginal Affairs proposed the development of a National Aboriginal Health Strategy (1989), leading to the appointment of a Working Party. Following the completion of its report, the ministers set up an Aboriginal Health Development Group in March 1989 to examine the Working Party Report and produce a further report for submission to those ministers (many of whom had changed in the interim). The National Aboriginal Health Strategy Working Party presented a rather jaundiced Aboriginal view of government involvement:

> Aboriginal people often feel that the motivation for government action in Aboriginal health comes as a response to intermittent political pressure, rather than from a commitment to effective long-term solutions for future generations. The art of the 'quick fix' seems to be the norm. Expedient gestures for Aboriginal problems are made by governments and any commitment lasts only until media attention has eased or until the next election. (1989 : xi)

Short-term political expediency is not compatible with long-term planning; it favours problems that are amenable to short-term solutions. The enthusiasm for constructing 'suicide-proof cells' at the height of media pressure associated with the Royal Commission into Aboriginal Deaths in Custody is a case in point. Further examples are the implementation of the prison-visitor scheme and the rapid decriminalisation of public intoxication in Western Australia, both of which have occurred without backup or field support in remote regions, where existing services are limited or nonexistent. The construction of problems to fit solutions is particularly seductive for health, where the medicalisation of social problems appeals to both political and health care delivery systems. Thus, 'problem drinking', as 'alcoholism', may be addressed through the provision of alcohol-treatment facilities; suicide and self-mutilation, as 'depression' or other emotional distress, will respond to psychiatric services; the battering and death of women, and abuse of children, as 'domestic violence', may be responded to with safe houses and women's refuges; Third World patterns of infant and child infectious diseases, as 'inadequate sanitation', precipitates more environmental health officers. Aborigines deserve equal access to all such services but, by themselves, such services are unlikely to have any substantial enduring impact beyond a veneer of purposeful activity.

Burgeoning bureaucracies

Entering the 1990s the most obvious high profile initiative is the Aboriginal and Torres Strait Islander Commission, replacing the Commonwealth Department of Aboriginal Affairs and the long-troubled Aboriginal Development Commission. It was conceived of as a representative structure linked to government agencies to provide programs and services aimed at social, economic and cultural development. The organisation will be overseen by 20 commissioners (17 elected and 3 nominated by the minister for Aboriginal Affairs), with local definition of priorities and programs in the hands of 60 Regional Councils (each with up to 20 members elected for three years by local Aboriginal groups) in 17 zones. While there may be few organisational alternatives, the structure again clearly replicates the ideals and norms, not only of the wider society, but of the governing bureaucracy. Numerous concerns have been voiced (Foundation for Aboriginal and Islander Research Action, 1990) and it remains to be seen what the 'bran nue dae' in Aboriginal Affairs brings.

Aborigines remain the most disadvantaged group in Australia. Most have experienced bureaucratic or institutional intrusion into their family or community life. Regardless of the political rhetoric of opportunity and empowerment, under whatever policy or platform, the structuring of Aboriginal lives continues. To suggest that this will not occur in the era of self-determination and self-management denies the institutional reliance of such policies and programs. Indeed, for Aborigines: 'a bureaucratically administered policy of self-management is a perfect paradoxical injunction' (Rose 1986 : 26). The differences that separate Aboriginal and institutional interests will not easily be resolved, given the bureaucratic priorities of institutional goals. However, regardless of the diversity of agendas of the agencies operating in the arena of Aboriginal Affairs, it is likely that most would identify as an ultimate goal some form of Aboriginal 'advancement' or 'development'. In the second half of this final chapter, 'development' as a planned process enacted upon a subordinate group, will be examined.

INDUCED CHANGE:
'DEVELOPMENT' AND ITS VICISSITUDES

'Development' has emerged as a Western panacea for the inequalities continuing in the aftermath of decolonisation. Every industrialised country has its development aid agency; multinational development banks thrive on it, and dozens of international organisations, including the United Nations, are committed to it. The purported goals of development are to eradicate poverty, to raise standards of living equal to those found in the industrialised countries, and to assure the provision of health services, education, clean water, food, housing, transportation and energy (Stiles 1987).

In this section a paradigm will be outlined that explores changing theory and practice internationally. Development, as commonly used, refers to a relationship between a dominant and subordinate group (which may be framed in other ways, for instance developed/ underdeveloped; First World/Third World; privileged/underprivileged; North/South) characterised by unilateral socio-economic change in the direction of, and facilitated by, the superordinate group. Consistent with this view, development is frequently construed in a limited hydrodynamic sense that presumes the existence of an entity (be it money, resources or technology) that can flow from one to the other. In reality, the relationship is based on power, the turbulent dynamics of which defy such simplistic analyses. Inherent in this usage is a paradox: in any relationship characterised by an asymmetry of power, that asymmetry must be emphasised by actions predicated on the actions of the empowered on the powerless. Or, to phrase it as a question: How is it possible to redress inequalities in terms of power through unilateral processes controlled by the empowered group?

The paradigm is based on international aid approaches, the historical forces involved directly and indirectly influencing policy in Australia. It is, thus, essential to understand the dynamics of change broadly in order to locate current domestic initiatives. Six levels emerge in this formulation (see table 15), each level defined by characteristics which are drawn from theories of psychological and social development. These are: the nature of growth of the dominant group (Land 1978); the control mechanisms by which the dominant group articulates its power; the cognitive schema that describes the logic used by the dominant group to explain the existing relationship (Piaget, in Brainerd 1978); the moral-ethical structure characteristic of the decision process of the dominant group (Kohlberg 1981); and, the nature of the responses of the disadvantaged and advantaged groups to the inequality of the relationship (Taylor & McKirnan 1984).[1] The discussion will involve use of several concepts that are functionally interrelated, their common denominator being a relationship to attribution theory, which will be briefly described.

ATTRIBUTION AND ALLIED THEORIES

According to attribution theory, the individual's analysis of events resulting from task success or failure leads to ascriptions that, in turn, affect subsequent task behaviour and expectations for success or failure. Such attributions affect achievement-oriented behaviour, and involve three dimensions (Abramson, Seligman and Teasdale 1978). The attribution may be stable or unstable, reflecting long-term or recurrent, versus short-term or intermittent expectations for its influence. It may be global (impacting on a wide variety of outcomes) or specific (having limited application). Finally, it may involve internal attributions that directly influence self-esteem, or external attributions that situate the 'locus of control' beyond the individual.

Locus of control is a concept derived from individual psychology, which proposes that the potential for the outcome of a behaviour to reinforce, positively or negatively, the preceding behaviour, is dependent on the degree to which the reinforcement is perceived as being contingent on the individual's behaviour — internal or external to her or his locus of control (Rotter 1966). Rotter pointed out that externality may be utilised as a defence against failure, and introduced in his initial work its relevance to social conditions:

> Perhaps the most important kind of data to assess the construct validity of the internal-external control dimension involves the attempts of people to better their life conditions, that is, to control their environment in important life situations. It is in this sense that the I-E scale appears to measure a psychological equivalent of the sociological concept of alienation, in the sense of powerlessness. (1966 : 19)

Rotter (1975) subsequently clarified that the dimension of control is not dichotomised, internality versus externality being on a continuum, with the nature of this dimension itself influenced by contingent factors. The relationship of locus of control to the sociological concept of alienation is relevant, and germane to the Aboriginal experience of cultural exclusion and its consequences for identity. Demonstrating the interconnectedness of these concepts, Seeman provided five alternative usages for alienation that invoke both locus of control and anomie:

> Powerlessness . . . the expectation or probability held by the individual that his own behavior cannot determine the occurrence of the outcomes, or reinforcements, he seeks.
> Meaninglessness . . . . the individual is unclear as to what he ought to believe — when the individual's minimal standards for clarity in decision-making are not met . . . the individual's choice among alternative beliefs has low 'confidence limits' . . . characterized by a low expectancy that satisfactory predictions about future outcomes of behavior can be made.
> Normlessness . . . a high expectancy that socially unapproved behaviors are required to achieve given goals.
> Isolation . . . those who assign low reward value to goals or beliefs that are typically highly valued in the given society.
> Self-estrangement . . . the degree of dependence of the given behavior upon anticipated future rewards, that is, upon rewards that lie outside the activity itself . . . the inability of the individual to find self-rewarding activities. (1959 : 783–790)

These concepts are interrelated, therefore, and will be used in the following discussion in defining the psychological antecedents and consequences of social change, specifically the model of inter-group relations of Taylor and McKirnan.

SOCIAL CHANGE AND DEVELOPMENT: A PARADIGM

The following schema examines the changing approaches to international development. Aboriginal Australia has itself been compared to the 'Third World' (Palmer & McKenna 1978 : xi). However, while there are clearly parallels in, for example, life expectancy (Thomson 1991), the patterns of mortality are quite different (English 1991), as are those of morbidity in which 'life-style' diseases and conditions are increasingly prominent. Comparisons between Aboriginal Australia and Third World societies should, thus, be undertaken with caution. In terms of disposable income and access to medical and other social services, there are substantial differences to Third World nations characterised by endemic poverty and absent or extremely limited social services. Regardless, the fundamental asymmetries of power between the impoverished nations of the Third World and the West, and between Aboriginal Australia and the dominant non-Aboriginal society, may be compared.

This model rests on four assumptions regarding paradigm-change, drawn from the work of Kuhn (1970):

1 'Development' will be used here to describe the relationship between two systems characterised by an asymmetry of power. The relationship is dynamic, each system itself engaged in an open-ended process of adaptive change unique to the external demands constraining its own growth.

2 Failing approaches change only when confronted by better-functioning initiatives incompatible with the existing theories.

3 Once accepted, development theories resist change in the short term.

4 However, in the long term they are themselves destabilising, as they tend to be inherently static patterns of assumptions, whereas the reality from which they are drawn, and on which they act, is dynamic.

Each level of the paradigm (see table 15) represents a set of characteristics of the relationship between the parties to the

Table 15 *A paradigm of development*

Period	Growth (Land)	Control mechanism	Cognition (Piaget)	Morality (Kohlberg)	Intergroup relations (Taylor & McKirnan)
Colonialism	Accretive	Territory	Pre-operational	Pre-conventional: rule of might	Stratified: ascribed group internal attributions
Neo-colonialism	Replicative	Resources	Pre-operational	Pre-conventional: instrumental	Emerging individualistic social ideology: individual internal attributions
Resource aid	Replicative	Development aid	Concrete-operational	Conventional	Social mobility: mobile (individual/ internal) vs immobile (individual/ external) attributions
Technical aid	Replicative	Development aid	Concrete-operational	Conventional	Social mobility: (as above)
Self-aid (PHC/Freire)	Replicative/ Mutualistic	Debt	Formal-operational	Post-conventional: situational	Consciousness raising: group external attributions
De-development (Illich)	Mutualistic		Trans-operational	Post-conventional: universal	Collective action: group attributions renounced, universal individual attributions

development process that, to varying degrees, prevail at a point in time. The progression is neither invariable nor uniform across populations, and particular approaches may include aspects of different levels. Within specific groups, movement may be recursive, reflecting inter-group, intra-group, and environmental forces that oppose change. At any level there will, therefore, be vestiges of the previous stages informing policy and decisions. The movement is towards an ideal: from subjugation to equality; from separatism to mutuality; from non-reflective to reflective policy; from the polarisation of power towards 'power sharing'. However, implicit in this last goal is a contradiction; power can only be distributed by those who have it or appropriate it, its redistribution to the out-group thus being resisted.

Level 1: Colonialism

Imperialism, secular or sacred, involves the extension of authority of one group over another. Growth of the dominant society is essentially accretive, or incremental. Land identified characteristics of accretive growth on a social level as: self-centred; absolutist; polarising; with little assimilation of feedback; and without connection to others, resulting in alienation. Power on this level is articulated through control of territory and people. Subject groups are perceived as different, and without the same rights and privileges as those with power. Justification of the relationship to appease the morality prevalent within the dominant society requires rationalisations. The colonised are portrayed as 'savages', 'children', 'animals', a variety of constructions that dehumanise. Such distorting thinking, while it may have been culturally informed, is characteristic of Piaget's preoperational thinking — egocentric, omnipotent, magical. At the same time that the 'rights of man' were debated with fervour in London, Paris, Madrid, or any of the colonial capitals during the periods of the greatest colonial expansion, the relationship of those same societies with their subject races was governed by the exercise of power. This is characteristic of Kohlberg's first stage of preconventional morality, the 'punishment and obedience orientation', in which the cooperation of the subject is motivated by the disparity in power ('might is right'). Rules are obeyed to avoid punishment; the value of human life and the value of objects conflated.

Inter-group relations are clearly stratified and entrenched. The subject group is defined by those in power such that: 'members of the disadvantaged group are led to believe that by virtue of their ascribed characteristics, they are responsible for their status' (Taylor, & McKirnan 1984 : 296). The potency of the power differential is such that the status of the subordinate group is attributed to their own group characteristics — an ascribed, group, attribution ('blaming the victim'). Social mobility is generally not a consideration, and the internalisation of the attributions leads to self-hate and self-deprecation. Development does not exist as a category of action at this level, the relationship being entirely exploitative, save at a utilitarian level of ministering to the minor needs of a subject race to preserve the status quo.

Level 2: Neocolonialism

Hastened by the disruption of two world wars, the chaos and social changes in Europe accelerated the demise of the colonial systems. Fanon (1967) suggested that forces from within the oppressed societies were mandatory for the humanitarian and reformist rhetoric in the capitals of the West to be translated into action. Even so, power shifted but slightly, being articulated through control of resources: cocoa, fruit, minerals — whatever a poor country had that was wanted. Direct or de facto control of the primary resources, land and people, remained essential. Growth is best considered replicative, the privileged group executing control through a clone power structure within the underprivileged host or subject society, with similar values, motivations and incentives. Control is, thus, exercised by proxy. Replicative social growth (of the dominant group), according to Land, involves cynicism, tentative acceptance of changed situations reflecting pre-formed opinions, and a lack of innovation. Positive feedback is accepted, but that which is negative is rejected; the feedback relationship being characterised by defensiveness, insecurity, fear of rebellion, and guilt.

To maintain the economic status quo and the unidirectional flow of resources, at the same time as espousing the rights of the newly decolonised peoples, also required distorting rationalisations. However, the moral-ethical dimension is more typical of Kohlberg's 'instrumental relativist orientation'. At this level, obedience is no longer obtained through exercising might — the subject group conforming, not to avoid punishment, but to obtain rewards. While the rewards proffered by the advanced groups are limited, they quickly become 'essential', at least for the proxy representatives of the dominant group.[2]

At this level ·inter-group relations reflect an emerging individualistic ideology. This is imperative for the dominant group, in need of subordinate representatives. A 'meritocracy' is supported by those in power, however: 'while group-based discrimination is increasingly viewed as illegitimate, individual based discrimination is considered legitimate even if many of those who are "individually" unable to compete belong to one specific group' (Taylor & McKirnan 1984 : 297). The dominant group supports a shift to internal, personal attributions of performance and, thus, of worth. Accordingly the ascription of blame also shifts to the individual, thus exonerating the dominant group, and holding the subordinate group 'individually' responsible for the continuing inequalities. At this point inter-group social comparisons are increased.

Development initiatives remain minimal, motivated primarily by political expediency and carrying a price. The dynamics of colonialism do not necessarily disappear, often articulated through 'internal colonialism'. The consequences are hardly different at the hands of the proxy representatives, who have appropriated the ethos of their former masters. Beginning in the immediate wake of decolonisation, the 'Third World War' now progresses across the globe, generally by states (created from colonies and supplied by the previous colonial powers) against the indigenous populations of the Fourth World — 'the nation peoples and their countries that exist beneath the imposed states' (Neitschmann 1987 : 2). Little has changed for those at the bottom.

Levels 3 and 4: Resource and Technical Aid

These two levels will be dealt with together as they reflect broadly similar dynamics, being differentiated solely by development strategy. The theoretical basis for these approaches followed from the reconstruction of the war-devastated economies of Germany and Japan following the Second World War. General George Marshall, American chief of staff during the war, who became Secretary of State following the cessation of hostilities, oversaw the dramatically successful European programs. Based on an infusion of resources, the rapid return to economic solvency of Germany and Japan suggested a similar approach elsewhere, and afforded major powers an avenue to exercise covert control in order to consolidate power. The United Nations facilitated this by assigning large areas as Trust Territories to previous colonial powers, which at times included military options (Micronesia, United States Trust Territory). The realities of geopolitics necessitated realigning the non-aligned, the newly liberated and economically undeveloped nation-states of Africa, Asia, and the Pacific. Regimes sympathetic to the worldview of the major power-brokers were mandatory to consolidate the various spheres of influence: growth remained replicative.

The mechanism of control became development aid itself. In the highly visible forum of the United Nations and its scions, a new sense of 'responsibility' towards those less fortunate emerged. Approval on this political stage demanded that resource-rich nations conform to avoid the disapproval and censure of the international community, a conventional morality (Kohlberg's 'interpersonal concordance' and 'society maintenance orientations'). The logic of the resource-aid approach is disarmingly simple: there is poverty; poverty is alleviated by resources. This concrete solution suggested a 'trickle down' effect; resources would be filtered through the national representatives to those in need, either through direct aid or economic development. In reality, dollars are as easily turned into swords as ploughshares, and the covert political agendas of the donor nations and aid agencies frequently supported such diversions (Clay 1987).

Relations with technology- and resource-poor societies were not completely dominated by self-interest. Recognising that those most in need were not benefiting from this resource-based approach, planners in donor countries shifted the focus of aid programs. It was not money that was needed, they argued, but knowledge and expertise. This did not substantially alter the paradigm that remained: ' "tree top" development, where the bureaucrats plan and peer down on their works from detached perches' (Stiles 1987 : 3). It only altered what was to trickle down. The Fulbright Act was introduced in the United States in 1946[3], and continued to exemplify this approach into the 1970s. By exposing selected (read, privileged) representatives of the target countries to the benefits of education and technology, it was surmised, they would, given adequate backup, return to their countries with their new expertise to initiate a chain reaction. Unfortunately, those selected were generally the elite representatives of the emplaced regimes and thus had the same agendas. Furthermore, with the seductive appeal of life in the West, not unexpectedly many refused to return, compounding rather than alleviating the situation by removing important human resources. The era of technological aid has been a manifest failure.

Inter-group relations at these two levels — resource and technical aid — show an increase in individual social mobility, which is, of necessity, a precursor to any collective action. Individuals able to take advantage of opportunities (such as those selected for foreign education) are generally derived from an elite, with the linguistic and cultural tools required to make the transition. Taylor and McKirnan suggest that there are two forms of such mobility. The first involves a change in personal characteristics allowing the individual to become a member of the dominant group (this generally is restricted to groups differentiated by modifiable factors such as language, social class, or cultural factors). The second strategy, where the differences are invariable (race, caste, sex), involves adoption of enough characteristics of the dominant group to be accepted by them, while remaining obviously members of the excluded group. For both aspiring groups the criteria of acceptance remain determined by those in power, and require, on some level, a repudiation of aspects of their previous identity.

Therefore, at these levels there is a predisposition to increasing polarisation within the subordinate group. Achievers attribute their social status to individual internal factors, which is corroborated by the characteristics ascribed to them by the dominant group. Those failing, or being obstructed in their attempts to gain access to and acceptance by the dominant group, attribute their failure to individual external factors — to exclusion. As the dominant society affirms the identity of the former group, and negatively assesses the latter, those capable of social mobility tend to increase contact (reinforcing those attributions), whereas those denied access minimise their inter-group relations. This fosters the subsequent development of intra-group attributions among those excluded. So, at these levels the power structure of the dominant group is replicated within the host society, co-opting their human resources to the task of maintaining that status quo and, in so doing, accentuating inequality. The emergence of an empowered minority predisposes to the production of intra-group asymmetries, leading to the internal replication of the inter-group dynamics of earlier levels.

Level 5: Self-aid

The growth of the so-called 'non-aligned nations' and their recognition that they could choose their 'benefactors', destabilised the previous political spheres of influence. Increasingly, organisations as well as nations wielded power, their control exercised through cumulative debt. The first radical departures in terms of development thinking occurred during the 1970s, with 'pour down' or 'trickle down' theorising replaced by 'trickle up' approaches based on 'grass-roots' development. The impetus for change came from within the power structures (such as United Nations, World Health Organization, World Bank), and from the underprivileged or oppressed groups (such movements as Liberation Theology and the work of the educationalist Paulo Freire [1968]).

From within the institutional systems a new horizon emerged at the 1978 Alma Ata conference of the World Health Organization, with the promulgation of 'primary health care' as the means to achieving 'health for all by the year 2000':

> Primary health care is essential health care based on practical, scientifically sound and socially acceptable methods and technology made universally accessible to individuals and families in the community through their full participation and at a cost that the community and country can afford at every stage of the development in the spirit of self-reliance and self-determination. (World Health Organization 1978 : 3)

Inherent in this definition is a more complex analysis of the problem, and solutions that go beyond the concrete hydrodynamic principles previously guiding policy, hence more characteristic of the problem-solving of Piagetian formal operational thinking. Likewise, presentation of the needs of the underprivileged in terms of universal human rights implies a principled morality. However, conformity to these principles is significantly influenced by an expectation of being judged before the international community, and there remains a relativism of values determined by national interest. It is, thus, best described by Kohlberg's first stage of post-conventional (principled) morality, the 'social contract orientation' — situational ethics.

The World Health Organization has had a major influence in shifting the focus to grass-roots development. Regardless, both governmental and non-governmental developmental aid agencies are invariably involved, and the development agencies themselves have evolved into empowered bureaucracies. In this sense elements of replicative growth persist; there are, however, certain features of mutual growth (Land) emerging in the relationship. Ideally, according to Land, at this level attempts to engage directly with the underprivileged groups involve increased openness, tolerance of ambiguity, working with others, an ability to deviate from a pre-determined course, the assimilation of positive and negative feedback, and interdependence.

That development agencies must work through other bureau-cracies to gain access to the indigenous populations designated as recipients of aid, reveals one of the major limitations of this approach. Just as welfare departments determine an ideal welfare recipient (Collmann 1988), there are ideal recipients of international aid.[4] The criteria are generally formulated by the donor agency and host government. There is, thus, a conflict between the ideals of grass-roots development and the reality:

> the tension between ideology and action so often observed in community programs emerges not simply because of problems of implementation, but because of a contradiction or inconsistency in the PHC concept itself. Community involvement, community participation, self-reliance and self determination are key elements of the Alma-Ata declaration and they are essential ingredients if PHC is to become a reality, but the structure of WHO efforts toward PHC has almost completely excluded any possibility of meaningful local participation and self determination. (Welsch 1988 : 1)

From within the ranks of the disadvantaged and oppressed, arti-culated by politically conscious intellectuals attempting to confront the structure of oppression, emerged the internal response. This is perhaps best exemplified by Liberation Theology and the trans-formation model of Paulo Freire (1968). Fundamental to this approach is an elevation of the awareness of those oppressed to their oppression, thus shifting the focus from resources to power. Through a questioning of their role (as victim, either of force or induced dependence), the foundations for indigenous social action are laid. This 'conscientization' or 'education for critical conscious-ness', requires an engagement of the parties based on a dialogue between equals. It confronts the disempowering of the oppressed that results from decision-making about their welfare that does not involve them as the primary decision-makers.

The focus for both these approaches to grass-roots development is the central involvement of the subordinate population in the process of change. In its most extreme interpretation it implies a total empowering of the minority or oppressed group in terms of decision-making about their future. In this regard, Smith (1987) asked four questions of development programs to ascertain their degree of autonomous control:

> 1 Is the indigenous community in control of the conceptualization, planning and implementation of their development? . . .
> 2 Does the indigenous community exercise control over its territory and over all the resources found within the limits of that territory? . . .
> 3 Does the program for the development promote self-sufficiency and economic independence of the indigenous community? . . .
> 4 Does the development process strengthen the social and cultural bonds of the community and affirm the sense of historical identity and cultural dignity of the community members? (1987 : 8–12)

Inter-group relations on this level are affected by the process of consciousness-raising. Many of those within the subordinate group capable of social mobility have used that advantage. By reinforcing the individual attribution of success for those who have assimilated, the dominant group may render them unavailable as agents of change. For the majority who remain excluded, status-enhancement is linked to the status of the group as a whole. There is, thus, a pressure from those among this group for recognition of the collectivity as the only valid identity. For them, status is increasingly defined in terms of this collectivity, as reflecting group attributes. Personal responsibility for failure is redefined in terms of discrimination.

These two quite different approaches represent the cutting edge of development activity in most settings today. Regardless of their limitations, they will persist along with elements of other levels, until an alternative is seen to prevail. Their failures are for different reasons. The approach typified by development agencies ('primary health care') is limited by its replication of pre-existing systems that entrench power in hierarchies. It cannot ultimately succeed in its lofty goals ('health for all by the year 2000') as it is forced to work through those very institutions (national agencies and governments) that perpetuate the vested power interests. The fiascos in the delivery of 'humanitarian aid' in Sudan and Ethiopia are but two instances from one region in desperate need of the clear priorities of those controlling access to their starving 'citizens'.

Autochthonous movements such as Liberation Theology are limited for a very different reason. The awareness by the oppressed of their oppression is, for the oppressors, clearly destabilising. The redefinition of the issue from resources to power is a political statement: hence the negative reactions of the Catholic Church to

Liberation Theology. Consequently, the responses of those in power are predictable — a redefinition of such activities as treason or insurgency. The main reason for the ultimate failure of 'education for critical consciousness' is that it is invariably unilateral.

Level 6: Dedevelopment

The trajectory of the development paradigm is towards an ideal. I have suggested that the previous level demonstrated a cognition that could be characterised in a Piagetian sense as formal operational. The final level of the paradigm demands a different analytic approach which could be termed 'post-formal', or 'trans-operational'. The fundamental shift is from being constrained by logic, to the acceptance of paradox as part of the cognitive process, as in theoretical physics, which offers the most obvious examples of the application of trans-operational cognition. Another example is the position of Ivan Illich. Thus far, resource reallocation has been unidirectional, evolving successively from no reallocation, to 'pour on', to 'trickle down', to 'trickle up' — with essentially little or no redistribution of power. For Illich (1977), any relationship which is based on the actions of one group on another (regardless of directionality) merely entrenches or enhances the asymmetry of power and concentrates power in elites — it is 'dedevelopment'. According to Illich (1972), deinstitutionalisation is mandatory if further impoverishment is not to occur. This position would seem an improbable ideal: How is it feasible, one may ask, to sustain development without the structures and mechanisms that have evolved to facilitate that task? However, what Illich is demanding is reflection by those in power; that the question to be asked first is not: What can this advantaged society do to that disadvantaged society? Instead, it is: What can it do both to itself and together, to address the imbalances? The dedevelopment, or development as paradox model, aspires to the ideals of mutualistic growth (Land) and reflects the 'universal ethical principle orientation' of Kohlberg, in which actions are responsive to internalised principles of justice, respect, and the universal value of human beings as individuals.

At this ideal level, the dimension of control is redundant, as such mutuality precludes a disparity of power. At its simplest it is the relinquishing of the advantages of power in favour of mutual growth. Inter-group relations are characterised by competition on an equal footing, leading to collective action. The wider social group is redefined in terms of similarities allowing maintenance of a common ideology which rejects group attributions, suggesting that every individual is accepted on her or his merits without any consideration of group origin or membership. Past inequalities are attributed to the dominant group, and the future is constructed in terms of internal characteristics of the collectivity.

Advocates of this approach to development are unlikely to be well received by the representatives of the privileged societies. Consequently, development must aspire to ideals without losing sight of the realities that determine suffering and constrain initiatives to alleviate it. On this pragmatic level, Goulet (1971) identified normative principles that should guide the elaboration of a valid ethic of development:

> The first has to do with things and may be phrased as a question: what is the relationship, if any, between the fullness of good and an abundance of goods? . . . the second concerns solidarity . . . genuine development can never take place until men agree to a worldwide plan for use and allocation of resources. The Mind pillar of the normative edifice is a position on technology and its relation to freedom and happiness. . . . Finally neither elitism alone nor populism alone is enough for political or social decision making. In ideal terms a continuum of alternatives exists — from autocracy, aristocracy and oligarchy, running through a broad, ill-charted middle terrain to the other pole of full communitarian participatory rule.

AND AUSTRALIAN ABORIGINES?

Is this schema applicable to the relationship between Aborigines and the majority culture in Australia during the last decade of the twentieth century? Can the experiences of indigenous peoples in Africa or Latin America provide meaningful insights relevant to those of the indigenous minority in Australia? The above schema represents but one interpretation. Overshadowed by the economic preoccupations of an advanced technocratic society, development in Aboriginal Australia has only recently gathered momentum as the inertia of the colonial relationship has been challenged. The utility of a schema such as this lies as much in its potential to stimulate questioning and debate as in its predictive capacity.

It is also important to locate the attitudes and approaches of non-Aboriginal Australians to the Aboriginal population under the same light as is being used, not least of all by Australians, to examine the rights of indigenous peoples elsewhere. Australia has, in this and many other regards, far too long remained isolated. In terms of prevailing attitudes to Aborigines this in part reflects an acute sensitivity to outside criticism. Australians are at pains to point out that Aborigines have access to the benefits available to the rest of the nation (of course, only recently), implicit in this being an attribution of personal, or at times group responsibility for their degraded lot.

These factors (action responsive, largely, to outside criticism; attribution pattern) define a locus on the development schema in terms of morality (conventional) and inter-group relations (social mobility). Superficially, non-Aboriginal attitudes to Aborigines changed dramatically during the late 1980s. Outrage voiced at the treatment of Aborigines at the hands of Europeans reached a crescendo during the first year of the Royal Commission into Aboriginal Deaths in Custody. Aborigines suddenly found friends who appeared willing to question their own role in the construction of a dispossessing and disempowering system.[5] However, the self-castigatory rhetoric has been inconsistently accompanied by engagement with Aborigines, other than those who had managed to enter into the stream of non-Aboriginal discourse. Current interventions remain guided by concrete thinking, reflecting a replicative social ethos and a conventional moral-ethical orientation. Control over Aborigines is certainly no less than before, articulated now through endemic welfare dependency in remote Australia, a situation of such concern that Perkins (1991a) stated:

> The time has come for us to break out of this unworthy enforced, western-dreamtime and charter a new course, not only for our people, and particularly for our children, but for our nation. We must throw off this yoke of welfare and the soul-destroying concept of welfare and the state of dependency which results from it. It is destroying us and will eventually do so completely. (1991a : 20)

These dynamics parallel those at the development aid level in the paradigm. The cutting edge of development in Aboriginal Australia remains at the levels defined internationally as resource aid/technical aid. Vestiges of the antecedent stages are also apparent: the battles over land and resources continue — the gains remain conditional.

This is not to imply that interventions at more advanced levels have not been contemplated or attempted. For instance, Brady (1990b) participated in research into Aboriginal social and psychological health in the South Australian Aboriginal community of Yalata. Responding to the concerns of Aboriginal communities through the 1970s regarding exploitative research, the multidisciplinary team set out to adapt the principles of Freire, specifically: to avoid imposing constructions of the problems investigated and the solutions arising from research; to involve the community in the research process; and to allow the subjects themselves to take control of acting on those problems. However, the mutual problematising proposed by Freire was not found to be appropriate in that setting. Brady suggested five factors contributing to the lack of success. First, regardless of the intent, mutual definition of the problems was not achieved. Second, while the South American subjects of Freire's initiatives are located in economic and sociopolitical systems that, through the inherent polarisation of wealth and power, encourage dissonance, dissatisfaction and dissent, Australian Aborigines in a welfare state are restrained by state-imposed 'assistencialism'. Freire has said of such 'assistencialism' that it is, 'an especially pernicious method of trying to vitiate popular participation in the historical process . . . by imposing silence and passivity [it] denies men conditions likely to develop or to "open" their consciousness' (in Brady 1990b : 19).

The third reason the approach failed, according to Brady, was that, as a heterogeneous collection of previously autonomous desert peoples brought together by circumstance, they lacked the cohesion necessary for a Freirian approach. The fourth factor was that, in this setting, problems tended to be accommodated to, thus preventing their objectification and the collective disapproval of the group necessary to the development of collective action. The ostensible purpose of the research was to investigate problems of delinquency and substance-abuse among Aboriginal youth, which leads to the last factor:

> the nature of interpersonal authority was such that although older people were treated with respect, particularly those knowledgeable about country, and ritual matters, they did not wield authority over others who were disorderly or unsociable in their actions. They were not empowered to deal with youthful offenders who disregarded the white Australian legal system. (1990b : 20)

In conclusion, Brady called for a more critical interrogation of the rhetoric of community empowerment. As suggested in her analysis, for underprivileged minorities in welfare societies, additional forces exist which resist change. Welfare dependency insidiously entraps, not only because it controls access to limited resources, but also because the fragile safety-net prevents the total and manifest failure of the system. In the tenuous existence of welfare survival, effort is expended and directed towards maintaining the status quo, rather than structural change.

Such artificially buoyed economies minimise dissonance, which is, according to Blum, created by 'conflicts between values, and from discrepancies that are seen, felt, or believed to exist between accomplishments attained under pursuit of value-derived goals and the matching, value-derived standards of expectation' (1981 : 42). Dissonance, in Blum's theory, gives rise to 'impetus', which he presented as the main determinant of social change (the others being structural controls, societal system pressures and self-regulation, and mobilisation). Impetus, directed towards the lessening of dissonance, is a primary and universal force. For Aborigines of remote Australia, the sharp transition from the paternalism of institution life to the paternalism of welfare dependence retarded the development of economic autonomy in communities by obviating the need for independent economic survival in a non-traditional world. Dissonance is further muted by the absence of a subjective reference point of autonomous existence that generates value-derived goals and expectations. It is, perhaps, extinguished by alcohol.

Welfare control also sequesters Aborigines on the peripheries of Australian society. This should not be understood as a rationalisation for a withdrawal of the existing liminal levels of funding (the argument that 'they have to hit bottom before they can find their feet'), but for a redirection. In a system that discourages substantial upward mobility, stifles dissonance, and prevents total collapse, Aborigines, particularly those of remote Australia, are too often suspended, immobile, impotent, and contained.

Looking ahead

Defining successful policies for the future is beyond the authority or bravado of this writer. However, it is clear that a movement towards a more sophisticated level of analysis and engagement is required. Regardless of Brady's experiences, and taking account of her caveats, on whatever level problems are addressed, it is essential to have an Aboriginal definition and articulation of problems, including prominently the insidious social controls of welfare reliance.

Hopefully, such movement would ultimately progress towards and include collective action involving Aborigines and non-Aborigines, with a shift within the dominant society from action motivated by self-blame (in itself indulgent and egocentric), or contingent on concern regarding exposure, towards mutualistic growth that values Aborigines and foregrounds their role in planning change.

In this regard, Perkins (1991b) has identified seven principles he considers necessary for the construction of a framework that Aborigines can use to create a template for the future. The first is the development of an Aboriginal economy that is no longer reliant on the 'false economy' of the welfare system. Second, he proposes a 'cultural renaissance' to consolidate and expand the Aboriginal base for collective action. Perkins's third principle involves confronting the bureaucratisation and duplication of Aboriginal organisations, from the community level up. The fourth requirement is a treaty, with acknowledgment of Aboriginal rights forming a basis for future negotiations with the government and its representatives. Fifth in his list, and essential to the development of independence and self-determination, is free education for Aborigines at all levels. The sixth issue, a national independent Aboriginal body, funded by Aborigines themselves and able to be accepted and operate within the framework of a multicultural society. Finally, Perkins emphasised the need for programs that generate employment for all Aborigines of working age.

The Nobel laureate, Carleton Gajdusek (1990) reflected these issues in commenting on the 'paradoxes of aspirations for and of children in remote and isolated cultures' (1990 : S59). He pointed out that while there is a common and hypocritical European position that defines culturally correct values for such 'primitive people', often construed as living in a paradisiacal environment from which they should not aspire to leave, in fact:

> the inhabitants of 'Paradise' — on Pacific atolls and island villages, surrounded by kinsmen, from the tropics to the arctic — want as youths to get into the 'action,' even if it be in urban slums and ghettos with all the loneliness, frustration, and anxiety of modern high-tech cosmopolitan urban life. (1990 : S59)

To suggest that they should not is, of course, another level of paternalism. Gajdusek presents humans as cultural improvisers, who should not be expected to be prisoners of an imposed, and stagnant, construction of culture. This is not to suggest invariable assimilation, as he points to the striving of all populations for a unique, and dynamic, ethnic identity. For Gajdusek, as for Perkins, education is critical. Real change demands more than simple grass-roots development, which on its own may lead to solutions that remain at the grass-roots — low-level change and further dependency:

> Instead, give them the ability to control their own destiny in industry, politics, business, and law, and they will buy and negotiate for their needs, as they can see them, in these 'humanitarian' fields of endeavour, where we gain for ourselves such self-satisfaction . . . for activities that have little impact on their future, and often cause them to be enslaved and subservient for longer. (1990 : S60)

These changes require an acknowledgement of the asymmetries in the distribution of power between groups, and a willingness to accept its redistribution. Like Brady (1990b), I am suspicious of the contemporary rhetoric of Aboriginal empowerment. The Aboriginal militancy associated with land rights suggested consciousness-raising involving Aborigines nationally. However, its subsequent transformation into a bureaucratic structure and process has muted its political potency, as may yet happen to the Aboriginal and Torres Strait Islander Commission, which must also contend with bureaucratic absorptive and replicative forces. In remote Australia, the demography of power is little altered; Kolig's comments on the Kimberley of the 1970s remain relevant:

> Aborigines nowadays still have next to no power. They are trapped in a situation in which their traditional means of procuring power are no longer seen as effective, and power is obtained now in the society at large in ways with which they are still partly unfamiliar or from which they are barred. (1982 : 26)

The asymmetries will not disappear in my lifetime: Aboriginal problems will remain on the agenda. The ideal situation of the elaborated paradigm involves 'mutual problematising', itself highly problematic. It requires that Aborigines as individuals and as a group are no longer the objects of pity or derision, or the subjects of welfare entrapment or development. It respects Aboriginal culture as a vibrant, dynamic entity evolving along a path determined by Aboriginal choices, requiring that Aborigines have both the rights and options to make such choices. This must include legislative assurances (land rights, treaty) and the provision of educational and political tools to make informed choices regarding functionally available opportunities. Are these issues on which all Aborigines would agree? Unlikely. Am I making assumptions, as a non-Aborigine, regarding issues to which I have no rightful access? I believe not. The asymmetries of power involve two parties. While the lines of power snaking across remote Australia converge only at a seemingly unreachable distance, at that horizon there is no longer an Aboriginal problem. It is an Australian problem.

NOTES

Chapter 9 is based in part on a previously published paper: 'Out of sight, out of mind — 2: Social and historical contexts of self-harmful behaviour among Aborigines of remote Australia'. *Social Science and Medicine 33 (6)*, 1991, 661–671.

1. The source theories for the discussion that follows are derived from the theories of Land (1978), Piaget (Brainerd 1978), Kohlberg (1981) and Taylor and McKirnan (1984). Their theories are central to this analysis and are duly recognised. In order to facilitate the smooth flow of the text they will not be repeatedly referenced save in quotation.
2. One of the best examples was the calculated American initiative to develop a climate of economic dependency in Micronesia during the 1960s and 1970s as a result of the 'Solomon report' (see chapter 6).
3. James William Fulbright, an American senator, subsequently rose to become chairman of the Senate Foreign Relations Committee from 1959–1974.
4. For instance, while Lesotho (formerly Basutoland) is clearly an underprivileged and underdeveloped country, the unparalleled level of activity by dozens of international aid agencies through the 1970s and early 1980s was largely due to the lack of constraints on aid programs. Lesotho was an 'ideal recipient country'.
5. Aboriginal society in Australia of the late 1980s was no longer politically or socially naive, or as desperately in need of friends as two decades earlier when Aborigines were emerging from the restrictions of assimilation policies. Thus, new friends were not necessarily welcomed uncritically. Dudgeon and Oxenham identified two groups for particular scrutiny. One was a group who have spent time in remote Australia, 'the "I've Got a Skin Name Too" Type' who:

   > are smug in their ownership of knowledge of 'real' Aboriginal people. They feel unrealistically privileged that they have skin names and acceptance by 'real' Aboriginal people, in fact many feel that they are more Aboriginal than Aboriginal people living in urban situations.

   The other group in question is 'the idealistic helpers' who 'have romanticised views about Aboriginal people and they endeavour to make Aboriginal people live out those ideals' (1988 : 4).

References

Abbie, A. A. 1970. *The original Australians.* Wellington: Reed.

Abramson, L. Y; Seligman, E. P; & Teasdale, J. D. 1978. Learned helplessness in humans: Critique and reformulation. *Journal of Abnormal Psychology 87 (1),* 49–74.

Aguilar, G. Z. 1964. Suspension of control: A sociocultural study on specific drinking habits and their psychiatric consequences. *Journal of Existential Psychology 4,* 245–253.

Akerman, K. 1979. The renascence of Aboriginal Law in the Kimberleys. In R. M. Berndt & C. H. Berndt (eds), *Aborigines of the West: Their past and their present* pp. 234–242. Perth: University of Western Australia Press.

Albrecht, P. G. 1974. The social and psychological reasons for the alcohol problem among Aborigines. In B. S. Hetzel, M. Dobbin, L. Lippmann & E. Eggleston (eds), *Better health for Aborigines? Report of a national seminar at Monash University* pp. 36–41. St Lucia: University of Queensland Press.

Alexander, K. (ed.). 1990. *Aboriginal alcohol use and related problems: Report and recommendations prepared by an Expert Working Group for the Royal Commission into Aboriginal Deaths in Custody.* Alcohol and Drug Foundation, Australia, Canberra.

Allen, M. 1967. *Male cults and secret initiations in Melanesia.* Melbourne: Melbourne University Press.

Alpert, M. A. 1985. Alcohol withdrawal syndromes: Recognition and pathogenesis. *Missouri Medicine 82,* 79–83.

Alroe, M. 1988. A Pygmalion complex among missionaries: The Catholic case in the Kimberley. In T. Swain & D. B. Rose (eds), *Aboriginal Australians and Christian missions: Ethnographic and historical studies* pp. 30–44. Adelaide: Australian Association for the Study of Religions.

American Psychiatric Association. 1987. *Diagnostic and statistical manual of mental disorders 3rd edition — revised.* Washington: American Psychiatric Association.

Anderson, C. 1989. Centralisation and group inequalities in north Queensland. In J. C. Altman (ed.), *Emergent inequalities in Aboriginal Australia* pp. 67–84. Oceania Monograph No. 38, University of Sydney.

288

Ariss, R. 1988. Writing black: The construction of an Aboriginal discourse. In J. R. Beckett (ed.), *Past and present: The construction of Aboriginality* pp. 131–146. Canberra: Aboriginal Studies Press.

Atkinson, J. 1990a. Violence in Aboriginal Australia: Colonisation and gender. *Aboriginal and Islander Health Worker Journal 14 (2)*, 5–21.

———. 1990b. Violence in Aboriginal Australia: Part 2. *Aboriginal and Islander Health Worker Journal 14 (3)*, 4–27.

Australian Bureau of Statistics. 1987. *Census 1986 — Aborigines and Torres Strait Islanders: Australia, States and Territories* (2499.0).

Awatere, D; Casswell, S; Cullen, H; Gilmore, L; & Kupenga, D. 1984. *Alcohol and the Maori people.* Alcohol Research Unit, University of Auckland, Auckland.

Bain, M. S. 1974. Alcohol use and traditional social control in Aboriginal society. In B. S. Hetzel, M. Dobbin, L. Lippmann & E. Eggleston (eds), *Better health for Aborigines: Report of a national seminar at Monash University* pp. 42–52. St Lucia: University of Queensland Press.

Bandler, F. 1989. *Turning the tide: A personal history of the Federal Council for Advancement of Aborigines and Torres Strait Islanders.* Canberra: Aboriginal Studies Press.

Barber, J. G; Punt, J; & Albers, J. 1988. Alcohol and power on Palm Island. *Australian Journal of Social Issues 23 (2)*, 87–101.

Barwick, D. 1978. 'And the lubras are ladies now'. In F. Gale (ed.), *Woman's role in Aboriginal society* 3rd edn pp. 51–63. Canberra: Australian Institute of Aboriginal Studies.

Basedow, H. 1932. Diseases of the Australian Aborigines. *Journal of Tropical Medicine and Hygiene 35 (12)*, 177–185.

Battye, J. S. (ed.). 1987 (1915). *The history of the North West of Australia embracing Kimberley, Gascoyne and Murchison Districts* (facsimile edn). Perth: Hesperian Press.

Beckett, J. 1988. The past and the present; the present and the past: Constructing a national Aboriginality. In J. Beckett (ed.), *Past and present: The construction of Aboriginality* pp. 191–217. Canberra: Aboriginal Studies Press.

Behr, J. 1985. Medical history of the Royal Flying Doctor Service of Australia — 1928–1984. Unpublished manuscript for the Royal Flying Doctor Service of Australia, Melbourne.

Bell, D. 1983. *Daughters of the Dreaming.* Melbourne: McPhee Gribble/George Allen & Unwin.

Bennett, S. 1985. The 1967 referendum. *Australian Aboriginal Studies 2*, 26–31.

———. 1989. *Aborigines and political power.* Sydney: Allen & Unwin.

Berger, P. & Luckmann, T. 1979. *The social construction of reality: A treatise in the sociology of knowledge.* London: Peregrine.

Berlin, I. N. 1985. Prevention of adolescent suicide among some native American tribes. In S. C. Feinstein, M. Sugar, A. H. Esman, J. G. Leary,

A. Z. Schwartzberg & A. D. Sorosky (eds), *Adolescent psychiatry: Vol. 1. Developmental and clinical studies* pp. 77–93. Chicago: University of Chicago Press.

Bernadt, M. W; Mumford, J; Taylor, C; Smith, B; & Murray, R. M. 1982. Comparison of questionnaire and laboratory tests in the detection of excessive drinking and alcoholism. *Lancet 1*, 325–328.

Berndt, C. H. 1979. Aboriginal women and the notion of the 'marginal man'. In R. M. Berndt & C. H. Berndt (eds), *Aborigines of the West: Their past and their present* pp. 28–38. Perth: University of Western Australia Press.

Berndt, R. M. 1977. Aboriginal identity: Reality or mirage. In R. M. Berndt (ed.), *Aborigines and change: Australia in the '70s* pp. 1–12. Canberra: Australian Institute of Aboriginal Studies.

Berndt, R. M. & Berndt, C. H. 1985. *The world of the first Australians.* Adelaide: Rigby.

——. 1988. Body and soul: More than an episode! In T. Swain & D. B. Rose (eds), *Aboriginal Australians and Christian missions: Ethnographic and historical studies* pp. 45–59. Adelaide: Australian Association for the Study of Religions.

Berrios, G. E. & Mohanna, A. M. 1990. Durkheim and French psychiatric views on suicide during the 19th century: A conceptual history. *British Journal of Psychiatry 156*, 1–9.

Berry, J. W. 1970. Marginality, stress and ethnic identification in an acculturated Aboriginal community. *Journal of Cross Cultural Psychology 1 (3)*, 239–252.

——. 1980. Introduction to methodology. In H. C. Triandis & J. W. Berry (eds), *Handbook of cross-cultural psychology, Vol. 2* pp. 1–28. Boston: Allyn & Bacon.

Bettelheim, B. 1955. *Symbolic wounds: Puberty rites and the envious male.* London: Thames and Hudson.

Biernoff, D. 1982. Psychiatric and anthropological interpretations of 'aberrant' behaviour in an Aboriginal community. In J. Reid (ed.), *Body land and spirit: Health and healing in Aboriginal society* pp. 131–153. St Lucia: University of Queensland Press.

Biles, D. 1988. *Research paper No. I: Preliminary analysis of current data base.* Royal Commission into Aboriginal Deaths in Custody, Canberra.

——. 1990. *Research paper No 15: International review of deaths in custody.* Royal Commission into Aboriginal Deaths in Custody, Canberra.

Biller, R. P. 1976. Disaggregating health promotion and health care: Policy initiatives that depend less on homogeneity assumptions and more on human uniqueness. Paper presented to the Conference on National Health Policy Issues, San Francisco, California. 12 February.

Blum, H. L. 1981. Planning as a preferred instrument for achieving social change. In H. L. Blum (ed.), *Planning for health: Generics for the eighties* pp. 39–85. New York: Human Sciences Press.

Blum, K; Noble, E. P; Sheridan, P. J; Montgomery, A; Ritchie, T; Jagadeeswaran, P; Nogami, H; Briggs, A. H; & Cohn, J. B. 1990. Allelic association of human dopamine D_2 receptor gene in alcoholism. *Journal of the American Medical Association 263 (15)*, 2055–2060.

Bolger, A. 1990. *Aboriginal women and violence: A report for the Criminology Research Council and the Northern Territory Commissioner of Police.* Australian National University, North Australian Research Unit, Darwin.

Born, D. O. 1970. Psychological adaptation and development under acculturative stress: Toward a general model. *Social Science and Medicine 3*, 529–547.

Bostock, J. 1924. Insanity in the Australian Aboriginal and its bearing on the evolution of mental disease. *Medical Journal of Australia July 5 (supplement)*, 459–464.

Boundy, C. A. P. 1977. *Aboriginal population of the Kimberley: A projection.* A report by the Regional Development Committee for the Office of the North-West, Perth.

Bowlby, J. 1988. Developmental psychiatry comes of age. *American Journal of Psychiatry 145 (1)*, 1–10.

Bowles, J. R. 1985. Suicide and attempted suicide in contemporary Western Samoa. In F. X. Hezel, D. H. Rubinstein & G. H. White (eds), *Culture, youth and suicide: Papers from an East-West Center conference* pp. 15–35. Honolulu: University of Hawaii Press.

Brady, M. 1988. *When the beer truck stopped: Drinking in a Northern Australian town.* Monograph of the Australian National University North Australia Research Unit, Darwin.

————. 1990a. Alcohol use and its effects upon Aboriginal women. In J. Vernon (ed.), *Alcohol and crime* pp. 135–147. Canberra: Australian Institute of Criminology.

————. 1990b. The problem with 'problematising research'. *Australian Aboriginal Studies 1*, 18–20.

————. 1991. *The health of young Aboriginal Australians: Social and cultural issues. Report for the National Youth Affairs Research Scheme.* Australian Institute of Aboriginal and Torres Strait Islander Studies, Canberra.

————. 1992a. *Heavy metal: The social meaning of petrol sniffing in Australia.* Canberra: Aboriginal Studies Press.

————. 1992b. Ethnography and understandings of Aboriginal drinking. *Journal of Drug Issues.* in press.

Brady, M. & Palmer, K. 1984. *Alcohol in the outback: Two studies of drinking.* Monograph of the Australian National University North Australian Research Unit, Darwin.

————. 1988. Dependency and assertiveness: Three waves of Christianity among Pitjantjatjara people at Ooldea and Yalata. In T. Swain & D. B. Rose (eds), *Aboriginal Australians and Christian missions: Ethnographic and historical studies* pp. 236–249. Adelaide: Australian Association for the Study of Religions.

Brainerd, C. J. 1978. *Piaget's theory of intelligence*. New York: Prentice Hall.

Brehm, S. S. & Brehm, J. W. 1981. *Psychological resilience: A theory of freedom and control*. New York: Academic Press.

Broadhurst, R. G. 1987. Imprisonment of the Aborigine in Western Australia, 1957–1985. In K. M. Hazelhurst (ed.), *Ivory scales: Black Australia and the Law* pp. 190–226. Sydney: New South Wales University Press.

Brody, E. B. 1966. Cultural exclusion, character and illness. *American Journal of Psychiatry 122 (2)*, 852–858.

Brown, S. A. & Schuckit, M. A. 1988. Changes in depression among abstinent alcoholics. *Journal of Studies on Alcohol 49 (5)*, 412–417.

Burbank, V. K. 1988. *Aboriginal adolescence: Maidenhood in an Australian community*. New Brunswick: Rutgers.

Burvill, P. W. 1975. Attempted suicide in the Perth statistical division, 1971–1972. *Australian and New Zealand Journal of Psychiatry 9 (4)*, 273–279.

Cadoret, R. & Winokur, G. 1974. Depression in alcoholism. *Annals of the New York Academy of Sciences 233*, 34–39.

Camus, A. 1975 (1942). *The myth of Sisyphus*. London: Penguin.

Cantor, C. H. & Dunne, M. P. 1990. Australian suicide data and the use of 'undetermined' death category (1968–1985). *Australian and New Zealand Journal of Psychiatry 24 (3)*, 381–384.

Cawte, J. [E.] 1972. *Cruel, poor and brutal nations*. Honolulu: University of Hawaii Press.

——. 1973. Why we slit the penis. In G. E. Kearney, P. R. de Lacey & G. R. Davidson (eds), *The psychology of Aboriginal Australians* pp. 380–394. Sydney: John Wiley.

——. 1974. *Medicine is the Law*. Honolulu: University of Hawaii Press.

——. 1984. Emic accounts of a mystery illness: The Groote Eylandt syndrome. *Australian and New Zealand Journal of Psychiatry 18*, 179–187.

Chesher, G. & Greeley, J. 1989. The effects of alcohol on mood. In J. Greeley & W. Gladstone (eds), *The effects of alcohol on cognitive, psychomotor, and affective functioning: Report and recommendations prepared by an expert working group for the Royal Commission Into Aboriginal Deaths in Custody* pp. 87–95. Sydney: National Drug and Alcohol Research Centre.

Chick, J; Kreitman, N; & Plant, N. 1982. Mean cell volume and gamma-glutamyl-transpeptidase as markers of drinking in working men. *Lancet 1*, 1249–1251.

Clay, J. W. 1987. Editorial: Grassroots development — more sunshine and rain, less seed. *Cultural Survival Quarterly 11 (1)*, 2.

Cleland, J. B. 1962. Disease in the Australian native. *Journal of Tropical Medicine and Hygiene 65*, 95–102.

Clement, C. 1987. *East Kimberley working paper No. 24: Pre-settlement intrusion into the East Kimberley*. East Kimberley Impact Assessment Project, Canberra.

Clifford, J. 1986. On ethnographic allegory. In J. Clifford & G. E. Marcus (eds), *Writing culture: The poetics and politics of ethnography* pp. 98–121. Berkeley: University of California Press.

Clinard, M. B. 1971. The theoretical implications of anomie and deviant behavior. In M. B. Clinard (ed.), *Anomie and deviant behaviour: A discussion and critique* pp. 1–56. London: Free Press.

Cloninger, C. R; Bohman, M; & Sigvardsson, S. 1981. Inheritance of alcohol abuse: Cross-fostering analysis of adopted men. *Archives of General Psychiatry 38*, 861–868.

Cloninger, C. R; Reich, T; Sigvardsson, S; von Knorring, A; & Bohman, M. 1988. Effects of changes in alcohol use between generations on inheritance of alcohol use. In R. M. Rose & J. Barret (eds), *Alcoholism: Origins and outcome* pp. 49–73. New York: Raven Press.

Cole, S. & Zuckerman, H. 1971. Inventory of empirical and theoretical studies of anomie. In M. B. Clinard (ed.), *Anomie and deviant behaviour: A discussion and critique* pp. 243–283. London: Free Press.

Collins, J. J. 1988. Suggested explanatory frameworks to clarify the alcohol use/violence relationship. *Contemporary Drug Problems 15*, 107–121.

Collmann, J. 1979a. Women, children, and the significance of the domestic group to urban Aborigines in Central Australia. *Ethnology 18*, 379–397.

———. 1979b. Social order and the exchange of liquor: A theory of drinking among Australian Aborigines. *Journal of Anthropological Research 35 (2)*, 208–224.

———. 1988. *Fringe-dwellers and welfare: The Aboriginal response to bureaucracy.* St Lucia: University of Queensland Press.

Cook, C. C. H. & Gurling, H. M. D. 1990. The genetic aspects of alcoholism and substance abuse: A review. In G. Edwards & M. Lader (eds), *The nature of drug dependence* pp. 75–102. Oxford: Oxford University Press.

Cook, C. E. 1923. *Report.* Health Department of Western Australia, File 888/1923.

———. 1974. Retrospect: 50 Years. Unpublished paper presented to the Association of State Medical Officers, Perth. 8 July.

Coombs, H. C. 1978. *Kulinma: Listening to Aboriginal Australians.* Canberra: Australian National University Press.

Coverley, A. A. M. 1933. Motion — Aborigines, treatment. *Western Australian Parliamentary Debates 90*, 639–647. 30 August.

Cowdy, G. O. 1970. Clinical psychiatric service to the Aborigines of the Northern Territory. *Australian and New Zealand Journal of Psychiatry 4 (1)*, 95–105.

d'Abbs, P. 1990. *Dry areas, alcohol and Aboriginal communities: A review of the Northern Territory Restricted Areas legislation.* Drug and Alcohol Bureau, Department of Health and Community Services and the Racing Gaming and Liquor Commission, Darwin.

Darwin, C. 1988 (1845). *The voyage of the Beagle.* New York: Mentor.

Dassori, A. M; Mezzich, J. E; & Keshavan, M. 1990. Suicidal indicators in schizophrenia. *Acta Psychiatrica Scandinavica 81*, 409–413.

Davidson, A. R. 1977. The emic-etic dilemma: Can methodology provide a solution in the absence of theory? In Y. P. Poortinga (ed.), *Basic problems in cross-cultural psychology* pp. 49–54. Amsterdam: Swets & Zeitlinger.

Davidson, W. S. 1978. *Havens of refuge: A history of leprosy in Western Australia.* Perth: University of Western Australia Press.

de Figueiredo, J. M. 1983. The law of sociocultural demoralization. *Social Psychiatry 18*, 73–78.

DeMaria, W. 1986. 'White welfare: Black entitlement' — the social security accesss controversy. *Aboriginal History 10 (1)*, 25–39.

Department of Native Welfare (W.A.). 1957–1972. *Annual reports.*

Devanesen, D; Furber, M; Hampton, D; Honari, M; Kinmonth, N; & Peach, H. G. 1986. *Health indicators in the Northern Territory.* Darwin: Government Printer.

Diekstra, R. F. W. 1989. Suicide and the attempted suicide: An international perspective. *Acta Psychiatrica Scandinavica 80 (suppl. 354)*, 1–24.

Doerner, K. 1981. *Madmen and the bourgeoisie: A social history of insanity and psychiatry.* Oxford: Blackwell.

Donaldson, T. 1985. Hearing the first Australians. In I. Donaldson & T. Donaldson (eds), *Seeing the first Australians* pp. 77–91. Sydney: George Allen & Unwin.

Donovan J. M. 1986. An etiologic model of alcoholism. *American Journal of Psychiatry 143 (1)*, 1–11.

Dorsch, M. M. & Roder, D. M. 1983. A comparison of Australian suicide rates in 1969–73 and 1976–80. *Australian and New Zealand Journal of Psychiatry 17*, 254–257.

Douglas, J. D. 1967. *The social meanings of suicide.* Princeton: Princeton University Press.

Drew, L. H. R. 1987. Beyond the disease concept of addiction: Towards an integration of the moral and scientific perspectives. *Australian Drug and Alcohol Review 6*, 45–48.

Duckworth, A. M. E; Foley-Jones, C. R; Lowe, P; & Maller, M. 1982. Imprisonment of Aborigines in North-Western Australia. *Australian and New Zealand Journal of Criminology 15*, 26–46.

Dudgeon, P. & Oxenham, D. 1988. The complexity of Aboriginal diversity: Identity and kindredness. Paper presented to the 'Learning my way conference', Perth. Centre for Aboriginal Studies, Curtin University of Technology.

Duquemin, A; d'Abbs, P; & Chalmers, E. 1991. *Making research into Aboriginal substance misuse issues more effective.* Working paper No. 4, National Drug and Alcohol Research Centre, Sydney.

Durack, M. 1969. *The rock and the sand.* London: Constable.

——— . 1975. *Sons in the saddle.* London: Corgi.

Durkheim, E. 1970 (1897). *Suicide: A study in sociology.* London: Routledge & Kegan Paul.

Eagleson, R. D. 1982. Variation in Aboriginal English. In R. D. Eagleson, S. Kaldor, & I. G. Malcolm (eds), *English and the Aboriginal child* pp. 11–30. Canberra: Curriculum Development Centre.

Eastwell, H. D. 1982. Voodoo death and the mechanism for dispatch of the dying in East Arnhem, Australia. *American Anthropologist 84*, 5–18.

———. 1988. The low risk of suicide among the Yolngu of the Northern Territory: The traditional pattern. *Medical Journal of Australia 148*, 338–340.

Eckermann, A-K. & Dowd, L. T. 1988. Structural violence and Aboriginal organisations in rural-urban Australia. *Journal of Legal Pluralism and Unofficial Law 27*, 55–77.

Edmunds, M. 1990. *Doing business: Socialisation, social relations, and social control in Aboriginal societies.* Discussion paper No. 2, Royal Commission into Aboriginal Deaths in Custody, Canberra.

Edwards, C. & Read, P. 1989. *The lost children.* Sydney: Doubleday.

Edwards, G. & Gross, M. M. 1976. Alcohol dependence: Provisional description of a clinical syndrome. *British Medical Journal 1*, 1058–1061.

Elkin, A. P. 1979. Aboriginal-European relations in Western Australia: An historical and personal record. In R. M. Berndt and C. H. Berndt (eds), *Aborigines of the West: Their past and their present* pp. 285–323. Perth: University of Western Australia Press.

English, B. 1991. The current state of Aboriginal health. *Aboriginal and Islander Health Worker Journal 15 (3)*, 6–8.

Fabrega, H. 1987. Psychiatric diagnosis: A cultural perspective. *Journal of Nervous and Mental Disease 175 (7)*, 383–394.

Fagan, P. 1991. Self-determination in action. In J. Reid & P. Trompf (eds), *The health of Aboriginal Australia* pp. 400–401. Sydney: Harcourt Brace Jovanovich.

Fanon, F. 1967. *The wretched of the earth.* Harmondsworth: Penguin.

Favazza, A. R. 1987. *Bodies under siege: Self-mutilation in culture and psychiatry.* Baltimore: Johns Hopkins University Press.

———. 1989. Normal and deviant self-mutilation: An essay-review. *Transcultural Psychiatric Research Review 26 (2)*, 113–127.

Felsman, J. K. 1989. Risk and resiliency in childhood: The lives of street children. In T. F. Dugan & R. Coles (eds), *The child in our times: Studies in the development of resiliency* pp. 56–80. New York: Brunner/Mazel.

Fisk, E. K. 1985. *The Aboriginal economy in town and country.* Sydney: George Allen & Unwin.

Flaherty, M. G. 1983. The national incidence of juvenile suicide in adult jails and juvenile detention centers. *Suicide and Life-Threatening Behavior 13 (2)*, 85–94.

Flanagan, R. J. 1988 (1888). *The Aborigines of Australia.* (facsimile edn). Brisbane: Boolorang.

Flood, J. 1983. *Archaeology of the dreamtime: The story of prehistoric Australia and her people*. Sydney: Collins.

Foley, G. 1982. Aboriginal community controlled health services: A short history. *Australian Institute of Aboriginal Studies, Aboriginal Health Project: Information Bulletin 2*, 13–15.

Foundation for Aboriginal and Islander Research Action (Qld). 1990. ATSIC: A limited step forward? *Aboriginal Law Bulletin 2 (43)*, 7–9.

Frances, R. J; Franklin, J; & Flavin, D. K. 1986. Suicide and alcoholism. In J. J. Mann & M. Stanley (eds), *Psychobiology of suicidal behaviour, Annals of the New York Academy of Sciences 487*, 316–326.

Freire, P. 1968. *Pedagogy of the oppressed*. New York: Seabury Press.

Gajdusek, C. 1990. Paradoxes of aspirations for and of children in primitive and isolated cultures. *Pediatric Research 27 (6)*, S59–S61.

Gale, F. 1978. Introduction. In F. Gale (ed.), *Woman's role in Aboriginal society* pp. 1–3. Canberra: Australian Institute of Aboriginal Studies.

Gault, E. I; Krupinski, J; & Stoller, A. 1970. Psychosocial problems of Aboriginal adolescents and their sociocultural environment. *Australian and New Zealand Journal of Psychiatry 4*: 174–181.

Gee, V; Webb, S. M; & Holman, C. D. 1989. *Perinatal statistics in Western Australia: Fifth annual report of the Western Australian Midwives' Notification System, 1987*. Health Department of Western Australia, Perth.

Gergen, K. J. 1986. Correspondence versus autonomy in the language of understanding human action. In D. W. Fiske & R. A. Schweder (eds), *Metatheory in social sciences: Pluralism and subjectivities* pp. 131–162. Chicago: University of Chicago Press.

Gibson, M. 1987. Anthropology and tradition: A contemporary Aboriginal viewpoint. Paper presented to the ANZAAS conference, Townsville.

Goedde, H. W. & Agarwal, D. P. 1987. Polymorphism of aldehyde dehydrogenase and alcohol sensitivity. *Enzyme 37 (1–2)*, 29–44.

Goldney, R. D. 1989. Suicide: The role of the media. *Australian and New Zealand Journal of Psychiatry 23*, 30–34.

Goldney, R. D. & Katsikitis, M. 1983. Cohort analysis of suicide rates in Australia. *Archives of General Psychiatry 40*, 71–74.

Goldstein, A. P. & Segall, M. H. 1983. *Aggression in global perspective*. New York: Pergamon.

Goodall, H. 1990. 'Saving the children': Gender and the colonization of Aboriginal children in NSW, 1788–1990. *Aboriginal Law Bulletin 2 (44)*, 6–9.

Goodman, R. A; Mercy, J. A; Loya, F; Rosenberg, M. L; Smith, J. C; Allen, N. H; Vargas, L; & Kolts, R. 1986. Alcohol use and interpersonal violence: Alcohol detected in homicide victims. *American Journal of Public Health 76 (2)*, 144–149.

Gould, R. A. 1970. Journey to Pulykara. *Natural History 75*, 57–66.

Goulet, D. 1971. *That third world: An introductory reader*. H. Cantel (ed.). New York: Macmillan.

Gracey, M. 1991. Health of Kimberley Aboriginal mothers and their infants and young children. *Medical Journal of Australia 155*, 98–402.

Gracey, M. & Spargo, R. M. 1987. The state of health of Aborigines in the Kimberley region. *Medical Journal of Australia 146 (4)*, 200–204.

Gracey, M; Sullivan, H; Burke, V; & Gacey, D. 1989. Factors which affect health, growth and nutrition in young children in remote Aboriginal communities. *Australian Paediatric Journal 25*, 322–323.

Gracey, M; Sullivan, H; & Spargo, R. 1988. Economic factors affecting Aboriginal health and health care. *Aboriginal Health Information Bulletin 9*, 36–39.

Gray, A. & Hogg, R. 1989. *Mortality of Aboriginal Australians in Western New South Wales, 1984–1987*. New South Wales Department of Health, Sydney.

Gray, A. & Smith, L. R. 1983. The size of the Aboriginal population. *Australian Aboriginal Studies 1*, 2–9.

Greeley, J. & Gladstone, W. (eds). 1989. *The effects of alcohol on cognitive, psychomotor, and affective functioning*. Monograph No. 8, National Drug and Alcohol Research Centre, Sydney.

Green, W. H; Campbell, M; & David, R. 1984. Psychosocial dwarfism: A critical review of the evidence. *Journal of the American Academy of Child Psychiatry 23 (1)*, 39–48.

Grey, G. 1983 (1841). *Expeditions in Western Australia, 1837-1839, Vol. 1* (facsimile edn). Perth: Hesperian Press.

Gribble, J. B. 1987 (1905). *Dark deeds in a sunny land, or blacks and whites in North-West Australia*, B. Tonkinson (ed.). Perth: University of Western Australia Press.

Griffiths, J. 1987. *Working paper No. 2 — Mining and exploration*. Kimberley Regional Planning Study report for the State Planning Commission and Department of Regional Development and the North West, Perth.

Gusfield, J. R. 1985. Social and cultural context of the drinking-driving event. *Journal of Studies on Alcohol 46 (Supplement No. 10, July)*, 70–77.

Gussow, Z. & Tracy, G. S. 1970. Stigma and the leprosy phenomenon: The social history of a disease in the nineteenth and twentieth centuries. *Bulletin of the History of Medicine 44 (5)*, 425–449.

Haebich, A. 1988. *For their own good: Aborigines and government in the Southwest of Western Australia, 1900–1940*. Perth: University of Western Australia Press.

Hamilton, A. 1981. *Nature and nurture: Aboriginal child-rearing in north-central Arnhem Land*. Canberra: Australian Institute of Aboriginal Studies.

Harding, T. W; De Arango, M. V; Baltazar, J; Climent, C. E; Ibrahim, H. H. A; Ladrigo-Ignacio, L; Murthy, R. S; Srinivasa, R; & Wig, N. N. 1980. Mental disorders in primary health care: A study of their frequency and diagnosis in four developing countries. *Psychological Medicine 19*, 231–241.

Harris, M; Sutherland, D; Cutter, G; & Ballangarry, L. 1987. Alcohol related hospital admissions in a country town. *Australian Drug and Alcohol Review 6*, 195–198.

Harrold, K. 1989. *The prevention and treatment of substance use with indigenous groups: A critique of the literature.* Alcohol and Drug Dependence Services, Queensland Department of Health, Brisbane.

Hasluck, P. 1961. *The policy of assimilation: Decisions of Commonwealth and State Ministers at the Native Welfare Conference, Canberra, January 26th and 27th.* Canberra: Government Publishing Service.

———. 1988. *Shadows of darkness: Aboriginal affairs, 1925–1965.* Melbourne: Melbourne University Press.

Hassan, R. & Carr, J. 1989. Changing patterns of suicide in Australia. *Australian and New Zealand Journal of Psychiatry 23*, 226–234.

Hayes, L. M. 1983. And darkness closes in . . . A national study of jail suicides. *Criminal Justice and Behavior 10 (4)*, 461–484.

Healy, B; Turpin, T; & Hamilton, M. 1985. Aboriginal drinking: A case study in inequality and disadvantage. *Australian Journal of Social Issues 20 (3)*, 191–208.

Healy, J. J. 1978. *Literature and the Aborigine in Australia, 1770–1975.* St Lucia: University of Queensland Press.

Heath, D. B. 1987. A decade of development in the anthropological study of alcohol use. In M. Douglas (ed.), *Constructive drinking: Perspectives on drink from anthropology* pp. 16–70. Cambridge: Cambridge University Press.

Hennessy, C. 1988. The National Aboriginal Mental Health Association. *Aboriginal Health Worker 12 (4)*, 3–6.

Hezel, F. X. 1984. Cultural patterns of Trukese suicides. *Ethnology 23 (3)*, 193–206.

Hicks, D. G. 1985. *Aboriginal morbidity and mortality in Western Australia: A comparative analysis of mortality and morbidity statistics including births, infant mortality and perinatal mortality in Aboriginals and non-Aboriginals in Western Australia, 1983.* Health Department of Western Australia, Perth.

Hitchcock, N. E; Gracey, M; Maller, R. A; & Spargo, R. M. 1987. Physical size of 1887 Aboriginal schoolchildren in the Kimberley region. *Medical Journal of Australia 146*, 415–419.

Holman, C. D. J; Quadros, C. F; Bucens, M. R; & Reid, P. M. 1987. Occurrence and distribution of hepatitis B infection in the Aboriginal population of Western Australia. *Australian and New Zealand Journal of Medicine 17*, 518–525

Hoskin, J. O; Friedman, M. I; & Cawte, J. E. 1969. A high incidence of suicide in a preliterate primitive society. *Psychiatry 32 (2)*, 200–210.

House of Representatives Standing Committee on Aboriginal Affairs. 1977. *Alcohol problems of Aboriginals: Final report.* Canberra: Australian Government Publishing Service.

Howard, M. C. 1981. *Aboriginal politics in Southwestern Australia*. Perth: University of Western Australia Press.

———. 1982. Introduction. In M. C. Howard (ed.), *Aboriginal power in Australian society* pp. 1–13. St Lucia: University of Queensland Press.

Huffer, V. 1980. *The sweetness of the fig: Aboriginal women in transition*. Sydney: New South Wales University Press.

Hughes, R. 1987. *The fatal shore*. London: Pan.

Human Rights and Equal Opportunity Commission. 1991. *Racist violence: Report of the National Inquiry into Racist Violence in Australia*. Canberra: Australian Government Publishing Service.

Hunt, H. 1981. Alcoholism among Aboriginal people. *Medical Journal of Australia 1 (2), (Special supplement No. 13)*, 1–3.

Hunt, S. 1986. *Spinifex and hessian: Women in North-West Australia, 1860–1900*. Perth: University of Western Australia Press.

———. 1987. The Gribble affair: A study in colonial politics. In J. B. Gribble, *Dark deeds in a sunny land, or blacks and whites in North-West Australia*, B. Tonkinson (ed.) pp. 62–73. Perth: University of Western Australia Press.

Hunter, E. M. & Allan, A. T. 1986. Psychiatric consultation in Micronesia: The question of organicity. *International Journal of Social Psychiatry 32 (4)*, 40–47.

Hunter, E; Hall, W; & Spargo, R. 1991. *The distribution and correlates of alcohol consumption in a remote Aboriginal population*. Monograph No 12, National Drug and Alcohol Research Centre, Sydney.

Illich, I. 1972. *Deschooling society*. New York: Perennial Library.

———. 1977 An exchange with Ivan Illich: Revolving development. *Reports Magazine*, April.

Jacobs, P. 1990. *Mister Neville*. Fremantle: Fremantle Arts Centre Press.

Jahoda, G. 1977. In pursuit of the emic-etic distinction: Can we ever capture it? In Y. P. Poortinga (ed.), *Basic problems in cross-cultural psychology* pp. 55–63. Amsterdam: Swets & Zeitlinger.

Jaynes, J. 1982. *The origin of consciousness in the breakdown of the bicameral mind*. Boston: Houghton & Mifflin.

Jebb, M. A. 1984. The lock hospitals experiment: Europeans, Aborigines and venereal disease. *Journal of Studies in Western Australian History 8*, 68–87.

Jellinek, E. M. 1977. The symbolism of drinking: A culture-historical approach. *Journal of Studies on Alcohol 38*, 852–866.

Jones, D. J. & Hill-Burnett, J. 1982. The political context of ethnogenesis: An Australian example. In M. C. Howard (ed.), *Aboriginal power in Australian society* pp. 214–246. St Lucia: University of Queensland Press.

Jones, I. H. 1971. Stereotyped aggression in a group of Australian Western Desert aborigines. *British Journal of Medical Psychology 44*, 259–265.

———. 1972. Psychiatric disorders among aborigines of the Australian Western Desert (II). *Social Science and Medicine 6 (2)*, 263–267.

————. 1977. Social unrest in an Aboriginal community. *Medical Journal of Australia 1 Suppl. (4)*, 5–7.

Jones, I. H. & Horne, D. J. 1973. Psychiatric disorders among aborigines of the Australian Western Desert: Further data and discussion. *Social Science and Medicine 7 (3)*, 219–228.

Jones, P. 1989. Ideas linking Aborigines and Fuegians: From Cook to the *Kulturkreis* school. *Australian Aboriginal Studies 2*, 2–13.

Jordan, D. F. 1988. Aboriginal identity: Uses of the past, problems for the future? In J. R. Beckett (ed.), *Past and present: The construction of Aboriginality* pp. 109–130. Canberra: Aboriginal Studies Press.

Kaberry, P. M. 1973 (1939). *Aboriginal woman: Sacred and profane*. New York: Gordon Press.

Kahn, M. W. 1982. Cultural clash and psychopathology in three Aboriginal cultures. *Academic Psychology Bulletin 4*, 553–561.

————. 1986. Psychosocial disorders of Aboriginal people of the United States and Australia. *Journal of Rural Community Psychology 7 (1)*, 45–59.

Kahn, M. W. & The Behavioural Health Team. 1980. Wife beating and cultural context: Prevalence in an Aboriginal and Islander community in Northern Australia. *American Journal of Community Psychology 8 (6)*, 727–731.

Kahn, M. W; Hunter, E; Heather, N; & Tebbutt, J. 1990. Australian Aborigines and alcohol: A review. *Drug and Alcohol Review 10*, 351–366.

Kamien, M. 1978. *The dark people of Bourke: A study of planned social change*. Canberra: Australian Institute of Aboriginal Studies.

Keeffe, K. 1988. Aboriginality: Resistance and persistence. *Australian Aboriginal Studies 1*, 67–81.

Kelly, H. A. & Weeks, S. A. 1991. Ear disease in three Aboriginal communities in Western Australia. *Medical Journal of Australia 154 (4)*, 240–245.

Kessler, R. C; Downey, G; Milavsky, J. R; & Stipp, H. 1988. Clustering of teenage suicides after news stories about suicides: A reconsideration. *American Journal of Psychiatry 145 (11)*, 1379–1383.

Khalidi, N. A. 1989. *Aboriginal mortality in Central Australia, 1975–77 to 1985–86: A comparative analysis of levels and trends*. Canberra: National Centre for Epidemiology and Population Health.

Kirk, R. L. 1981. *Aboriginal man adapting: The human biology of Australian Aborigines*. London: Clarendon Press.

Kleinman, A. 1987. Anthropology and psychiatry: The role of culture in cross-cultural research on illness. *British Journal of Psychiatry 151*, 447–454.

Kleinman, A. & Good. B. 1985. Introduction. In A. Kleinman & B. Good (eds), *Culture and depression: Studies in the anthropology and cross-cultural psychiatry of affect and disorder* pp. 1–33. Berkeley: University of California Press.

Koepping, K-P. 1988. Nativistic movements in Aboriginal Australia: Creative adjustment, protest or regeneration of tradition. In T. Swain & D. B. Rose (eds), *Aboriginal Australians and Christian missions: Ethnographic and historical studies* pp. 397–411. Adelaide: Australian Association for the Study of Religions.

Kohlberg, L. 1981. *The philosophy of moral development, Vol. 1*. New York: Harper and Row.

Kolig, E. 1977. From tribesman to citizen. In R. M. Berndt (ed.), *Aborigines and change: Australia in the '70s* pp. 33–53. Canberra: Australian Institute of Aboriginal Studies.

———. 1978. Dialectics of Aboriginal life-space. In M. C. Howard (ed.), *'Whitefella business': Aborigines in Australian politics* pp. 49–79. Philadelphia: The Institute for the Study of Human Issues.

———. 1979. Captain Cook in the Western Kimberleys. In R. M. Berndt & C. H. Berndt (eds), *Aborigines of the West: Their past and their present* pp. 274–284. Perth: University of Western Australia Press.

———. 1982. An obituary for ritual power. In M. C. Howard (ed.), *Aboriginal power in Australian society* pp. 14–31. St Lucia: University of Queensland Press.

———. 1987. *The Noonkanbah story*. Dunedin: University of Otago Press.

———. 1988. Mission not accomplished: Christianity in the Kimberleys. In T. Swain & D. B. Rose (eds), *Aboriginal Australians and Christian missions: Ethnographic and historical studies* pp. 376–390. Adelaide: Australian Association for the Study of Religions.

———. 1989. The powers that be and those who aspire to them: Power, knowledge and reputation in Australian Aboriginal society. In J. C. Altman (ed.), *Emergent inequalities in Aboriginal Australia* pp. 43–66. Oceania Monograph No. 38, University of Sydney.

Kosky, R. 1987. Is suicidal behaviour increasing among Australian youth? *Medical Journal of Australia 147*, 164–169.

Kuhn, T. 1970. *The structure of scientific revolution*. Chicago: University of Chicago Press.

Lake, P. 1989. Alcohol and cigarette use by urban Aboriginal people. *Aboriginal Health Information Bulletin 11*, 20–22.

Land, G. 1978. *Grow or die*. New York: Delta Books.

Lands, M. (ed.). 1987. Mayi: *Some bush fruits of Dampierland*. Broome: Magabala Books.

Langton, M. 1989. Seeing the grog for what it is. *Land Rights News*, March 29.

Larsen, K. S. 1979. Social crisis and Aboriginal alcohol abuse. *Australian Journal of Social Issues 14 (2)*, 143–160.

———. 1980. Aboriginal group identification and problem drinking. *Australian Psychologist 15 (3)*, 385–392.

Laughlin, C. D. & Brady, I. A. 1978. Introduction: Diaphysis and change in human populations. In C. D. Laughlin & I. A. Brady (eds),

Extinction and survival in human populations pp. 1–48. New York: Columbia University Press.

Lester, D. & Yang, B. 1991. The relationship between divorce, unemployment and female participation in the labour force and suicide rates in Australia and America. *Australian and New Zealand Journal of Psychiatry 25*, 519–523.

LeVine, R. A. 1982. *Culture, behavior and personality: An introduction to the comparative study of psychological adaptation.* New York: Aldine.

Lewis, M. 1988. From blue light clinic to Nightingale centre, a brief history of the Sydney STD centre and its forerunners, Part 1: Venereal diseases in Europe and in Australia from colonization to 1945. *Venereology 1 (1)*, 3–9.

Lincoln, R. A; Najman, J. M; Wilson, P. R; & Matis, C. E. 1983. Mortality rates in 14 Queensland Aboriginal communities. *Medical Journal of Australia 1 (8)*, 357–360.

Lipsedge, M. 1989. Cultural influences on psychiatry. *Current Opinion in Psychiatry 2*, 267–272.

Littlewood, R. & Lipsedge, M. 1989. *Aliens and alienists: Ethnic minorities and psychiatry* 2nd edn. London: Unwin Hyman.

Long, J. V. F. & Vaillant, G. E. 1989. Escape from the underclass. In T. F. Dugan & R. Coles (eds), *The child in our times: Studies in the development of resiliency* pp. 200–213. New York: Brunner/Mazel.

Long, T. 1979. The development of government Aboriginal policy: The effect of administrative changes, 1829–1977. In R. M. Berndt & C. H. Berndt (eds), *Aborigines of the West: Their past and their present* pp. 357–366. Perth: University of Western Australia Press.

Lyon, P. 1990. *What everyone knows about Alice: A report on the impact of alcohol abuse on the town of Alice Springs.* Report for the Tangentyere Council, Alice Springs.

MacAndrew, C. & Edgerton, R. B. 1969. *Drunken comportment: A social explanation.* Chicago: Aldine.

McCarthy, P. D. & Walsh, D. 1975. Suicide in Dublin: I. The under-reporting of suicide and the consequences for national statistics. *British Journal of Psychiatry 126*, 301–308.

McClure, G. M. G. 1984a. Recent trends in suicide among the young. *British Journal of Psychiatry 144*, 134–138.

————. 1984b. Trends in suicide rates for England and Wales 1975–80. *British Journal of Psychiatry 144*, 119–126.

McCorquodale, J. C. 1985. Aborigines: A history of law and injustice, 1829–1985. PhD thesis, University of New England.

McDonald, D. 1990. *Research Paper No. 13. National police custody survey, August 1988, national report.* Royal Commission into Aboriginal Deaths in Custody, Canberra.

McGrath, A. 1987. *'Born in the cattle': Aborigines in cattle country.* Sydney: Allen & Unwin.

McKelson, K. 1979. Nadya Nadya country. In R. M. Berndt & C. H. Berndt (eds), *Aborigines of the West: Their past and their present* pp. 214–223. Perth: University of Western Australia Press.

Macknight, C. C. (ed.). 1969. *The farthest coast: A selection of writings relating to the history of the northern coast of Australia.* Melbourne: Melbourne University Press.

McLeod, D. W. (n.d.). *How the West was lost: The native question in the development of Western Australia.* Perth: Nomads Charitable and Educational Foundation.

MacPherson, C. & MacPherson, L. 1985. Suicide in Western Samoa: A sociological Perspective. In F. X. Hezel, D. H. Rubinstein & G. H. White (eds), *Culture, youth and suicide: Papers from an East-West Center conference* pp. 36–73. Honolulu: University of Hawaii Press.

Maddock, K. 1977. Two laws in one community. In R. M. Berndt (ed.), *Aborigines and change: Australia in the '70s* pp. 13–32. Canberra: Australian Institute of Aboriginal Studies.

Marchant, L. R. 1981. *Aboriginal Administration in Western Australia, 1886–1905.* Canberra: Australian Institute of Aboriginal Studies.

————. 1988. *An island unto itself: William Dampier & New Holland.* Perth: Hesperian Press.

Marinovich, N; Larsson, O; & Barber, K. 1976. Comparative metabolism rates of ethanol in adults of Aboriginal and European descent. *Medical Journal of Australia 1 Suppl (3)*, 44–46.

Marshall, M. 1979. *Weekend warriors: Alcohol in a Micronesian culture.* Palo Alto: Mayfield Press.

————. 1983. 'Four hundred rabbits': An anthropological view of ethanol as a disinhibitor. In R. Room & G. Collins (eds), *Disinhibition: Nature and meaning of the link, N.I.A.A. Research monograph No. 12, proceedings of a conference held in February 1981* pp. 186–204. Berkeley: U.S. Department of Health and Human Services.

————. 1987. 'Young men's work': Alcohol use in the contemporary Pacific. In A. B. Robillard & A. J. Marsella (eds), *Contemporary issues in mental health research in the Pacific Islands* pp. 72–93. Honolulu: Social Science Research Unit.

Marx, E. 1976. *The social context of violent behaviour: A social anthropological study in an Israeli immigrant town.* London: Routledge & Kegan Paul.

May, P. [A.] 1982. Substance abuse and American Indians: Prevalence and susceptibility. *International Journal of the Addictions 17 (7)*, 1185–1206.

————. 1987. Suicide and self-destruction among American Indian youths. *Journal of the National Center for American Indian and Alaskan Mental Health Research 1 (1)*, 52–69.

Maynard, M. 1985. Projections of melancholy. In I. Donaldson & T. Donaldson (eds), *Seeing the first Australians* pp. 92–109. Sydney: George Allen & Unwin.

Meggitt, M. J. 1962. *Desert people: A study of the Walbiri Aborigines of Central Australia.* Sydney: Angus and Robertson.

Menninger, K. 1938. *Man against himself.* New York: Harvest.

Merlan, F. 1988. Gender in Aboriginal social life: A review. In R. M. Berndt & R. Tonkinson (eds), *Social anthropology and Australian Aboriginal studies: A contemporary overview* pp. 15–76. Canberra: Australian Studies Press.

———. 1989. Emergent inequalities in Aboriginal Australia: An introduction. In J. C. Altman (ed.), *Emergent inequalities in Aboriginal Australia* pp. 1–16. Oceania Monograph No. 38, University of Sydney.

Merton, R. K. 1971. Anomie, anomia, and social interaction: Contexts of deviant behavior. In M. B. Clinard (ed.), *Anomie and deviant behaviour: A discussion and critique* pp. 213–242. London: Free Press.

Midford, R. 1991. The decriminalisation of public drunkenness in Western Australia. *Aboriginal Law Bulletin 2 (51)*, 18–20.

Ministry of National Health and Welfare (Canada). 1989. *Alcohol in Canada.* Ministry of Health and Welfare, Ottawa.

Mol, H. 1982. *The firm and the formless: Religion and identity in Aboriginal Australia.* Waterloo: Wilfred Laurier University Press.

Mollica, R. F; Wyshak, G; de Marneffe, D; Khuon, F; & Lavelle, J. 1987. Indochinese versions of the Hopkins Symptom Checklist-25: A screening instrument for the psychiatric care of refugees. *American Journal of Psychiatry 144 (4)*, 497–500.

Montagu, A. 1974 (1937). *Coming into being among the Australian Aborigines: The procreative beliefs of the Australian Aborigines.* London: Routlege & Kegan Paul.

Morris, B. 1988. The politics of identity: From Aborigines to the first Australian. In J. R. Beckett (ed.), *Past and present: The construction of Aboriginality* pp. 63–86. Canberra: Aboriginal Studies Press.

Morrison, J. 1976. The origins of the practice of circumcision and subincision among the Australian Aborigines. *Medical Journal of Australia 21*, 125–127.

Moseley, H. D. 1935. *Report of the Royal Commission appointed to investigate, report, and advise upon matters in relation to the condition and treatment of Aborigines.* Perth: Government Printer.

Mounsey, C. F. 1979. Aboriginal education — A new dawning. In R. M. Berndt & C. H. Berndt (eds), *Aborigines of the West: Their past and their present* pp. 395–405. Perth: University of Western Australia Press.

Mullen, P. E. 1991. Jealousy: The pathology of passion. *British Journal of Psychiatry 158*, 593–601.

Mulvaney, D. J. 1985. The Darwinian perspective. In I. Donaldson & T. Donaldson (eds), *Seeing the first Australians* pp. 68–75. Sydney: George Allen & Unwin.

———. 1989. *Encounters in place: Outsiders and Aboriginal Australians 1606–1985.* St Lucia: University of Queensland Press.

Munch, P. A. 1974. Anarchy and anomie in an atomistic community. *Man, Journal of the Royal Anthropological Institute 9 (2)*, 243–261.

Murphy, G. E; Armstrong, J. W; Hermele, S. L; Fischer, J. R; & Clendenin, W. W. 1979. Suicide and alcoholism. Interpersonal loss confirmed as a predictor. *Archives of General Psychiatry 36*, 65–69.

Murphy, G. E; Lindesay, J; & Grundy, E. 1986. 60 years of suicide in England and Wales: A cohort study. *Archives of General Psychiatry 43*, 969–976.

Murphy, G. E. & Wetzel, R. D. 1980. Suicide risk by birth cohort in the United States, 1949–1974. *Archives of General Psychiatry 37*, 519–523.

Myers, F. R. 1979. Emotions and the self: A theory of personhood and political order among Pintupi Aborigines. *Ethos 7 (4)*, 343–370.

————. 1982. Ideology and experience: The cultural basis of politics in Pintupi life. In M. C. Howard (ed.), *Aboriginal power in Australian society* pp. 79–114. St Lucia: University of Queensland Press.

————. 1986. *Pintupi country, Pintupi self: Sentiment, place, and politics among Western Desert Aborigines.* Canberra: Australian Institute of Aboriginal Studies.

Nandy, A. 1983. *The intimate enemy: Loss and recovery of self under colonialism.* Delhi: Oxford University Press.

Nathan, P. & Japanangka, D. L. 1983. *Health business: A report for the Central Australian Aboriginal Congress.* Melbourne: Heinemann.

National Aboriginal Health Strategy Working Party. 1989. *A national Aboriginal health strategy.* Canberra: Department of Aboriginal Affairs.

National Health and Medical Research Council. 1987. *Is there a safe level of daily consumption of alcohol for men and women? Recommendations regarding responsible drinking behaviour.* Canberra: Australian Government Publishing Service.

National Task Force on Suicide in Canada. 1987. *Suicide in Canada.* Mental Health Division, Health Services and Promotion Branch, Health and Welfare Canada, Ottawa.

Neitschmann, B. 1987. The third world war. *Cultural Survival Quarterly 11 (3)*, 1–16.

Nichter, M. 1981. Idioms of distress: Alternatives in the expression of psychosocial distress: A case study from South India. *Culture, Medicine and Psychiatry 5*, 379–408.

Nurcombe, B. 1970. Deprivation: An essay in definition with special consideration of the Australian Aboriginal. Unpublished manuscript, introduction to the work of the Preschool Enrichment Centre, Bourke.

————. 1976. *Children of the dispossessed.* Honolulu, University of Hawaii Press.

Obeyesekere, G. 1970. The idiom of demonic possession: A case study. *Social Science and Medicine 4*, 97–111.

O'Brian, P. 1988. *Joseph Banks: A life.* London: Collins Harvill.

O'Connor, R. 1984. Alcohol and contingent drunkenness in Central Australia. *Australian Journal of Social Issues 19 (3)*, 173–183.

O'Dea, D. J. 1989. *Report of the inquiry into the death of Hugh Wodulan*. Royal Commission into Aboriginal Deaths in Custody, Canberra.

———. 1990. *Report of the inquiry into the death of Stanley Brown*. Royal Commission into Aboriginal Deaths in Custody, Canberra.

O'Dea, K; Spargo, R. M; & Akerman, K. 1980. The effects of transition from traditional to urban life-style on the insulin secretory response in Australian Aborigines. *Diabetes Care 3 (1)*, 31–37.

O'Dea, K; Spargo, R. M; & Nestel, P. I. 1982. Impact of Westernization on carbohydrate and lipid metabolism in Australian Aborigines. *Diabetologica 22*, 148–153.

Oetting, E. R; Beauvais, F; & Edwards, R. 1988. Alcohol and Indian youth: Social and psychological correlates and prevention. *Journal of Drug Issues 18 (1)*, 87–101.

Oliver, D. 1985. Reducing suicide in Western Samoa. In F. X. Hezel, D. H. Rubinstein & G. H. White (eds), *Culture, youth and suicide: Papers from an East-West Center conference* pp. 74–87. Honolulu: University of Hawaii Press.

Orru, M. 1986. Anomy and reason in the English renaissance. *Journal of the History of Ideas 47 (2)*, 177–196.

Paddy, E; Paddy, S; & Smith, M. 1987. Boonja bardak korn: *All trees are good for something*. Report for the Western Australian Museum Anthropology Department, Perth.

Palmer, K. & McKenna, C. 1978. *Somewhere between black and white: The story of an Aboriginal Australian*. Melbourne: Macmillan.

Perkins, C. 1991a. An open letter from Charles Perkins — Part 1. *Aboriginal and Islander Health Worker Journal 15 (2)*, 19–27.

———. 1991b. An open letter from Charles Perkins — Part 2. *Aboriginal and Islander Health Worker Journal 15 (3)*, 24–26.

Peters, R. 1981. Suicidal behavior among native Americans: An annotated bibliography. *White Cloud Journal 2 (3)*, 9–20.

Peterson, N. 1970. Buluwandi: A Central Australian ceremony for the resolution of conflict. In R. M. Berndt (ed.), *Australian Aboriginal Anthropology* pp. 200–215. Perth: University of Western Australia Press.

———. 1977. Aboriginal involvement with the Australian economy in the Central Reserve during the winter of 1970. In R. M. Berndt (ed.), *Aborigines and change: Australia in the '70s* pp. 136–146. Canberra: Australian Institute of Aboriginal Studies.

Petheram, R. J. & Kok, B. 1986. *Plants of the Kimberley region of Western Australia*. Perth: University of Western Australia Press.

Pettinati, H. M; Sugerman, A. A; & Maurer, H. S. 1982. Four year MMPI changes in abstinent and drinking alcoholics. *Alcoholism: Clinical and Experimental Research 6 (4)*, 487–494.

Pfeffer, C. R. 1986. Suicide prevention: Current efficacy and future promise. In J. J. Mann & M. Stanley (eds), *Psychobiology of suicidal behavior*, *Annals of the New York Academy of Sciences 487*, 341–350.

Phillips, D. P. & Carstensen, L. 1986. Clustering of teenage suicides after television news stories about suicide. *New England Journal of Medicine* 315 (11), 685–689.

Pine, C. J. 1981. Suicide in American Indian and Alaskan native tradition. *White Cloud Journal 2 (3)*, 3–8.

Polloi, A. H. 1985. Suicide in Palau. In F. X. Hezel, D. H. Rubinstein & G. H. White (eds), *Culture, youth and suicide: Papers from an East-West Center conference* pp. 125–138. Honolulu: University of Hawaii Press.

Poole, F. J. P. 1985. Among the boughs of the hanging tree: Male suicide among the Bimin-Kuskusmin of Papua New Guinea. In F. X. Hezel, D. H. Rubinstein & G. H. White (eds), *Culture, youth and suicide: Papers from an East-West Center conference* pp. 152–181. Honolulu: University of Hawaii Press.

Prokopec, M. 1979. Demographic and morphological aspects of the Roonka population, *Archeological and Physical Anthropology in Oceania 14 (1)*, 11–26.

Radford, A. J; Harris, R. D; Brice, G. A; Van der Byl, M; Monten, H; Matters, D; Neeson, M; Bryan, L; & Hassan, R. 1990. *Taking control: A joint study of Aboriginal social health in Adelaide with particular reference to stress and destructive behaviours, 1988–1989*. Monograph No. 7, Department of Primary Health Care, Flinders University of South Australia.

Read, P. 1981. *The stolen generations: The removal of Aboriginal children in New South Wales 1883–1969*. Occasional paper No 1. Ministry of Aboriginal Affairs, Sydney.

——. 1988. *A hundred years war*. Sydney: Australian National University Press.

Reich, W. 1981. Psychiatric diagnosis as an ethical problem. In S. Bloch & P. Chodoff (eds), *Psychiatric ethics*. Oxford: Oxford University Press.

Reid, J. 1979. Health as harmony, sickness as conflict. *Hemisphere 23 (4)*, 194–199.

——. 1983. *Sorcerers and healing spirits: Continuity and change in an Aboriginal medical system*. Canberra: Australian National University Press.

Reser, J. [P.] 1989a. *Research paper No. 9. The design of safe and humane police cells: A discussion of some issues relating to Aboriginal people in police custody*. Royal Commission into Aboriginal Deaths in Custody, Canberra.

——. 1989b. Australian Aboriginal suicide deaths in custody: Cultural context and cluster evidence. *Australian Psychologist 24 (3)*, 325–324.

——. 1990a. The cultural context of Aboriginal suicide: Myths meanings and critical analysis. *Oceania 61 (2)*, 177–184.

——. 1990b. A perspective on the causes and cultural context of violence in Aboriginal communities in North Queensland. Unpublished report for the Royal Commission into Aboriginal Deaths in Custody, Canberra.

————. 1991a. Aboriginal mental health: Conflicting cultural perspectives. In J. Reid & P. Trompf (eds), *The health of Aboriginal Australia* pp. 218–291. Sydney, Harcourt Brace Jovanovich.

————. 1991b. The 'socio-cultural' argument and constructions of 'Aboriginal violence': A critical review of Hunter (1991). *Australian Psychologist 26 (3)*, 209–214.

Reser, J. P. & Eastwell, H. D. 1981. Labelling and cultural expectations: The shaping of a sorcery syndrome in Aboriginal Australia. *Journal of Nervous and Mental Disease 169 (5)*, 303–310.

Reynolds, H. 1982. *The other side of the frontier: Aboriginal resistance to the European invasion of Australia.* Ringwood: Penguin.

Rich, C. L; Warsradt, G. M; Nemiroff, R. A; Fowler, R. C; & Young, D. 1991. Suicide stressors and the life cycle. *American Journal of Psychiatry 148 (4)*, 524–527.

Ricoeur, P. 1984. The creativity of language. In R. Kearney (ed.), *Dialogues with contemporary continental thinkers: The phenomenological heritage* pp. 15–46. Manchester: Manchester University Press.

Roberts, D; Gracey, M; & Spargo, R. M. 1988. Growth and morbidity in children in a remote Aboriginal community in north-west Australia. *Medical Journal of Australia 148*, 68–71.

Robillard, A. B. 1987. Introduction. In A. B. Robillard & A. J. Marsella (eds), *Contemporary issues in mental health research in the Pacific Islands* pp. v–xix. Honolulu: Social Science Research Institute.

Robins, E. 1986. Psychosis and suicide. *Biological Psychiatry 21*, 665–672.

Robinson, G. 1990. Separation, retaliation and suicide: Mourning and the conflicts of young Tiwi men. *Oceania 60 (3)*, 161–178.

Robinson, M. V. 1973. Change and adjustment among the Bardi of Sunday Island, North-Western Australia. M.A. thesis, University of Western Australia, Perth.

Robinson, M. V. & Yu, P. 1975. *A note on* kuns: *An Aboriginal card game from the North-West of Western Australia.* Department of Aboriginal Affairs Newsletter, 2 (3), 41–49.

Roheim, G. 1974. *Children of the desert: The western tribes of Central Australia,* edited by W. Muensterberger. New York: Basic Books.

Room, R. 1984. Alcohol and ethnography: A case of problem deflation? *Current Anthropology 25 (2)*, 169–191.

Rose, D. B. 1986. Passive violence. *Australian Aboriginal Studies 1*, 24–30.

Rose, F. G. G. 1987. *The traditional mode of production of the Australian Aborigines.* Sydney: Angus & Robertson.

Rosenberg, M. 1979. *Conceiving the self.* New York: Basic Books.

Rotter, J. B. 1966. Generalized expectancies for internal versus external control of reinforcement. *Psychological Monographs 80 (1, whole No. 609).*

————. 1975. Some problems and misconceptions related to the construct of internal versus external control of reinforcement. *Journal of Consulting and Clinical Psychology 43 (1)*, 56–67.

Rowley, C. D. 1972a. *The remote Aborigines*. Melbourne: Pelican Books.

———. 1972b. *The destruction of Aboriginal society*. Melbourne: Pelican Books.

———. 1972c. *Outcasts in White Australia*. Melbourne: Pelican Books.

Royal Commission into Aboriginal Deaths in Custody. 1988. *Interim report*. Canberra: Australian Government Publishing Service.

———. 1991. *Final report*. Canberra: Australian Government Publishing Service.

Rubinstein, D. H. 1983. Epidemic suicide among Micronesian adolescents. *Social Science and Medicine 17 (10)*, 657–665.

———. 1987. Cultural patterns and contagion: Epidemic suicide among Micronesian youth. In A. B. Robillard & A. J. Marsella (eds), *Contemporary issues in mental health research in the Pacific Islands* pp. 127–148. Honolulu: Social Science Research Institute.

Rutter, M. 1987. Psychological resilience and protective mechanisms. *American Journal of Orthopsychiatry 57 (3)*, 316–331.

Ryan, W. 1971. *Blaming the victim*. New York: Random House.

Sackett, L. 1977. Liquor and the Law: Wiluna, Western Australia. In R. M. Berndt (ed.), *Aborigines and change: Australia in the '70s* pp. 90–99. Canberra: Australian Institute of Aboriginal Studies.

———. 1988. Resisting arrests: Drinking, development and discipline in a desert context. *Social Analysis 24*, 66–84.

Saggers, S. & Gray, D. 1991. Policy and practice in Aboriginal health. In J. Reid & P. Trompf (eds), *The health of Aboriginal Australia* pp. 381–420. Sydney: Harcourt Brace Jovanovich.

Sainsbury, P. & Jenkins, J. S. 1982. The accuracy of officially reported suicide statistics for purposes of epidemiological research. *Journal of Epidemiology and Community Health 36*, 43–48.

Sambo, L. 1988. *Survey of alcohol and other drug use among Aboriginal people in Esperance*. Esperance Aboriginal Corporation, Esperance.

Sandefur, J. & Sandefur, J. 1980. Pidgin and Creole in the Kimberleys, Western Australia. *Australian Institute of Aboriginal Studies Newsletter 14 (September)*, 31–37.

Sandison, A. T. 1980. Notes on some skeletal changes in pre-European contact Australian Aborigines. *Journal of Human Evolution 9*, 45–47.

Sansom, B. 1977. Aborigines and alcohol: A fringe-camp example. *Australian Journal of Alcohol and Drug Dependence 4 (2)*, 58–62.

———. 1980. *The camp at Wallaby Cross: Aboriginal fringe dwellers in Darwin*. Canberra: Australian Institute of Aboriginal Studies.

———. 1982. The Aboriginal commonality. In R. M. Berndt (ed.) *Aboriginal sites, rights and resource development*. Perth: University of Western Australia Press.

Saunders, J. 1989. The clinical pharmacology of alcohol. In J. Greeley & W. Gladstone (eds) *The effects of alcohol on cognitive, psychomotor, and affective functioning: Report and recommendations prepared by an* expert working group for the Royal Commission into Aboriginal Deaths in Custody pp. 6-14. Sydney: National Drug and Alcohol Research Centre.

Schopenhauer, A. 1962 (1851 as *Parerga and Paralipomena*). On suicide. In *The essential Schopenhauer* pp. 97-101. London: Unwin.

Schuckit, M. A. 1986. Genetic and clinical implications of alcoholism and affective disorder. *American Journal of Psychiatry 143 (2)*, 140-147.

Seeman, M. 1959. On the meaning of alienation. *American Sociological Review 24*, 783-791.

Shaw, B. 1981. *My country of the pelican dreaming: The life of an Australian Aborigine of the Gadjerong, Grant Ngabidj, 1904-1977*. Canberra: Australian Institute of Aboriginal Studies.

Shoemaker, A. 1989. *Black words, white page: Aboriginal literature 1929-1988*. St Lucia: University of Queensland Press.

Shore, J. H. 1975. American Indian suicide: Fact and fantasy. *Psychiatry 38*, 86-91.

Shore, J. H. & Manson, S. 1983. American Indian psychiatric and social problems. *Transcultural Psychiatry Research Review 20*, 159-180.

Skowron, S. & Smith, D. I. 1986. Survey of homelessness, alcohol consumption and related problems amongst Aboriginals in the Hedland area. Unpublished paper, Western Australian Alcohol and Drug Authority, Perth.

Smith, B. 1989. *The concept of 'community' in Aboriginal policy and service delivery*. Occasional paper No. 1., North Australian Development Unit, Darwin.

———. 1990. *Aboriginal income maintenance: Policy and legislation*. Occasional paper No. 4., North Australian Development Unit, Darwin.

Smith, D. I; Singh, H; & Singh, M. N. 1987. *Survey of Aboriginal alcohol consumption and related problems at Wiluna, Western Australia*. Western Australian Alcohol and Drug Authority, Perth.

Smith, R. C. 1987. Indigenous autonomy for grassroots development. *Cultural Survival Quarterly 11 (1)*, 8-12.

Smith, R. [M.] 1991. *Urbanization and the effects of alcohol on the nutrition and health of Aboriginal children in the Kimberley region of Western Australia*. Paper presented to the Urbanization and Nutritional Problems of Children Conference, Perth, May 12.

Smith, R. [M.]; Hunter, E; Spargo, R; & Hall, W. 1990. *Feedback: A summary of research findings on health and lifestyle presented to Kimberley Aboriginal communities*. CSIRO Division of Human Nutrition, Adelaide.

Smith, R. M; Spargo, R. M; Hunter, E. M; King, R. A; Correll, R. L; Craig, I. H; & Nestel, P. J. 1992. Prevalence of hypertension in Kimberley Aborigines and its relationship to ischaemic heart disease: An age-stratified random survey. *Medical Journal of Australia 156*, 557-562.

Smyth, R. 1989. *Research paper No. 4. The Aboriginal and Torres Strait Islander population*. Royal Commission into Aboriginal Deaths in Custody, Canberra.

Sommerlad, E. A. & Berry, J. W. 1970. The role of ethnic identification in distinguishing between attitudes towards assimilation and integration of a minority racial group. *Human Relations 23 (1)*, 23–29.

Spargo, R. M. 1981. Address to the Victorian Section of the Royal Flying Doctor Service. *Royal Flying Doctor Service: Victorian Section Bulletin 3 (3)*, 1–7.

Spencer, B. & Gillen, F. J. 1968 (1899). *The native tribes of Central Australia*. New York: Dover Publications.

Spencer, J. 1986. Letter: Use of SRQ in primary care situations. *British Journal of Psychiatry 148*, 479–480.

Spiro, M. E. 1984. Some reflections on cultural determinism and relativism with special reference to emotion and reason. In R. A. Shweder & R. A. LeVine (eds), *Culture theory: Essays on mind, self and emotion* pp. 323–346. Cambridge: Cambridge University Press.

Stanner, W. E. H. 1979. *White man got no dreaming: Essays 1938–1973*. Canberra: Australian National University Press.

Stiles, D. 1987. Classical versus grassroots development. *Cultural Survival Quarterly 11 (1)*, 3–7.

Strehlow, T. G. H. 1970. Geography and the totemic landscape in Central Australia: A functional study. In R. M. Berndt (ed.), *Australian Aboriginal anthropology* pp. 92–140. Perth: University of Western Australia Press.

Sturgess, D. & Brennan, F. 1982. The health of Alwyn Peter. *Aboriginal Health Worker 6 (1)*, 42–47.

Sykes, R. B. 1989. *Black majority*. Hawthorne: Hudson.

Tatz, C. 1979. *Race politics in Australia: Aborigines, politics and law*. Armidale: University of New England Publishing Unit.

———. 1980. Aboriginality as civilization. *Australian Quarterly 52 (3)*, 352–362.

———. 1983. Aborigines in the age of atonement. *Australian Quarterly 55 (3)*, 291–306.

———. 1987. *Aborigines in sport*. Bedford Park: The Australian Society for Sports History.

———. 1989. *Aboriginal juvenile crime in Western Australia*. Report to the Cabinet Sub-Committee on Crime Prevention, Perth.

Taylor, D. M. & McKirnan, D. J. 1984. A five-stage model of intergroup relations. *British Journal of Psychology 23*, 291–300.

Tench, W. 1979 (1793). *Sydney's first four years: A narrative of the expedition to Botany Bay and a complete account of the settlement at Port Jackson*. Sydney: Library of Australian History.

Thomson, N. 1985. Review of available Aboriginal mortality data, 1980–1982. *Medical Journal of Australia 143 (9)*, S46–49.

————. 1991. Recent trends in Aboriginal mortality. *Medical Journal of Australia 154 (4)*, 235–239.

Thomson, N. & English, B. 1990. *Drug use and related problems among Aborigines: Current and potential data sources.* Draft report to the National Drug Abuse Information Centre. Australian Institute of Health, Canberra.

Thomson, N. & Merrifield, P. 1988. *Aboriginal health, an annotated bibliography.* Canberra: Australian Institute of Aboriginal Studies.

Thomson, N. & Smith, L. 1985. An analysis of Aboriginal mortality in NSW country regions, 1980–1981. *Medical Journal of Australia 143 (9)*, S49–54.

Tonkinson, R. 1982. Outside the power of the dreaming: Paternalism and permissiveness in an Aboriginal settlement. In M. C. Howard (ed.), *Aboriginal power in Australian society* pp. 115–130. St Lucia: University of Queensland Press.

Trainor, D. E. 1973 (6 September). Brutality towards Australian Aboriginal — Western Australia style. Report to the Senate Standing Committee on Social Environment, Perth. *Senate*, 1245–1256.

Tsai, L. 1989. *The problem of suicide among Inuit youth.* Report for the Pauktuutit Inuit Women's Association, Ottawa.

Vaszolyi, E. 1979. Kimberley languages: Past and present. In R. M. Berndt & C. H. Berndt (eds), *Aborigines of the West: Their past and their present* pp. 252–260. Perth: University of Western Australia Press.

von Sturmer, J. 1984. Interpretations and directions. In The Australian Institute of Aboriginal Studies (eds), *Aborigines and uranium: Consolidated report to the Minister for Aboriginal Affairs on the social impact of uranium mining on the Aborigines of the Northern Territory* pp. 261–291. Canberra: Government Publishing Service.

Walsh, B. W. & Rosen, P. 1985. Self-mutilation and contagion: An empirical test. *American Journal of Psychiatry 142 (2)*, 119–120.

Walsh, B; Walsh, D; & Whelan, B. 1975. Suicide in Dublin: II. The influence of some social and medical factors on coroner's verdicts. *British Journal of Psychiatry 126*, 309–312.

Wan, S. P; Soderdahl, D. W; & Blight E. M. 1985. Non-psychotic genital mutilation. *Urology 26 (3)*, 286–287.

Warner, W. L. 1969 (1937). *A black civilization: A social study of an Australian tribe.* Gloucester: Peter Smith.

Watson, C; Fleming, J; & Alexander, K. 1988. *A survey of drug use patterns in Northern Territory Aboriginal communities: 1986–1987.* Northern Territory Department of Health and Community Services, Drug and Alcohol Bureau, Darwin.

Watson, E. L. G. 1946. *But to what purpose: The autobiography of a contemporary.* London: The Crescent Press.

Watts, T. D. & Lewis, R. G. 1988. Alcoholism and Native American youth: An overview. *Journal of Drug Issues 18 (1)*, 69–89.

Weir, I. 1959. The flying doctor service of Western Australia, 1935–1959, Unpublished paper for Graylands Teacher's College, Perth.

Welsch, R. L. 1988. Primary health care: A Papua New Guinea example. *Cultural Survival Quarterly 12 (1)*, 1–4.

White, G. M. 1985. Suicide and culture: Island views. In F. X. Hezel, D. H. Rubinstein & G. H. White (eds), *Culture, youth and suicide: Papers from an East-West Center conference* pp. 1–14. Honolulu: University of Hawaii Press.

Williams, M. 1986. *1986 survey of drug and alcohol use by Aboriginal school students in New South Wales*. New South Wales Aboriginal Education Consultative Group, Sydney.

Wilson, P. R. 1985. *Black death, white hands*. Sydney: Allen & Unwin.

Winchel, R. M. & Stanley, M. 1991. Self-injurious behavior: A review of the behavior and biology of self-mutilation. *American Journal of Psychiatry 148 (3)*, 306–317.

Woenne, S. T. 1979. 'The true state of affairs': Commissions of inquiry concerning Western Australian Aborigines. In R. M. Berndt & C. H. Berndt (eds), *Aborigines of the West: Their past and their present* pp. 324–356. Perth: University of Western Australia Press.

World Health Organization. 1975. *International statistical classification of diseases, injuries and causes of death (ninth revision)*. Geneva: World Health Organization.

———. 1978. *Report of the International Conference on Primary Health Care, Alma Ata, U.S.S.R., September 1978*. Geneva: World Health Organization.

Wundersitz, J; Bailey-Harris, R; & Gale, F. 1990. Aboriginal youth and juvenile justice in South Australia. *Aboriginal Law Bulletin 2 (44)*, 12–14.

Yates, A. 1987. Current status and future directions of research on the American Indian child. *American Journal of Psychiatry 144 (9)*, 1135–1142.

Index